MULTICULTURAL BRITAIN

KIERAN CONNELL

Multicultural Britain

A People's History

HURST & COMPANY, LONDON

First published in the United Kingdom in 2024 by
C. Hurst & Co. (Publishers) Ltd.,
New Wing, Somerset House, Strand,
London, WC2R 1LA
© Kieran Connell, 2024
All rights reserved.
Printed in the United Kingdom.

The right of Kieran Connell to be identified as the author of this publication is asserted by him in accordance with the Copyright, Designs and Patents Act, 1988.

A Cataloguing-in-Publication data record for this book is available from the British Library.

ISBN: 9781911723516

www.hurstpublishers.com

Printed in Great Britain by Bell & Bain Ltd, Glasgow

For C & F

CONTENTS

List of Illustrations   ix
A Note on the Text   xv

Introduction   1
1. Brown Babies: 1940s Cardiff   27
2. Colour Bars: 1950s Nottingham   73
3. Red Lights: 1960s Balsall Heath   121
4. Black Powers: 1980s Bradford   175
5. White Flights: 1990s Balsall Heath   221
Epilogue   269

Notes   287
Select Bibliography   337
Acknowledgements   369
Index   373

LIST OF ILLUSTRATIONS

Figure 1: The author in Sparkhill Park, 21 September 1996. Photo copyright © Kieran Connell.   21

Figure 2: Somalian café, Tiger Bay. From anon., 'Down the Bay', *Picture Post*, 22 April 1950. Photo by Bert Hardy, copyright © Getty Images.   60

Figure 3: Cardiff RFC, 1949. Bill Douglas, middle row second from left. Photo courtesy of Cardiff Rugby Museum and the family of Bleddyn Williams.   65

Figure 4: Eric Irons, Nell Irons and children, c. 1995. Photo courtesy of the Irons family.   118

Figure 5: 'The Street', Balsall Heath, c. 1968. Photograph by Janet Mendelsohn, © Janet Mendelsohn/ The Cadbury Research Library, University of Birmingham.   122

Figure 6: 'The Street', Balsall Heath, c. 1968. Photograph by Janet Mendelsohn, © Janet Mendelsohn/ The Cadbury Research Library, University of Birmingham.   139

Figure 7: 'The Street', Balsall Heath, c. 1968. Photograph by Janet Mendelsohn, © Janet Mendelsohn/ The Cadbury Research Library, University of Birmingham.   139

LIST OF ILLUSTRATIONS

Figure 8: Untitled, Balsall Heath, c. 1968. Photograph by Janet Mendelsohn, © Janet Mendelsohn/ The Cadbury Research Library, University of Birmingham. 141

Figure 9: 'The Street', Balsall Heath, c. 1967. Photograph by Janet Mendelsohn, © Janet Mendelsohn/ Cadbury Research Library, University of Birmingham. 142

Figure 10: Untitled, Balsall Heath, c. 1968. Photograph by Janet Mendelsohn, © Janet Mendelsohn/ Cadbury Research Library, University of Birmingham. 143

Figure 11: Untitled, Balsall Heath, c. 1968. Photograph by Janet Mendelsohn, © Janet Mendelsohn/ Cadbury Research Library, University of Birmingham. 143

Figure 12: 'The Street', Balsall Heath, c. 1968. Photograph by Janet Mendelsohn, © Janet Mendelsohn/ Cadbury Research Library, University of Birmingham. 143

Figure 13: Untitled, Balsall Heath, c. 1968. Photograph by Janet Mendelsohn, © Janet Mendelsohn/Cadbury Research Library, University of Birmingham. 144

Figure 14: 'The Street', Balsall Heath, c. 1968. Photograph by Janet Mendelsohn, © Janet Mendelsohn/ Cadbury Research Library, University of Birmingham. 145

Figure 15: 'The Street', Balsall Heath, c. 1968. Photograph by Janet Mendelsohn, © Janet Mendelsohn/ Cadbury Research Library, University of Birmingham. 146

LIST OF ILLUSTRATIONS

Figure 16: Untitled, Balsall Heath, c. 1968. Photograph by Janet Mendelsohn, © Janet Mendelsohn/ Cadbury Research Library, University of Birmingham. 148

Figure 17: 'The Street', Balsall Heath, c. 1968. Photograph by Janet Mendelsohn, © Janet Mendelsohn/ Cadbury Research Library, University of Birmingham. 149

Figure 18: 'The Street', Balsall Heath, c. 1968. Photograph by Janet Mendelsohn, © Janet Mendelsohn/ Cadbury Research Library, University of Birmingham. 149

Figure 19: Untitled, Balsall Heath, c. 1968. Photograph by Janet Mendelsohn, © Janet Mendelsohn/ Cadbury Research Library, University of Birmingham. 151

Figure 20: Untitled, Balsall Heath, c. 1968. Photograph by Janet Mendelsohn, © Janet Mendelsohn/Cadbury Research Library, University of Birmingham. 151

Figure 21: 'The Street', Balsall Heath, c. 1968. Photograph by Janet Mendelsohn, © Janet Mendelsohn/ Cadbury Research Library, University of Birmingham. 154

Figure 22: 'The Street', Balsall Heath, c. 1968. Photograph by Janet Mendelsohn, © Janet Mendelsohn/ Cadbury Research Library, University of Birmingham. 154

Figure 23: 'Kathleen on the Street', Balsall Heath, c. 1968. Photograph by Janet Mendelsohn, © Janet Mendelsohn/Cadbury Research Library, University of Birmingham. 155

LIST OF ILLUSTRATIONS

Figure 24: Untitled, Balsall Heath, c. 1968. Photograph by Janet Mendelsohn, © Janet Mendelsohn/Cadbury Research Library, University of Birmingham.   156

Figure 25: 'Kathleen at the Hospital', Balsall Heath, c. 1968. Photograph by Janet Mendelsohn, © Janet Mendelsohn/Cadbury Research Library, University of Birmingham.   157

Figure 26: 'Salim at the Hospital', Balsall Heath, c. 1968. Photograph by Janet Mendelsohn, © Janet Mendelsohn/Cadbury Research Library, University of Birmingham.   157

Figure 27: 'Visiting Salim's Mother', Birmingham, c. 1968. Photograph by Janet Mendelsohn, © Janet Mendelsohn/Cadbury Research Library, University of Birmingham.   159

Figure 28: 'Visiting Kathleen's Mother', Birmingham, c. 1968. Photograph by Janet Mendelsohn, © Janet Mendelsohn/Cadbury Research Library, University of Birmingham.   159

Figure 29: 'Kathleen and Salim at Home', Balsall Heath, c. 1968. Photograph by Janet Mendelsohn, © Janet Mendelsohn/Cadbury Research Library, University of Birmingham.

Figure 30: 'Kathleen', c. 1968. Photograph by Janet Mendelsohn, © Janet Mendelsohn/Cadbury Research Library, University of Birmingham.   166

Figure 31: 'Kathleen at Home With Newborn Baby', Balsall Heath, c. 1968. Photograph by Janet Mendelsohn, © Janet Mendelsohn/Cadbury Research Library, University of Birmingham.   170

LIST OF ILLUSTRATIONS

Figure 32: Balsall Heath, c. mid-1990s. Photograph by Birmingham Mail, © Trinity Mirror.   236

Figure 33: Raja Brothers Supermarket, Balsall Heath, c. 2010. Photograph © Balsall Heath Local History Society.   265

A NOTE ON THE TEXT

In this book, I draw on a wide range of historical sources—newspaper reports, magazine articles, fieldwork conducted by social scientists, campaign leaflets, interviews, letters, speeches, acts of parliament, photographs, memoirs, novels—to try to reconstruct the experiences of, and attitudes towards, ethnically diverse communities across four British cities at different points in time. These are the tools of the social historian's craft. But by drawing on such material there will be times throughout this book where the reader is confronted with instances of overt racism. The intention here is not to legitimise the kind of actions and language that, belatedly (and only partially), had begun to be criminalised in Britain in the mid-1960s. Rather, it is to shine a light on the shifting nature of British racism to demonstrate the day-to-day effects it had—and continues to have—on ethnic minority groups. The form of racism evolves, as the journalist and writer Gary Younge has argued, "even as the nature of the resistance and rebellion [to racism] will evolve with it". We cannot know for sure where these struggles will take us in the future. In what follows, I hope to contribute to a better understanding of their past.

INTRODUCTION

My first kiss was with a girl called Bushra. It must have been in the mid-1990s, because I was no more than ten or eleven years old and still at junior school in Balsall Heath, a diverse neighbourhood barely two miles south of Birmingham city centre. I am not sure exactly how the kiss came about. I was playing football with my friend Ben, who was in the year above me at school and whose mother was friends with mine. Word must have got out that Bushra and I *wanted* to kiss; I remember us standing in front of a crowd of kids cheering us on, in the yard outside her house—one of those new-build council houses with identikit front walls.

Bushra was beautiful. Her big, sparkling eyes were the colour of hazelnuts. Her hair was hidden beneath a *hijab*. We were both nervous. I had never kissed a girl before, and I remember her saying that her dad would kill her. In the end, we agreed that I would just give her a kiss on the cheek. Nevertheless, the crowd around us cheered and whooped as I leaned in. I can still recall the softness of her skin on my lips.

It's difficult to say how unusual it was at this point for a white boy like me to have had his first kiss with a girl like Bushra, whose parents were from Yemen. Bushra's anxiety, and the excitement of our friends, might have been exacerbated by the fact she was Muslim and I was a *gora* ('white person'); then again, this could just as easily have been driven by the first stirrings of puberty in our soon-to-be teenage bodies. Balsall Heath and Sparkhill, the neighbouring district where I lived, were poor, dilapidated, and sometimes rough. If these were simply features of everyday life, so, too, was the ethnic diversity around me. From the vantage point of my childhood self—when my mother dropped me off with my Pakistani childminder each day, or later when I went to school past the Asian shops that lined Ladypool Road and Stoney Lane—our neighbourhood seemed no more remarkable than the cars that passed by in the streets or the lollipop ladies who guided us across them.

The memories of that time that are closest to the surface often revolve around Sufyaan, my classmate, near-neighbour and best friend. Even now I can readily picture myself eating fish and chips at his house and watching him roll a handful of chips into a gigantic ball of mashed potato; playing cricket in his back garden with a tennis ball, and smashing a six straight through his parents' living-room window; and holding his hand as we tried to teach ourselves to roller-skate from the top end of our road (mine) to the bottom end (Sufyaan's). Like Bushra and most of my classmates, Sufyaan's family had migrated from Britain's former colonies. In the case of Sufyaan's family, this was from the Indian sub-continent. For others in my class it was Yemen, Jamaica, Kenya and beyond.

I was among a minority of children at school who spoke English as a first language, and an even smaller minority of white pupils. From the late 1950s onwards in Britain, it became apparent that accelerating inner-city ethnic diversity was not going to be a temporary situation. This was a nightmare scenario for a growing number of politicians and other commentators, who positioned themselves as quasi-prophets warning of the malaise that, in their view, inevitably awaited the country because of its "open-door"

INTRODUCTION

immigration policy. The most influential among these was undoubtedly Enoch Powell, who, in 1968, as the Conservative Shadow Defence Minister and MP for Wolverhampton South West, delivered what became known as his "Rivers of Blood" speech in a Birmingham hotel (barely two miles from Balsall Heath), in which he talked of his white constituents having been rendered "strangers in their own country", their "wives unable to obtain hospital beds in childbirth, their children unable to obtain school places, their homes and neighbourhoods changed beyond recognition". The inflammatory nature of this speech led to Powell's immediate sacking from the Shadow Cabinet. But in the same year, one opinion poll suggested that 80 per cent of white parents in Britain would have concerns about there being a single black or Asian pupil in their own child's classroom. And Powell's narrative of white victimhood at the hands of an external and supposedly alien 'invasion' would be repeated, with different inflections and particular targets in mind, at regular intervals over the subsequent fifty years.[1]

These anxieties were felt most acutely in Britain, France, the Netherlands, and other one-time imperial nations, where growing populations of formerly colonial peoples coincided with (and acted as the unsuspecting reminders of) the rapid decolonisation taking place since the Second World War. Political concerns about race, immigration and 'multiculturalism' were bound up with what the cultural theorist Paul Gilroy—whose mother the teacher and writer Beryl Gilroy migrated to Britain from British Guiana in 1951—has called "postcolonial melancholia", whereby formerly imperial societies simultaneously struggled to process both the loss of empire and its ongoing legacy in the present day. In this context, the term *multiculturalism* and its derivatives took on a particular resonance. They became watchwords that, especially following the 11 September 2001 terrorist attacks on the World Trade Center in New York City and the subsequent "War on Terror", apparently encapsulated everything that was understood to be wrong with the presence in these countries of increasingly diverse populations.²

In The Netherlands, for example, the right-wing Party for Freedom's 2010 election manifesto called for the Dutch political establishment to take responsibility for the creation of a "multicultural nightmare", part of a wider agenda supposedly concerned with "imposing even more Islam on us in order to take away every memory of an independent and recognisable Netherlands". The following year, UK Prime Minister David Cameron criticised what he called "the doctrine of state multiculturalism" which, in his view, had "encouraged different cultures to live separate lives, apart from each other and apart from the mainstream".³

Then, following his central role in the ultimately successful campaign for Britain to leave the European Union, and offering his own analysis of the causes of the March 2017 terrorist attacks on Westminster Bridge in London, the former UK Independence Party (UKIP) leader Nigel Farage pointed the finger at the Labour Government under Tony Blair, whose supposed commitment to multiculturalism Farage regarded as setting the scene for the problems Britain would encounter for 100 years. The problem with multiculturalism, Farage argued, echoing and amplifying the arguments made six years earlier by Cameron, was not only that it divided communities. It had, Farage claimed, created a "fifth column" of Islamic extremists across Europe. "Frankly," Farage concluded, making his scapegoat explicit, "if you open your door to uncontrolled immigration from Middle Eastern countries, you are inviting in terrorism".⁴

Variations of this depiction of a "clash of civilisations" between East and West were repeated by politicians across the political spectrum from the German Chancellor Angela Merkel and the one-time Labour Home Secretary David Blunkett to Nick Griffin, the former leader of the neo-Nazi British National Party.

INTRODUCTION

Their prominence not only demonstrates the extent to which the events of 9/11 and the subsequent neo-imperial conflicts in the Middle East made Muslim communities the primary focus of fears about immigration in the West; they also reveal an enduring inability on the part of the body politic to come up with a language that incorporates the social reality of ethnic diversity—the world I inhabited in 1990s Balsall Heath—into a coherent political vision.

Multiculturalism has been used by politicians to stand in for a much broader set of concerns. But the term has different meanings. It can refer specifically to a set of policies that were rolled out in Britain from the 1970s onwards—particularly by Labour-run local authorities such as the Greater London Council—that were designed to provide the space and finances to enable particular ethnic groups to celebrate cultural traditions or religious practices. In spite of the doctrinaire philosophy evoked by the "ism", the strategies of multiculturalism vary considerably from context to context. In Britain, they often meant the provision of small grants to voluntary groups in inner-city areas for arts projects and cultural festivals, or for the maintenance of community buildings. But *multiculturalism* can also refer to a concrete reality, a dynamic whereby "different cultural communities live together and attempt to build a common life while retaining something of their 'original' identity". This understanding is necessarily connected to immigration, but takes in themes such as the process of settlement, the formation of community structures, the establishment of new relationships, and the shifting dynamic brought about by the emergence of new generations of ethnic minorities who are born in the 'host' country. While events at Westminster cast an important shadow over the story I tell in *Multicultural Britain*, I am primarily focused on unearthing *a social history of multiculturalism*, or what one writer has referred to as "actually existing multiculturalism": the interactions that took place at different points in time as cultural difference was negotiated in everyday life, between neighbours, co-workers, school friends, lovers, or casual acquaintances.[5]

A major theme in this history is necessarily that of immigration—from Pakistan, as in the case of Sufyaan's family; from Yemen, as in the case of Bushra's; or from elsewhere across Britain's once-sprawling empire. This included immigration from Ireland, Britain's oldest colony, which had approached the level of 60,000 people per year by the late-1950s and which, a generation earlier, included the arrival of my own great-grandparents, James and Susanna Connell, from County Cork in pre-independence Ireland. It also included tens of thousands of immigrants from Germany, Italy and elsewhere in mainland Europe, as well as the arrival of refugees who had either survived the brutality of the Nazi atrocities or else found themselves displaced following the post-war redrawing of national boundaries in the east of the continent. And this is a story that also includes Britain's indigenous white population.[6]

We too often think of 'multicultural Britain' as something that exclusively concerns black or Asian communities. Certainly, immigrants from the Caribbean, East and West Africa, and the Indian subcontinent became the largest and most visible ethnic minorities to make their home in Britain. They experienced the most overt discrimination and had to fight the hardest for political representation and against the inequality they encountered in almost every area of their lives. These groups are the indispensable heart of this book. But it is also important not to lose sight of the active role 'white society' played in the making of multicultural Britain. This could mean white immigration to Britain from across Europe, or internal migrations from Scotland, Wales, and rural England into Britain's major cities. Yet it must also mean white society taking ownership of the history of white racism; white ignorance; what the writer Reni Eddo-Lodge has

INTRODUCTION

emphasised as "white privilege"; and, at certain points, white decency and communality.[7]

In this book I foreground an understanding of *multiculturalism* as a pluralistic historical process. I want to get at the nature and 'feel' of different multicultural communities—what it was like to live in them on a daily basis—from the vantage points of those who shaped them. And this necessarily includes the white shopkeeper in 1960s Birmingham who railed against "coloured people coming into this country and taking jobs off our own countrypeople", alongside the Arab founder of a mosque in 1940s Cardiff, the Jamaican founder of a social club in 1950s Nottingham, and the Pakistani community organiser in 1980s Bradford.[8]

For this modern history of multicultural Britain, my focus is the seventy-year period from the end of the Second World War to the first decades of the twenty-first century. If the years after 1945 saw immigration to Britain increase dramatically, by the turn of the century Britain was engaged in what the Jamaican-born British intellectual Stuart Hall called a "drift" towards the multicultural. Hall argued that by the 1990s ethnic diversity was becoming recognised as "a natural and inevitable part of the 'scene'", despite continued hostility towards immigration and the persistent threat of racial violence. The interactions that happened organically between groups on a daily basis drove this recognition, often in untidy, unpredictable ways at the community level. Relationships occurred between immigrants from places as disparate as Kashmir on the disputed India-Pakistan border, Kingston in Jamaica or Galway in Ireland; a rapidly expanding ethnic minority population born and brought up in Britain grew in influence, working out what it meant to be black Britons, British Asians, or "Afropeans" whilst retaining a commitment to various diasporic inheritances; and quotidian encounters took place, such as a kiss between the daughter of Yemeni immigrants and the great-grandson of Irish immigrants. Such scenes continued to be the source of considerable anxiety for many observers. From the 1950s onwards, various politicians laid claim to the far-right mantra that Britain should be kept 'for the British'. But as they did so, they missed the fundamental nature of the changes that were taking place around them. Even if there were a dwindling number of areas in Britain relatively untouched by ethnic diversity, by the new millennium the genie was already out of the bottle. As a result of what was happening in Balsall Heath, Sparkhill, and similar neighbourhoods the length and breadth of the country, Britain had become multicultural. In this book, I set out to understand how this came about.[9]

* * *

The arrival of the *Empire Windrush* at Tilbury Docks on 22 June 1948, and the disembarkation of some 500 Jamaican immigrants, is commonly presented as the starting point for ethnic diversity in Britain—undoubtedly aided by the eminently visual spectacle, captured by waiting news cameras and journalists, of hundreds of predominately black men coming ashore in Essex dressed in formal suits, kipper ties and fedora hats. As the authors Trevor and Mike Phillips remarked on the fiftieth anniversary of the ship's arrival, "the *Windrush* has become a symbol for all those occasions when we, or any of the other black people who have become part of the British nation, stepped off our separate gangplanks". But this symbolism has arguably worked to conceal as much as it reveals. For example, alongside the 500 Jamaicans on board, half of whom spent their first nights in Britain in an underground air-raid shelter in London, were more than sixty displaced people from Poland who, following the end of the Second World War, had found themselves in the Americas and may well have boarded the *Windrush* in Tampico, Mexico or Havana, Cuba, where the ship made stops *en route* to Tilbury. There were passengers from the British colonies of Uganda and

INTRODUCTION

Kenya as well as Trinidad, St Lucia, and British Guiana. The docking of the *Windrush* was more accurately a multicultural arrival rather than solely a Jamaican one.[10]

Moreover, contrary to the idea (which quickly took root) that the Jamaican arrivals were setting foot in Britain for the first time, many of those black passengers were, in fact, *returning* to Britain, having served in the British army and been stationed at military bases across the UK during the war. The continued focus on the *Windrush* as an imaginary starting point has also worked to obscure the small but significant ethnic minority presence in Britain well before June 1948. London was a long-standing destination for black students, writers, and other travellers from across the empire, as well as port cities such as Cardiff where, from the mid-nineteenth century onwards, the international demand for British coal meant that an expanded shipping industry was a source of employment for labourers across Britain's colonies (see Chapter One).

This is not to downplay the contributions made by those we have come to refer to as "the *Windrush* generation". Rather, it is to highlight the kinds of contradictions that seem to run right through the history of multicultural Britain. For example, a gaping disparity soon became apparent between the way ethnic-minority immigrants often felt about Britain before their arrival, and the treatment they encountered subsequently as they went about trying to make lives for themselves in British cities. This disparity was felt most strongly by immigrants from the Caribbean, where the colonial structures that had helped shape their formative experiences often produced an especially powerful attachment to an imperialistic vision of 'Britishness'. As one Caribbean immigrant reflected in the late 1990s: "We were brought up that we are British, we were brought up [to think] that England is your 'mother country', and we were brought up to respect the royal family."[11]

Indeed, with the passing of the British Nationality Act in July 1948, this affinity to Britain was formally enshrined in law. The Act gave citizens in Britain's colonies and former colonies—including the onetime imperial jewel, India, which, with Partition and the formation of Pakistan, gained independence from the Crown in August 1947—the same legal right to live and work in Britain as those who had been born in the UK. The aim was to encourage the arrival of the cheap labour force that, in the context of a declining birth rate and rising emigration out of the country, was urgently required to rebuild Britain's decaying infrastructure—including the establishment of the National Health Service (NHS), founded just weeks before the British Nationality Act received royal assent.[12]

But as the number of ethnic minorities in Britain increased by more than 500,000 between the late 1940s and early 1960s, the hostility they encountered also snowballed. This was seen most clearly with the pervasive nature of the British 'colour bar', in which landlords, employers, bouncers, hoteliers, and other gatekeepers who wanted to prevent the unwanted encroachment of "coloured" immigrants into their worlds simply barred black or Asian people from entry (see Chapter Two). Such attitudes went hand in hand with the widespread ignorance immigrants encountered about their home countries, and the historic connection they had to the imperial 'mother country'. The trauma experienced by black and South Asian immigrants in the context of their early encounters in Britain is one of the dominant themes of the historical archive. As one immigrant in Nottingham explained in the early 1970s, the missionaries and teachers had given "a very misleading impression [of Britain]. Discrimination came as a big shock. We had it in Jamaica but we didn't expect it here." An Asian bus conductor in the same city likewise emphasised that most white people did not like Indians; if you were Indian, white people would not even sit next to you on the bus.

INTRODUCTION

Whatever the deep-rooted nature of their own connection to Britain, another Caribbean immigrant argued, the vast majority of white people "don't want to understand us". No matter the centuries of colonisation and the economic imperatives of the post-war reconstruction effort; the fact was, he concluded, the British "don't want us here".[13]

Contradictions such as these are present in almost every landmark moment in the making of multicultural Britain. They are there, for instance, in Enoch Powell's trajectory from an unflinching commitment to the British Empire (born in part from his wartime service in colonial India) to a brand of nationalism that, by the post-colonial 1960s, attempted to elide Britain's bloody legacy of colonisation and instead foreground an immensely powerful narrative of white victimhood at home, at the hands of a 'non-white' and therefore fundamentally alien incursion. They are there in the followers of the neo-Nazi National Front (NF), who waged a campaign of intimidation against black and Asian communities in the 1970s and '80s, but whose 'skinhead' style aped a look that had initially emerged in British inner cities out of a desire among white youths to mimic the Jamaican 'rude boy' style made visible by the growing popularity of Jamaican ska music. And, in a later period, they are there in the striking difference between two David Camerons.[14]

The better-known David Cameron is the one who, as Prime Minister and in the context of ongoing concerns about Islamic terrorism, immigration, and racial segregation, positioned himself as a vocal opponent of multiculturalism. With an eye on the growing influence of Farage's UKIP, it was this standpoint that—overseen by Cameron's Home Secretary and eventual successor as Prime Minister, Theresa May—led to the implementation of policies designed to create a "Hostile Environment" for illegal immigrants, including benefit sanctions, the loss of access to the NHS, and deportation. This approach culminated in 2018 with the eruption of the *Windrush* scandal. Dozens of black British citizens who had accompanied their parents to Britain on boats like the *Windrush*, and whose right to reside in Britain had been enshrined under the British Nationality Act, were found to have been wrongfully deported back to countries in which many had not set foot for more than five decades.[15]

Yet this David Cameron had been preceded by another, often forgotten incarnation who, as leader of the Conservative opposition, was keen to extenuate his multicultural credentials by paying a visit to Balsall Heath. Drawn to the area because of the success of a community campaign to reduce crime, he posed for the cameras in summer 2007 by sampling a portion of chicken tikka bites at the Karachi Café and volunteering for a stint on the tills at the local Raja Brothers supermarket—just around the corner from where I went to school. He stayed overnight at the home of Abdullah Rehman, a prominent local activist who later explained that Cameron wanted to talk with a "normal Asian family", hear about their family values and learn about "community cohesion". Afterwards, Cameron reflected on his time in Balsall Heath in an article for a national newspaper. He argued that the largely Muslim communities he had encountered there—many of whom would subsequently become the target of key Hostile Environment policies such as immigration checks from landlords, banks, and NHS workers—epitomised what he understood to be the "British values" of hospitality, tolerance, and generosity. "Not for the first time," Cameron wrote, "I found myself thinking that it is mainstream Britain which needs to integrate more with the British Asian way of life, not the other way around." Even accounting for the grubbiness of *realpolitik*, Cameron's was a journey of some distance. But as Stuart Hall has argued, it is often on such "piquant, fragile and bizarre paradoxes" that the history of multicultural Britain has turned.[16]

What follows is a series of snapshots, seen from a bottom-up perspective, of the experience of multicultural Britain in particu-

INTRODUCTION

lar places at different points in time. This includes immigration from all over the world; settlement, and the formation of new relationships; racism and other kinds of hostility, as well as the impact of deep-rooted structural inequalities in areas such as housing and employment; and the establishment of new communities as the children, grandchildren and great-grandchildren of those who shaped the fledgling multicultural encounters of the 1940s and '50s reached maturity in the context of a changing set of socio-political circumstances.

In the chapters that follow, I take readers on a journey across multicultural Britain. I begin in the late 1940s, in the Tiger Bay district of Cardiff, one of Britain's oldest multicultural communities. If it was Cardiff's emergence in the mid-nineteenth century as a major port that brought labourers from all over the world to the city, it was, I argue in Chapter One, imperialistic ideas about race that often structured the Tiger Bay milieu—proliferating concerns over what was understood to be "darkest Cardiff", but also internal community dynamics and the often-messy relationships that developed between ethnically diverse segments of the population. Chapter Two enters into St Ann's in Nottingham, a neighbourhood that made headlines around the world in August 1958 with a serious outbreak of racial violence. Groups of white men initiated the strife, taking issue with the sight of Caribbean immigrants apparently in romantic relationships with white women; they reportedly attacked them with cries of "lynch the blacks". Yet in the context of the gathering pace of decolonisation and concurrent anxieties about Britain's place in the world, the problem of white racism somehow came to be understood as an issue that should be remedied by stemming the growth of Britain's "coloured" population. The origins of what would become "Powellism" can be found in the political response to what happened on the streets of 1950s Nottingham.

Chapter Three takes the reader some fifty miles southwest to 1960s Balsall Heath, the area where I would later attend school.

MULTICULTURAL BRITAIN

In the 1960s, the neighbourhood was notorious as the site of one of the country's largest red-light districts, which not only catered for many newly arrived immigrant men, but was also shaped by a number of ethnic minorities acting as pimps to dozens of women—the vast majority of whom were white. Here I focus on one particularly ambiguous relationship between a South Asian man and a white woman of Irish heritage, and show how its parameters exemplified the broader contradictions I see as being at the heart of the making of multicultural Britain.

In my penultimate chapter, I head north to Bradford in the 1970s and '80s. By focussing on the area of education and the experiences of Bradford's large Muslim population in particular, we are able to see the enduring impact of white racism in Britain and the continued reach of Powellism. By examining a campaign that was waged against the racist headteacher of a school in the Manningham district of the city, we can also recognise the extent to which ethnic minority communities have had to take direct political action themselves in order to overcome the impact of racism on their everyday lives.

Finally, I return to the Balsall Heath of my childhood, and reconstruct the milieu I inhabited with friends like Sufyaan at the turn of the millennium. My own experiences as a white schoolboy here becomes a central part of the narrative. By returning to Balsall Heath, which I situate in relation to the broader context of an ultimately successful campaign led by the local Asian community to eradicate Balsall Heath's sex industry, I move the narrative towards the present day. In so doing, I look for clues as to where, amid the fallout from the 2016 Brexit vote and the influence of successive iterations of the far right, the future of multicultural Britain may lie.

An obvious absence here is London, a city which, perhaps more than any other, has been an integral feature of Britain's multicultural drift. Yet because of the size of its population (it has

INTRODUCTION

six times as many people as Birmingham, Britain's second city), its geographic spread (it takes at least ninety minutes to drive from Enfield in the north of the city to Croydon in the south, while a similar journey across Bradford takes no more than a quarter of that time), and its status as a financial, cultural, transport, and political centre, the nature of multicultural London is very different to that of the rest of Britain. In the 1950s and '60s, in areas such as Brixton in the south and Notting Hill in the northwest, various "coloured quarters" had emerged as visible features of the London geography. In smaller cities such as Cardiff and Nottingham, by contrast, there were generally just one. Thus, in addition to London's spatial reach and status as an imperial capital with a long tradition of population fluidity, immigrants to London encountered a particular set of circumstances there that were not available elsewhere in the country.[17]

The fact that many existing histories implicitly conflate Britain with London, moreover, means that a skewed picture has emerged, with very little to say about the experience of ethnic diversity away from the capital. "People in London ... don't know what [is] happening in the room next to them, far more the street," the narrator reflects in *The Lonely Londoners* (1956), a semi-autobiographical novel by Samuel Selvon, the Trinidadian writer who migrated to London in 1950. "London is a place like that. It divides up into little worlds, and you stay in the world you belong to and you don't know anything about what happening in the other ones except what you read in the papers." There were, of course, similar themes at play along class and race lines in smaller cities, but the size and reach of each competing world was dramatically reduced. There was much less scope to pass unnoticed as a newly arrived black or Asian immigrant in Nottingham (population in 1961: 312,000) than in London (population that same year: 8.1 million). As one Caribbean immigrant reflected in Cardiff in the early 1940s, London was "the sort of place where anything might happen and no one takes any particular notice of it ... [but] if it happens *here*, there is a hell-of-a-baloo."[18]

What was it like to navigate Cardiff as an Arab or Caribbean seafarer in the late 1940s, almost two decades before racial discrimination was formally (if partially) made illegal in Britain? How did the white residents of Nottingham view the city's growing ethnic minority population? What was it like to be in a mixed-race relationship in 1960s Birmingham? How were the children of such relationships treated, and how did they see themselves? What kinds of politics emerged out of multicultural communities, as ethnic diversity increased and the needs of particular groups—including the growing number of ethnic minorities born in Britain—changed over time? In seeking answers to these questions, a number of themes have emerged as threads that, as I move in and out of different cities at different moments across the second half of the twentieth century, run right through this book.

One is the spatial element of Britain's multicultural drift. This does not only mean the importance of avoiding what one writer has referred to as the "Brixtonization" of the history of multicultural Britain. It also means paying attention to the topographical spaces around which the spectacle of increasing ethnic diversity played out—something which, for most of the period under consideration in *Multicultural Britain*, meant the inner areas of Britain's major cities. It was no coincidence that these areas were marked by the poorest-quality housing, which private landlords commonly sought to exploit by cramming immigrants and their families into single rooms, often in houses with a solitary (outside) toilet and no hot water. The overt discrimination that faced immigrants in the housing market—and particularly the "NO BLACKS, NO IRISH, NO DOGS" signs that immigrants remember being posted in the windows of residences in the 1950s and

INTRODUCTION

'60s—became symbolic of the spectrum of discrimination faced by ethnic minorities in the post-war period.[19]

It is also a recurring trope in the chapters that follow. But what emerges at the same time is a less well-documented process: how inner-city spaces were physically transformed as consecutive generations of ethnically diverse communities sought to establish themselves in Britain. This transformation was generally a response to the need to provide essential services that were simply not otherwise available—the formation of mosques or other places of worship; shops that sold food from 'back home'; cafés that cooked it; cinemas that played Bollywood movies; community centres that provided advice and help for new arrivals. These establishments were important on their own terms, but they often took on a greater level of significance in the context of tensions around the colour bar. They became safe spaces away from the hostility of the indigenous white population, and at times acted as the springboard for the emergence of more overtly political organisations that aimed to address the issues faced by ethnic minorities in Britain. They were about turning Britain's dilapidated inner-city spaces into community-orientated *places*. In many ways, the names of such establishments—the Café Cairo, the Kashmir Coffee Bar, the Coloured International Athletic Club, Zaff's Halal Diner—were embodiments of Britain's contradictory, uneven, but nevertheless resolute drift towards the multicultural.[20]

Alongside this is the centrality of the themes of love, sex, and intimacy. Sex in particular—and especially the prospect of sex between white women and black men—propelled some of the earliest, most fraught anxieties in Britain about increasing ethnic diversity. During the Second World War and in its immediate aftermath, for instance, a sustained moral panic broke out over the sexual relationships that were apparently developing between white women and some of the more than 200,000 black troops from the United States and the West Indies who were, at various points, stationed across Britain during the conflict. If such relationships became the focus of widespread media coverage, they also caught the attention of politicians and wartime authorities, whose ostensible concerns about the spread of venereal disease were bound up with much more fundamental anxieties about racial purity that were shaped by the ideologies underpinning the British colonial project. In this context, it is unsurprising that the perceived threat of miscegenation struck a nerve with a significant section of the British population more generally—particularly where the consequences of sexual liaisons were made visible by the birth of so-called "half-caste" babies. "I do not think I would ... avoid social or business relations with coloured people," one respondent to a social survey reflected in the 1940s. But on the other hand, he admitted that he felt "very strongly about intimate relations with coloured folks". In his view, the time had come for the "laws of the land [to] prohibit intermarriage of white people with coloured". The prominence of such attitudes helps undermine the notion that was often peddled by British wartime propaganda that, in contrast to Nazi Germany, the British public maintained a modishly egalitarian attitude towards race. As demonstrated by the St Ann's riots, as well as by the more serious unrest that took place just days later in Notting Hill in London (also sparked by white hostility toward people in mixed-race relationships), the effects of these attitudes continued to be felt in multicultural communities well into the 1950s and beyond.[21]

However, as well as underpinning such moments of tension, love and sex were also behind some of the most embryonic instances of multicultural interaction. Whether this meant the scores of white women from Cardiff who, in October 1945, overwhelmed an American army base in order to embrace their African American sweethearts, the Jamaican immigrant who met

INTRODUCTION

the white woman who would become his wife while asking for directions outside Nottingham's train station, or the complicated relationship between a South Asian immigrant and his Anglo-Irish partner in Balsall Heath, romantic liaisons could open up spaces for conversations and the development of cross-cultural understanding. Given these relationships often took place in the context of the inner city, class was an important dynamic here. It was often the poorest white people who lived next door to newly arrived immigrants from Pakistan or East Africa. If they could, many white residents moved out of the inner city to the more affluent (and therefore whiter) suburbs—a process American sociologists referred to as "white flight". Many also became the constituents of politicians like Powell, whose narrative of white victimhood chimed with the way they experienced the rapidity of changes taking place around them. But others adapted to these changes, and, in order to navigate their increasingly multicultural surroundings, were forced to develop some level of familiarity, a kind of rough and ready competency with the types of cross-cultural interactions that, more and more, were becoming an everyday feature of life in Britain's inner cities—with the establishment of new relationships, and also more generally with the kind of quotidian sociability that rarely makes it into the history books: on the street, in cafés and bars, in the local shop, and at the school gates.

Women have played a particularly important (if often overlooked) role in this process. In Balsall Heath, for instance, the arrival of large numbers of single men from overseas acted as a significant boon to the mainly white women who worked in Britain's expanding sex industries. As well as providing paid-for sexual favours, sex workers sometimes entered into closer relationships with immigrant clients, and in so doing become valued as sources of information about British customs and ways of life—how to shop around for the best value, what to do if you get sick. In turn, such women were given a window into the impact that widespread racial discrimination had on ethnic minorities in Britain—one that was, particularly in the early years, rarely provided by politicians or the media. For example, in the late 1960s, a young white woman in Balsall Heath rationalised her decision to begin working as a prostitute by referencing the effect that racism had on her black lover (who subsequently also became her pimp). She remembered accompanying him to factories and other places of work where there were advertised vacancies, and him applying for those jobs. But on realising the applicant was black, the employers would simply claim the vacancies had already been filled. Another white woman in the same neighbourhood, whose partner was from Jamaica, likewise spoke of her determination to send her daughter away to boarding school because of the problems she felt mixed-race children could otherwise face. "We wouldn't have bothered so much if they were white or even full coloured," she reflected. "But with them being half-castes it's much harder for them."[22]

In the first decades of the twenty-first century, people of mixed race have become one of the fastest-growing ethnic groups in Britain. Whereas at the time of the St Ann's riots in 1958, surveys showed that more than seventy per cent of the population disapproved of the idea of mixed-race marriages, by 2012 that figure had collapsed to fifteen per cent. On their own, such statistics can seem trite and meaningless. They conceal the fact that, like the racism encountered by ethnic minorities more generally, discrimination faced by those who were once referred to as "half-caste" remains *in situ*. But when taken in relation to the spectrum of social, cultural, political, and geographic changes encapsulated by Britain's multicultural drift, the statistics can help us get a handle on the momentous nature of the transformations brought about in Britain in the seven decades that have passed since the docking of the *Empire Windrush*. In the pages

INTRODUCTION

that follow, I bring to the surface the conditions that helped prepare the ground for this phenomenon, and the gamut of relationships sparked between newly arrived immigrants, members of the indigenous population, and, as the decades wore on, the ethnically diverse British-born inhabitants of multicultural communities across the country.[23]

When I try to interrogate my relationship to these themes, it is to a photograph of my friends and me in Sparkhill Park on 21 September 1996 (my eleventh birthday) that I often turn (Fig. 1). My mother had kept it in a dog-eared folder of drawings and other mementos attesting to the happiness of my early childhood. As the photograph suggests, this was a happy moment for me. All my closest friends from school had come to celebrate with a game of football, including Ben and Sufyaan; in the background, Sufyaan's mother and younger siblings can also be seen looking on. But as I examine the image now, I also see that my eleventh birthday was a significant turning point in my own

Figure 1: The author in Sparkhill Park, 21 September 1996. Photo copyright © Kieran Connell.

trajectory into adulthood. It was a sliding-doors moment that belies the conviviality of a late-summer kick around in the park. At the insistence of my father (back row left), I had just started at a different secondary school from the one most of my Balsall Heath friends were attending. It had a better academic reputation and was a few miles further south, closer to my dad's home in a slightly more well-to-do part of town. By anyone's standards, this was also a multicultural school, with a particularly large South Asian presence, but it also included a substantial white working-class population—a segment of society that, while present in my world, I had yet to encounter *en masse*. I began to make new friends, none of whom lived near Balsall Heath. By the time I packed my bags to leave Birmingham for university, seven years later, I had lost touch with most of the people from my childhood world—with Bushra, with Sufyaan, and with almost everyone who came to celebrate my eleventh birthday on that day in 1996.

Given the obvious proximity I have to my subject, I have had to acknowledge that *Multicultural Britain* is strongly influenced by my own formative relationships. Writing it has caused me to return to them—not only with friends such as Sufyaan, but also with my parents, both of whom had arrived in Birmingham with histories of migration. These were completely different paths from those followed by the families of most of my childhood friends. On my mother's side, my great-grandparents from County Cork had, in the 1910s, embarked on the well-worn journey from Ireland to England in search of work. My maternal grandmother, meanwhile, had grown up in Germany, and moved to Britain as a child when her father found work at a plastics factory in Lancashire in 1926. Later, while at university in Liverpool, she met my grandfather, who, in 1952, moved the family to live in the north of Ireland. Two decades later, having crossed the Irish Sea once more to attend university, my mother finally settled in Birmingham.

INTRODUCTION

For my father, the migration that characterised his life was an internal one. He had grown up in Nuneaton, a small mining town in the East Midlands that would be blighted by the growing speed of deindustrialisation. Disillusioned with life in the provinces, he moved to Birmingham in his late teens. That city is a mere half-hour by train from Nuneaton. But the cultural differences my father encountered there were nevertheless significant. He gravitated towards the inner cities, so different from Nuneaton and far away from the hysterical pronouncements about Britain's supposedly bleak future as a multiracial society; these places were the breeding ground for the emergence of an arts scene that, across a range of forms, provided alternative perspectives on the growth of multicultural Britain. Prior to fatherhood, this scene occupied most of my dad's time as an employee of an arts centre in Small Heath, a neighbourhood of Birmingham two miles northeast of Balsall Heath and just beyond the city's central mosque.

My intellectual interests have been guided by these currents. But my opportunities in life have also been shaped by the relative privilege of my background, compared to many of my childhood friends. As I navigated the increasingly white spaces of secondary school, sixth form and university, I could call on the advantages that came from having two university-educated parents at home; my own white privilege also allowed me to sidestep the vicious effects of racial discrimination that, in myriad forms—structurally, economically, politically, and socially—continues to affect the lives of ethnic minorities in Britain, and often bars them from entering the best universities, the best jobs, the positions of power.

In some ways, my own move away from Balsall Heath was an alternative form of white flight from the inner cities. But whereas most white residents who left them in the 1950s and '60s were fleeing the shock induced by the arrival of widespread ethnic diversity, in the late 1990s I was gravitating away from what—for me—was the *familiarity* of the multicultural inner city. This was something which I had experienced more properly as a dislocation, especially in those early, pubescent years. As Didier Eribon has argued, "whatever you have uprooted yourself from or been uprooted from still endures as an integral part of who or what you are". My work as a historian is informed by this tension, and an ongoing conversation with my childhood experiences in Balsall Heath. Indeed, it is the main reason I decided to write this book.[24]

As I have suggested, the story of Britain's multicultural drift is, at heart, a contradictory one. It could equally be understood as a case of 'two steps forward, one step back'. For example: when, in November 1945, hordes of young, white women in Cardiff were held back by police at the train station as they sought to see off their black boyfriends returning to the United States, this event followed a shrill outcry just two months earlier over what was deemed to be the transgressive behaviour of many of the same girls as they sought out encounters with their lovers in what the press described as the "indescribable filth" of an area around Cardiff's military barracks that was soon christened "Burma Road". Or consider the story of Balsall Heath's red-light district, which expanded during the 1950s owing to the growing number of single black and Asian men and continued to grow in the 1960s and '70s, often as a result of the problematic relationships some of these men established with young, white women; and which, finally, was eradicated in the 1990s thanks primarily to a campaign fought by the area's increasingly devout Muslim population—a section of the community that was initially fêted by politicians such as David Cameron for their voluntary work, but which was itself very quickly made the object of a moral panic around "home-grown" terrorism and the dangers of segregated communities.[25]

INTRODUCTION

Such is the contradictory nature of what I refer to as the dialectics of multiculturalism. In many respects, it could not be any other way. *Multicultural Britain* charts the long, unstable, and often difficult historical process of ethnically diverse populations weaving themselves, their cultures, and their politics into the fabric of Britain's major cities. Often powered in the first instance by sex and love, it is a story also indelibly bound up with the legacies of colonialism, empire, and the accelerating forces of globalisation. What follows is just one chapter in the much larger story of the making of modern Britain. But it is one in which—no matter the particularities of our own familial backgrounds and childhood experiences—we all have a stake.[26]

1

BROWN BABIES

1940s CARDIFF

My road to Tiger Bay began in New York City. I had made the journey across the Atlantic to follow in the footsteps of St Clair Drake, the African American anthropologist who, in the late 1940s, made the same trip in reverse when he set out to research Cardiff's Tiger Bay in light of its reputation as one of Britain's oldest multicultural communities. By the time he left for Britain, Drake's academic reputation had been established by the publication of *Black Metropolis* (1945), an epic, 800-page study of the African American community of the South Side district of Chicago that he co-authored with the researcher Horace Cayton. After Drake's death in 1990, his 100-box archive was donated to a branch of the New York Public Library in Harlem. So it was, then, that over a four-week period I wrapped up warm against the crisp New York winter and made a daily commute to Harlem to find out what this pioneering American social scientist made of Tiger Bay, a neighbourhood that, to many white onlookers in 1940s Britain, was otherwise known as "darkest Cardiff", "negroland", or simply "niggertown".[1]

MULTICULTURAL BRITAIN

As ever when I find myself in a major US city, while in New York I often felt disorientated by the abrasiveness of American street culture. While more than a decade of austerity has put Britain on a similar path, poverty always comes across as a more overt presence in the United States, where people are forced to hold open the doors of 7-Elevens and hang around subway stations in the hope of scraping together a few dollars in spare change. It is also hard to avoid the racialised nature of poverty in the States, particularly in a city like New York. This fact was illuminated by the daily commute I made to see Drake's papers from the Airbnb flat I had rented—against my better judgement—in the hipsterized Williamsburg district of Brooklyn. Every morning, I would squeeze into a packed L train at Bedford Avenue, surrounded mostly by white people in bright-coloured beanies, expensive-looking glasses, and brilliant-white cordless earphones. Having made the short journey under the East River, most passengers disembarked at Union Square. The crowds would disperse out into Midtown Manhattan or down towards the Financial District, but I would make my way to the No. 3 train that would take me northwards to Harlem. This time, the carriage would be emptier and much less white, and there were often men trying to sleep horizontally on the seats.

My lack of familiarity with the rhythms of American urban life became apparent when I got off the subway at 125th Street, across the road from the library. As I alighted, people would ask me to hold open the platform barrier in the hope that they might get a free ride; and when I emerged from the subway, blinking into the winter sunshine, there were middle-aged men passed out by the side of the road. Now, after a journey of barely forty minutes, it sometimes seemed as though I was the only white person around.

One day, I bought an espresso at a branch of Dunkin Donuts. In the queue to order, I took pity on a middle-aged man who was going from table to table trying to hustle enough money for a cup of coffee. I asked him what he wanted and ordered it: a large coffee and a chocolate-coated donut. When it arrived, the man took it and silently headed for the exit. "That's the trouble with these people," the Indian man behind the till said, catching my eye. "They're just not human." Maybe the server sensed my own lack of sure-footedness about the way things worked in New York. It was also possible that, as seemingly one of the few white people who frequented this branch of Dunkin Donuts, he was trying to establish common ground by denigrating the impoverished and quite possibly homeless black man for whom I had just bought breakfast. But there was anger in his eyes, and he almost spat the words out; I had the impression he meant what he said. At the very least, I thought as I navigated New York in the waning Trump presidency—just before the murder of George Floyd in May 2020 provided another, tragic spark in the global take-up of the Black Lives Matter movement—it was a reminder of racism's central but complicated position at the heart of the American sensibility. I downed my espresso and decided that, in future, I would buy breakfast from the Hispanic diner around the corner.

When St Clair Drake set sail for Cardiff in the summer of 1947, racism was even more embedded within the social fabric of the country he was leaving behind. If *Black Metropolis* was Drake's and Cayton's *magnum opus*, what gave it its punch was the detail with which they demonstrated the brutality of what was referred to as America's "colour line". By 1940, 1.5 million African Americans had left the Jim Crow South in search of prosperity in the ostensibly more egalitarian North. But what they found was that while racial segregation was not written into law, it was nevertheless a *de facto* feature of the way cities like New York and Chicago were organised. African Americans found themselves effectively confined to neighbourhoods such as Harlem and the South Side, which had the worst-quality housing and, because of chronic overcrowding, were often hotbeds of disease.

When black people attempted to buy property outside the "black belt", they were repeatedly targeted by white vigilante groups, which, in Chicago, led to the 1919 race riots and a series of arson attacks on black people's homes throughout the 1920s and '30s. White homeowners signed quasi-legal documents in which they agreed never to rent or sell their property to an African American, while at work black people were vastly over-represented in both unskilled jobs and unemployment rates. The colour line was, for all intents and purposes, a form of racial segregation by another name.²

Cardiff's Tiger Bay was also beset by overcrowding, disease, and, at different points, high unemployment and rioting. But what distinguished it from the South Side, Drake knew, was the Bay's reputation for racial mixing. Fuelled by the global demand for Welsh coal, by the late-nineteenth century Tiger Bay had become a major stop-off for the ethnically diverse band of labourers who manned the global merchant-shipping industry, and who often arrived in Britain from its colonies in Africa, the Middle East, the West Indies, and elsewhere. In 1938, there were more foreign and ethnic-minority seamen living in Tiger Bay than in all Britain's other port areas put together, alongside an additional population of 40,000 "floating" seamen who passed through the area on an annual basis. By the 1940s, over half the Bay's 6,000 residents were from ethnic-minority backgrounds, and one reporter calculated that there were more than forty-five different nationalities in residence, from Arabs, Somalis, and Haitians to those whose "race mixtures" were somehow too difficult to name. Visiting the Bay, the reporter concluded, was like embarking on a voyage around the world.³

It was a scandal that erupted during the tail-end of the Second World War that prompted Drake to uproot himself from the

BROWN BABIES: 1940s CARDIFF

American Midwest to this surprisingly cosmopolitan square-mile corner of South Wales. In the context of the unprecedented diversity brought about in Britain by the conflict—the hundreds of thousands Italian and German prisoners of war, for example, the 250,000 Irish immigrants who also arrived in Britain during the conflict, as well as the three million American troops who were at different points stationed across the country—the controversy centred on reports of a growing number of African American GIs who, while stationed in Britain at military bases such as Maindy Barracks in Cardiff, were purportedly embarking on sexual relationships with local white women. Unsurprisingly, these relationships—and, even more alarmingly for many observers, the growing population of mixed-race babies reportedly being fathered by black troops—struck a nerve with the American public. At that time the US Army remained a racially segregated force, and the prospect of interracial mingling in Britain threatened to damage diplomatic relations between the States and its key ally. But more than this, as Drake made clear in *Black Metropolis*, in both the South and the North, sex was conceptualised as one of the key frontiers of the American colour line. Echoing the temper of some of the crudest legislation of the Jim Crow era, Drake found that in Chicago it was commonly believed that the presence of a single drop of black blood was enough to "taint" a white person's racial stock. It was therefore necessary to preserve the colour line to maintain the "purity" of the white race. With this milieu as his point of reference, Drake began his seven-month stint in Britain in order to understand the nature of a neighbourhood where, at the very least, the lines seemed to be less clearly drawn.[4]

If Drake was hoping for a multicultural utopia in Cardiff, he was to be disappointed. What he encountered was the ubiquitous nature of racism and ideas about race in late-colonial Britain. The way in which the Bay was viewed by politicians, journalists, and other commentators was underpinned by a fusion of racial and sexual anxieties that echoed the world Drake had left behind in Chicago. There were fears about the supposedly limitless potential of criminality and violence among Tiger Bay's ethnic-minority population, concerns about the sexuality of black men and the threat this posed to white women, and most fundamentally, worries about the spectre of inter-ethnic sex and a charged fascination with what was understood to be the aberration of "brown babies".

In the years after the conflict, especially following the 1947 declaration of Indian independence, there were signs that Britain's once-sprawling empire was beginning to erode. But the ideas about race and racial characteristics that buttressed Britain's imperial project remained pervasive. Although these were the product of irrational fictions and pseudoscience of the crudest kind, Drake also found that their dominance in British culture created concrete situations that the diverse inhabitants of the Bay were, again and again, forced to come up against in their everyday lives.

This is what the Martiniquan theorist, psychiatrist, and anti-colonial activist Frantz Fanon would later describe as the crippling "fact of blackness": in their daily lives, visibly "different" people were forced to carry the "thousand details, anecdotes [and] stories" that were at the heart of racial thinking in majority-white societies, and bound up with colonialism and the legacies of slavery. Thus Tiger Bay's ethnic-minority residents not only had to deal with the brutal effects of direct racism; in spite of the concerted efforts of world-weary local activists to refute the stereotypes published in newspaper exposés, they themselves could begin to think racially. Like the Indian server in that Harlem branch of Dunkin Donuts, they could begin to internalise the fictions that underpinned the ideology of race.[5]

Drake's field notes—and the 300-page PhD he would eventually complete on race relations in Britain (but never publish)—

demonstrate just how integral race was to the social fabric of late-imperial Britain. But the more I read of his work, the more I could see a parallel formation in Cardiff—one that echoed a central intervention made by Drake and Cayton in *Black Metropolis*. It went without saying that, in the "black belt" of South Side Chicago, racism dominated black people's lives; it was the effective cage in which such communities were held. But Drake and Cayton were just as keen to highlight an equally real, parallel reality they referred to as the "metropolis". If places such as the South Side were racialised ghettos beset with the consequences of structural discrimination, the metropolis represented the social and commercial bonds that people were nevertheless able to make for themselves in such areas. In essence, it represented the lives that people fought to create in spite of the lived consequences of racism: places of worship, dive bars, dice rooms, political associations, chitterling diners, and cabaret joints; hustling, thinking, political organising, love-making and "having a good time". The metropolis was both a "struggle for liberty" and a "tenacious clinging to life".[6]

In Cardiff, Drake found it difficult to get past the "fact of blackness" as, in different ways, they brought themselves to bear on Tiger Bay's ethnically diverse population. But I began to see that—hidden away in Drake's field notes, or buried in the footnotes of his doctorate—there were also unmistakable signs of metropolitan community life. There was the presence of political organisations such as the Colonial Defence Association, which in the 1920s had played a major role in fighting for the rights of ethnic-minority seamen but, by the 1940s, was struggling to reckon with an increasingly powerful, heterogeneous anti-colonial movement that had set the energies of activists off in competing directions. There was the 1947 opening of a permanent mosque in the Bay, replete with traditional Islamic minarets, the green flag of Islam, and banners with the message *la ilaha ilallah*

MULTICULTURAL BRITAIN

("There is no god but God"). There were the mixed-race youths who frequented a local sports club, the West Indian-run boarding house that catered for visiting seamen of different ethnicities, and local cafés with names such as Cairo and Chop Suey that sold groceries alongside cups of tea and glasses of diluted whisky, and reportedly had backrooms set aside for illicit sexual liaisons.

What follows in this chapter demonstrates the relentless presence of racism in 1940s Britain, and the related influence of ideas about race—the "fact of blackness". But it is testament to the dialectical nature of the making of multicultural Britain that Drake simultaneously provided a window onto a metropolis in its infancy—one that was attempting to solidify its foundations. These were far from perfect. But they were indeed foundations, and it was upon them that the future of multicultural Britain would one day be built.

Tiger Bay, 1947

Having arrived in Cardiff in the summer of 1947, St. Clair Drake recorded in his diary his initial impressions of Bute Street, Tiger Bay's main thoroughfare. It was lined with more than two dozen cafés in the space of 300 yards, seamen's boarding houses, barbers, shops selling naval uniforms, sea boots, and other seafaring equipment, and at least one pub to every street. To Drake's eyes the names of these establishments—Ebony Café (named after the popular African American magazine), Cairo Lodging House, Singapore Café, Satar's Arab Lodging House, Sande Fjord Café, Chop Suey Café—spoke to the global nature of Tiger Bay, and made the area a rival to the Maltese, Greek and Arab owned cafés that in the same period lined Cable Street in London's East End. Drake was equally struck by the diversity of the people around him. At one junction, he watched as a street performer entertained a crowd of more than thirty people, eight of whom were "recognisably coloured" (although it seemed to Drake that, in contrast to the world he had left behind in Chicago, he was the only one bothering to make any such distinctions).

Further down towards Loudoun Square, Tiger Bay's central hub, the diversity became even more pronounced. In a park, Drake spotted a blonde toddler playing with a black girl of the same age, and a white woman with an Arab man. The latter picked up one of the children lovingly, leaving the others to continue playing in the mud. Nearby, Drake noticed a smartly dressed girl he guessed was no more than eight years old, looking after two dark-skinned toddlers, and a black boy of twelve pushing a friend in what looked like a homemade wheelbarrow. Men walked past briskly in fezzes, with badges bearing the insignia MN (Merchant Navy) on their collars; many of the women wore brightly coloured turbans. At the northern end of Bute Street was a newly-built stucco mosque with truncated minarets and neon Arabic lettering. At the opposite end of the community, Drake noticed a sign with directions to the nearby maternity clinic, printed in both English and Arabic.[7]

"The professor", as Drake's subjects referred to him, soon became a familiar presence as he attended cricket matches put on by the Coloured International Athletic Club or sat down for tea with the Yemeni *shaykh* of the Bay's mosque. Drake initially felt a sense of disorientation that mirrored my own awkwardness in New York. On his first morning in Cardiff he wasn't sure whether or not to tip his hotel maid, and he never seemed to understand the appeal of cricket among his West Indian associates in particular. But the overall ease with which he assimilated into Bay life was no doubt helped by the fact that during the war, African Americans had become a regular presence in the area— mainly as a result of the various black US Army units stationed nearby on bases such as Maindy Barracks and Fairford in Gloucestershire. One Tiger Bay resident remembered a steady stream of black GIs arriving almost every weekend, drawn to the area's reputation as Britain's primary "coloured quarter" in the hope that this would allow them to enjoy its nightlife without any of the hostility that could greet them elsewhere in the country. There were an estimated 240,000 African American troops stationed across the UK at different points during the conflict. Photographs show black GIs sitting in Cardiff's Loudoun Square, dressed in sports jackets and high-waisted slacks. In one photo, two men pose for the camera by drinking a celebratory bottle of VP wine; in another, a GI poses awkwardly in the sunshine next to a young white woman in a knee-length floral dress.[8]

The possibilities evoked by such images, especially the latter, caught the attention of the chattering classes on both sides of the Atlantic. In the US, media interest in Britain's growing mixed-race population—and the role that American troops might have played in contributing to it—was shaped by intense domestic debates about the prevalence of racial segregation in the army, the Jim Crow South and the "colour-lined" North. Tiger Bay was just like the Yamacraw seaport in Savannah, Georgia, an American journalist told readers, except for one important distinction: "the free mixing of all the races". It was reported that in Tiger Bay, an area just two blocks wide and ten long, there lived citizens of almost every corner of Britain's empire, "infinitely varied in colour, culture, race and creed". More shocking to American readers would have been the story of the growing population of illegitimate "mulatto" babies, the product of relationships between African American GIs and local white women. According to *Time* Magazine, as many as 500 such children faced severe social and economic difficulties in Britain. Where the fathers acknowledged paternity, the mothers of these children were entitled to financial support from the US Army amounting to $85 per month. But this was often disputed, and in any case the support was withdrawn once soldiers had been demobilised in the US. Another American journalist, on a visit to Cardiff, described encountering a mixed-race baby in abject poverty who stared at him with worried eyes and was forced to suck on the leather strap of an old shoe. Some mixed-race children did seem to be well-cared for, the journalist admitted, and over and again he was told that white mothers would not part with their "brown babies". But this belied the fact that the vast majority were, in his view, either neglected or maltreated; Britain's "half-caste" population would, he predicted, go on to lead "rootless lives, with little hope of a secure future".[9]

The sex appeal that black GIs found they had in Britain stemmed at least in part from the popular understanding, particularly in the provinces, that American "negroes" represented a sense of exotic, modish urbanity—particularly with the perception, gleaned from the popularity of Hollywood movies and jazz, that African Americans could dance the jitterbug much better than their white counterparts. In some ways, this was a precursor to the later appeal hip-hop culture found—in terms of music, but also with regard to style and language—among white and South Asian children at British schools such as the one I attended in Birmingham. For African American soldiers stationed in Britain during the war, their romantic encounters were a central feature of their later recollections of wartime experiences. Wilbur Young, for example, who had joined the US Army in 1943 and received his training in the segregated military town of Norfolk, Virginia, found himself stationed in Newport, Wales during the conflict—a twenty-minute drive from Cardiff. In an interview conducted in 1946, Young remembered how his black unit seemed to fit in nicely with Welsh life. Appreciating the "sing-song" nature of the Welsh accent—and the peculiar way locals would say *aye* instead of *yes*—Young insisted that a number of marriages between black GIs and white women took place "right off the bat", in spite of the US Army's formal requirement that any such arrangement be approved by a commanding officer (and the fact that interracial marriages remained illegal in many US states). When Young's company was moved to a barracks thirty-five miles away in Bristol, some of the men managed to find a truck to drive them all back over the River Severn to see their sweethearts. When this was not possible, the women would get on trains to see them. There were even rivalries between the women of Newport and Bristol over the attentions of particular men, Young claimed; on occasion there were as many as three women waiting for a single soldier outside a camp, and the soldier in question would be forced to make his excuses and send word that he was out on detail.[10]

It would be tempting to dismiss such testimony as exaggerated bravado. But relationships did form between black troops and local women in Wales and the southwest of England and, charged by the relentlessness of the wartime experience, these could be experienced with acute intensity. In Bristol in the early hours of an August morning in 1945, for instance, when word began to spread that American troops would soon be returning home, a posse of women aged between seventeen and twenty-five descended on a military base that housed four companies of black soldiers. The women besieged the barracks with a chorus of "Don't Fence Me In"—a popular wartime song that featured in the movie *Hollywood Canteen* (1944)—while the soldiers reportedly broke down the barbed wire that surrounded their quarters so that the women could enter. Within minutes, hundreds of couples were seen kissing and embracing. There were similar scenes at Cardiff's train station in November where, in spite of the NO PLATFORM TICKET notices posted around the premises, scores of women found a way to join their African American lovers on the platform, where there was much good humoured banter. When the whistle signalled that it was time for the soldiers to leave aboard their train, policemen who had been deployed to manage the situation struggled to prevent the women from attempting to depart with them.[11]

The very public nature of scenes such as this one put wartime authorities in Britain in an uncomfortable position. On one hand, fantastical notions of British decency and a supposedly egalitarian attitude towards race stemming from the imperial "family of nations" served as useful propaganda that could be contrasted with the atrocities being committed by Nazi Germany. The Colonial Office was likewise particularly keen to cling to a Kafkaesque image of imperial Britain as the harbinger of racial equality in order to dampen down anti-colonial sentiment across the empire. On the other hand, the British Government was equally determined not to antagonise the United States, and worried that the relative ability of black GIs to enter into predominately white establishments—notwithstanding the expansion of Britain's "colour bar"—would, given the US Army's policy of segregation, cause diplomatic tensions that could hinder the Allied war effort. In addition, there was the inconvenient reality that, whatever the diplomatic considerations of the UK Government, there were also a substantial number of British politicians and other commentators who found the prospect of inter-ethnic relations—whether sexual or otherwise—distasteful on their own terms.[12]

In Cardiff, things came to a head in September 1945 with a sustained moral panic over the scenes taking place around Maindy Barracks, just over three miles north of Tiger Bay. There, GIs allegedly arranged sexual encounters with their girlfriends in the park next to the barracks, which had apparently also become a prominent area of solicitation for sex workers. According to reports, dozens of young women had begun to sleep rough in the park, with the majority having followed troops from base to base. The area of the park closest to the barracks was described as being one of "indescribable filth", strewn with women's underwear and lice-ridden mattresses. The iron railings that surrounded the park had purportedly been bent apart so that the women could bed down for the night in the nearby bushes. A park employee claimed that he had even seen a woman soliciting black soldiers dressed in nothing but a skirt.

To begin with, the local press laid the blame for such activity squarely with the women concerned. Tying into the well-established trope of the 'fallen' woman, one Welsh newspaper explained how "girl tramps" had become a "menace to Wales" and suggested that the best solution might be to simply round up the women and send them for institutional treatment. But there was a racial undercurrent to much of the reportage. The lane that separated the park and the barracks and connected Gelligaer Street to the south and New Zealand Road to the north was soon christened "Burma Road". This was a popular wartime postal acronym for "Be Undressed and Ready, My Angel" that—in referencing the real Burma Road, which connected China to British Burma—implicitly referenced perceived moral waywardness in the colonies and the idea that "jungle behaviour" had arrived in Britain. One resident of the terraced housing that surrounded Maindy Barracks complained to the press that his daughter had become afraid to leave the house because a black GI had recently followed her home. The problem was, the resident explained, black troops now thought that all white girls were the same.[13]

With the end of the conflict in Europe perhaps emboldening those who had previously been persuaded to hold back their reservations about the presence of African American soldiers in Britain, emphasis increasingly shifted to the role that black GIs played in the establishment of Cardiff's Burma Road. The controversy wore on, reaching a crescendo in mid-September when Cardiff's Lord Mayor described the situation as a disgrace to the city and advocated the immediate removal of African American troops. Siding with the mayor, Cardiff's veteran Chief Constable

BROWN BABIES: 1940s CARDIFF

James A. Wilson, who was in his twenty-fifth year in the job, laid his cards on the table: "It is on account of the coloured troops that these lapses of moral rectitude have occurred. The coloured troops are a truculent lot of people with the civil police and we have had trouble dealing with them. Until these coloured troops are removed from Cardiff", Wilson declared, "this type of woman will still persist in hanging about".[14]

A number of African American GIs wrote to the press anonymously in shock at the sudden way in which race had been made the central feature of the Burma Road scandal. One soldier accused Wilson of having created "undesirable thoughts" towards African American soldiers in Wales, while another explained how he had "never felt more down and sick on any subject connected with the British and Americans at the present moment"; the whole episode had, the soldier suggested, led to "minute elements of friendship" being "blown asunder". More experienced observers of the treatment of Cardiff's ethnic-minority population would surely have been less surprised. The eventual response to Burma Road, and the link that Wilson and others made between the supposed collapse in the established moral order and the presence of an "alien" black population had, in fact, been conditioned by decades of hostility and state-sponsored racism towards Cardiff's ethnic-minority population—the vast majority of whom, of course, lived in Tiger Bay. In many ways, the only surprise was that it took Wilson and others so long to turn their attention towards the African American companies stationed at Maindy Barracks during the latter part of the war.[15]

The flashpoints in this history were largely determined by the status of the labour market in the shipping industry. During the First World War—and as American employers in cities such as Chicago would do with African American labourers from the South following the end of the conflict—shipping companies filled the increasingly severe manpower gap created by the war with cheap labour from China and Britain's colonies in the Caribbean, Somaliland, and elsewhere. The return of British soldiers at the end of the war contributed to a labour surplus, along with a perception that workers who looked or spoke differently were not only undercutting wages but were also—having often formed relationships with local white women during the war—a source of sexual competition. In the hot summer of 1919, these tensions erupted with a major outbreak of rioting in Tiger Bay, the initial spark for which was a gang of returning white soldiers targeting a group of black men who had been out with their white wives in central Cardiff. During the subsequent unrest, which followed similar disturbances earlier in the year in the port areas of South Shields and Liverpool, and pre-empted the Chicago race riots Drake described in *Black Metropolis* by a month, black-owned property in Tiger Bay was vandalised and looted, and white mobs attacked black passers-by with cries of "Come on and set about them!" Over four days, an estimated £3,000 worth of damage was done to property—the equivalent of more than £125,000 in 2023. Three people lost their lives—a black man from a fractured skull, a white man from a slit throat, and another white man who had been shot through the heart.[16]

What was striking about the response to the unrest was not just the way in which, despite the fact that the events were propelled by white lynch mobs, they somehow reinforced the Bay's reputation as "niggertown"; even more damaging was the extent to which the British Government, in an unholy alliance with the Seamen's Union and the demands of the major shipping companies, subsequently showed themselves willing to institutionalise the prejudice that had fuelled the white rioters in Cardiff and elsewhere in the first place. The Government introduced brazenly discriminatory Aliens Orders in 1920 and again in 1925 which targeted ethnic-minority seamen specifically by requiring them to prove their right of entry into Britain and to register with the authorities as aliens—although large numbers were citizens of the British Empire and had earlier been actively encouraged to fill Britain's wartime labour shortage. The Orders emboldened rather than placated opposition to the presence of 'non-white' workers in Britain's seaports. In 1929, for instance, rehearsing the argument he would later make against the presence of African American GIs in Cardiff (and wilfully ignoring the role the Aliens Orders played in exacerbating the growth in unemployment among ethnic minorities in the city), Chief Constable Wilson made his position clear: "British West Indians and West Africans ... are men who dislike work," he claimed. "They are dissolute, thieves, inveterate gamesters, the associates of prostitutes and strongly suspected of living on their immoral earnings." While he regarded Somalis as "a fairly intelligent race", he thought of them as "truculent and vicious". West Africans, meanwhile, were to Wilson's mind "of an inferior order and almost primitive in their habits". In the absence of mass deportation, he argued, the best way to avoid future problems in Britain would be to follow the lead of apartheid South Africa and make interracial sex a formal crime.[17]

Anxieties around sex and miscegenation were indeed a central feature of these narratives, and often functioned in such a way as to deny any agency whatsoever to the white women who were deemed unlucky enough to have fallen in love with black men. Black seamen simply came into contact with white women in the Bay, one report explained, primarily those who were of "loose moral character", and it wasn't long before a growing number of "half caste" babies were brought into the world.[18]

Dovetailing with this sexualised anxiety was an equally powerful understanding of race that exposed the presence of a telling kind of doublethink in imperial Britain. On one hand, commentators showed themselves to be fully on board with the hierarchical racial logic of empire; at the same time, on the other hand, they were at pains to disavow Britain's history of colonial expansionism as providing any possible justification for the presence of black, Asian, or Arab people in places such as Tiger Bay. The essential problem, one report lamented, was that Cardiff's "coloured" population was "being made to adopt a standard of civilisation they cannot be expected to understand". A 1935 editorial in the *Western Mail and South Wales News*, the leading newspaper in Wales, slapped down those who argued that "inasmuch as the white man has staked claims in the black man's country, the black man is entitled to settle wherever he chooses in the Empire". Such an interpretation was to ignore a "clash of civilisations and ethical standards a thousand years apart". The problem, as one journalist saw it, was that Tiger Bay had become "a community of unsophisticated strangers, many of whom are unable to adjust themselves happily to the complexities of our civilisation". Whatever the reasons for the difficulties the Bay faced, the *Western Mail and South Wales News* concluded, the moment had been reached where "we can no longer tolerate that burden on our doorsteps".[19]

If these ideas abated during the Second World War, it is unsurprising that they returned with such intensity so soon after Britain's role in the conflict came to an end—particularly when returning British soldiers once again squeezed the main source of employment in Tiger Bay. Economic downturns contributing to the scapegoating of minority communities was a pattern that would be repeated throughout the history of multicultural Britain. During the war, the media focus on the Bay continued, and the neighbourhood also began to attract a growing number of academics who would shape what later became the thriving field of "race relations". While these scholars were generally committed to repudiating any notion of biologically distinct 'races', their writings nevertheless often reproduced many of the broader assumptions of racial thinking in the high-imperial era.

BROWN BABIES: 1940s CARDIFF

"Whiteness" was implicitly equated with "'civilised' virtues", one historian noted; it was something against which ethnic-minority subjects were to be "measured and found wanting". Thus, according to the white English anthropologist Kenneth Little, who conducted field research in Cardiff in the early 1940s, the number of 'non-white' skins were so plentiful in Tiger Bay that first-time visitors could be excused for mistaking the district for a foreign land. The Bay's ethnic minority population comprised "racially distinctive strangers" whose "racial characteristics" were fundamentally alien. Little found that the "half castes" had a light-hearted demeanour that verged on irresponsibility, and that the Arabs were primarily religious rather than political. The African and Caribbean population, meanwhile, which Little emphasised was made up of people with the darkest skins, was apparently characterised by a distinctive combination of masculinity and socio-economic austerity.[20]

Little's "facts of blackness" differed from the Chief Constable's focus on what he saw as the "immorality", "truculence", and "viciousness" of the Bay's ethnic-minority community. Unsurprisingly, though, his conclusions were strongly refuted by local black activists, who accused Little of slander worthy of a "sick pseudo-biologist". Mindful of this hostility to outsiders, when St Clair Drake arrived in Cardiff in 1947 he attempted to side with these activists, and tried to foreground a different side to Bay life away from the stereotype of "darkest Cardiff". Yet his work also attests to how much the kind of racial thinking that structured external representations of and policies towards Tiger Bay's residents also had an active presence within the community. To begin with, residents were evidently well aware of what they understood to be the connection between race and status in the Bay. Drake observed this as having manifested itself as a "rank order based on power and prestige *vis-à-vis* the larger white community", with the Arab community at the front of the pack and the West Indians coming just behind. However, whereas in societies such as colonial Jamaica the primary focus was on the relative lightness of skin pigmentation, in the post-war Bay the wider anxieties over interracial sex—and the events around Maindy Road Barracks in particular—had placed its "half caste" residents at the bottom of the community's racial hierarchy.[21]

"Half castes" were undisputed "symbols of immorality", Drake wrote in his field diary. He had encountered a similar situation on a visit to Liverpool, 150 miles north of Cardiff. Liverpool had been a central European port in the transatlantic slave trade and was home to a small black and mixed-race population consisting largely of servants and students as far back as the early-1800s. Yet the stigma around "brown babies" persisted. In fact, it was so acute during Drake's stay in the city that some infants were reportedly abandoned by their parents and handed over to the African Churches Mission, a "coloured centre" styled as a "haven of refuge for stranded Africans" that had been established at 122–24 Hill Street by the charismatic Nigerian preacher and former factory worker Daniels Ekarte in 1931.[22]

In Tiger Bay, the specific nature of the ethnic composition of mixed-ethnicity children was often critical. One white woman, for example, was reportedly indignant at hearing her son was being bullied at school for having a "nigger" father when, in fact, everyone knew his father was Arab. Those who were themselves of mixed ethnicity, meanwhile, found that they were often the recipients of abuse from all sides. One of Drake's interviewees, Roger Burnham—who was born in the early 1900s to a black seaman from St Vincent in the Caribbean and a mixed-ethnicity woman from Southampton—found that as soon as he left the Bay he was regularly subject to cries of "look at the black man" or "look at the nigger" as he passed by on the street. The geographic nature of racial discrimination—and the way black or Arab residents were much more visible once they crossed over the Canal Parade Bridge and headed into Central Cardiff—was also emphasised by a Somali man who was photographed by the English documentary photographer Bert Hardy in the post-war years. "If I go up into town, say to the pictures," the man explained, "everyone looks at me as if I left some buttons undone"; leaving the confines of the Bay meant having to come into contact with people who behaved as though "they believe we've got horns under our hats". But Burnham found that within the Bay, his mixed ethnicity meant that those with darker skins, who were more attuned to the nuances of the area's racial hierarchy, also subjected him to abuse. As Drake overheard one black resident saying, "these half castes could make something of themselves if they had any initiative". For Burnham, West Indians looked down on people who were not deemed to be "fully" West Indian. "You know", he confided in Drake, "I wish I was one thing or the other. It would be better to be all West Indian or all White."[23]

There was a messiness to the way in which this kind of racial thinking was worked through in the minds of those Bay residents, something exemplified by another of Drake's interviewees: Mrs Edwards, the black proprietor of a Tiger Bay boarding house who had been born in Britain in the early 1900s to a West Indian father and a black British mother. Prior to the Second World War such boarding houses were generally segregated along ethnic lines, with particular establishments catering for Arabs, Indians, Somalis, or "Negroes". (British establishments often also catered for white seamen from Spain, Portugal, or Scandinavia rather than black boarders from the British Empire, thus demonstrating the fickleness of British attitudes towards any notion of trans-imperial kinship.) Edwards's establishment, by contrast, placed no restrictions on who would be accommodated. Drake described the scene that greeted him as he entered into her premises to take tea with her and her guests. Ali, a Somali boarder, was sitting at the head of the dining room table alongside two men from the West Indies who, like hundreds of others in this period, had entered the UK as stowaways on ships. Both the men were drinking coffee and eating buttered bread and cheese. Soon after Drake arrived a Jamaican boarder walked in and settled down to a heavy stew.[24]

In her interview with Drake, Edwards described herself as "all coloured and proud of it". She was likewise explicit about the racism that black people experienced in Cardiff. The Welsh simply did not like black people, she explained. "They are taught young, too. The mothers tell the children [that] when they're bad the black man will get them if they don't behave." Reinforcing the emphasis placed on the politics of geography by both Burnham and Bert Hardy's anonymous Somali subject, Edwards explained that as soon as you left the Bay people were liable to nudge each other when you passed by and say, "there goes a black" or "there goes a darky". And there was also a class dynamic to Edwards's understanding of the city's racial politics. She was, for example, critical of the white women who were married to black or Arab men, whom she noticed never seemed to go anywhere with their husbands. The consensus, Edwards argued, was that such women were ashamed of their partners. They wanted "money, but not the man". In spite of her nuanced dissection of the way in which racism was perpetuated from generation to generation in Cardiff, as well as her ownership of one of the few ethnically-mixed boarding houses in the Bay, Edwards reserved her most jarring criticism for the neighbourhood's Muslims. Echoing what would become the familiar, racialised anxieties around hygiene and perceptions of cultural incompatibility as immigration to Britain increased in the 1950s (and presumably talking out of earshot of Ali, her Somalian boarder), Edwards complained about the noise the Muslim community had made during a recent festival in the Bay, that they kept goats by the Glamorganshire Canal and had even tried to keep them in the park until a warden had stopped them. "Dirty old Arabs," she exclaimed. "They're so dirty!"[25]

I found it difficult to read these comments and not recall some of the racism I had witnessed occasionally when I was at school—particularly when I moved to my comparatively white secondary school, and especially when the so-called "War on Terror" helped give credence to the damaging fiction that Islam was somehow incompatible with the basic values of "the West". But it is worth remembering that the late-1940s were as close to the brazenly discriminatory Aliens Orders of the 1920s as to the belated introduction of legislation designed to address the social effect of racism in 1965. While she accused Arabs of being "dirty", elsewhere in her conversation with Drake, Mrs Edwards pivoted to maternal (if undoubtedly patronising) language to describe the area's Somalian community: "they're very nice, aren't they?" she mused, her question perhaps betraying a lack of confidence in her own ability to find the right language; "Just like big children, aren't they?" Drake also noticed that race was a source of jocularity within the Edwards household, a kind of light-hearted banter that offered an outlet for a deeper malaise. On one occasion, for example, Mrs Edwards remarked that she might one day like to visit Africa, to which her son responded: "Don't go there. You're black enough already."[26]

Drake found this kind of discourse to be a pervasive feature of life in the Bay. Here was the West Indian ship's cook recounting a story about a group of Arabs who supposedly tried to cook a sheep with its bowels still in as evidence of a lack of hygiene among "those dirty Muslims"; here was the warden of the Bay's Colonial Centre who was reluctant to admit people of mixed ethnicity because they did not "take discipline"; here were the commonplace references to African seamen as "cannibals", "heathens", or "savages". While the joking that took place may have been a way of contesting the seemingly unassailable nature of racial thinking in Britain, racism was also a way for certain sections of the community to reinforce what they saw as their superior position within the Bay's racial hierarchy.[27]

From the post-war moral panic around Maindy Barracks and the views of Chief Constable Wilson over more than twenty-five years, to the steady stream of newspaper exposés of Britain's 'half-caste' problem and a growing literature produced by white sociologists of 'race relations', ideas about race structured how Tiger Bay was viewed by white society. This was also a feature of the Bay's profane culture. Just as Fanon found that a "thousand details, anecdotes [and] stories" had somehow begun to creep into his own consciousness and "fix" his sense of self, so too were the residents of Tiger Bay forced to navigate the practical consequences of the centrality of racial thinking in late-imperial Britain. But beyond the control of figures such as Wilson and the view of journalists from either side of the Atlantic Ocean, developments in the community's political and particularly its social life were beginning to undermine the reach of such ideas. Drake referred to these as the vibrant metropolis within the ghetto, something that, in his view, regarding the people he encountered on the South Side of Chicago, represented concrete evidence of a particular kind of freedom—the "freedom to erect a community in their own image". The racial thinking that permeated the empire exercised a powerful influence in the post-war Bay. But it is at the level of everyday politics and leisure in the Tiger Bay "metropolis" that we can see how residents were—in the absence of constructive assistance from the state—beginning to feel out the practicalities of multicultural living.[28]

"A scene of brilliant colour": the Tiger Bay Metropolis

Race as an everyday feature of life in the Bay coincided with wider tensions, particularly between Muslim residents and black sections of the population that regarded their own longstanding presence in the Bay as giving them a more authentic claim to the community. "Why can't darkies stick together like the Arabs?" one black activist complained to Drake. "They've came here since we did, and now look, they've got all the stores. What have we darkies got? Nothing!" Drake's arrival in the Bay certainly coincided with a period of political fragmentation in the area. Organisations such as the Colonial Defence Association, which had been established in 1927 by the Guyanese seaman and Communist organiser Harry O'Connell, and which had played a leading role in marshalling community resistance to the Aliens Orders of the 1920s, were by the late 1940s in decline.[29]

O'Connell—whom Drake described as being short and wiry, with a closely cropped head of greying hair—first came to Cardiff in the early 1910s and joined the Communist Party in the aftermath of the 1919 race riots. One associate remembered him as "a very fine seaman comrade" and a "totally devoted and energetic Communist of the finest quality", though O'Connell's unwillingness to depart from the Party line—and in particular, his refusal to cede primacy to race over class struggles—was a source of discord among his peers even before the war. In the late 1930s, O'Connell fell out with the League of Coloured Peoples, a moderate campaign group that had been formed by the Jamaican physician Harold Moody in London in 1931 and, for a brief period, was also gaining a foothold in the Bay. O'Connell characterised Moody as a "misleader" whose focus on race was such that he believed black people could never do anything wrong. By 1947, however, O'Connell's once-powerful Colonial Defence Association was, by his own admission, largely defunct. For O'Connell, a key reason for this was the difficulty he purportedly encountered in working with the local Muslim community. There was resentment towards the local Yemeni *shaykh*, Abdullah Ali al-Hakimi, who was seen to be suspiciously willing to maintain a close proximity to the British state. For O'Connell, however, the issue with the Muslim community was more straightforward: it was simply "hard to understand what [they] are really thinking".[30]

There were more than 2,000 Muslims in the Bay, though it was the 700-strong Yemeni Sufi community that, by the late 1940s, exercised the most political power. Al-Hakimi was undoubtedly the prime mover in this respect. He had arrived in Britain from the Yemeni port city of Aden in 1936 and played a key role in the establishment of Cardiff's Islamic Society, as well as—at numbers 17–19 Peel Street, a stone's throw from the Bay's main Bute Street thoroughfare—the Cardiff mosque, the first purpose-built mosque in Wales. Later, he also established his own Arabic newspaper, *al-Salam*, which was the first of its kind in Britain.[31]

To Drake, al-Hakimi came across as "a venerable gentleman" as he walked around the Bay dressed in a green turban and white robe. He was educated, well-travelled, and was known to retain significant business interests in Aden, which had been annexed from the rest of Yemen by the British in 1839. Local resentment at al-Hakimi's apparent influence stemmed from the speed at which he won governmental support for the rebuilding of the mosque after it was severely damaged by the German Blitz in January 1941. First, al-Hakimi secured planning permission for a temporary wooden structure on the same site, which was opened in July 1943. Then, with the help of both Colonial Office and British Council funds, he gained permission for a much more expansive, permanent structure that was designed by the Cardiff architect Osborne V. Webb and dedicated in September 1947. The new building was bookended on either side by rows of terraced houses, had windows carved in the shape of traditional minarets, two small domes, and external walls painted light yellow; the green flag of Islam, adorned with white Arabic letters, hung over the entrance. According to *Picture Post*, at the mosque's dedication ceremony processions of worshippers carried flags and banners and recited prayers as they went. Hundreds of local residents gathered to hear the *shaykh* deliver an open-air address, and tea was handed out to everyone, including the passers-by who had stopped to watch. Inside the mosque, scores of people dressed in flame-red or brilliant green turbans and long, loose robes sat barefoot on brightly-coloured Eastern carpets. The event was summarised by *Picture Post* as "a scene of brilliant colour", and was attended by dignitaries including the Lord Mayors of Cardiff, Barry and Newport as well as Hafiz Wahba, the Saudi ambassador to Britain. Even Prime Minister Clement Attlee was reportedly on the original guest list.[32]

There was an unmistakable strain of Orientalism to *Picture Post's* reportage of what was understood to be the essential exoticness of a mosque built amid the rundown streets of working-class Cardiff. But from the vantage point of the early twenty-first century—where for more than twenty years the popular press and politicians alike have played a key role in amplifying hostility towards British Muslims—the overwhelmingly positive nature of the article's journalistic tone stands out. And given the spectacle of the mosque's dedication, as well as the financial support al-Hakimi was able to attract, it was probably inevitable that long-standing local activists such as O'Connell would also take notice.

Belying Kenneth Little's assumption that the Arab community was largely apolitical, al-Hakimi proved an effective political operator. At the end of an interview he conducted with Drake, for example, and perhaps mindful of the public impact that the work of an American academic could have, al-Hakimi emphasised that he wanted the professor to know that Cardiff's Muslim population had been accorded "every courtesy" and that the Government and local community had been "very kind to them". Al-Hakimi had played an important role in the "Islamization" of the seafaring Muslim community in Cardiff, and in making

Islamic celebrations a visible part of public life. In Drake's analysis, his broader influence was bound up with the Bay's racial hierarchy, and the fact Arabs were aware that their relatively light skin gave them particular advantages in Britain. For others, however, the reasons the British were so willing to support Cardiff's Arab population were more about the pragmatism of *realpolitik*, and the British Government's determination to outstrip competition from the United States by cultivating tactical relations with oil-rich states in the Middle East. Without the oil dynamic, one observer reflected, "them big wigs wouldn't even look at those damned black faces".[33]

While oil may have been a factor, it is more likely the authorities viewed al-Hakimi as a "representative" community leader who could be a useful ally in addressing issues such as rising unemployment among the Muslim seafaring community. Whatever the nature of the politicking behind the scenes, the reopening of the Cardiff mosque was a poignant moment. It showed a willingness on behalf of the state to offer both financial and political support to a section of its ethnic-minority population in a manner that would only begin to become commonplace in Britain in the 1970s. But the extravagance of the dedication ceremony also masked—perhaps even to those who, like O'Connell, were embedded in the Tiger Bay political scene—increasing divisions within the Muslim community itself.

These were primarily manifest in disputes between the Bay's Arab population and the some 200 permanently domiciled Somalis who also resided in the neighbourhood. Drake suggested the disputes partially stemmed from the ethnic differences between the two communities. While both spoke Arabic, for example, for Somalis this was primarily a religious rather than a vernacular language, which Drake observed sometimes led to misunderstandings. There were also differences in religious interpretations, something that came to a head over the decision to erect the new Peel Street mosque with financial assistance from the British authorities. Some Somalian community leaders, particularly Tualla Muhammad—who was born in Berbera, the port city and onetime capital of Somaliland, worked as a ship's fireman, and was an active player in the Somali Youth League, which was established in 1943 to agitate for Somalian independence—argued that money from "unbelievers" should never have been used to construct an Islamic building. The dispute was eventually mediated by an Islamic scholar at King Fuad I University in Cairo, whose conclusion was clear-cut: "since the infidel's bombs had destroyed the mosque, let the infidels rebuild it". Yet there remained suggestions that the Somalian community would seek to establish its own mosque, much to the dismay of *Shaykh* al-Hakimi who—having himself married a mixed-race woman in Cardiff—was at pains to emphasise the inclusive nature of his worldview. "We are all Muslims," he explained in his interview with Drake. "The secretary of this [Islamic] society is a Somali and many Somalis pray here ... There are no racial or tribal distinctions in Islam."[34]

In Drake's view, what these disputes were really about was the extent to which the shifting post-war geopolitical climate was increasingly also being played out in microcosm in the square-mile neighbourhood of the Bay. The willingness of the Arab community to openly embrace the British state, he argued, was connected to the role that Britain had begun to play in opposing Zionist expansion into Palestine at the outbreak of the 1947–49 Arab–Israeli War. The Bay's Somalian political leadership, in contrast, was focused on campaigning for the removal of Italy from any administrative influence on its former colony in Somaliland, as well as the more radical platform for the formation of an independent Greater Somalia that would encompass the Somalian populations in neighbouring Kenya and Ethiopia. Britain's imperial status and the powerful forces of post-war anticolonialism were, in other words, effectively pulling the Bay's Muslim community in separate directions. Arabs gravitated towards strategic support for the British as the colonial power apparently best-placed to halt the partition of Palestine and the subsequent displacement of more than 720,000 Palestinian people (to Arabs this became known as the *Nakba* or catastrophe). But for Tualla Muhammad and other Somali activists, it meant an emphasis on both the immediate political goal of removing the defeated colonial power of Italy from the region, alongside the more ambitious project of Somalian nationalism. It was a twin approach captured by the slogans held aloft on banners by those members of the Somali Youth League who took part in Cardiff's May Day parade of 1948: no return of the colonies to Italy, down with political expediency, Somalis demand a united Somalia and Somalia *ha nolato*—long live freedom.[35]

It is unclear whether or not these concerns resonated more generally in the Bay, beyond particularly committed individuals such as O'Connell, al-Hakimi, and Muhammad. Arab-run shops such as Khalid Salah's on Christina Street, just off Loudoun Square, often had SAVE PALESTINE collection boxes on display alongside portraits of prominent Palestinian nationalists such as Amin al-Husseini, the former Mufti of Jerusalem. Al-Hakimi's position as a *shaykh* likewise also meant that he was a particularly prominent presence in the lives of visiting Arab seamen who were new to the Bay. He was not only a spiritual leader, but also "relates his followers to the great unknown 'white world' of Britain; he keeps their money while they are away; he gets them jobs when they need them; he gets them out of trouble when they are in it". But he was also someone who, during his interview with Drake, abruptly broke off the conversation when a news report about the Palestinian conflict came on the wireless, and paced around the room, leaving Drake to watch awkwardly, taking notes.[36]

BROWN BABIES: 1940s CARDIFF

Similarly, while in the late 1940s O'Connell fought campaigns against the discriminatory practices of the shipping companies, he also hung a chrome portrait of Stalin on his dining-room wall and, by his own admission, spent a good deal of time trying to break up organisations he deemed to be Trotskyist or otherwise politically impure. In many ways, the rivalries between political organisations were about different activists' competing visions of what winning the peace should look like—in South Wales, but also in relation to a global political climate that was changing at a rate of knots. But these were political aspirations, and as such were not necessarily rooted in the everyday rhythms of life in the Tiger Bay metropolis. For most people, Drake observed, day-to-day life did not mean breaking up Trotskyist organisations or plotting to establish an alternative place of worship. Rather, it meant lounging around in boarding houses, drinking and gambling—whether in illegal bookies, or simply on the street.[37]

It is the career of Alan Sheppard—a Guyanese seaman, prominent local organiser, and contemporary of Harry O'Connell—who embodied this tension between the political and the social. Sheppard had arrived in the Bay in the early 1920s as a fully-fledged activist, having previously been imprisoned for "stirring up the natives" in Mozambique, where he claimed to have been subject to beatings so bad he lost all his teeth. With his "seedy" clothing and weather-beaten cap, his was the polar opposite of the near-regal image projected by *Shaykh* al-Hakimi. Drake thought Sheppard's bombastic style of speaking and tendency to wander around with socialist newspapers tucked under his arm gave him all the trappings of the classic "proletarian intellectual". Alongside O'Connell, Sheppard had been regarded as one of the elite black Communists in Cardiff but had been expelled from the Party in 1945 for perceived Trotskyist tendencies. His politics were certainly distinguished by a commitment to racial alongside class-based struggles, and Sheppard gravitated particularly to the Pan-Africanism of Marcus Garvey, which was being developed by black intellectuals such as the Trinidadian writer C. L. R. James in dialogue with the work of Trotsky. But having been involved in the campaigns against the implementation of the Aliens Acts of the 1920s, and while continuing to maintain some connection to the largely dormant Colonial Defence Association in the 1940s, his expulsion from the Communist Party seemingly moved Sheppard towards less overtly political activity. He ran a newspaper shop, which acted as a front for his illegal bookmaking business (betting shops were not legalised in Britain until 1961). He also became the key player in the running of the Coloured International Athletic Club (CIAC), which began life as a cricket club but, under O'Connell's guidance, expanded to include rugby, athletics, table tennis, and other activities. The Club had a formal membership of around fifty, the vast majority of whom were men under the age of thirty. Drake saw that the members respected Sheppard, but not, he believed, because of his passion for politics. For example, Sheppard kept a library at the Club consisting of a range of Marxist and pan-African material, of which he continually urged people to make use. But as Drake dryly noted in his field diary, such admonishments were rarely heeded.[38]

The transient nature of life in a sailor town must have been a barrier to sustained political mobilisation, beyond moments of acute crisis such as the 1919 riots or the Aliens Acts of the 1920s. As one local resident explained to Drake, "going to sea helps to bring down the organisations here. You don't know what happens when you're away. And when you're here you're just apt to have a good time." The Bay's leisure scene was particularly important to visiting seamen who, though flush with earnings from their most recent job at sea, did not want to venture too far from their lodgings in local boarding houses because of the racism that faced ethnic minorities in central Cardiff.

BROWN BABIES: 1940s CARDIFF

Locally, the available options included the Sailors Institutes, which provided cheap meals and places to sit and talk or write letters home. But these were predominately white establishments that, depending on who was running them on a given day, could be hostile to "coloured" seamen. There was also the Bute Town Social and Welfare Club, which hosted regular dances attended by a mix of British-born black men, unmarried women of mixed ethnicity, West Indian, African, and Arab visiting seamen and a handful of white seamen—each of whom, upon entering the club, passed a framed photograph of the African American performer Paul Robeson and spent the evening jitterbugging to music played alternately by a phonograph and a live piano. There were the after-parties that lasted until dawn in rented flats above the shops and pubs of Bute Street and which were often the site of transactions between visiting seamen and sex workers. And there were the scores of local cafés, which, because of their long opening hours, relative affordability, and varied services, were perhaps the most popular recreational haunts in Tiger Bay, for locals and visitors alike.[39]

This milieu is reminiscent of the world often evoked by Claude McKay, the Jamaican-born writer who was a central figure in the Harlem Renaissance of the 1920s and who, throughout his life, made many transatlantic journeys to Europe—often to Marseilles, where much of his fiction is set. In books like *Romance in Marseilles*, the action often takes place in seedy bars frequented by hustlers, immigrant peddlers, and seamen from all over the world. In McKay's Marseilles, newly minted sailors arrive in the port city's "coloured colony" high from having finished a long stretch at sea, compete for the attention of beautiful "mulatto" prostitutes, get into fistfights over money or, just as likely, buy the patrons of a particular establishment bottles of *vins mousseux*. In Cardiff, Kenneth Little described the scene that greeted you as you opened the door to one of Tiger Bay's many cafés-*cum*-bars in the 1940s: there would be a large, semi-clean room with a few tables and chairs dotted about and a strong smell of food in the air; a counter selling groceries alongside hot food, cups of tea, lemonade, and anything from Australian wine, methylated spirits, and "near beer" to diluted whisky at seven shillings a cup; the sound of a wireless radio could be heard from an adjacent room. In one photograph (Fig. 2), taken inside a Somali-owned café by Bert Hardy in 1950, a group of Somali men sit around a table in double-breasted suits drinking tea and smoking cigarettes, the formality of the men's appearance contrasting with the rundown room around them—rickety-looking table, dingy curtains, dog-eared cupboards.[40]

Some proprietors clearly envisaged their establishments as places that combined everyday sociability with more formal cultural interventions in the community. The Café Cairo on Bute Street was run by Ali Salaman, a Yemeni immigrant, and his wife

Figure 2: Somalian café, Tiger Bay. From anon., 'Down the Bay', *Picture Post*, 22 April 1950. Photo by Bert Hardy, copyright © Getty Images.

Olive, who was white, from the Welsh valleys and fluent in Arabic. It simultaneously functioned as a boarding house, an Arabic school, and a temporary place of worship for local Muslims following the bombing of the Peel Street mosque in 1941. But it was more common for such establishments to play a facilitating role in the Bay's underground economy. They could be used as sites for games of "craps", a popular pastime among the area's African American and West Indian population, on which sums as large as £20 could be bet—though more often this took place on the street, usually on the corner of Sophia Street and Old Angelina Street a few steps north of Loudoun Square; a lookout would be positioned nearby to keep an eye out for the police.[41]

The Bay's café culture was most strongly associated with prostitution, particularly in the aftermath of anxieties during the interwar period over the extent of the illicit activities taking place in establishments run by some of the local Maltese population. Then, egged on by a series of sensationalist reports in the press, Chief Constable Wilson added Maltese men to his ever-expanding list of racialised bogeymen—this time as a result of what he perceived to be the immorality of Maltese café owners/pimps who facilitated prostitution on their property between ethnic-minority seamen and white women who were ostensibly employed as waitresses. The focus on Maltese-run cafés continued sporadically into the 1940s and '50s, both in the Bay and in the "coloured quarters" that had emerged in the East End of London and elsewhere. In the early 1940s, Little reported that visiting seamen were often drawn to such establishments because alcohol could be purchased up to 11pm—one hour later than the pubs. They got "doped up" and often made use of the back room many cafés kept free for "immoral purposes". There were times, Drake acknowledged, when prosaic encounters in cafés could lead to lasting relationships. But more often, he claimed—echoing

McKay's evocation of life in the dive bars of Marseilles—visiting seamen could find themselves cheated by hustlers, robbed by prostitutes, and beaten up in barfights.[42]

With his proprietorship of one of the two illegal bookmakers in the Bay, Alan Sheppard was part of this underground scene. On one occasion, Drake visited Sheppard's premises in the hope of conducting an interview with him, only to find him on the phone, relaying the racing results through a window. Although the Cardiff authorities were less draconian in the prosecution of illegal bookmaking than elsewhere, their focus on Tiger Bay tied into longstanding puritanical narratives in Britain that connected gambling and vice to perceptions of "un-Christian" depravity in the colonies. Another time Drake encountered Sheppard just after the latter had been fined £50 by the authorities for running an illegal gambling house—a breach that Sheppard attempted to justify in class-based terms. "Gambling has always been thought of in this country as a gentleman's game," he explained; the authorities in Britain simply "haven't wanted the bloody poor man to do it."[43]

Sheppard's activities stood in contrast to those who, like O'Connell, viewed their politics as an exercise in ideological purity. "How can a gambler win anybody's respect?" one observer asked of Sheppard. "I know he has to live, and ... at least he isn't selling women, and that's to his credit. But you can't win respect if you're down there in the pig pen." Sheppard's CIAC ("Kayaks" to its regulars) was in keeping with his wider aura of disreputability. It was based in an old, ramshackle building, the entrance to which was down a poorly lit alleyway, beneath an inconspicuous, barely legible sign. On being taken to the clubhouse for the first time, one visitor was heard to remark: "My God, what a dive. What are we going into? Is it safe?"[44]

It is clear from his field notes that Drake spent a good deal of time hanging around Sheppard and the CIAC regulars. Perhaps the gritty nature of the clubhouse reminded Drake of the semi-legal watering holes he got to know during his research in Chicago. Drake reported that, on an average evening, people sat around drinking or playing games of billiards, cards, or table tennis. Although this was tame compared to the novels of Claude McKay, the significance of what went on in "Kayaks" must have been particularly clear to an African American anthropologist used to dealing with the impact of the United States colour line.

Although Drake observed that an incessant amount of ribbing went on among CIAC members—on the playing field, in the car returning home, and in the post-mortems of the games that took place on street corners and at the clubhouse—the Club was a multicultural endeavour. It brought together various Tiger Bay cliques, but particularly an older generation of West Indian men like Sheppard and a "younger set" that was primarily British-born, and often of mixed ethnicity. While the clubhouse was a shared space, Drake noticed that a shift in the balance of power seemed to be taking place—away from Sheppard and towards these younger, mixed-race members, who were seemingly intent on turning the Club into a much more 'respectable' enterprise. This meant the younger set gravitating not towards the Pan-Africanism favoured by Sheppard, the orthodox communism of O'Connell, or the anti-colonial nationalism of Tualla Muhammad, but towards a much more conservative, status-orientated emphasis that Drake described as a form of "British steadiness".[45]

This trend was doubtless influenced by the pervasiveness of racial stereotypes around "half-castes" in mid-century Britain, and a concurrent desire to upend them by foregrounding dominant perceptions of white "respectability". But it was also a sign that the Bay's racial hierarchy was, at times, implicitly reinforced by an older generation of activists who, like Sheppard, bore the scars induced by decades of political campaigning. "These half-castes just haven't learned how to cooperate with anybody,"

Sheppard confided to Drake as the influence of the CIAC younger set increased. "They weren't supposed to go off and do anything on their own."[46]

What took place at the Club was, in many ways, indicative of the unruly nature of the Bay's multicultural metropolis. The CIAC brought together different segments of the Bay community, but to Drake's eyes, as the influence of the mixed-race younger set grew, it was also a space where—perhaps to the chagrin of Sheppard himself—the established racial hierarchy that put "half-castes" firmly at the bottom of the pile was being turned on its head. More than this, the CIAC was run by a West Indian Marxist who sought to encourage members to read up on the politics of Pan-Africanism, but whose influence was being superseded by those whose worldviews seemed almost bourgeois in nature, and concerned primarily with projecting an image of respectable upward mobility.

Drake recorded a visit to the home of one prominent member of the younger set, who was born in Trinidad but had attended school in the Bay in the early 1920s. Drake noticed a framed photograph of a white teenager on a mantelpiece, at which his host laughed. "That's my wife's sister's child," Drake was told. "He's English! His sister is the smart one. She's just about to finish secondary school!" While Drake observed that Sheppard was admired by the younger set for his knowledge of cricket and rugby, as well as his enthusiastic work for the organisation, others functioned as more authentic success symbols in this milieu. Sheppard was described as old fashioned, stern, and critical; someone who "expected you to listen and not to question". In contrast, the most important success symbol for the younger members of the CIAC—the person Drake identified as embodying the "British steadiness" privileged by the younger set—was Bill Douglas (Fig. 3), who was born in Britain in 1917 to a West Indian father and a white mother, had attained the rank of captain

BROWN BABIES: 1940s CARDIFF

Figure 3: Cardiff RFC, 1949. Bill Douglas, middle row second from left. Photo courtesy of Cardiff Rugby Museum and the family of Bleddyn Williams.

in a paratrooper division during the war and, alongside his mother, ran a local grocery shop.[47]

Drake described Douglas as being above average in height, with light-brown skin and a shock of brown hair that was neatly parted on the left. Between 1947 and 1951, Douglas became one of the earliest black players to play for Cardiff Rugby Club, making thirty-nine first team appearances as a prop and flanker during a period of sustained success for the team. In the spring of 1948, organised by its increasingly confident younger members, the CIAC hosted a black-tie banquet to celebrate his burgeoning success. The occasion was understood by local members to be a historic event—never before had an ethnic minority organisation in Tiger Bay hosted a white group on such a large scale. The event was held not at the dingy clubhouse, but in the convention room of a city-centre hotel that had been rented specifically for the occasion. The Cardiff Rugby Club was represented by a number of white administrators as well as two white players, Cliff Davis and Willie Jones. Perhaps driven by these symbols of British 'respectability', there was a concurrent anxiety among the younger members of the Club that the event be handled in a "proper fashion". A British–Arab member, whose skin was so light he was reportedly able to pass for white, was put in charge of publicising the occasion. Announcements were posted in local shop windows, and—although none of the younger set expressed much interest in his attendance—Sheppard volunteered to take part as the event's master of ceremonies.[48]

On the evening in question, Drake recorded in his diary what transpired. He entered the hotel without any of the stares or comments that might ordinarily greet someone from an ethnic minority background in central Cardiff. In the hotel lobby, he spotted five white girls and two black girls chatting with a group of four white boys. Further on, four or five boys of mixed ethnicity were trying to set up a large keg of beer. Sheppard was initially sceptical about the event but had nevertheless tried to make himself presentable. His seedy clothes and weather-worn hat had been replaced with a newly pressed suit, and he had been to the barber for a haircut and a shave. Prior to the guests arriving, the members of the organising committee reminded Sheppard that he would have to toast the King—preferably after the guests had finished their meal and before they had begun to light their smokes. "I have never toasted any bloody king and I don't intend to now," Drake overheard Sheppard respond, though the younger members "shushed him ... and pleaded with him not to spoil the affair."[49]

After the meal had been served—by an all-white waiting staff, Drake noted—Sheppard began his speech. "The kind of sport a country has [is] no better than the kind of local players it produces," he remarked. He declared himself "glad to present some boys who had grown up on cricket and rugby and who are now bringing honour to their club, their community and their city". And he duly toasted the King, which was greeted with "knowing grins among the Tiger Bay boys at this great sacrifice of principle".

The short remarks of Bill Douglas himself, though, best encapsulated the spirit of the evening as envisaged by the younger set. "It's good to see a Cardiff team with both black and white faces," he stated. "I'm proud to represent Tiger Bay where I was born." A three-piece ensemble—piano, drums, and trumpet—was then formed by two members of the CIAC and one of the white players from the Cardiff rugby team. The guests then danced around with no evidence of any colour-bar induced awkwardness to the American entertainer Arthur Godfrey's 1947 hit "Too Fat Polka". The event finished at 10pm, Drake observed, at which point there were handshakes all round. Then, after a brief period spent hanging around, not knowing what to do next, the Club's younger set began to trickle back down to the Bay.[50]

Reading Drake's description of this event, and notwithstanding the pressed suits, black ties, and toasts to the King, there was something touching about the modesty of the event that had been put on by the Tiger Bay younger set. Although it was an ethnically mixed ceremony to celebrate the success of a mixed-race rugby player, and although it took place in the immediate aftermath of widespread concerns about the growing population of "brown babies" in Britain, there were no hyperbolic references to Tiger Bay as the setting for a happy-go-lucky story of multicultural conviviality. Indeed, this was a narrative that only emerged much later, as part of the Cardiff heritage industry's retrospective portrayal of life in the Bay. In this telling, the Bay is presented not as "darkest Cardiff", an alien enclave where the number of interracial relationships was testament to the gamut of sexual and criminal transgressions. Rather, it was a neighbourhood that was to be celebrated for its supposed ability to combine "traditional" forms of working-class community—the sense that "everyone lives as an extended family and knows everyone else intimately"—with a kind of cosmopolitan colour-blindness that was positioned as being radically ahead of its time.[51]

For one prominent chronicler and former resident, writing in 1997, the Tiger Bay of the 1940s and '50s was indicative of "an advanced form of social existence"; it was a "racially heterogeneous community" where people "lived together [in] intra-cultural harmony". This idea became increasingly prominent in works of amateur history, online blogs, and even in the pages of the same local newspapers that had, over decades, been key proponents of the racialised image of Tiger Bay as the setting for a "clash of civilisations and ethical standards a thousand years apart". And it is surely not coincidental that they proliferated—often around the totemic image of the pop singer Shirley Bassey, who was born in the Bay in 1937 to a Nigerian father and an English mother—at the very moment that the last physical remnants of the neighbourhood I have described in this chapter had almost completely slipped from view.[52]

Following the decline of the British shipping industry in the 1950s and the formal closure of the docks in 1964, a series of urban-redevelopment initiatives rendered the area's topography unrecognisable. In the 1960s, a programme of slum clearance replaced the Bay's terraced houses, cafés, and seafaring shops with tower blocks and maisonettes with neat front gardens. In 1988, one writer went in search of Tiger Bay for a new book and was disappointed to find that all that remained was a windswept, practically deserted council estate. By the turn of the century, the Bay had been transformed once more into what developers now called the Cardiff Bay Barrage, a £2 billion "wonderland" consisting of a freshwater lake on the site of what had once been the docks; office blocks; luxury apartments; and a shopping mall that promised a "festival of retail". During my own visit I stayed at a Holiday Inn that overlooked one of the many now-defunct canals that had once been key arteries in the service of Cardiff docks; to get to Bute Street I had to walk around a massive development of apartment blocks that was promoted to passers-by with advertising boards featuring attractive white people smiling cosmetic, carefree smiles. The landmarks that had defined the Tiger Bay Drake knew were gone; as the bulldozers moved in, the project to rescue its overlooked history became increasingly urgent.[53]

It is easy to sympathise with nostalgic representations of life in Tiger Bay that have sought to overcome the potency of the stereotypical view of the area that, for decades, has been lodged in the popular imaginary—through film, literature, magazine articles, and a stream of sensationalist newspaper exposés. But in the determination to present life in the Bay as a kind of multicultural idyll, the extent and impact of racism in mid-century, late-imperial Britain is overlooked. With his experience of mapping in vivid detail the extent of the Chicago colour line, and in light of his status as one of very few African American anthropologists, it is not surprising that Drake was alert to the presence of racial thinking in the Bay. But as I sat in Harlem looking through his archive day after day, it still made for difficult reading to see how integral racial discrimination actually was to the worldview of many of the people Drake encountered—to white individuals such as Cardiff's long serving chief constable, but also to people from ethnic-minority backgrounds, who themselves would have been victims of racial discrimination, but who nevertheless saw racism as a cheap way of advancing their own cause within the confines of the Bay's racial hierarchy.

In some ways, it would have been difficult for this to have been any other way. Although India achieved independence in

MULTICULTURAL BRITAIN

1947, during Drake's time in Cardiff the British Empire continued to stretch across nations, time zones, and continents. The racial fictions that were a central feature of it not only structured how those in the metropole viewed the colonies; they were also a feature of how colonial societies were structured internally. This meant that as seamen arrived in Tiger Bay from Yemen, British Guiana, Somalia, and far beyond, they brought with them their own understandings of race. As I would find out on the rest of my journey through the history of multicultural Britain, the entrenched nature of British racism maintained its hold long after the empire had gone. The "thousand details, anecdotes [and] stories" that Fanon characterised as the "fact of blackness" would continue to make themselves felt.

Perhaps this is why Drake was drawn to the prosaic sociability that took place at Alan Sheppard's Coloured International Athletic Club, as opposed to the titillating stories that emanated from inside the Bay's cafés, bars, and boarding houses. Such establishments may have been sources of sexier material. They were surely prime examples of Drake's definition of a "metropolis" within a city, and the importance of "love-making, hustling and having a good time" when it came to surviving life in a racially and economically segregated ghetto. The CIAC represented something slightly different. The direction in which the "younger set" was taking it was not in keeping with Sheppard's definition of what radical politics looked like. And it avoided the more formal anti-colonial manoeuvrings that were dividing the seasoned activists. Yet there surely is something important about a group of mixed-race people rejecting the hostility directed at them in 1940s Britain and, in defiance, trying to articulate a sense of pride in their own formations. It was an example of the kind of limited but significant freedoms that Drake saw as powering the metropolis: "the freedom to erect a community in their own image". Maybe this was the reason the younger set seemed so determined that Sheppard—against all his better political instincts—raise a glass to the King at the event they had organised to celebrate the success of Bill Douglas, one of their own who had made it big. In their own small way, this was part of reimagining what it meant to be British.

2

COLOUR BARS

1950s NOTTINGHAM

I arrived in Nottingham first thing on a warm July morning. My train had taken me through Luton, where the rows of red-brick terraced houses were overlooked by a mosque, its gold minarets glittering in the early-morning sun. At Kettering I changed trains and overheard an Irish builder chatting to his colleagues as he fixed the station lights on the platform opposite. It was already a beautiful day; as we pulled into Nottingham, I watched the train's shadow slide smoothly over concrete and jitter across deep-green foliage and overhanging trees. In the city I encountered, all around me were the sights that have become ordinary, barely-acknowledged symbols of diversity in modern Britain. As I dodged the kids who buzzed about on the council's network of bright-yellow rental scooters, I passed curry houses and Indian 'street food' joints, Turkish take-outs and posters that promised the cheapest rates for sending parcels to the Caribbean. Later, over coffee and a croissant outside a branch of Café Nero, I people-watched: a Nigerian man in a Barcelona shirt with 'Nouri' on the back rushed by, talking on his wireless headphones; a young black woman with long nail extensions almost bumped into an elderly white couple in sandals and cricket hats, already struggling with the morning heat. One afternoon, while I was admiring the city's Irish Centre on Wilford Street, a black woman thrusted into my hand a leaflet with good news from the Pentecostal church next door. Nottingham was still a mostly white city, certainly when compared to my hometown of Birmingham. But if first impressions were anything to go by, it also seemed emblematic of how far Britain had drifted towards the multicultural.

The Nottingham that confronted post-war immigrants was a different world. Unlike Tiger Bay, before the Second World War Nottingham's ethnically-diverse population was miniscule. In the mid-nineteenth century, when the Irish were the largest ethnic minority group in Britain, Nottingham had an Irish population of 1,500 people. In 1931, meanwhile, there were 238 people in the city who had been born in British colonies in the West Indies or the Indian sub-continent—0.08 per cent of Nottingham's total population. It was only in the fifteen years after the end of the war that a significant ethnic minority presence began to form, most of which was made up of people who had emigrated from the West Indies. They were attracted by the prospect of work in Nottingham's lace and hosiery industries, in its munitions factories and coal mines, on its buses and trains or at Raleigh Industries, one of the largest bicycle manufacturers in the world. And what they encountered in Nottingham was an unmistakably white scene. In impoverished districts like St Ann's in the north of the city—where, largely because of discrimination in the housing sector, ethnic minorities were often forced to settle—this was also wrapped up with class and a sense of community that, compared with the fluidity of life in Tiger Bay, was marked by its insularity. This was a world where everybody knew everyone, and gossip would spread along the cobbled streets like electricity through a circuit. It was a world where the butchers on St Ann's Well Road would let you run a tab until pay day, and the chippy on Alfred Street handed out free scraps to schoolchildren. It was a world of clocking in on a Monday, of cafés that sold plates of liver and onions and working-men's clubs where you could have a few pints with the regulars before beginning a night shift.[1]

The white, working-class landscapes of 1950s Nottingham were famously evoked by the Nottingham-born novelist Alan Sillitoe in *Saturday Night and Sunday Morning* (1958). The novel revolves around the character of Arthur Seaton, an "angry young man" whose attempts to refuse the conventions of his close-knit community mainly involve hard drinking, fighting and sexual conquests. As I read Sillitoe, I kept thinking of my father's family in the town of Nuneaton, an hour south of Nottingham. Nuneaton is a quarter of the size of Nottingham, though the two places do have a shared history of coal-mining as an important source of employment (and locals have similar, slack-jawed accents). So far as I know, Dad never adopted the escapist tactics of Arthur Seaton. But he did feel the need to leave the restrictions of his own upbringing and, in the late-1960s, became the first member of his immediate family to leave Nuneaton for good.

When we were children, my father would take us on daytrips to visit our grandma Dorothy in Nuneaton, or to attend wedding or funeral receptions at the local Conservative Club. It was the memories of these occasions that I found coming to mind as I was reading *Saturday Night and Sunday Morning*. It often seemed that Dad (and, by extension, my brother and I) were treated with a kind of suspicion by our Nuneaton family. Just as there is in *Saturday Night*, there was wariness of anything deemed unorthodox, and a mistrust of "out-groups" that, in my case, usually meant a stream of questions about when I was finally going to finish studying and start earning some money.

Travelling from our home in Birmingham, you also could not avoid noticing the relative whiteness of Nuneaton. And even as a child, I remember feeling Dad's discomfort when his elderly mother would on occasions make disparaging comments about the Asian families who had moved in down the road.[2]

I haven't set foot in Nuneaton since the death of my father in 2013. But it was Nuneaton that was with me as I walked the balmy streets of Nottingham, trying to picture the atmosphere that faced those early pioneers of multicultural Britain. In 1958, the number of black and Asian residents of Nottingham had reached 3,000. This was still only one per cent of the city's total population. But these communities found that their visibility was exacerbated by their concentration in particular parts of the city—especially St Ann's, which in August 1958 was the scene of the most serious outbreak of race rioting in Britain since the unrest that took place in Cardiff and other port cities in 1919.[3]

What hung over the 1958 unrest was the issue of permanence. On the one hand, when the British Nationality Act was passed in 1948, giving citizens across Britain's current and former colonies the equal right to live and work in the 'mother country', the political calculation was that it would be a way of slowing the anti-colonial sentiment that in 1947 led to Indian independence, while simultaneously facilitating the arrival of the cheap labour force that was desperately needed to rebuild Britain's infrastructure and expand its welfare state. Citizens of the colonies might come for a few years to help in Britain's hour of need, as they had done during the war. But no one was in any doubt that they would eventually want to go back from where they had come. On the other hand, most 'colonial' immigrants themselves never intended to make Britain their permanent home. In the interviews they conducted with journalists, sociologists and later historians, or in the memoirs some would come to write about their lives in Britain, the comment you see repeated again and again is that the plan was always to return to India, Jamaica, Pakistan, or Barbados after a few years of banking the generous cheques that people presumed they would quickly be able to earn. The 1950s was the period in which, on both sides, these theories began to unravel.[4]

From the vantage-point of white Britain, the gradual realisation that Britain had opened its doors to a permanent and expanding black presence was made more traumatic by the pace of change more generally. In neighbourhoods like St Ann's, rising wages and the expanding consumer and leisure sectors of the economy provided a bizarre juxtaposition with the decrepit state of local housing, which visitors to the area likened to a scene from a Dickens novel. The increased availability of better-paid jobs and rising disposable incomes, meanwhile, helped young people emerge as a distinct, increasingly rebellious section of society. With their Brylcreemed quiffs and "Edwardian" style of long jackets, tight trousers and "brothel creeper" shoes, the behaviour of Britain's so-called "Teddy Boys" became a major source of public concern. But the pre-eminent issue was the status of Britain's once-dominant empire, which—between Indian independence, that of the Gold Coast (now Ghana) in 1957, Somaliland, Cyprus and Nigeria in 1960, and the rise of anti-colonial nationalism elsewhere—was coming apart at the seams. As Britain was changing domestically, the empire was becoming intertwined with a sense of loss and unease about the erosion of Britain's former glories, a feeling that Britain was not only losing its global territories but was also "dying by the mind". Empire was becoming a profoundly uncomfortable memory, "a past from which people wanted to run", observed Stuart Hall— who made the journey from Jamaica to Britain in 1951—but were being prevented from doing so by the growing number of living, breathing symbols of empire who were moving in next door, walking the same streets and applying for the same jobs.[5]

MULTICULTURAL BRITAIN

It was in regional, predominately white cities like Nottingham that this tension often played out most spectacularly. As black and Asian immigration increased across the country—particularly after 1953, when employers including the NHS went out of their way to encourage further migration from the colonies—ethnic minorities found that their visibility in white Nottingham made them the immediate object of verbal abuse. It was also clear that sections of the white community were prepared to act on their opposition to the prospect of a permanent (and expanding) population of "dark strangers". In Nottingham, the letters KBW (Keep Britain White) began to appear on white-washed walls. Signs began to appear in the windows of the bed and breakfasts that lined Goldsmith Street and Shakespeare Street on the outskirts of the city centre, or on the doors of the pubs in St Ann's: "Rooms available. No Blacks or Niggers", "No coloured person will be served here". Black people who applied for jobs were brazenly told by managers they did not want black people in the office, while those who were able to find jobs were nicknamed "Sambo" or pushed about and told, "you should not be doing this job!" White Britain was not simply retreating behind its net-curtains, as Hall put it with regard to his own initial impressions of Oxford and London. The expansion of Britain's colour bar demonstrated that sections of white Britain were prepared to go on the attack.[6]

This was the backdrop to the riots in St Ann's on the weekends of the 23 and 30 August 1958, in the hot tail-end of what had hitherto been a miserably overcast summer. As had happened in Tiger Bay and other port-districts in summer 1919, thousands of white men descended on St Ann's Well Road with the intention of "finding some niggers". A black man out with his white partner was mobbed by an angry crowd with cries of "go back to your own country", while another group chanted "let's lynch them" as they set upon a car full of West Indian immigrants. With the windows of black people's homes smashed in by bricks and a black man who had to be taken to hospital having been stabbed in the back, most commentators agreed it was a miracle that no one was killed.[7]

What happened in St Ann's—alongside the even more serious events that took place just days later in Notting Hill in London—seemed to offer proof that the preconceptions many colonial immigrants had of Britain as a place where they would be welcomed as imperial citizens were way off the mark. In the weeks after the unrest, ethnic minorities in Nottingham went about their lives in a fog of anxiety. Many did not venture out at night, or only walked the streets in groups. As one Jamaican immigrant reflected, "any coloured man who was living near St Ann's Well Road in those times and says that he was not scared, is telling you a lie". And the riots also propelled the racism that was an everyday feature of neighbourhoods like St Ann's to re-emerge in the political mainstream. In spite of the fact the unrest was driven in the first instance by white rioters with the intention of attacking black people, in the months and years that followed it gradually became accepted that what in essence was a problem of white racism could (and should) be remedied by stemming the growth of Britain's "coloured" population. In 1962, the same year the one-time colonies of Uganda, Jamaica and Trinidad secured their independence, the first restrictions on immigration to Britain since the principle of free movement was enshrined by the 1948 Nationality Act were introduced by Harold Macmillan's Conservative Government. Like the Aliens Orders of the 1920s, the 1962 Commonwealth Immigrants Act made it more difficult specifically for immigrants from the West Indies, South Asia and Africa to enter into the country; "blackness", as the journalist Peter Fryer put it, had become "officially equated with second-class citizenship". To other observers, meanwhile, the passing of the 1962 Act was the moment Britain's colour bar was formally enshrined in law.[8]

MULTICULTURAL BRITAIN

White Nottingham

In 1944, Eric Irons—who had been born in Spanish Town in 1921 and was the youngest of three siblings—prepared to leave Jamaica for the first time and set sail for Britain. He was disillusioned with his job as an apprentice tailor, even if—with unemployment on the island running at 40 per cent—he was lucky to have a job at all. Having heard that citizens across the empire were being encouraged to join in the final throes of the war effort, he volunteered to serve with the Royal Air Force (RAF). Before making his way to Kingston, where the *SS Cuba* was waiting to take him across the Atlantic Ocean, his father gifted him a Parker pen to remind him to write home; his mother gave him a Bible. When the time came for Irons to leave, the lyrics to a popular song by the Jamaican "mento" folklorists Slim and Sam were playing in his head—"England has got to win that war, to raa-raa-raa/So Jamaicans are ready to fight, to raaa-raaa-raa/Hitler is a son of a bitch/to rip, to rip to raa-raa-raa". On board, he was issued with his regulation "Mae West" lifejacket, a bright-yellow waistcoat that consisted of inflatable pockets on either side of the user's chest. As the *Cuba's* engines started, he made his way to the top deck and watched the Jamaica of his youth gradually slip from view.[9]

Irons arrived at Greenock dock south of Glasgow on a gloomy Sunday morning in November. In his half-finished (and never published) memoir, he recalled his shock at the conditions that faced him. Although he had prepared himself for the climate, Irons still struggled with the reality of icy footpaths, hail, snow, a sun that appeared to radiate cold rather than heat and—as Stuart Hall saw it—light that seemed "permanently stuck halfway to dusk". Like many West Indian immigrants of his generation, he also found it difficult to get used to the everyday sights and sounds of late-industrial Britain. Although he had been born in Port-of-Spain, Irons spent his formative years living on a two-acre farm in rural Portland in the north-east, surrounded by cassava plants, fowl, goats, pigs and a cat to ward off lizards and mice. His family house had clay floors and a wattle and daub thatched roof; Irons would play cricket with balls made from rags and bats from coconut bough. In Britain, however, as he made his way from Glasgow to military bases across the country, he mistook rows of terraced houses with smoking chimneys for factories. It almost seemed as though the buildings were frowning; the only way he could tell there was someone living inside was that the curtains opened and shut. It was a long way from the mythical image of a "green and pleasant land" that had been drilled into Irons' generation in colonial Jamaica. In this context, Britain was not merely a place, but a heritage mythologised by the recital of songs like "Rule Britannia" and "There Will Always Be an England", the annual celebration of Empire Day and the King's birthday, and a school curriculum that fetishised the activities of imperial "heroes" like Clive of India and Rhodes of Africa.[10]

Although Irons' experiences were shaped by his status as an RAF serviceman, his was a trajectory that anticipated the generation of West Indian immigrants who migrated to Britain over the subsequent decade on boats like the *Windrush* (Trinidad to Tilbury Docks via Jamaica, Mexico, Cuba and Bermuda), the *Captain Verdic* (Jamaica to Southampton via Italy) and the *Escalla* (Jamaica to Southampton via the Dominican Republic). With the option of moving to America severely curtailed by the introduction of restrictive immigration legislation in 1952, across the West Indies the growing appeal of migrating to the "mother country" was referred to as "England fever". You saved up for your ticket, which could cost anything from £28 to £75 from travel agents like Chin Yee's on Old Hope Road in East Kingston. You packed a suitcase full of knitted woollen jumpers and a holdall with bammy (baked cassava) and coconut drops (coconut sweet cake) for the journey. On board, you gravitated towards the other West Indian passengers, and soon began ribbing one another about which island had the best beaches, the best climate or the best schools. As the days went by and the prospect of arrival become more real, those who had already spent time in Britain grew in stature, and were tapped for practical guidance about what to do: how did you get to Paddington Station? Were the newspaper reports of a housing shortage in Britain accurate? What were the "limeys" really like? When the ship dropped its anchor and the time finally came for you to disembark, you went back down below deck and composed yourself. You put on your Sunday best, straightened your tie and made your way out for your papers to be checked. The white officials treated you with a sense of bewilderment. Did you really want to leave the sun and the sand of the Caribbean, where it was summer all year around, for cold, grey Britain—Britain of all places? You tried to crouch further into your clothes, and rubbed your hands together to keep them warm. Eventually, you found your way to the train station and set off for the address you had been given by a friend who had made the journey before you, which was written down on an airmail envelope you had kept. On the way, you marvelled at the factories that made the shaving blades you used at home. You ordered a cup of tea, and tried to work out what was meant by the question "with or without"?[11]

Like most arrivals from the West Indies, it did not take long for Eric Irons to realise that race was going to be an integral feature of his life in Britain. Part of this was coming to terms with the weirdness of seeing poor white people—white road sweepers, white bin men, white porters, white children begging for chocolate. Such sights were simply unimaginable in the "pigmentocracy" of the colonial West Indies, where white skin almost always meant greater social and economic capital. And if white people were often poor in Britain, they could also be shockingly ignorant, especially when it came to the status of "colonials" like Irons. Irons found that the average Briton was unable to find Jamaica on the map, let alone distinguish between the different islands that made up the West Indies. For him, black people seemed to be typecast as either unsophisticated African tribespeople or the product of some missionary Christian institution; upon meeting Irons the first thing white people would usually do was ask where he learnt to speak such good English.[12]

It would be hard to overstate the impact of the visibility of black and Asian immigrants in Britain, particularly in cities like Nottingham. In Glasgow, where Irons initially arrived, there was at least a small but significant ethnic minority presence stretching back to the nineteenth century. In the 1930s, the city could boast an Indian population of approaching 600 people—largely made up of "pedlars" who earnt a living by selling ties, socks, shirts, aprons and other items directly to people's houses. During the early part of the Second World War, Glasgow's multicultural profile expanded still further with the recruitment of forestry workers from the West Indies and British Honduras (now Belize) to help meet the need for domestically produced timber during the conflict. The lack of a comparable ethnically diverse presence in cities like Nottingham made the situation encountered by immigrants of Irons' generation even more pronounced. They were moving from countries where they had always been in the majority to a society where, in almost every setting, they were vastly outnumbered by white people. They had become unavoidably visible as members of the "minority race" and, as Fanon found when he moved from Martinique to Lyon, this meant having to carry the weight of the "fact of blackness" at any moment. In some ways, it was the unpredictability of British racism that made it most difficult to deal with. In the close-knit, working-class neighbourhoods to which black immigrants arrived, a contradictory picture emerged. The hostility towards "niggers", "Paddies", "Yids" and other outsiders was unmissable. But there could also be a generosity of spirit, a willingness (as the literary critic Richard Hoggart recalled of his own upbringing in Leeds) to live and let live, rub along and "tek people as y' find 'em".[13]

For example, the only "non-white" character in Alan Sillitoe's *Saturday Night and Sunday Morning* is Sam, a soldier from the Gold Coast who comes to stay with the extended family of the novel's protagonist, Arthur, for Christmas. Over the course of a single chapter, Sillitoe builds the tension around the prospect of Sam coming face-to-face with the racialised hostilities of white Nottingham. When Sam doesn't turn up on time, Arthur and his cousin Bert head into town to look for him. They grumble about Sam probably thinking telegrams are sent by "tom-tom" and quickly give up waiting—"I'm not going to freeze to death running after a Zulu". By the time they get home Sam is already there, and facing questions from Arthur's cousins: could he read and write? Did he believe in God? Was his girlfriend as black as the ace of spades? Yet as the novel progresses, the expected conflict never materialises. Instead, when someone asks for half-crown contributions towards a crate of ale, Arthur's aunt Ada insists that Sam, as the guest, is exempt. When they go to the pub and Sam offers to buy a round of drinks, he is shouted down. Back at home, a camp-bed has been made up for Sam upstairs, and the next morning—much to the annoyance of Arthur's younger cousins—Sam is served three eggs for breakfast. On his final night, Arthur's cousins ask Sam to promise to write to them from Africa and take it in turns to kiss him under the mistletoe.[14]

It's a telling depiction of the British double-standard on race, something that—as the Barbadian writer George Lamming observed—differed markedly from the much more clear-cut situation that faced African Americans in the United States (whether in the Jim Crow South or the "colour lined" North). Sillitoe's portrayal is reminiscent of the behaviour of English football fans in recent years, who have demonstrated an apparently unrivalled capacity to celebrate goals by one of the most multicultural teams in Europe and sing songs about their love of vindaloo curry, while in the next breath boo their own team for taking the knee as a symbolic protest against racism. As one West Indian immigrant told a white researcher in Nottingham, "you people change like the weather". And the duplicitous nature of British racism was also a defining feature of Eric Irons' first few years in Britain.[15]

When he arrived at a makeshift military base at Butlin's holiday camp in Filey in North-East Yorkshire, Irons was called a "nigger" by one of his fellow soldiers. The locals, meanwhile, literally ran away at the sight of the black troops walking around town. Later, on a trip to Nottingham, Irons was set upon by eight white men who shouted, "you black bastard, what have you got to say for yourself?" But Irons also found he was met with benevolence and the kind of sexualised fascination from young, working-class women that also contributed to the number of inter-racial relationships in wartime Cardiff. Having just got off the train on another trip to Nottingham, Irons noticed two young white women window-shopping. Lost amid the bomb damage along Drury Hill, and hoping to get to the Navy, Army and Air Force Institutes (NAFFI) on Fletcher Gate, he stopped to ask them for directions. The women offered to walk him there in person. One of them, Irons remembered, was silent the whole way; her hair was so dark he initially thought she could have been Indian. When they arrived, Irons politely thanked them and turned to the woman with beautiful dark hair. Her name was Nell Kelham, and she worked at a box factory. Would she like to go with him to the pictures? Soon, Irons was spending most of his weekends with Kelham in Nottingham. By day they went for long walks along the canal or in Colwick Park on the outskirts of the city; by night they danced the jitterbug or the jive at the NAFFI. When he wasn't in his RAF uniform, Irons would wear a pin-striped suit, with wide lapels and a kipper tie, his hair parted on the left-hand side. Kelham, with her jet-black hair, high cheekbones, and "reefer" coat, looked like the Indian-born actress Vivien Leigh. In 1946, and with the blessing of Kelham's parents Marie (a cleaner) and Harry (a railway goods porter), the couple married at Nottingham registry office on Shakespeare Street; with Irons' discharge from the RAF finally on the horizon, three years later they moved into their first home together at 1A Pennyfoot Street, on the outskirts of Nottingham city centre and a ten-minute walk from St Ann's.[16]

During the war and the years that followed it, what helped facilitate the contradictory treatment of Britain's black population was the idea that they were only going to be a temporary presence. They were thought of as a cohort of "coloured guests", as one magazine christened them, who—like the character of Sam in *Saturday Night*, who only appears in a single chapter of the novel—would one day disappear without a trace. Up to a point, Britain's mythologised, supposedly inclusive wartime spirit helped keep a lid on these contradictions. But as we saw in the previous chapter, cracks very quickly began to appear. In 1943, the upmarket Imperial Hotel in London's Russell Square famously refused entry to the Trinidadian cricketer Learie Constantine on the grounds that his presence would offend the hotel's American clientele (Constantine later successfully sued the hotel for breach of contract). Five years later in Nottingham, the white manager of the city's labour hostels, where many newly-arrived immigrants found temporary accommodation, urged his superiors to take action against those West Indian tenants who he saw as asserting a "childish" pride in their British citizenship and had the audacity to claim privileges on the basis of it.[17]

By the mid-1950s, with the belated end of wartime rationing and a black presence expanding at a rate of 40,000 immigrants a year, the duplicitous attitude of white Britain was revealing itself in technicolour. Ainsley Grant, for instance, was from Jamaica and in the 1950s lived in the Robin Hood Chase district of Nottingham. He recalled approaching a group of white colleagues on the street one evening, who at work he thought he was on friendly terms with: these were people he talked with, shared tea-breaks with and even travelled on buses to and from work with. But on the street, his co-workers spontaneously berated him with chants of "black bastard". Shaken, Grant spent the night dreading going to work again the next morning, only to find that the very same people came up to him as if nothing happened, ready for a chat. As one of the characters explains in *The Emigrants*, George Lamming's 1954 novel that was based on his experience migrating to Britain from Barbados, it was important not to get fooled by any sweet talk or smiles from white people: "behin' that smile...the teeth they show does bite. An' they won't leave you till they get rid o you, chase you out of the country, or suck yuh blood like a blasted jumbie". In the 1950s, it was the idea that the growing black population were guests who were increasingly outstaying their welcome that prepared the ground for the expansion of Britain's colour bar.[18]

This was shaped on a haphazard basis by the determination of particular employers, landlords and other gatekeepers to put their hostility towards the black presence into practice. The West Indian immigrants who arrived in Nottingham in the early-1950s recalled having their applications for promotion mysteriously rejected, finding out that they were being paid less than white co-workers for doing the same job, or inquiring about accommodation and being openly told by landlords, "we don't want you 'ere". Ainsley Grant, a qualified machinist, was offered a job in a factory—but only if he was willing to sweep the floors. To begin with, there could be attempts to offer excuses, or deflect responsibility onto other people. It was never the person who answered the door who had a problem with black applicants, but rather husbands, lodgers, co-workers and neighbours. On one occasion, Eric Irons remembered, his wife Nell found their eldest son—a mixed-race child, and as such perhaps the clearest threat to the idea that ethnic minorities would only ever be temporary guests in Britain—in the school playground surrounded by white children chanting "blackie, blackie". He was told by the watching teachers it was just a case of children playing.[19]

Irons himself—having lived in Nottingham since the 1940s, and having eventually secured a job at an ordnance depot in Chilwell on the outskirts of the city—was increasingly treated by newly-arrived immigrants as an elder statesman, a first port-of-call for help navigating Nottingham. In February 1952 this role was formalised with the establishment (initially out of Irons' own front room) of the Cosmopolitan Social Club, which aimed to be a focal point for the city's growing population of black immigrants—a kind of East Midlands version of Alan Sheppard's Coloured International Athletic Club in Tiger Bay, and part of a growing network of immigrant-run social clubs in places like Handsworth in Birmingham, Moss Side in Manchester, Brixton in London and other centres of West Indian immigration across the country. In 1956, the Cosmopolitan Club moved to a premises at 279 Alfred Street in Nottingham city centre and was renamed the Colonial and Social Welfare Club. It was through the connections he made at the club that Irons began to be invited into the homes of West Indians living in St Ann's, and grew increasingly distressed by what seemed like the uniformity of the conditions they faced: the families or groups of single men sharing single rooms in decrepit, overcrowded houses; the single gas stove on the landing that would be used by an entire household, on which overflowing water from a saucepan would fry and sizzle; the damp washing that would be hung around a single oil heater; the outside toilets that were in total darkness because the bulb had not been replaced. Having initially encountered racism on an ad-hoc, inter-personal basis, it had become impossible for Irons to miss what had evidently become the structural nature of the problem.[20]

In Brixton in South London, the researcher Sheila Patterson reported the existence of what she called "coloured premiums" in the housing market in this period, whereby the owners of decaying properties in unfashionable streets would seek to take advantage of the desperation of black buyers by raising the asking price. In Nottingham, discrimination in the private sector was matched by the activities of the local council, which had a policy of purchasing sub-standard houses in areas like St Ann's with the explicit intention of housing newly-arrived immigrants in them. In the area of employment, meanwhile, Britain's trade unions had emerged as a key bulwark against any attempt to fill the labour shortage with black workers. A perennial obstacle faced by West Indian immigrants—almost a quarter of whom arrived in Britain with some professional or managerial experience—was that they were excluded from white-collar jobs and forced to take positions for which they were over-qualified. And even in the sectors of the economy where labour was in particularly short supply, black applicants could often find that they were also omitted. In the mid-1950s, for instance, the labour shortage on Britain's buses was so acute the British Transport Commission sent officials to Barbados, Britain's oldest colony in the West Indies, to encourage further immigration. The Commission offered to loan prospective immigrants two-thirds of the cost of their journey to Britain if they committed to working on the buses for at least a year. In Nottingham alone at this time there were 200 vacancies on the buses. However, aping tactics that had earlier been deployed by white transport workers in West Bromwich, local members of the Transport and General Workers Union spoke out in favour of a colour bar. Tellingly alluding to the familiar obsession with inter-racial sex, the union declared that employing black men in a position where they would be in close contact with white women would be a recipe for "immorality". The matter was made worse by the fact it was widely understood black immigrants had a "chip on their shoulder", could not add up and were incapable of taking discipline. Whatever promises the Government had made in Barbados, the union concluded that the only ethical solution was to continue to bar black workers from the job.[21]

It was a situation that contrasted with the experiences of the thousands of Irish immigrants who found their way "across the water" to Nottingham in the same period in search of work. In the early days, signs did appear on some establishments with slogans like "No Irishmen Served Here", and Irish immigrants could also find it difficult to communicate given the respective thickness of some Irish and Nottinghamshire accents. Irish immigrants, particularly those who came from rural parts of the country, often struggled to adapt to the pace and noise of factory work. But most Irish immigrants nevertheless found work easily—as waitresses at Lyon's Tea House on Long Row, for instance, or as construction workers building the M1 motorway from Hertfordshire to Northamptonshire. One survey suggested that 60 per cent of Irish immigrants had a job within a week of their arrival in Britain, and 90 per cent had done so within a month. The popular Irish folk song "McAlpine's Fusiliers", which spread around construction sites across Britain from the 1940s onwards and was subsequently popularised by the Irish folk band the Dubliners, was a mythologised evocation of life as an Irish labourer in Britain, many of whom found work with the Robert

COLOUR BARS: 1950s NOTTINGHAM

McAlpine construction company. "As down the glen came McAlpine's men with their shovels slung behind them", the song went. "Twas in the pub that they drank their sub and out in the spike you'll find them/they sweated blood and they washed down mud with pints and quarts of beer/and now we're on the road again with McAlpine's fusiliers."[22]

Unlike black or Asian immigrants, the Irish were treated as both insiders and outsiders in Britain. They were often stereotyped as being lazy, drunk, stupid and backward. But they were also white, European, English speakers—and therefore familiar. The colour bar was, by definition, structured by race. As the production manager of a Nottingham textiles factory told the press in 1956, among his employees there were most definitely strong feelings against "colonial workers", a term which in the 1950s had become synonymous with "non-white" immigrants. His response was to introduce a form of segregation in the workplace along the lines of Jim Crow America or South Africa, where apartheid was formally enshrined into law in 1948. Around the same time at a factory in nearby Derbyshire, two hundred white employees withdrew their labour to protest the firm's decision to employ a new Pakistani worker, Mohammed Ghulam, to add to the six other ethnic minority men it had taken on in the preceding years. "All our members are determined", the factory's union secretary declared. "The seven Coloured men must go." Ghulam was eventually dismissed from his job. In the Nottingham factory, meanwhile, white and black employees were split up into entirely different sections and black workers paid three times less than their white counterparts. In the context of Britain's labour shortage, ethnic minority labour was a necessity in many parts of the economy. But the interests of white employees and customers were paramount. The colour bar was what most white workers wanted, the Secretary of the Nottingham branch of the National Union of Manufacturers concluded; "far from creating racist feelings, it satisfies both sides".[23]

By the summer of 1958, one observer argued it was no longer feasible to dismiss the colour bar as a series of isolated incidents; it was instead part of a pattern that was threatening to engulf the whole of the Midlands. And it was the young, white, garishly-dressed Teddy Boys who took it upon themselves to extend the colour bar into a broader campaign of intimidation against Britain's black population. The "Teds" were one of Britain's earliest youth subcultures, forerunners of the later mod and punk scenes. Their style was influenced by the zoot suits commonly worn by the Hispanic population of Los Angeles in the 1940s, made notorious by the anti-Mexican violence that took place in that city in June 1943. Teddy Boys also enthusiastically embraced the rise of rock and roll, a genre that—before it was appropriated by white performers like Elvis Presley, Gene Vincent and British acts like Marty Wilde, and long before it became the subject of an apparently never-ending series of nostalgic television documentaries—emerged out of a fusion of African American blues and gospel. Like the skinheads a generation later, then, the Teddy Boys were shaped by cross-cultural, trans-Atlantic movements. But they were also characterised by a defensive emphasis on community and a strong sense of territoriality, something which often led them towards verbal and physical attacks on anyone who was deemed to be part of an "out-group".[24]

In London, there were reports of Teddy Boys targeting Greek Cypriot immigrants as well as members of a West Indian community that numbered 7,000 in Notting Hill alone. In white Nottingham, however, the visibility of the 3,000 black immigrants in the city, most of whom lived in St Ann's, made them easy targets. The Teddy Boys felt they had a licence to beat black people, one local official told the press, simply because they constituted the section of society that everyone hated. For the Dominican-born journalist Edward Scobie, who was sent to Nottingham on an assignment for *Tribune* magazine in summer 1958, it was obvious that the Teddy Boys on St Ann's Well

Road—the "white hoodlums", as Scobie called them—had become a law unto themselves. They were armed with daggers and warned that black people would be attacked if they congregated in groups. Walking around St Ann's, Scobie was intimidated by gangs of Teds who purposefully brushed against him in the hope he would make a wrong move. Further down the street, Scobie saw groups of youths doing the same thing to an elderly black man. And there was hostility from other locals, including white mothers and the passers-by who refused to even speak to Scobie when he asked for directions to his hotel. Even the disingenuous smiles that initially greeted black immigrants had vanished; the only reason he wasn't jumped, Scobie reasoned, was because it was still early in the afternoon.[25]

Incidents of "black-burying", as local Teddy Boys referred to it, were indeed piling up. A black man was set upon in St Ann's by a group of Teds one evening as he visited a late-night pharmacy to collect a prescription for his wife, while Eric Irons remembered that a gang of white youths had tried to set fire to a Jamaican man in the toilets of the Robin Hood Chase Pub at 140 St Ann's Well Road. Bricks began to be hurled through the windows of black people's homes. Then, on the evening of 23 August 1958, there was an altercation in the Chase after a black man was told by a white onlooker to "lay off" the white woman he was talking to. The scuffle spilled out onto the streets around the pub, and the crowds quickly swelled with white people screaming that they were going to "kill niggers". It was, a West Indian resident of St Ann's later explained, as if they were hunting badgers in the woods. "In the pub they said, 'Let's go hunt the niggers'...then they went out for the kill."[26]

White riots

There were more than 1,500 people involved in the first night's unrest in Nottingham on 23 August, mostly gangs of Teddy

Boys, drinkers at nearby pubs and dozens of onlookers who watched the violence like motorists passing a crash. To those black immigrants drinking in the Chase or walking the streets around it, the gravity of the situation quickly became obvious. Many attempted to flee down the alleyways that threaded the rows of terraced housing on St Ann's Well Road and Curzon Street. With cries of "go back to your own country", they were chased by mobs of white men carrying broken bottles, knives and razors. In the immediate aftermath of the violence, however, the public's understanding of what had taken place was dominated by the privileged position of white eyewitnesses in the media; black perspectives were almost entirely absent. And it was the harrowing experiences of the white couples who were out for a Saturday night drink only to find themselves caught up in the riots that were made to symbolise the shocking depravity of what had taken place. Mary Lowndes, a mother of two and resident of nearby Little John Street, told how she saw her husband being punched from one side of the road to the other by a group of "darkies", while a resident of Beacon Street on the other side of St Ann's Well Road described how she had become separated from her husband during the affray, only to find him bleeding from ear to ear by the side of the road. His throat had been cut. Another white woman told reporters she knew something was wrong when she felt something sharp in her arm. Before she was knocked into a doorway, she caught sight of her husband on the floor beneath a pile of black men. When they ran off, her husband stood up, pulled a knife from his back and threw it to the ground.[27]

Having quelled the unrest, Nottingham's Chief Constable, the South African-born Captain Athelstan Popkess, made explicit what should already have been obvious, namely that it was white racists who were the initial and primary aggressors in the affray. "The crowd that had gathered were mostly white and they were hostile to the many coloured people in the area", Popkess told journalists, before explaining that the police had even deemed it necessary to take a number of black men into protective custody for their own safety. But the centrality of the accounts by white participants—and in particular the respectable white couples who, reporters were keen to point out, resided in carefully maintained terraced houses—meant that a narrative of black aggression (and thereby black culpability) quickly took root. Shaped by the racialised hostility towards the black presence more generally, an alarming picture was painted of West Indian men running amok, brandishing knives, and attacking anyone in sight. It was, in the view of another white eye-witness, behaviour that was quite simply "not the work of humans".[28]

The corollary to the idea of black aggression was the notion of white victimhood, something that was articulated most clearly by the Lowndeses in the days that followed the first bout of rioting. Mary Lowndes gave a series of interviews to the press, in which she advanced the theory that the riots were planned by the black community in advance as part of an "anti-white demonstration". Lowndes called for black men—who she accused of drinking spirits until they didn't know what they were doing—to be banned from the local pubs. Her husband, meanwhile, claimed he was afraid to leave his wife and children alone in the house. In the days after the unrest, Fred Alsopp, the licensee of the Chase, heeded Mary Lowdes' call for the extension of the colour bar in St Ann's by barring black people from entry. A sign was placed on the pub's door: "Owing to recent disturbances", it read, "no coloured person will be served here". Alsopp claimed never to have been a supporter of the colour bar prior to taking over the running of the Chase. "But oh boy", he remarked, "what a lot of trouble these coloured men can cause".[29]

The unrest brought the national spotlight onto Nottingham. National newspapers sent their correspondents on assignments to

St Ann's with a remit to understand the deeper reasons for what had happened. At this point, some space began to be given to black voices and the impact of rampant racism brought to bear by the colour bar and sharpened by the Teddy Boys' campaign of street harassment. A Jamaican barber told a reporter there was widespread disillusionment with the police among the black population, and what was seen as a reluctance to hold to account the white perpetrators of the attacks. He recalled a friend who had been so badly beaten by a gang of Teddy Boys he had been taken to hospital, only to be informed by the police that his assailants simply could not be found; "but let a coloured man attack a white man", the barber wryly observed, "and the police will move heaven and earth to find him". For the most part, though—and following on from the acute anxieties over miscegenation that St Clair Drake encountered in 1940s Cardiff—reporters hit on the twin pillars of sexual and economic jealousy as the primary causes for the unrest.[30]

On the one hand, there was distaste among the white residents of St Ann's at the number of black men who, like Eric Irons, had entered into relationships with local white women. There was the widespread belief that St Ann's had a "woman problem", one correspondent explained, which was taken to mean the suspicion that any inter-racial relationship was in fact a front for a prostitution racket. It was seemingly impossible to conceive of mixed relationships in any other way. If you were married to a black man, a white woman who was herself in a relationship with a Jamaican immigrant explained, everyone treated you as though you were a common prostitute. And at the same time as this, on the other hand, the ability of some immigrants to purchase their own radiograms, cars and houses irked white residents. This was particularly the case in the context of a worsening economic landscape and an unemployment rate across the country that by the time of the riots had risen to more than 500,000 people (it was unclear why this should prevent those ethnic minorities who could afford to do so from purchasing particular items). The two issues became conflated, with the supposed involvement of black men in prostitution understood to be the only conceivable explanation for their apparent economic prosperity. The riots were a simple case of envy, the white proprietor of a local cigarette shop on the corner of Peas Hill Road and St Ann's Well Road explained. "White people see these coloured men rolling around in large sleek cars and they get worked up about it because they haven't got the same themselves."[31]

It is difficult to think of the white crowd that descended on the Chase as anything other than a lynch mob along Southern American lines, particularly as this was the kind of language that many of the white participants in the unrest used themselves. And the charge of "nigger hunting in England" was made even clearer by what took place in St Ann's the following weekend. In light of the simmering resentment towards the black population and the dominance of white perspectives in the media—alongside the steady drip-drip of news of worsening inter-racial tensions in London—further violence on the streets of Nottingham looked like an inevitability. When this came to pass on Saturday 30 August, however, no one anticipated that this would end up being an all-white affair. This was partly as a result of the conciliatory stance taken by Eric Irons, who—in the week after the initial disturbances, and using the connections he had built up through his Colonial and Social Welfare Club—urged ethnic minorities in the area to stay indoors during the evenings while tensions were high. It meant that when a crowd of 4,000 people—more than double the number involved in the unrest of the previous week—assembled in St Ann's after last orders at the local pubs, with chants of "let's get the blacks", there was barely a black person in sight.[32]

Upon hearing of the disturbances, three West Indian men at a nearby house party did attempt to drive to the scene. The driver of the car worked with Irons in Chilwell, and later told Irons he had set off with the intention of showing the rioters that "if they want to be nasty, we can be nasty as well". But on its arrival, the car was immediately rushed by angry crowds, who hammered on the windows and attempted to overturn it until the police intervened, ordered the driver to "go like hell" and the driver was able to accelerate away. With members of the crowd openly discussing raiding black people's homes, the 100 police officers that had been deployed to the area began mobilising. From the makeshift headquarters that had been set up at St Ann's Church, they frisked anyone who looked like a Teddy Boy and, to loud jeers from the crowds, bundled those found with weapons into the back of waiting black Marias. Traffic was diverted off St Ann's Well Road, and the police formed a human shield to prevent the unrest from spreading. The rioters began to shout, "It is the niggers we are after, let us get after them". Having turned on the police, however, the crowd increasingly fought with one another. By 11.30 p.m., with the use of strong-arm tactics that reportedly even led to a journalist being punched on the chin by an officer, the police had largely regained control of the situation. Officers removed their helmets and stood about wiping their brows. Finally, they set off to process the dozens of suspects due to spend a night in the cells.[33]

In total, twenty-four white men were charged and eventually either jailed for three months or fined for their part in the rioting—a relatively small number perhaps explained by the challenge the police faced in controlling a crowd as large as that which had formed in St Ann's. And the men's passage through the courts revealed a growing disagreement between the authorities, the media and broader public over the exact nature of the violence. Captain Popkess was determined that the unrest should not be thought of as a race riot and went out of his way to praise the restraint shown by the black population. In court, and picking up from Popkess' description of the rioters as "irresponsible Teddy Boys and persons who had had a lot to drink", the prosecution likened the rioters to a Saturday night crowd gone wrong; they were simply badly-behaved louts who had had too much to drink.[34]

If this chimed with the broader moral panic around Teddy Boys in the 1950s—one newspaper editorial saw the unrest in Nottingham as evidence Britain was living though a new "hooligan age"—it ignored the obvious fact that, by their own admission, a significant proportion of the crowd that descended on St Ann's were there with the primary ambition of hurting black people. And the decision of the authorities to prevent them from doing so also fed into the perverse idea—initially established by the media's laser-like focus on white perspectives of the first night's unrest in Nottingham—that, in spite of the colour bar, incidents of "black burying" and two nights of racist rioting, and in spite of the attacks on black people's homes that continued in the weeks after the riots, it was the white population who were the real victims. When the sentences of five of the perpetrators were read out in court, for example, there were gasps and screams from the public gallery. One woman fainted, while another exclaimed "what about the dirty black dogs? They have started all the trouble, but you can't catch them".[35]

As the dust settled in Nottingham, the black population closed ranks. Black residents of St Ann's slept with milk bottles next to the bed, so that if a brick were to shatter through the window at night they would have something ready to throw back. They began to strategise about what to do in case their houses were set on fire, and wondered whether it would be feasible to seek refuge in France. The West Indian driver of the car that was rushed by the rioters emigrated to Canada. John Wray, who arrived in Nottingham from Jamaica at the beginning of summer 1958, told of his shock at having come to Britain to "climb up" in society, only to find that each evening he was on the receiving end of racist remarks from white people as they passed by his window. One report noted that well into the autumn there was a reluctance on the part of Nottingham's black population to leave their homes after dark. Such stories did attract sympathy from concerned citizens elsewhere in the country. A correspondent wrote to the *Manchester Guardian* in the aftermath of the riots to emphasise that the danger of racism came not from a Saturday night fight in Nottingham but from the media's distorted reporting of it, and the emphasis placed on sexual jealousy between white and black communities. A woman from the King's Road area of London, who was married to a Nigerian immigrant, sang the praises of the West Indian bus conductors in her neighbourhood, whose behaviour she saw as being in stark contrast to white conductors who seemed to have given up any pretence of friendliness. The correspondent urged readers to recognise that Britain's growing black population were not only fleeing poverty and mostly working in unskilled, poorly paid jobs, but were also adding "their own warm gaiety to our daily lives". Yet these were all too rare voices. And what had happened in Nottingham was quickly overshadowed by the growing intensity of the violence taking place 120 miles south in the Notting Hill district of West London.[36]

In Notting Hill, it was the prospect of miscegenation that once again provided a major catalyst in the unrest. One flashpoint came when the Swedish immigrant and part-time prostitute Majbritt Morrison was spotted with her Jamaican husband Raymond near Latimer Road Tube Station, not far from the house they shared on Bramley Road. The violence began as an unwanted attempt to "protect" a white woman, but Morrison defended her husband against the crowds, and her home was later pelted with milk bottles for the crime of being a "black man's trollop". It then became, over a four-day period, a concerted attack on one of the largest West Indian communities in the country. Over the bank holiday weekend in late August and into the following week black passers-by were beaten up and sometimes even stabbed; a West African student who was on a visit to the area from Derby was attacked by a crowd of 200 people with cries of "lynch him", and was forced to take refuge in a nearby greengrocer's; a prominent West Indian café was ransacked by a crowd of 800 people that it took more than 30 police officers to clear. By the Monday, there were even reports that the number 28 bus from Wandsworth to Kensington had become packed with crowds eager to join in the "nigger run".[37]

What distinguished the unrest in London from what happened in Nottingham was the prominent role played by the far right and in particular the Union Movement, a hotchpotch of extremist groups that was headed by the veteran fascist Oswald Mosley, who as leader of the British Union of Fascists in the 1930s had sought to do for Britain what Mussolini had done for Italy. Mosley's Union Movement set up shop at the Kensington Park Hotel on Ladbroke Grove (just around the corner from a Jewish synagogue), posted Keep Britain White posters on lampposts and held meetings in pubs and outside tube stations to ramp up local hostility towards the black presence. The aim was not simply to clamp down on black and Asian immigration. In order to avoid places like Notting Hill becoming "Little Harlems"—a geographical reference point that was widely used to signify the supposed dangers posed by the emergence of the increasingly-diverse inner city—the Union Movement called for all black and Asian migrants to be deported back to their countries of origin.[38]

What happened in Notting Hill—right on the doorstep of the editors of the nation's major newspapers at Fleet Street—further anchored the way in which the earlier events in Nottingham were understood. There were few mainstream politicians in

Britain willing to support Oswald Mosley's call for the repatriation of black and Asian immigrants. The Board of Deputies of British Jews expressed its fear that the riots could lead to a resurgence of fascism in Britain. But when in 1959 Mosley stood for election in North Kensington, the constituency which encompassed Notting Hill, the electorate largely ignored him. For the first time in his career he lost his electoral deposit (but Mosely did receive eight per cent of the vote, meaning that one in twelve voters agreed with Mosley that the local black population should be removed). Yet the far right's success in whipping up tensions in London made the line that had earlier been taken in Nottingham by Captain Popkess—namely that the unrest was down to too many irresponsible young people who had simply had too much to drink—even more implausible. This was especially the case as the events of 1958 began to make headlines around the world, including in places internationally recognised as primary examples of entrenched racism *in extremis*. In South Africa, for example, there was anticipation that the riots would force Britain to reign in its criticism of racial apartheid. In Little Rock, Arkansas, meanwhile, the state governor Orval Faubus had just one year earlier made the incendiary decision to bring in the Arkansas National Guard to prevent black students from entering white schools in an attempt to block the mandated desegregation of US education. Now, British journalists in Little Rock found that white residents were approaching them with the word *Nottingham* on their lips. And upon hearing of the unrest in Britain, Governor Faubus himself had a message for the British authorities: "we have sympathy for you".[39]

There remained an inability on the part of the media and the authorities to put an accurate label on what happened in Nottingham and Notting Hill. Rather than "white riots" or "racist riots", it was "race riots"—a term more open to interpretation—that became conventional. And picking up the baton from the far-right, the notion of race rioting in Britain—and the prospect of racial strife along South African or American lines—became ammunition for those more mainstream politicians who were opposed to Britain's gradual drift towards the multicultural. Cyril Osborne, a kind of prototype Enoch Powell who had himself grown up in Nottingham and in 1945 became MP for the largely white market town of Louth in Lincolnshire, warned that unless action was taken, Britain was "sowing the seeds of another Little Rock". It was a disturbing prospect, particularly for those who still clung to the fairy-tale image of Britain as an egalitarian beacon of liberty and tolerance. The reputation of the United States had been severely tarnished as a result of what had happened at Little Rock, one campaign group declared in October 1958; "for the UK to be laid open to similar charges would disillusion many who look to Britain as a tolerant corner of an intolerant world". Osborne's solution—the immediate introduction of restrictions on immigration, and especially "coloured" immigration—was contentious. But it did have the advantage of allowing the body politic to sidestep the inconvenient truth of the extent of Britain's problem with racism: the colour bars at work, in the pubs, or in the housing sector, the verbal abuse, the bricks through windows, the physical attacks and the thousands of white people who gathered in two major cities with expressed ambition of "getting at the blacks" and "keeping Britain white". Perversely, the approach to dealing with the issue of white racism increasingly became finding ways of clamping down on "non-white" immigration. The steady erosion over a period of decades of the principles of the 1948 British Nationality Act began with the political response to the violence on the streets of St Ann's and Notting Hill.[40]

Black Skins, White Prejudice

The remarkable thing about the Government's position on the rioting is just how conspicuous it was by its absence. There was no official statement from either the Prime Minister or his Home Secretary, R. A. Butler, until the worst of the unrest was over. No one from Government bothered to visit the areas that were affected, and there were no immediate assurances that the black British citizens who were the targets of the violence would be protected. From the point of view of Britain's black population, this vacuum was filled by the leaders of what remained the British colonies in the Caribbean five thousand miles away—and particularly Norman Manley, Jamaica's Chief Minister and an eventual architect of Jamaican independence. Alongside Karl LaCorbiniere, the Deputy Prime Minister of the Federal West Indies, Manley touched down in London on 5 September, and immediately held a press conference that he used to play on British anxieties about how the disturbances were being viewed geopolitically. The rioting was a big deal, of "tremendous world importance", Manley told the media. Referencing Orval Faubus' apparent sympathies for the British Government in light of the unrest, Manley argued that anything that allowed the leaders of Little Rock, Arkansas to smirk on the world stage was nothing short of a disaster.[41]

Days later, Manley made for Notting Hill and Nottingham. With his three-piece suit and shock of white hair, he cut an unmissable figure as he toured the rioting hot spots of St Mark's Road in London and St Ann's Well Road in Nottingham. Manley was mobbed. In Nottingham, he couldn't move more than three feet without a West Indian immigrant stopping him to shake his hand. Frank Jackson, a Jamaican painter who lived in St Ann's, told Manley there were rumours Teddy Boys were arming themselves with rocks and weapons ahead of a third prospective attack in St Ann's on Saturday night (it never materialised). Manley was invited into people's houses for cups of tea, and later stopped for a drink at a local wine and spirits shop. Finally, at the invitation of Eric Irons, he addressed a packed audience of West Indian immigrants at the Colonial and Social Welfare Club at 279 Alfred Street—barely half a mile from the Chase pub at 140 St Ann's Well Road, where black people were now barred from entry.[42]

It was a stuffy, windowless room and, not helped by the dozens of conversations he had had earlier in the day, Manley was suffering with laryngitis. But nevertheless, he rose to the occasion. He struck a balance between optimism that conditions for Britain's black population would one day improve and the desperately-needed official recognition of the severity of the racism that had become an everyday part of black people's lives. He stressed that he saw it as his duty to visit both Notting Hill and Nottingham—not only to provide encouragement but also, in the context of the silence from the British authorities, "to let both you and England know that you have a Government of your own". While Manley had found that there were large numbers of white citizens who supported the cause of the black population and were disgusted by the rioting, he argued those who claimed there was no racial prejudice in Britain were just fooling themselves. "You have the right to be here", Manley reminded his audience, and—putting into words what was gradually becoming obvious, to West Indian immigrants but also to the white residents of neighbourhoods like St Ann's—"you are going to stay". His audience erupted into loud cheers. "Your trouble will not be over a day and a night", Manley concluded. "The night is over, but with the dawn we have a tremendous amount of work to do. I want you to know", Manley emphasised, that "we in the West Indies are with you every step of the way".[43]

In the weeks and months after his visit, there was a concerted effort on the part of Britain's black communities to take up Manley's challenge. Notting Hill, in particular, became a hive of black cultural and political activity, with the formation of many of the organisations out of which the British Black Power movement would eventually emerge. In winter 1959 the chain-smoking Trinidadian journalist and Communist activist Claudia Jones established the inaugural Notting Hill carnival which, within the limitations of a poorly-heated public hall, featured dances, beauty pageants and performances by calypso bands, the aim of which was to "wash the taste of Notting Hill and Nottingham out of our mouths". Notting Hill was becoming an urban epicentre, for black Britain but also for growing numbers of well-meaning white activists and sociologists looking to improve race relations. Nottingham was a much more low-key affair, but fledgling activists likewise set about trying to find ways of establishing a sense of West Indian culture in the city. The management of the Colonial and Social Welfare Club described Manley's visit as a much-needed tonic for it to redouble its efforts to further the social, cultural and physical well-being of its members. Regular social activities were arranged at its premises on Alfred Street. This included access to the latest newspapers from Jamaica and Guiana, the establishment of cricket and dominoes teams, performances by steel bands and a weekly Saturday night dance to the latest calypso and jazz records played by a local sound system. By 1960, the Club had also obtained funds from the local council to allow a group of ethnic minority schoolchildren to attend a free Christmas performance of *The Happiest Day of Your Life* at the Nottingham Playhouse.[44]

By this point, Eric Irons himself had been tapped up by the local authorities for the newly-created position of Organiser for Educational Work Among the Coloured Communities. In a pattern that would be repeated across the country with alarming regularity over the latter half of the twentieth century, the council claimed it had been caught unawares by the severity of the rioting. "The violence made us realise that something had been lurking about that we knew nothing about", a spokesperson admitted; in the aftermath of the riots, the intention was to set about repairing Nottingham's tarnished image.[45]

COLOUR BARS: 1950s NOTTINGHAM

It is telling that hitherto, the council's work in this area was largely restricted to its Consultative Committee for the Welfare of Coloured People, which had been established in 1954 out of the council's offices at 45 Castle Gate with the ambition of helping ethnic minorities become "ordinary, useful citizens" and adapting to the "English way of life". This kind of language, the misplaced assumption that black citizens of empire would know nothing of life in the "mother country", and that, initially, the Committee was made up entirely of white people, indicated the paternalistic, neo-colonial nature of the debate about race in this period—even in liberal, ostensibly well-meaning circles. It also showed how far the narrative that the white violence of 1958 was somehow the responsibility of the black presence was filtering into the mainstream. Irons was positioned as a would-be interpreter between the local authority and Nottingham's growing ethnic minority population. He accepted the position because he recognised the importance of ethnic minorities having someone they could look upon as a friend in high places in the city. In the council's eyes, however, Irons was the official leader of the city's ethnic minority population, a kind of Mr Fix-It who was presumed to speak for the entirety of Nottingham's "coloured" residents—which by this time also included some 1,000 South Asian immigrants. With his RAF credentials, sharp-suits and long-standing presence in Nottingham, he was a man with whom business could be done. The role of the "community leader"—which would dominate race relations policies in Britain for decades—was born.[46]

It is almost laughable how inadequate the council's post-riots initiatives were as a response to the broader issues encountered by black and Asian immigrants in 1950s Nottingham—notwithstanding the involvement of Irons. But at the same time, as I was leafing through the records of the Consultative Committee in Nottinghamshire archives, with the diversity of modern

107

Nottingham buzzing around me outside, there was also something moving about the tentativeness of their activities. Here, for example, was a member of the International Friendship League inviting local black teenagers to his house in the leafy suburb of Basford to listen to his collection of gramophone records; here was a request for volunteers to visit the homes of local ethnic minorities, to ensure they were OK; here was a Pakistani resident who had written to the Committee asking them if they would facilitate a debate with local university students, on a subject of their choosing; and here were the invitations to the Committee's Christmas party, which was open to children from any background in Nottingham and consisted of a menu of tea, instant coffee, mince pies and sausage rolls (the inability of devout Muslims to eat pork was apparently not considered), as well as activities including tombola and a white elephant auction. These events were little more than gestures, given the structural problems that faced Nottingham's ethnic minority population. In late 1958, for instance, the unemployment rate for West Indians in the city had reached thirteen per cent—more than six times the national average. But I wondered whether one might see in these small-scale, earnest and ultimately inadequate gestures the tentative beginnings of an increasing familiarity with, and even respect for ethnic diversity in Britain; not so much "drifting", as "creeping" multiculturalism.[47]

Whatever its intentions, in late 1958 Nottingham's Consultative Committee was swimming against the tide. The hostility towards "coloured" immigrants—expressed most explicitly by the cries of the white rioters on the streets of St Ann's and Notting Hill—was entering the political mainstream. In part, this was a result of the silence of Harold Macmillan's Conservative Government as the unrest was unfolding. This absence left those who saw the rioting as a symptom of Britain's post-war immigration policies free to set the tone of the debate.

COLOUR BARS: 1950s NOTTINGHAM

The Labour MP for Nottingham North, James Harrison, was first out of the traps. He fed into the idea that the unrest could be explained in connection to the worsening economic landscape, and argued it was madness to allow indiscriminate immigration into what was supposedly already an over-crowded island (652,000 people left Britain over the course of the 1950s, mostly for Australia, New Zealand and Canada). The Conservative MP for Nottingham Central, Lieutenant Colonel J. K. Cordeaux, backed up his Labour opponent by calling for the immediate introduction of restrictions on immigration; in his view, the riots had simply emphasised the severity of what was already a major problem. This was the period in which the immigration debate was becoming intertwined in the public imagination with race. And what the Nottingham MPs left unsaid, the tabloids made explicit. An editorial in *The People* generously made it clear that Britain's black and Asian population could not be blamed for the colour of their skin. However, the sad truth was, the paper claimed, they had the misfortune of coming from "backwards countries" with "a very different way of life from ours"; it was therefore inevitable that such immigrants would worsen conditions in inner-city neighbourhoods and, in the process, offend their new neighbours; the riots in St Ann's and Notting Hill should be seen as the "lunatic and criminal result of our failure to tackle the colour problem". The *Daily Mirror* agreed that too many "coloured no-goods" had been allowed into Britain—from the West Indies in particular. And the reality was, the paper claimed—irrespective of the worsening unemployment rate across the country and the ongoing impact of the British colour bar—these people had not come to work. Rather, the *Mirror* concluded, they simply wanted to take advantage of what they saw as Britain's "milk-and-honey welfare state, with its golden pavements, pensions for all and false teeth on the cheap".[48]

MULTICULTURAL BRITAIN

What is striking about these narratives is how often variations of them have been repeated by politicians, sections of the British media and the broader public across the latter part of the twentieth century and into the first decades of the twenty-first. The concern that Britain is an "over-crowded" island with too many ill-suited foreigners "scrounging" benefits off the state was not only a feature of the many letters of support Enoch Powell received following his 1968 "Rivers of Blood" speech, but was also a prominent part of the referendum on Britain's membership of the European Union almost five decades later. In 1958, establishing a pattern that would recur time and again in British politics, the absence of principled leadership from Government on issues around race and ethnic diversity meant the terms of the debate were being set by the far right. The media was effectively echoing the stance taken by Oswald Mosley's Union Movement, a spokesperson for the group went as far as to argue. Anyone who says, "restrict immigration" and "deport undesirables" were simply repeating, parrot like, what the Union Movement had been calling for five years ago.[49]

The Government did eventually try to regain control of the situation. It stressed it would focus on the impartial enforcement of the law with utmost precision. But in positioning itself as the neutral arbiters of law and order, it wholly failed to engage with the question of racism. And more than that, the Government's pretensions to impartiality were undermined by its admission that it had for some time been looking into the feasibility of restricting immigration from Britain's colonies and former colonies. It was, in effect, an official endorsement of the idea that the white riots had been caused by the black and Asian presence. At this point, the cross-party consensus that the introduction of immigration controls would fatally damage the unity of the Commonwealth and Britain's supposed reputation for tolerance (not to mention its future ability to access a cheap labour force) was just about holding. And there were some, such as the Labour Party chairman Tom Driberg, who were willing to call out the bizarre irrationality of the line that equated white racism with a "colour problem". How could there be such a problem in Britain, Driberg wondered, given that ethnic minorities accounted for just four out of every 1,000 people? Surely, he argued, the real problem was "not black skins, but white prejudice". Yet by the end of 1958, it was obvious that the emboldened and expanding anti-immigration lobby was not going away. By the end of the decade, the introduction of some kind of restriction on immigration was beginning to look like an inevitability.[50]

In the months and years that followed the riots, the self-anointed leaders of the campaign for immigration controls—Cyril Osborne and Norman Pannell, the Conservative MP for Liverpool Kirkdale who had himself been an immigrant for many years in colonial Nigeria—took their case to the nation. They positioned themselves as noble speakers of truth to power, politicians who, unlike the majority of their peers, were not prepared to turn away from a problem they saw as having the potential to blight the lives of their children and grandchildren. "Coloured immigrants" (a term which Osborne clarified he was using loosely, so as to encompass Britain's Maltese and Cypriot population) were like sticks of dynamite and, like real dynamite, became more dangerous as they accumulated in greater numbers. The issue had become critical, Osborne claimed; "some foolishly applied or accidental spark could ignite the whole lot". Osborne and his backers drew on a ragbag of contradictory arguments that were mobilised at different points depending on their audience. Each of the West Indian nations had policies in place that prevented immigrants from moving freely from island to island. Why shouldn't Britain do the same? In the event of another recession, the Trade Unions would impose a "last in, first out" policy, and the resulting rise in black unemployment would inevitably mean trouble. The absence of immigration controls would make the colour bar more, not less pervasive.

But there were occasions when the mask slipped, and the true basis for the campaign was revealed. For Martin Lindsay, the Conservative MP for the affluent, white town of Solihull—a constituency just outside Birmingham's city limits where in 2001 my friends and I studied for our A Levels—the problem wasn't that there were presently 200,000 ethnic minority immigrants in Britain. It was that this number would soon become 500,000, and that in turn would soon become a million. It was in this light, Lindsay argued, that people should ask themselves whether they really wanted Britain to become a "multiracial community". It was a rhetorical statement, but one to which Cyril Osborne provided an answer. In a letter to *The Times*, Osborne laid it on thick. If immigration rates were permitted unchecked, he wrote, by the turn of the century "there would be more black than white people in England". The English would face the indignity of being forced to "exist in their own country only on sufferance from the Afro-Asians". White Britain was on the cusp of being dispossessed and turning into a "chocolate coloured" society. Such a situation could not, Osborne warned, be allowed to happen. The problems as Osborne understood them in Britain's housing sector, in its schools, in the National Health Service and in its rising crime rates, "shout too loudly to be ignored".[51]

In response, Nottingham's Consultative Committee for the Welfare of Coloured People wrote a politely-worded letter to *The Times* correcting Osborne's claims. Based on the research the Committee had done in the city, it was clear that the situation in its schools and hospitals was made no worse by the presence of ethnic minorities. Indeed, a large number of employers in Nottingham would cease to be going concerns without black and Asian workers, while if anything crime rates were lower in areas with large ethnic minority populations than they were in predominately white communities. Increasingly, however, the facts no longer seemed to matter. In summer 1961, one opinion poll showed that 67 per cent of the public now favoured the introduction of restrictions on "non-white" immigration.[52]

In November 1961, the Commonwealth Immigrants Bill was brought before parliament. It would introduce a tiered immigration system, privileging prospective immigrants who already had jobs lined up in Britain or those who had particular skills that were deemed useful, and drastically reducing all unskilled immigration from the West Indies and South Asia. Irish immigrants, the vast majority of whom were unskilled but white, would be exempt. The straightforward aim, as one civil servant admitted behind the scenes, was to cut "coloured" immigration and leave prospective white immigrants with the same rights that they had enjoyed before. As the Home Secretary, R. A. Butler, told his colleagues, the Act would "operate on coloured people almost exclusively". Symbolising just how far the Government had fallen down the far-right rabbit hole, in a nod to the proposals made by Oswald Mosley's Union Movement the Bill also allowed for the deportation of Commonwealth immigrants convicted of a crime within five years of their arrival in Britain. The Commonwealth Immigrants Act came into force in July 1962—the same month the UK Government passed the Jamaica Independence Act, which formally marked an end to colonial rule in Jamaica. For the Labour leader Hugh Gaitskell, the Immigrants Act was a "miserable, shameful, shabby" piece of legislation. It was, he said, probably the first victory the fascists had ever won in Britain. Gaitskell declared that the Act would widely be seen as the moment the colour bar was entrenched in law. As the antiracist activist Ambalavaner Sivanandan put it, the passing of the Act meant that "a British citizen was not completely a British citizen when he was a black British citizen". The racism that powered Britain's colour bar and the 1958 white riots had, in effect, become institutionalised.[53]

MULTICULTURAL BRITAIN

The introduction of the Commonwealth Immigrants Act set in motion what would become a depressingly familiar process whereby the Government, instead of defending the rights of whichever ethnic minority community was being vilified that year, passed legislation designed to appeal to white voters who on the questions of race and immigration were apparently drifting ever further to the right. But even judging the tactic by the criteria of its own architects—in essence, the hope that formalising racism would sweep the broader, societal problem under the carpet—it is an approach that has, more often than not, resulted in failure. Following the 1964 general election, for example— which gave Labour a majority of just four seats—it became clear that the introduction of the Immigrants Act had simply paved the way for demands for even more extreme controls on immigration. Although it had won the election, Labour was spooked by the idea that anti-immigration, anti-black sentiment had cost it votes among its core constituency—and never more so than in Smethwick in the Midlands, where the Conservative candidate Peter Griffiths had won a shock victory over the high-profile Labour incumbent Patrick Gordon-Walker with the aid of his unofficial slogan, "if you want a nigger for a neighbour, vote Labour". It was a slogan that, Government officials noted, was increasingly being fly posted onto walls and bus stops all over the region. By this time, the black and Asian population of Nottingham had risen to 8,000 and, according to one survey, 80 per cent of the electorate as a whole now believed there were too many immigrants in Britain. Within a year of taking office, Labour duly abandoned its opposition to the Immigrants Act. Although the party declared it remained committed to outlawing racial discrimination, it simultaneously found ways of strengthening an Act that, just three years earlier, it had decried as amounting to a legislative colour bar. In 1968—ten years on from the Union Movement's demand in the wake of the

COLOUR BARS: 1950s NOTTINGHAM

Nottingham and Notting Hill unrest that all "coloured" immigrants be deported—Enoch Powell, a one-time contender for the leadership of the Conservative Party whose Wolverhampton constituency neighboured Smethwick, was calling for the establishment of a ministry for the repatriation of immigrants. By the 1970s, the National Front was arguing that all West Indian immigrants in Britain should be forcibly repatriated to Guyana.[54]

It is hard to avoid the impression of a black community under siege in 1950s Nottingham. The riots had brought to the surface a level of racism that echoed news reports on the crises in both apartheid South Africa and the deep south of America. In London, this arguably reached its nadir when in May 1959 Kelso Cochrane, a 32-year-old Antiguan carpenter, was stabbed to death by a gang of white youths who had attacked him as he was walking home. Two years later, in August 1961, the kind of scenes that had played out on the streets of Nottingham and Notting Hill reached the Cannon Street neighbourhood of Middlesborough. Almost three years to the day from the riots of 1958, thousands of white men were reported to have vandalised homes owned by the town's 400 strong Pakistani population and attacked the Taj Mahal café and a local shop—both were businesses that were run by Pakistani and Arab men alongside their white wives. In this light, what was remarkable was the extent to which a series of political opportunists—from Oswald Mosley, Cyril Osborne and Enoch Powell to a host of other, lesser-known characters—sought to turn issues like the colour bar and racist violence into a story about white victimhood. I thought of Mary Lowndes, the white resident of St Ann's whose eye-witness account of the riots—and demand for the extension of the colour bar as a result of them—helped anchor how the unrest was understood. It was a narrative that had a particular potency in a country which had once possessed an empire that famously encompassed a quarter of the world's land mass and six hundred million people, but was now unravelling. And it was a symbol of the state's disorientation over the imperial legacy and the arrival of growing numbers of formerly colonial people in Britain that the colour bar was not outlawed until 1965. Even then, this only applied to racial discrimination in what was vaguely described as "places of public resort". Racial discrimination in the workplace and in housing—the two primary pillars of Britain's colour bar—was not made illegal until 1968.[55]

In this context, it can be difficult to see the organic social connections that were nevertheless developing in 1950s Britain, "across the fortifications of the Colour Bar". But my trip to Nottingham allowed me glimpses of an alternative, more promising kind of atmosphere—brief flashes of the seeds of Britain's drift towards the multicultural that, in the 1950s, were sown in parallel to the increasingly powerful anti-immigrant, "anti-coloured" lobby. You could see this, for example, in the decision by one London resident to write to a national newspaper in the wake of the Nottingham riots to highlight what she experienced as the warmth of the West Indian immigrants around her. It is there in the members of the public who, however hesitantly, moved to invite black immigrants into their houses to listen to records or set up debates between university students and a local Pakistani group. It is there in Irons' activities with the Colonial and Social Welfare Club, and—picking up from the Norman Manley's insistence in the wake of the riots that West Indian immigrants would not be returning home any time soon—his attempts to anchor Nottingham's black community around performances by steel bands and weekly dances to the latest calypso records. And perhaps most importantly, following on from the situation in 1940s Cardiff, the roots of Britain's multicultural drift can also be seen in the growing numbers of mixed-race relationships in Nottingham. Even as their presence acted as one of the sparks for two weekends of violence, these relationships

COLOUR BARS: 1950s NOTTINGHAM

offered perhaps the clearest indication of what Britain's multicultural future might one day look like.[56]

In his memoir, Eric Irons describes the moment he first met the parents of his future wife Nell Kelham, the girl with the jet-black hair. The couple had been due to meet for their regular weekend date at the NAFFI, but Kelham had not shown up. It was a Sunday afternoon, and Irons would soon have to return to his duties with the RAF. Worried about her well-being (and anxious that he may have been stood up), Irons plucked up the courage to knock on the Kelhams' door. Nell was out, but her mother, Marie, invited Irons inside. Immediately she began scolding Irons for the impact his relationship with Nell was having on the Kelhams' family life. "So you are the Eric who is making our lives a misery", she said, as Nell's father Harry sat silently in the corner of the room, reading the newspaper. "My husband and I work very hard, and Saturday night is the only time we go out together and whenever you are in Nottingham there is no peace in this house if we don't give up our evening so that she can go out with you". Irons remained silent. He thought he could see the play of a smile beginning to emerge at the corners of Marie's lips. "Besides", she continued, "I don't go to bed until my daughter comes home. What kind of young man are you keeping my daughter out until the early hours of the morning? I will be glad when the two of you get married and done away with it so we can have some peace". Irons stood there uncomfortably, not knowing what to say. Marie allowed herself to smile. "You've just missed her", she said. Irons thanked her, and headed back to the NAFFI where he found Nell waiting.[57]

On my last day in Nottingham, I made my way up the Woodborough Road, which runs parallel to St Ann's Well Road, the scene of the worst of the rioting in 1958. I was heading to meet with Eric and Nell Irons' adult children to talk about their long since deceased parents. We had arranged to have tea at the house of Irons' son, Ben, who lived at the top of a steep hill. It was still uncomfortably hot in Nottingham, and by the time I arrived at Ben's place I was so sweaty I had to use the bathroom so I could splash cold water on my face. I wasn't sure what I hoped to get out of the meeting. I knew that as an RAF veteran and longstanding "community leader" who was awarded both an OBE and the Jamaican Badge of Honour, Irons was an outlier when it came to the experiences of most ethnic minorities in 1950s Britain. His children were either not born in the 1950s or else too young to remember that time; it was unlikely they would be able to add much to what I already knew.

We talked for a bit about their experiences as mixed-race children, their mother's insistence that the best response to racism was to turn the other cheek, and their father's advice that if reasoning didn't work, the only thing left to do was to get physical. Paul Irons, the eldest of Eric's children, said that as a young man he had struggled with his identity. "I used to ask these

Figure 4: Eric Irons, Nell Irons and children, c. 1995. Photo courtesy of the Irons family.

questions—"'Am I black, or am I white?'" In the end, he gave up searching for a label. "I am a mixture", he concluded; "I adore the bit my mum gave me, and I adore the bit my dad gave me". Someone brought in some biscuits, and the conversation drifted to the situation in present-day Nottingham. Ben told me about his grandchildren, who had light skin, blonde hair and blue eyes but continued to identify with the black heritage given to them by their great-grandfather Eric. Everyone agreed that, with the diversity of modern Nottingham, it was even more difficult to categorise their grandchildren's generation. I thought of my own impressions of Nottingham, the trendy Indian restaurants, the black Pentecostal churches, the Irish centre on Wilford Street. For Ben, his grandchildren were part of a melting pot that was simply inconceivable when he was growing up in the city. We finished our tea, and there was an awkward silence as I fiddled with my voice recorder. I thanked them all and made my way back out into the heat to begin the long trudge back to Nottingham train station.[58]

3

RED LIGHTS

1960s BALSALL HEATH

For a long time I did not seriously engage with my childhood experiences in Balsall Heath. In the late-1990s, a few years after I started secondary school, my mother moved us from our terraced house near Sparkhill Park and into Moseley. It is a neighbourhood less than a mile south, but as the epicentre of Birmingham's intelligentsia, and with a correspondingly high number of coffee shops and organic food establishments, it felt a world away. At my new school, most of the friends I made already knew each other from the suburban primary schools they had attended, and I often felt uneasy about telling people I had gone to school in Balsall Heath. As I got older, I returned to the neighbourhood only sporadically, maybe to eat in one of the Asian restaurants that constituted what by now was marketed as Birmingham's "balti triangle". One time, I ran into an old classmate from Balsall Heath working at just such a restaurant. We studiously avoided each other all night, presumably each feeling uncomfortable at the distance that had been created by the divergence of our lives. Occasionally, a headline on a website would

Figure 5: 'The Street', Balsall Heath, c. 1968. Photograph by Janet Mendelsohn, © Janet Mendelsohn/The Cadbury Research Library, University of Birmingham.

catch my attention, such as with David Cameron's first visit to the area in 2007, the year I graduated from university. But I would quickly scroll on, distracted by other things.

It took the arrival of a parcel that had been sent from the other side of the Atlantic Ocean for me to re-engage with the neighbourhood where I had spent many of my formative years. The package had been sent by Janet Mendelsohn, a retired film producer and Harvard *alumna* who between 1967 and 1969 had been a postgraduate student at the Centre for Contemporary Cultural Studies (CCCS), the radical academic department established at Birmingham University in 1964 by Stuart Hall and Richard Hoggart. I had written to Mendelsohn about a project I was involved with on the history of the CCCS. She had carried the archive from her time in Birmingham around with her for more than forty years. But now she was suffering from ill-health.

RED LIGHTS: 1960s BALSALL HEATH

So yes, Mendelsohn wrote back, she would like me to take it off her hands.[1]

It transpired that, owing to her interest in the lives of Britain's immigrant communities, while she was in the UK Mendelsohn spent most of her time in Balsall Heath. And her approach to academic research was in keeping with what Hall always saw as the experimental nature of cultural studies. Inside the box marked "airmail" were over sixty black-and-white photographs of life in 1960s Balsall Heath, plus thousands more negatives. Alongside these were transcripts of interviews Mendelsohn had conducted with residents of the area—mostly with people who seemed to be involved with what was, by the late-1960s, a red-light district of national repute. There were also the early drafts of a photo-essay Mendelsohn had published in a university magazine, based on the photographs of and interviews with a mixed-race couple she got to know in Balsall Heath—Kathleen, the child of Irish immigrants, and Salim, who was born in Pakistan but had grown up in the British colony of Kenya.[2] Given Mendelsohn was documenting the same streets that, in the 1990s, I walked along daily on my way to school, it was impossible not to be excited by this unusual blend of anthropology, journalism and documentary photography.[3]

To make the twenty-minute walk from my mother's house in Moseley back down to Balsall Heath means for the most part following a single road. There's a moment when the terrain shifts and it becomes clear you have entered the inner-city; the coffee shops are replaced by fast-food joints like DFC Chicken, which for as long as I can remember has been sandwiched in between a Bangladeshi Islamic Centre on one side and a major site of fly-tipping on the other. To order your chicken and chips in DFC you often have to walk past a pile of overflowing bin bags and discarded furniture that would be unimaginable in Moseley. (I have long suspected that the city council prioritises refuse collection along class lines.)

MULTICULTURAL BRITAIN

Coming to Balsall Heath the other way, from Birmingham city centre, involves a bus ride from town. You can get the 35 from outside the futuristic Selfridges building, which opened in 2003 as part of an expensive redevelopment of the Bull Ring shopping centre. The bus crosses the inner-ring road, which after its completion in 1971 became the *de facto* dividing line between the city's commercial hub and its residential neighbourhoods. Once past Birmingham Central Mosque—which became the largest mosque in Western Europe when it opened in 1975— you arrive onto the backstreets of Balsall Heath. The bus winds its way up Clevedon Road, not far from the Clock and the Old Mo, the last two surviving pubs in the area. On the left is Apna Ghar (our house), a multi-faith care home for elderly people; on the right is Aziz supermarket, which is more accurately a corner shop the signage of which is sponsored by the Scottish soft drinks company Irn-Bru.

When I imagine this topography, in my mind's eye I still see it from the vantage point of the smoke-filled top deck of the number 35. It was the arrival of Janet Mendelsohn's photographs that led me towards a different perspective. Her pictures remind us that Britain's "street-level multiculturalism", as the writer and photographer Johny Pitts has called it, is not a modern phenomenon. Her images show how, in going about the challenging process of putting down roots, immigrant communities were transforming the physical landscapes of areas like Balsall Heath with the establishment of cafés, cinemas and other businesses designed to cater for the needs of people who had uprooted themselves halfway around the world. We came across similar themes in 1940s Tiger Bay. By the 1960s, however, this was something that was not restricted to the "sailortowns" populated by an ethnically-disparate band of transient seamen.[4]

In part this was due to the conjuncture in which Mendelsohn was conducting her research. As we saw in the previous chapter, in

RED LIGHTS: 1960s BALSALL HEATH

1962 the Conservative Government introduced the Commonwealth Immigrants Act, a key moment in what would become the long, undignified post-war history of attempts at limiting immigration to Britain. But in the short term, at least, the Act had the opposite impact to what was intended. It forced those immigrants who were already in Britain to decide whether to return home, as many had always intended to do, and reunite with family members and friends many of whom would soon be prevented from settling in Britain. But this would mean doing so without having made themselves financially secure in the way that immigrants often hoped they would. The alternative was to stop thinking of themselves as temporary sojourners in Britain and start imagining themselves as settlers. It was the latter option that many people opted for.

When Mendelsohn arrived in Birmingham in 1967, the number of immigrants in the city from Britain's former colonies in the Caribbean, East Africa and the Indian sub-continent—most of whom came from the Punjab on the Indian-Pakistan border, as well as the Mirpur district of Pakistan—had reached 50,000, almost double what it had been in 1961. It was not hard to see where the appeal of starting a new life in *Vilayet* ("foreign place" or Britain specifically) lay. In 1960, for example, the construction of the Mangla dam on the outskirts of Mirpur had displaced an estimated 100,000 people from their homes. The average weekly wage in Mirpur at this time was equivalent to 40 pence a week; in Birmingham, by contrast, Pakistani immigrants could expect to take home a weekly wage of upwards of £13. By 1963, across Britain the "non-white" population had grown to 500,000 people, while in Birmingham there were 22 schools where the number of immigrant pupils was between 16 and 70 per cent. In order to "beat the ban", the men who had often initially migrated by themselves had arranged for wives, children and other "dependent" family members to join them. They began looking into the possibility of purchasing homes that would be big enough to fit their families in. And they set up businesses that they hoped could one day pay for them.[5]

Two such businesses are a recurring feature of Mendelsohn's photography: the Kashmir Coffee Bar and the Pyar Ka Sagar (sea of love), both of which were cafés situated on what became the 35 bus route on Clevedon Road. Establishments like these are forgotten emblems of Britain's gradual transformation into the multicultural society we know today. But it was a different kind of business that gave Balsall Heath its notoriety in the 1960s and which, in Mendelsohn's work, leads us towards a much less comfortable example of ethnic diversity at the level of the street: the area's sex-industry, which included more than 200 sex workers operating out of a single square mile, a concentration that made Balsall Heath a rival to the much more established commercial sex scenes in London's Soho or Notting Hill.

Balsall Heath did not have the national and indeed international infamy of Notting Hill in particular. Following on from the central role that anxieties about miscegenation had played during the 1958 white riots, in 1963 the area was caught up in the scandal around the Conservative Secretary of State for War John Profumo's extramarital affair with the call-girl-*cum*-model Christine Keeler when it transpired that the latter had also been in a number of relationships with black men in Notting Hill's criminal underworld. The involvement of some black and Asian men in Britain's sex industry, whether as clients of sex workers or their pimps, was often just one more stick used to beat Britain's "non-white" population with. Mendelsohn's archive allows us to get at the complicated, often blurred nature of the relationships that some ethnic minority men formed with the generally white women who worked as prostitutes in Balsall Heath. At times they seemed to function in a kind of grey area between mutual dependency, exploitation, and love. And the relationships were often

RED LIGHTS: 1960s BALSALL HEATH

abusive, leaving lasting damage on many of the women involved. It's another example of the contradictory ebbs and flows of multicultural Britain. Mendelsohn's photographs are a record of a key moment in the making of multicultural Britain, as black, Asian and other immigrants—in the decade after the riots of 1958, and in spite of the ongoing impact of racism—moved towards some degree of permanence. Yet they also suggest that, for a minority of men, the need to become established went hand in hand with them entering into problematic relationships with white women. However jarring, this was also a part of what street-level multiculturalism looked like in practice.[6]

In the 1960s, according to one resident, Balsall Heath had become a neighbourhood where it was exceptional to be white. Such statements were wildly inaccurate—three in four residents of Balsall Heath were white at this time, even accounting for the 13 per cent of such residents who were Irish—and were typical of the shrill nature of the debate around "race relations" in 1960s Britain, in the context of the unprocessed trauma caused by decolonisation. But what Mendelsohn's photographs do capture is the extent to which the inner-areas of Britain's major cities were becoming increasingly multicultural. By 1966, Balsall Heath had the largest concentration of immigrants of any neighbourhood in Birmingham, with a quarter of Balsall Heath residents having been born in the so-called "New Commonwealth"—the term used to refer to newly-independent countries in the Caribbean, Africa and Asia. In light of this, the media often referred to Balsall Heath as Birmingham's "coloured colony". Yet in many ways what was happening there was paradigmatic of a broader set of changes that, within decades, would affect almost every part of the city. And, contrary to the often-hysterical narratives that could be found in the media's reporting of events in 1960s Balsall Heath, it is possible to see in Mendelsohn's work a growing familiarity with increasing ethnic diversity, something hinted at through quotidian encounters on Balsall Heath's streets, in front gardens, inside cafés, and in the complex relationships between couples like Salim and Kathleen, Mendelsohn's key photographic subjects. This was taking place just as the steady permeation of social racism was being amplified by Enoch Powell, who built on the narratives that had earlier been articulated by Cyril Osborne and others in the aftermath of the 1958 riots. In 1967, Powell vigorously opposed a campaign by Sikh employees in his Wolverhampton constituency to allow them to wear turbans while working on the city's buses. In April 1968 Powell gave his "Rivers of Blood" speech in a central Birmingham hotel, while Mendelsohn was photographing the streets of Balsall Heath barely three miles down the road.[7]

Mendelsohn's work has led me back to Balsall Heath. In some ways, the genesis of this book was the package she sent from Massachusetts. In the years since its arrival, I have found it impossible to impose any singular, reassuringly straightforward narrative on her photography. But this is in keeping with what was an ambiguous moment of transition as, to a backdrop of social change and growing political hostility towards black and Asian immigrants in particular, the residents of neighbourhoods like Balsall Heath went about the complicated business of day-to-day cohabitation.

1960s Balsall Heath

By the time Janet Mendelsohn arrived in Balsall Heath in September 1967, the growth in the immigrant population from Britain's former colonies, along with the belated realisation among its body politic that this was not going to be a temporary state of affairs, had combined to create a new set of anxieties around multicultural Britain in which the question of geography became central. The emphasis on the supposed alienness that

RED LIGHTS: 1960s BALSALL HEATH

characterised representations of Tiger Bay in the 1940s persisted, alongside a focus on sex. But by the 1960s concerns about miscegenation had been fused with broader panics about the role that growing ethnic diversity was seen to have played in the expansion of Britain's underground sexual economies—and nowhere more than in red-light districts like Balsall Heath. What also changed in the 1960s, certainly when it came to major cities like Birmingham and London, was that it was becoming increasingly difficult to conceptualise the issue in terms of a singular "coloured quarter"; in the big conurbations, at least, ethnic diversity was by this point simply too widespread for that. The focus instead shifted onto the inner city, a term that had become intimately associated with issues such as crime, violence, vice and other racialised euphemisms following its importation from the fraught climate around race relations in urban America.[8]

Throughout the 1960s, the inner areas of Britain's major cities were more accurately slums. In 1967, for example, more than 60 per cent of residents in Balsall Heath lacked the exclusive use of a hot tap or toilet, while the area's topography still bore the wartime scars inflicted by German bombing campaigns, which had targeted the city's motor and munitions factories. The neighbourhood's decaying housing stock, meanwhile, continued to be monetised by "shark" landlords. More than 21 per cent of households in Balsall Heath were classified as overcrowded, and up to six families could be found occupying a single house. The situation was made worse for newly arrived immigrants by the local authority's policy that council housing could only be allocated to people who had been in the UK for a minimum of five years (this was subsequently reduced to two years). One resident described the impression that decay had worked its way into the walls of houses in Balsall Heath, with damp having made the mortar bulge in the shape of half-melons. But in the popular fantasy, the ethnically diverse communities who now inhabited

Britain's inner cities had become indelibly associated with the dilapidation of the geography around them. And this was fused with a potent nostalgia for the supposed respectability of these areas in a bygone, more simplistic time—before the suffering and social changes precipitated by the Second World War and, by extension, before the arrival of widespread ethnic diversity.[9]

The Balsall Heath of the 1960s was a locus for journalists who seemed inexorably drawn to the neighbourhood's potential for voyeuristic narratives of sex and immorality. One reporter described a walk through the area as a "salutary experience" with rowdy crowds assembled at street corners and men accosted by prostitutes as many as five times on a single outing. The streets themselves were "mean and dirty", in marked contrast to the Balsall Heath of the pre-war years, which was supposedly a good-class area full of respectable, hard-working, professional people who resided in the imposing homes that once belonged to the Victorian middle class. While there might be a few such residents left, "something has happened in the last few years to make them reluctant to admit that they live in Balsall Heath". That something was, of course, the growth of the area's immigrant population and all the associated problems that these communities were thought to bring. Echoing the colonial motifs often deployed by reporters in the 1940s, journalists explained that immigrants had arrived unprepared and unsuited to "the British way of life". The immigrant presence had supposedly transformed Balsall Heath into a ghetto along American lines. With a growing population of people from all over the world, once well-to-do residences had become disreputable lodging houses and centres of vice. By the 1960s, prostitutes could be seen brazenly soliciting at all hours of the day by standing in gardens or doorways, posing at windows and even cruising around in cars. One onlooker suggested that there was in fact little need for solicitation; as night fell, queues of men suppos-

RED LIGHTS: 1960s BALSALL HEATH

edly formed outside brothels. It was a situation that, to the mind of one Birmingham councillor, seriously threatened the city's "high standards of decency". For another local politician, Balsall Heath had become more reminiscent of nocturnal Turkey or Morocco than of anything Birmingham had been used to.[10]

These perspectives had a symbiotic relationship with the everyday racism that faced black and Asian immigrants in their professional and social lives. As important as the media's role was in creating a climate of hostility towards the ethnic minority presence—one academic felt moved to remind reporters that "the immigrants did not bring the slums brick by brick in their fibre suitcases or their cheap airline bags"—it was the steady drip-drip of microaggressions that was an even more damaging problem. First, there was the graffiti. Slogans like "blacks go home", "keep Africa black, keep Britain White" and, following Powell's April 1968 speech in Birmingham, "Enoch was right" are a recurring feature of film footage of the city in this period, and acted as daily reminders of the hostility that was potentially around every corner. Then there was the animosity that could characterise personal relationships. In *The Colony*, for instance, the filmmaker Phillip Donnellan's 1964 documentary about the black experience in Birmingham, Stan Crooke, an immigrant from St Kitts who worked as a signalman for British Rail, emphasised the hurtful duplicity of British racism that had also struck black immigrants in 1950s Nottingham. He saw his white colleagues daily, they would discuss issues relating to the job, they would travel on the same trains. But any trace of amenability would evaporate as soon as the train arrived at a station. At this point, Crooke explained, "all confab ends; we don't even walk ten yards together on the station platform". This was the kind of discrimination whereby invitations from colleagues to go for a cigarette break or a drink after work never materialised, or if you invited your white colleagues to your home for dinner, they simply did not show up. For another of Donnellan's black interviewees, such interactions were daily reminders that, on a fundamental level, he would always be perceived as a stranger in Britain. To the mind of most white people, the interviewee concluded, the very concept of a black Brummie—hinted at by the presence of the kind of hybridised Jamaican-Brummie accents I had grown accustomed to among some of my friends' parents—was impossible; it was like trying to mix water with oil.[11]

This discrimination extended to other, less immediately visible immigrant communities in Birmingham. A common target was the city's Irish population, which expanded rapidly in the 1950s, partly because of a scheme by Birmingham Transport Department to recruit Irish staff to work on the city's buses, as well as efforts by local factories to entice Irish labourers by offering to provide temporary accommodation and travel expenses. Throughout the decade dozens of Irish immigrants arrived in the city on a weekly basis, often on board the 05.30 train from Holyhead in Wales, where the ferry from Dún Laoghaire docked. By 1961, there were 644,400 Irish immigrants in England and 58,000 in Birmingham alone—more than half of all overseas immigrants living in the city. The size of the population meant that the Birmingham Irish community had become increasingly rooted. Tens of thousands of people attended the annual St Patrick's Day Parade following its inaugural procession in 1952; newspapers like the *Irish Press* were commonly found in local newsagents and in Irish pubs last orders would often be drunk to the sound of traditional Irish ballads like "The Wild Colonial Boy", accompanied by an Irish button accordion. Pubs like the Mermaid on the Stratford Road also began to function as informal job centres for the many Irishmen who found casual work as "lump" or illegally subcontracted labourers on building sites across Birmingham (by the end of the century, with the area's demographics having shifted once more, the Mermaid had become an Indian restaurant).[12]

RED LIGHTS: 1960s BALSALL HEATH

By 1965, it was estimated that one in every six births in the city were to couples with at least one Irish-born parent; at this time, a sixth of the entire population of the Republic of Ireland was living in Britain. The Irish scene in Birmingham was substantial, even if it was not quite as vibrant as Camden or Kilburn, key hubs for the Irish community in London which boasted an Irish Centre and half a dozen Irish dancehalls which could fill to capacity with hundreds of dancers five nights a week. Yet the ongoing currency of imperial stereotypes regarding the "wild Irish" meant that the presence of Irish people in neighbourhoods like Balsall Heath—particularly Catholics—chimed with the broader understanding that the dilapidation of the once-respectable inner city was intimately connected to its increasingly multicultural profile. This was a trope in media representations of the problem, such as the outcry in autumn 1965 over the reported levels of Irish drunkenness in Birmingham, which centred on the dubious finding that more than half of all charges for being drunk and disorderly in the city that year were attributed to people with Irish names (the longstanding history of Irish migration to Birmingham, stretching back at least to the Irish Famine in the mid-nineteenth century, meant that a significant proportion of these people would likely never have set foot in Ireland). Meanwhile, for the authors of a 1967 study of Sparkbrook, an inner-city district of Birmingham a little over a mile away from Balsall Heath and home to some 5,000 Irish immigrants, these prejudices were also a recurring feature of internal community dynamics. English residents there told how the Irish were supposedly riven with sectarian animosity, liable to getting "boozed up to their eye-balls" and prone to fighting one another in the streets. Such hostilities became even more pronounced with the escalation of the Troubles in the north of Ireland in the 1970s.[13]

The violence followed the burgeoning campaign for civil rights among the minority Catholic population in the north, which had endured systemic discrimination in the electoral system, in housing and in employment since the establishment of Northern Ireland in 1921. In October 1968 my maternal grandfather, who in the early-1950s relocated from England to the island of Ireland—the inverse journey that his own parents had made thirty years earlier—took part in a student protest in Belfast against the treatment of Catholics by the police, which culminated in 2,000 people staging an impromptu sit-in in Belfast city centre. By the 1970s, with the British Army having been deployed to the north of Ireland and violence worsening, the paramilitary Irish Republican Army (IRA) embarked on a bombing campaign in England, which on 21 November 1974 killed 21 people and injured a further 200 in explosions at two Birmingham city centre pubs. In the aftermath, there were reports of British employees refusing to take shifts with Irish colleagues, and shops refusing to stock Irish goods. Indeed, the anti-Irish sentiment that was aroused by the pub bombings was so intense that the city's St Patrick's Day parade was not held for the next 22 years. Prior to this, hostility to the Irish was more accurately an accumulated set of stereotypes and resentments against the social problems the Irish community was understood to have brought to the city. And in Balsall Heath in summer 1968, this became enmeshed with opposition to the presence of some twenty families from the Irish Traveller community who had camped on a derelict site between Sherborne Road and what would become Birmingham's inner ring road or "concrete collar". It was a stone's throw from Highgate Tower, a high-rise tower block which opened in 1965 and housed many one-time residents of Balsall Heath's slums.[14]

Irish "tinkers", as they were derogatorily referred to, were a growing presence in post-war Britain, where they hoped they might be able to pass for members of the settled Irish community and thus gain a more profitable foothold in the construction and scrap metal industries. In practice, what they often found was that they were the victims of hostility from many sides: from English travellers, who resented the additional competition for income; from the settled Irish population, whose views on Travellers were often informed by the widespread stigmatisation of nomadic communities in Ireland; and from other local residents in Birmingham, as well as the authorities, where there was a racialised view of Travellers as being fundamentally untrustworthy, unhygienic and potentially criminal.

In Balsall Heath, the proximity of the Traveller camp to a school led to concern among residents that the safety of their children was in jeopardy. In early September 1968 some 250 parents petitioned the city council stating that they would refuse to send their children to school unless the Traveller camp was immediately removed. The parents enjoyed support in high places. Dennis Howell, the Labour MP for Small Heath and a parliamentary under-secretary at the Education Ministry, declared himself to be "amazed at the filth and degrading state of the tinkers' site" in Balsall Heath which was, he claimed, "the most filthy and disgusting I have ever seen". Local officials aggravated the situation by alleging the extreme tactics Travellers would employ to avoid eviction. According to one public health inspector, this included deliberately breaking a family member's arm in the hope that the medical attention required would delay proceedings. Few Travellers were given a platform in the media's coverage of the events, but those who did make themselves heard were at pains to emphasise the impact that societal discrimination had—on Irish Travellers in particular, but also on members of the Irish community in Britain more generally. One member of the Balsall Heath settlement talked of being "hounded around" by the authorities: "for years now we have been treated worse than dogs, and it is about time someone realised our need". And in spite of the fact Irish Travellers often spoke in *shelta* (Irish Traveller slang), it also became clear that the settlement in Balsall Heath had grown to include a number of Irish immigrants who were not from the Traveller community but had been forced to join the site due to an inability to find accommodation elsewhere. "I have not always lived in a caravan", Jim Maloney, an immigrant from Dublin was quoted as saying. "But if you are a foreigner in this country and have no particular trade to your fingertips...what else is there?"[15]

The lengths to which the city council went to remove the Traveller site is emblematic of how acutely anxieties about the changing inner city were felt in the late-1960s—and how far this had come to be associated with an outside, alien presence. On 15 September a convoy of 100 police officers and 50 bailiffs arrived in Balsall Heath and set about forcibly moving the Travellers on. The site was cleared in a matter of hours, at which point bulldozers were called on to dig what was described as an "anti-Tinker ditch" around the site, in order to prevent the Travellers from returning. It was as if, in that late summer of 1968, the removal of the settlement had in the minds of the authorities become a test case for their ability to deal with the wider malaise that the inner city was understood to be in. "Thank God it's over", Alderman Albert Shaw, the chairman of Birmingham's Public Works Committee told the press. The council would, Shaw explained, try to find a site for the Travellers elsewhere. But wherever this was, he reassured his constituents, it would be outside the city boundaries.[16]

The visibility of this Traveller community had in some respects put them on a similar plane to the black and Asian population of Balsall Heath; they had become scapegoats for the neighbourhood's transition from respectable, middle-class community to a "decayed warren of mean and dirty streets". Hostility towards the Irish erupted at particular moments of crisis and was intertwined with the pervasive issue of having to inhabit what one writer has

RED LIGHTS: 1960s BALSALL HEATH

referred to as the "perceptual prison" created by the enduring presence of colonial stereotypes about "Irishness". But there can be little doubt that it was specifically *racial* minorities who bore the brunt of community tensions. As we saw in Chapter One, in the late imperial period the nature of British racism was marked by a particular kind of doublethink: on the one hand, an unquestioned belief in the essential worthiness of the imperial project, and a commitment to the racial hierarchies that underpinned it; and on the other, a near-absolute refusal to countenance the idea that this same project provided any justification for the black and Asian citizens of colonised nations to take up residence in the imperial mother country. Decolonisation accelerated in the 1960s—by the time Mendelsohn arrived in Birmingham, nations including Jamaica (1962), Kenya (1963), Malta (1964) and The Gambia (1965) had all declared their independence. In this light, and in the context of the changing inner-city, the kind of mental gymnastics we encountered in 1940s Cardiff had reached near-Olympian proportions.[17]

In 1965, Associated Television sent the journalist Kenneth Hill to conduct a series of vox-pops with residents of what he repeatedly referred to as the Balsall Heath "colony". There he came across a housewife in her late twenties, who reflected that she got on with the Irish but had not had much to do with "coloured immigrants" and would be afraid of ever having to approach one. He interviewed Terry Szotowicz, who was born in Poland, migrated to Britain at the end of the Second World War and ran a tailor shop in Balsall Heath. Twenty years earlier, the thousands of Polish fighters who had escaped the Nazis by travelling to Britain to volunteer in the war effort were often the focus of hostility from the British-born population, who repeatedly told pollsters they believed the Polish had outstayed their welcome. By 1965, Szotowicz was vocalising similar sentiments towards the ethnically-diverse residents of Balsall Heath. He told

Hill he would not like to live where he worked. He did not think much of the neighbourhood; there were simply "too many coloured faces".[18]

Hill also interviewed an unnamed white, middle-aged shopkeeper with a thin face, thick-rimmed spectacles and black hair slicked back from his face. The shopkeeper had lived in Balsall Heath for fourteen years and had run his shop for half that time. With his emphasis on the arrival of black and Asian immigrants as the chief cause of the problems that faced the area, and his hope that, like those Irish Travellers who were ultimately removed from their settlement just off Sherborne Road, the immigrant population would one day be forced out—no matter what the economic cost to his own livelihood—his was in many ways a textbook example of the perverse, hypocritical logic of racism as it habitually functioned in the dilapidated, inner-city geographies of 1960s Britain. When asked by Hill how he felt when he first noticed immigrants arriving in Balsall Heath, the shopkeeper replied:

SHOPKEEPER: Prejudiced against them coming in to the country.
HILL: You didn't warm to them?
SHOPKEEPER: No I did not.
HILL: Why not?
SHOPKEEPER: Well I don't hold with coloured people coming into this country and taking jobs off our own countrypeople...
HILL: What about your shop, are they good for business here?
SHOPKEEPER: Oh, they're good for business, they spend money, they don't quibble over the price or anything like that.
HILL: And how do you correlate that with your feelings...you're prejudiced against them and yet you take money off them...
SHOPKEEPER: Well you have to live with the problem don't you ...the quicker they move out of this district the better... it will take the degrade out of Balsall Heath, won't it, because it's got a bad

RED LIGHTS: 1960s BALSALL HEATH

name at the moment. When you speak to someone and they ask you where you come from you say "Balsall Heath" they say "oh, blackie district".

HILL: Yes...is it only the immigrants...I mean, are there other problems, there's vice is there not?

SHOPKEEPER: There's plenty of vice, oh yes, lots of vice. You can see them walking down here every day...soliciting.

HILL: And the vice, has this got anything to do with the immigrants do you think?

SHOPKEEPER: I should imagine so, yes. They attract it.[19]

Janet Mendelsohn's Balsall Heath

Figures 6–7: 'The street', Balsall Heath, c. 1968. Photograph by Janet Mendelsohn, © Janet Mendelsohn/The Cadbury Research Library, University of Birmingham.

Given its growing ubiquity, Janet Mendelsohn must have been tempted to photograph scenes that reinforced the idea that Britain's multicultural inner cities had become virtual no-go areas—places where, as Powell put it in his Birmingham speech (and as Kenneth Hill's shopkeeper implicitly referenced throughout his interview), white people had been made to feel like "strangers in their own country". Mendelsohn's work certainly shows how urban decay continued to blight areas like Balsall

Heath, a full ten years after the Conservative Prime Minister Harold Macmillan's hubristic declaration that, with the belated end of wartime rationing and a growing economy, "most of our people have never had it so good". Fig. 6 echoes a recurring trope in documentary photography from this time that emphasises the social impact of poverty by picturing its effects on the lives of children. The kids are playing on the remnants of a site that had been bombed during the Second World War, behind a row of terraced houses on Clevedon Road—200 yards from where the Irish Travellers had camped in summer 1968. The litter and discarded bits of machinery on the ground, alongside the dirt that has turned the girl's dress a grimy shade of grey, are potent symbols of poverty and inequality. Fig. 7 similarly depicts a Balsall Heath landscape that is literally crumbling: three young children are playing with the bricks that have come loose from a garden wall; one of them, a toddler, is entirely naked.[20]

More often, though, Mendelsohn focused on the kind of cross-cultural interactions that went against the Powellite vision of an immigrant invasion that had, Powell claimed, placed Britain on an irreversible path towards the kind of racial violence playing out in the United States. For a long time after I first saw Mendelsohn's work, the image that I kept returning to was her picture of a group of children playing together on a garden wall (Fig. 5). I studied the photo many times, set it as the background to my laptop, and tried to extrapolate meaning from the cheeky grins of the black and Asian girls in the foreground, and the harassed look on the white woman's face at the rear. It was not only that this one image provided such a clear contrast to the dystopian vision of multicultural Britain presented by the media and some politicians. It was also because, had Mendelsohn arrived in the neighbourhood thirty years later, that could well have been me posing for her camera, playing with Sufyaan, our younger brothers and other friends from the neighbourhood.

RED LIGHTS: 1960s BALSALL HEATH

Photographs like this convey a process referred to as hybridisation: the coming together of different cultures, practices and diasporic traditions, often in the context of confined geographic spaces like inner cities. Fig. 8, for instance, juxtaposes a view of the Wallace Inn pub on the corner of Longmore Street and Balsall Heath Road with the interior of the halal butchers opposite. In Fig. 9, meanwhile, an Asian man in a turban poses for Mendelsohn beneath an advertisement for a soft drink depicting a woman drinking provocatively through a straw. The photo was taken on Clevedon Road—just across from where the Apna Ghar care home now is, and a few hundred yards from the Aziz "supermarket". The battered poster above the man's right shoulder in Fig. 9, advertising an event to mark the fifth anniversary of Jamaican independence, dates the photograph to August 1967, a fledging moment in the tentative emergence of post-colonial Britain.[21]

Figure 8: Untitled, Balsall Heath, c. 1968. Photograph by Janet Mendelsohn, © Janet Mendelsohn/The Cadbury Research Library, University of Birmingham.

MULTICULTURAL BRITAIN

Figure 9: 'The Street', Balsall Heath, c. 1967. Photograph by Janet Mendelsohn, © Janet Mendelsohn/Cadbury Research Library, University of Birmingham.

While some of these images—particularly Figs 8 and 9—are perhaps a little too neatly staged, as if Mendelsohn was self-consciously setting out to shoot photos that would act as counterpoints to the images of the inner city that were published in the tabloid newspapers, elsewhere her work does get at a more organic, kinetic sense of hybridity in Balsall Heath. As with much documentary photography from this period, it was children who—filled with intrigue and often lacking the self-consciousness of adults around cameras—acted as a recurring subject. Figs 10–13 testify to the importance of themes like proximity and tactility for young people in the multicultural inner city. They demonstrate how, particularly for its younger residents, cross-

RED LIGHTS: 1960s BALSALL HEATH

Figures 10–11: Untitled, Balsall Heath, c. 1968. Photograph by Janet Mendelsohn, © Janet Mendelsohn/Cadbury Research Library, University of Birmingham.

Figure 12: 'The Street', Balsall Heath, c. 1968. Photograph by Janet Mendelsohn, © Janet Mendelsohn/Cadbury Research Library, University of Birmingham.

Figure 13: Untitled, Balsall Heath, c. 1968. Photograph by Janet Mendelsohn, © Janet Mendelsohn/Cadbury Research Library, University of Birmingham.

cultural interactions had become routinised in the daily navigations of inner-city life—playing out on the street, a game of football, crossing the road on the way to school. Whatever was going on in parallel to these images politically—the interventions of Powell, the introduction of legislation designed to curb black and Asian immigration and, by the end of the 1960s, the growing influence of the far-right National Front (NF)–Mendelsohn's work shows that at street level, multicultural interactions had become a near-unavoidable feature of inner-city life.[22]

By the time I started primary school, Balsall Heath had been through various phases of urban renewal. This drastically altered its topography, as slum housing was pulled down to be replaced

RED LIGHTS: 1960s BALSALL HEATH

Figure 14: 'The Street', Balsall Heath, c. 1968. Photograph by Janet Mendelsohn, © Janet Mendelsohn/Cadbury Research Library, University of Birmingham.

by tower blocks and modern terraced houses. Some of the roads Mendelsohn photographed—including the notorious Varna Road, which was the main site of prostitution in the 1960s and was consequently divided by town planners into two cul-de-sacs in order to prevent the return of kerb crawlers—simply ceased to exist. During Mendelsohn's time in the area, buildings were vanishing from the landscape, signalled by the appearance of shutters on windows or a spray-painted red cross on a building's front-door. Fig. 14 alludes to the sense of helplessness residents could feel at the regeneration process, which was often dictated from the top down with minimal consultation with the people that it would actually affect: "we're off after 25 years", signs on the soon-to-be-demolished clothes shop in the photograph read, "you'll miss us we'll miss you", "they've got us out". In spite of the poor living conditions that made urban regeneration necessary in the first place, residents of working-class areas like Balsall Heath often resented being moved away from longstanding community ties and into the modern, better-equipped but somehow cold and lifeless tower blocks or housing estates that had become an increasingly common feature of Britain's cityscapes. Many photographers operating at this time were drawn to what has been described as the "slow violence" of housing dispossession: the removal of slum-housing is a feature of Shirley Baker's photographs of Manchester and Salford, of Nick Hedges' work (commissioned by the homelessness charity Shelter) in Birmingham, Liverpool, and Glasgow, and of Roger Mayne's photographs of northwest London. What is different about Mendelsohn's photographs, though, is the way she also captured an often-overlooked, parallel process: the extent to which immigrant communities had

Figure 15: 'The Street', Balsall Heath, c. 1968. Photograph by Janet Mendelsohn, © Janet Mendelsohn/Cadbury Research Library, University of Birmingham.

RED LIGHTS: 1960s BALSALL HEATH

been undertaking their own changes to the built environment of Britain's inner cities.[23]

These were primarily sites of leisure or retail. Immigrant entrepreneurs quickly recognised that, if these communities and their descendants were going to be a permanent fixture in areas like Balsall Heath, there was money to be made in the provision of goods and services that were not being offered elsewhere. Cinemas were particularly important in this respect. The growth in television ownership in Britain and the arrival in 1955 of a commercial television channel meant that local cinemas outside city centres increasingly struggled to survive. But in an era before VHS machines, satellite television and DVDs, such cinemas could work by catering for the niche but growing demand among South-Asian immigrants for films from the golden age of Indian cinema in the years after independence. Fig. 15 shows a group of suited-and-booted men leaving one such establishment in Balsall Heath. A similar business model was applied to other areas of the economy. Uncle's Continental Stores, for example, was based at 78 Highgate Road and established by Santokh Singh, a Punjabi immigrant who arrived in Birmingham in 1958. It was one of a growing number of shops that—following on from the pioneering Indian establishments that had begun to appear in inter-war London—were opened in the 1950s and 60s in order to meet the demand for *dhaniya, garam masala, ghee* and other foodstuffs essential to Asian cuisine but unavailable in mainstream establishments. And then there were the cafés, the two most popular of which were situated on Clevedon Road, less than a mile away from Uncle's: the Kashmir Coffee Bar, and the Pyar Ka Sagar café and restaurant (Figs 16–18).[24]

When I try to imagine what such establishments were like, I often picture the Shereen Kadah (sweet pumpkin) curry house on the Moseley Road, an old haunt opposite what is now DFC Chicken which was established in 1962 and continues to do a

Figure 16: Untitled, Balsall Heath, c. 1968. Photograph by Janet Mendelsohn, © Janet Mendelsohn/Cadbury Research Library, University of Birmingham.

brisk early-morning trade in breakfast *falooda* to Asian taxi drivers who have just finished the night shift. But the way in which such spaces operated in the 1960s—long before "going for an Indian" would become such a mainstay in the culinary lives of white diners, and at a time when "the stink of curry" was often cited by white inhabitants of the inner city as a major source of resentment against their newly-arrived South Asian neighbours—was much more wide-ranging than the functional importance of a place that sells cheap samosas. This is made clear by *Émigré Journeys*, the novel by the Pakistani writer Abdullah Hussein, who was one of the earliest writers to seek to evoke the experiences of working-class Muslims in Britain, and drew upon his own experiences of migrating to Britain in his mid-thirties in 1966. The novel is set in an anonymous district of Birmingham, though given the centrality of prostitution to the story Hussein was likely evoking Balsall Heath and the surrounding areas. In

RED LIGHTS: 1960s BALSALL HEATH

Figures 17–18: 'The Street', Balsall Heath, c. 1968. Photograph by Janet Mendelsohn, © Janet Mendelsohn/ Cadbury Research Library, University of Birmingham.

the novel, cafés are depicted as key community hubs, places where people met up to pass the time and collect information about how it was possible to make a living in Britain. They stayed open late so that men working lengthy hours would have a place to go for a cheap meal after a shift. They functioned both as a first point-of-call for new arrivals in Birmingham, as well as places where you could listen to songs from Indian films, *ghazals* (poems) and *qawwalis* (devotional songs).[25]

Cinemas occupied an even more privileged position in Hussein's telling; they come across as providing immigrants with a near-spiritual connection to their homes in the Indian subcontinent that took on further significance in the context of the alienation many people felt in Britain; like being in a mosque or temple, the cinema was a place where you became a different version of yourself. You packed a bag full of *parathas*, polished your shoes and, in defiance of any stares you might get from white passers-by, you wore your *shalwar kameez, kurta, chaddar, turban, lungi* and anything else you may have been too afraid to wear during the working week. While at the cinema, Hussein wrote in *Émigré Journeys*, the on-screen sight of "our actors and actresses, our jokes, romantic stories, the scenery of our land... the culture of our dreams" simultaneously entertained and "wrenched our souls". Once the film had finished and the lights went on, Hussein's narrator, engulfed with emotion, would often forget where he was. It was an experience enough to make grown men cry "as if suffering from a terrible disease".[26]

By the late 1960s, one writer estimated that there were 200 Asian-run cinemas across the country, and that the industry was worth over £1 million a year. For one Asian immigrant, it was the separateness of such spaces from white society that was their most important characteristic: "people just wanted to go where they could talk in their own language...rather than going to learn how to pronounce English to a *gora*". But as Figs 19–20 show, when it came to cafés like the Kashmir and the Pyar Ka Sagar this did not preclude them from having a mixed clientele. Such establishments provided the backdrop to points of interaction between different segments of the neighbourhood—in the small-talk in the queue to order, or over a shared joke at a cramped

RED LIGHTS: 1960s BALSALL HEATH

Figure 19: Untitled, Balsall Heath, c. 1968. Photograph by Janet Mendelsohn, © Janet Mendelsohn/Cadbury Research Library, University of Birmingham.

Figure 20: Untitled, Balsall Heath, c. 1968. Photograph by Janet Mendelsohn, © Janet Mendelsohn/Cadbury Research Library, University of Birmingham.

table in the wait for it to arrive. Certainly, by the late-1960s, these businesses were projecting a greater degree of cultural assertiveness among Balsall Heath's South-Asian communities in particular. Prior to Mendelsohn's arrival in Birmingham, for example, the owners of the Pyar Ka Sagar had hired Kafait Shah, a Lahore-born artist, to paint a series of murals both inside and outside the café based on scenes from the 1961 Indian film from which the café took its name.[27]

Shah had arrived in Birmingham in 1965 and, like many South-Asian men, initially earned his living at a Black Country foundry, an industry which by the 1960s had become increasingly reliant on Asian labour. But as his artistic reputation grew, Shah found that he was in demand for commissions from cafés, cinemas, restaurants and other immigrant-run establishments. Shah claimed that his paintings from *Pyar Ka Sagar*—at the heart of which was a love story between characters played by the Punjabi actor Rajendra Kumar and the Bombay-born "queen of tragedy" Meena Kumari—for a time helped make the café famous enough that people would come from outside Balsall Heath just to see his artwork. As Fig. 17 shows, his work was indeed striking. Like the large lettering on the signage of the Kashmir café, or the poster outside the cinema advertising the show-times for *Upkar*, a 1967 film about the India-Pakistan war, what is noteworthy about Shah's work for the Pyar Ka Sagar is its visibility. Uncle's, Kashmir and other establishments were of course themselves temporary and under threat, not least from the process of slum clearance. Yet their presence also projects an entirely different message to "they've got us out". Rather, these establishments are indicative of an increasing level of cultural self-confidence, and a community inserting itself *into* Balsall Heath's fabric.[28]

Mendelsohn must have been a conspicuous presence in late-1960s Balsall Heath, especially given that the area's sex industry was so widespread. One female journalist on assignment to the

RED LIGHTS: 1960s BALSALL HEATH

area in 1967 told her readers that she felt like a stranger in a crowd, ever conscious of the male gazes that seemed to be coming at her from all sides. This perhaps explains why in Mendelsohn's street photography prostitution is for the most part examined indirectly. Seeing it often requires us as viewers to have prior knowledge of the extent of the area's red-light district, and that in some cases it purportedly operated out of the area's immigrant-run cafés. Armed with this information, the portrait of a young woman walking down the street, seen from the vantagepoint of a group of boys (Fig. 21), take on extra meaning. In its capturing of what looks like a transaction taking place outside the Kashmir Coffee Bar, Fig. 22 is perhaps the most overt example of prostitution in Mendelsohn's street photography.

It's not clear whether, as she took such photographs, Mendelsohn also felt like a stranger in the crowd, or (more likely) whether she saw herself as an intrepid *flaneuse*, wandering (and mapping) the urban sprawl around her. By the time I got to know her, Mendelsohn's illness had meant that she was unable to remember almost anything about her time in Birmingham, save for the influence that Stuart Hall and his Centre for Contemporary Cultural Studies had on her work. While her camera may have helped her ward off unwanted male attention, it was her status as a young woman that perhaps allowed her to win the trust of some of the women who were involved in the sex industry—something that distinguishes her work from that of her (mostly male) photographic contemporaries. Mendelsohn's focus on sex work also takes us towards a much more uncomfortable example of how increasing ethnic diversity could be experienced.[29]

Red Lights

Fig. 23 encapsulates many of Mendelsohn's core photographic interests. There's the sense of confidence communicated by the

Figures 21–22: 'The Street', Balsall Heath, c. 1968. Photograph by Janet Mendelsohn, © Janet Mendelsohn/ Cadbury Research Library, University of Birmingham.

RED LIGHTS: 1960s BALSALL HEATH

Figure 23: 'Kathleen on the Street', Balsall Heath, c. 1968. Photograph by Janet Mendelsohn, © Janet Mendelsohn/Cadbury Research Library, University of Birmingham.

Kashmir Coffee Bar's bold signage on Clevedon Road—the idea that immigrant communities, pushed into a decision with the passing of increasingly-strict immigration controls, were beginning to think of themselves as a permanent presence in Britain. There's the closeness to the everyday navigation of the multicultural inner city, as people waited at bus stops and congregated on street corners. And there's the often-destabilising effects of male gazes on women, seen in Fig. 23 with the aggressive way that the man in the centre of the photograph—leaning in, his eyes shielded behind a pair of dark sunglasses—is staring at the group of white women assembled outside the Kashmir.

The woman in Fig. 23 standing with her arms folded and her back to the man in the sunglasses is Kathleen, the 23-year-old woman of Irish descent who became Mendelsohn's main subject. It's easy to see why, from Mendelsohn's point of view, Kathleen

MULTICULTURAL BRITAIN

Figure 24: Untitled, Balsall Heath, c. 1968. Photograph by Janet Mendelsohn, © Janet Mendelsohn/Cadbury Research Library, University of Birmingham.

took up more and more of her film. Kathleen was beautiful. This not only made her photogenic. It must also have stood out against the poverty and the general dilapidation of Balsall Heath which, for an American student from Harvard, was likely to have been especially disarming. There is also a pensiveness to many of Kathleen's expressions, a sense of mournfulness that hints at a difficult life being lived out beyond the frame. However, what is most apparent about these photographs is the closeness between photographer and subject. Mendelsohn was there to document Kathleen's domestic life, the trips she took to the park with her two-year old daughter, and her outings to the shops and pub. Mendelsohn was even present at the hospital to photograph the birth of Kathleen's two children (Figs 25–26).

Kathleen was shaped by Balsall Heath's hybridised street culture. She was one of a number of women of Irish descent who

RED LIGHTS: 1960s BALSALL HEATH

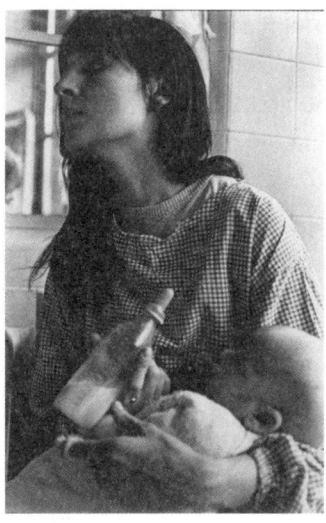

Figure 25: 'Kathleen at the Hospital', Balsall Heath, c. 1968. Photograph by Janet Mendelsohn, © Janet Mendelsohn/Cadbury Research Library, University of Birmingham.

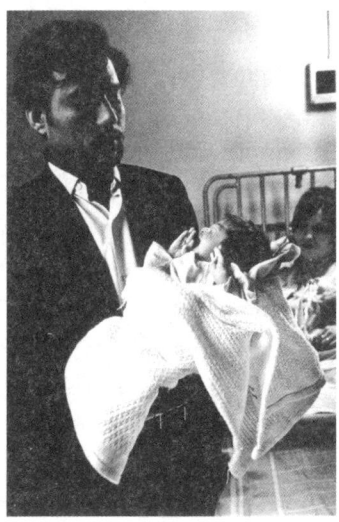

Figure 26: 'Salim at the Hospital', Balsall Heath, c. 1968. Photograph by Janet Mendelsohn, © Janet Mendelsohn/Cadbury Research Library, University of Birmingham.

were "living in concubinage", as the author of one report for the Catholic church in Ireland put it, with immigrant men of other nationalities in the area. The father of her children was her Pakistani lover, Salim, who is seen posing stiffly with the couple's daughter in Fig. 26. Elsewhere (Fig. 24), Mendelsohn photographs a woman applying make-up to Kathleen in a way that resembles the feminine aesthetic of Indian cinema, embodied by actresses like Meena Kumari and evoked by Kafait Shar's mural inside the Pyar Ka Sagar. Mendelsohn also followed the couple into the homes of their respective mothers. Figs 27 and 28 are almost mirror images of one another. Both Kathleen and Salim are surrounded by younger siblings or other family members. There is a religious dimension to both pictures, symbolised by the crucifix on the wall at Kathleen's mother's house, and by the *Shayla* (head scarf) worn by Salim's mother. And in both photographs there is a strain to the way in which each mother is engaging with their elder children. Salim's mother strikes a classically matriarchal pose, drying her hands on her patterned *shalwar kameez* as she watches her son playing with his younger siblings; in Fig. 28, meanwhile, the playfulness of the young boys in the foreground is set against the unease in the face of both Kathleen (at the rear of the photo) and her mother (to the left), who are looking neither at the camera nor each other. However, the most remarkable of all Mendelsohn's photographs of Kathleen and Salim—the one that brings home just how close she got to them—is her picture of the couple in bed together (Fig. 29). The image is again powered by competing gazes, and the way that Salim has turned away from Kathleen so as to meet Mendelsohn's camera head-on.[30]

In Balsall Heath, given the area's growing diversity was dominated by men in this period, it was inevitable that the monetisation of sex was often also racialised. In 1967, more than 80 per cent of the women arrested for solicitation in the neighbourhood

RED LIGHTS: 1960s BALSALL HEATH

Figure 27: 'Visiting Salim's Mother', Birmingham, c. 1968. Photograph by Janet Mendelsohn, © Janet Mendelsohn/Cadbury Research Library, University of Birmingham.

Figure 28: 'Visiting Kathleen's Mother', Birmingham, c. 1968. Photograph by Janet Mendelsohn, © Janet Mendelsohn/Cadbury Research Library, University of Birmingham.

Figure 29: 'Kathleen and Salim at Home', Balsall Heath, c. 1968. Photograph by Janet Mendelsohn, © Janet Mendelsohn/Cadbury Research Library, University of Birmingham.

were white. Concurrently, for every 1,000 men in Birmingham who had been born in the "New Commonwealth", there were just 577 women from the same background. As late as 1970, among the South-Asian population in the city men outnumbered women by 75 to one. While the situation was changing, it is not surprising that the entrepreneurial drivers of Britain's underground sexual economies spotted that a market existed among the large numbers of single men who, whether through issues of language or the broader pervasiveness of racial discrimination that had created Britain's "enclosed landscape" for immigrants, often found themselves cut adrift from wider society.[31]

In Bradford in West Yorkshire, one Pakistani immigrant told an interviewer about the relief he felt when, in the early-1970s and at the age of thirty, he had sex for the first time with a white woman he had met at a small pub in the Lumb Lane area of the

RED LIGHTS: 1960s BALSALL HEATH

city, itself a red-light district. She was the first woman who had ever "encouraged" him, the man remembered, and soon the couple got married. But the relationship was strained, and eventually ended when the man was informed by the police that his wife had twenty-three prior convictions for solicitation. In Abdullah Hussein's *Émigré Journeys*, meanwhile, the novel's narrator evokes the mechanical response to the social alienation experienced by a household of largely Pakistani men. Following the narrator's arrival in the house, the visit of a prostitute was quickly established as a core part of the weekly routine on a Sunday evening, following the household's group outing to the cinema. The men pooled their money together to pay for the services of three women, who took it in turns to visit the house each week. Every Sunday a woman would arrive and immediately make her way up to prepare a room that had been set aside for the occasion. The men then queued up along the landing and down the stairs, alongside the pictures of Indian actresses that had been cut out by the men from magazines and pasted onto the walls. First came two Mirpuris and a Hafizabadi, who were respected in the house for their dedication to the offering of *namaz* (prayers) five times a day. They were followed by the men whose seniority was based on the length of time each had resided in the house. Finally came the Bengalis, whose low status came from the fact that, even if they had been in Britain longer than some of their housemates, they were outnumbered by Punjabis by fifteen to two. The men would initially stand in line and talk in hushed voices, as you might do upon entering a mosque for a *janaza* (funeral). Then, as the familiarity to the situation increased and the proceedings began, the joking started and voices got louder. Afterwards, the men put their shillings in the meter for the hot bath, which would be used in the same order of privilege. Then, the house would be filled the sounds of the *namazis* in prayer, "weepy and repentant, begging forgiveness", while the rest of the men played cards.[32]

Even here in this transactional milieu, though, it is possible to see how women, in particular, were beginning to work through the issue of race in ways that belied the growing hostility to immigration which, by summer 1968, was increasingly orbiting around the totemic figure of Enoch Powell. Later on in *Émigré Journeys*, for instance, the novel's narrator depicts the astonishment felt by the men in the house as one of their number, Hussain Shah, begins a relationship with Mary, a Newcastle-born woman who the men presume is a local prostitute. The first night Mary stays in the house—which is also the first time any woman had stayed over with one of the men—Shah's housemates tiptoe about and listen at his door in order to understand the exact nature of an event that, to the narrator, "felt as if the sanctity of the house had been violated". The men—the majority of whom are in the country illegally—worry that Mary could be a *shaitan* (devil) working as a police informant; in "our close, protected world a crack had opened and through it were looking two foreign eyes, shaking our foundations". However, Mary quickly becomes friendly with her new lover's housemates, installs lightbulbs in hitherto-empty sockets, nurses one of their number through a hangover and even learns how to cook Pakistani cuisine. In turn, the men soon begin to pluck up the courage to wish her good night or ask her how she is feeling. Mary becomes a source of guidance, taking them on trips to the shops and encouraging the men—who would otherwise have been inclined to get such public activities over with as soon as possible, their illegal status gnawing at them "like a rat inside [a] skull"—to look around for the best value-for-money. In one shop, Mary gets into an argument with the shopkeeper over the price of items that she suggests can be bought much more cheaply across the road. "Who wants customers like you?", the shopkeeper responds, her eyes fixed specifically on Mary's two Asian associates. "All customers are like us here", Mary responded. "It's toffee-nosed shopkeepers like you we don't want".[33]

RED LIGHTS: 1960s BALSALL HEATH

Mendelsohn interviewed various women who were involved in Balsall Heath's sex industry. Like the character of Mary in *Émigré Journeys*, what is noticeable is how these women often showed a sensitivity to the discrimination that was faced by their ethnic minority lovers in a way that was often lacking in mainstream discourse in late-1960s Britain. Chrissy, for example, had been in a convent until she was eighteen and had started working as a prostitute at the age of twenty-one. She admitted that there were ethnic minority men working as pimps in Balsall Heath, but defended them by arguing this was forced on them by the impact of the colour bar. The job vacancies that were advertised in Birmingham's factories and warehouses had simply vanished by the time Chrissy's black partner applied for them, she told Mendelsohn. As a result of this, Chrissy claimed, men like her partner "drifted in" to pimping.

Another woman, Laura, told Mendelsohn she had herself begun prostituting to pay the school fees of her daughter, who was enrolled at a boarding school on Bristol Road, a short walk from Mendelsohn's flat near the university campus in the middle-class (and largely white) district of Edgbaston. Laura's partner, the Jamaican John Dyer, one of the city's most prolific pimps, was serving a prison sentence in the late-1960s and if Laura did not find a way of paying the school fees, she explained, "he'll go mad". For Laura, it was her children's mixed-race ethnicity that was the primary justification for the lengths to which she was prepared to go to meet her daughter's school fees. It wouldn't have mattered if her daughter was white or "full coloured", Laura declared. It was the ongoing stigma around "half-castes"—a leftover from the anxieties around "brown babies" we encountered in 1940s Cardiff—that to Laura's mind required that her daughter be sent to boarding school. For Chrissy, meanwhile, it was her partner's attempts to make her bring up a daughter from another relationship that saw her moving towards a more critical interpretation of his activities. The child was "as black as coal", Chrissy confided in Mendelsohn, whose status as an interviewer and a university student perhaps meant that, like St Clair Drake in Cardiff, she was respected as a possible source of guidance. "That's bad, isn't it really?" Chrissy asked. What would her own children say about it when they grew up? "He should think of me...don't you think?"[34]

There were observers who argued that it was white women like Laura and Chrissy who were responsible for turning their black and Asian boyfriends into pimps. In *Absolute Beginners*, for instance, the white writer and London *flaneur* Colin MacInnes' 1959 novel set in an increasingly diverse corner of West London, the narrator explains how he saw the process playing out. Single immigrant men arrived in Britain keen to form new relationships but unable to distinguish between "good" white women and "bad"; then, like the Pakistani man who lost his virginity with a woman he met in a Bradford pub, they quickly enter into relationships with the only "class" of women often willing to associate with them—the white prostitutes who worked the inner-city red light districts that black and Asian immigrants were beginning to call home. The idea that the "coloured man drives the girl out and beats her if she will not go is dramatic", the narrator of *Absolute Beginners* explains, "but, so far as I know, unfounded".[35]

This may have been the conclusion that MacInnes himself came to, based on his own proximity to London's sex industries (where he was himself an occasional user of male prostitutes and was known to have a particular preference for black men). But his gendered perspective perhaps meant he was blind to the abusive dimensions of what was taking place around him. Certainly, the threat of male violence hangs over much of the testimony Mendelsohn gathered from 1960s Balsall Heath. This was hinted at in Laura's concern that her partner John Dyer would "go mad" if she did not find a way of paying her daughter's school fees, and

RED LIGHTS: 1960s BALSALL HEATH

by the implication that Chrissy had been forced by her partner to bring up a child he had fathered with another woman. But it was made explicit by an interview Mendelsohn conducted with Paven, a South-Asian resident of Balsall Heath who openly admitted that he was a pimp. "I used to come in", Paven boasted to Mendelsohn in reference to one of "his" women, and the "first thing I'd do is belt her. For nothing. Kick her...anything. They get too cheeky if you don't. She used to tell me what to do and this and that. Then one day I got mad—I bashed her with a broomstick. Ever since then she never got too big-headed".[36]

In the photo-essay Mendelsohn published in 1969, she makes it clear that Kathleen had supported Salim for years. Mendelsohn also interviewed Kathleen's mother, who emphasised what she saw as the true nature of her daughter's relationship with Salim. Kathleen, her mother explained, used to be the best of her children. She never went out and, when her mother left the house would have it cleaned up and had the kettle boiling for a cup of tea. To the mind of her mother, the reason for Kathleen's apparent turn away from her upbringing was simple: "she was made to do it through Salim". The power of this testimony is intensified when read alongside Mendelsohn's pictures. Fig. 30, for instance, shows a woman Mendelsohn identifies as Kathleen, sitting alone at a window.[37]

What was it like for Mendelsohn, a 23-year-old, white American Harvard graduate armed with two cameras (a Leica M3 and a Nikon F), wandering the streets of a working class, increasingly multicultural red light district in 1960s Birmingham? Partly because of the mystery that surrounded this hitherto-forgotten body of work, after Mendelsohn's parcel arrived it quickly became clear that there was enough interest in her photography for a major exhibition. This eventually opened in January 2016 at the Ikon Gallery, next door to the Pret-a-Manger, Wagamama and other chains that now make up Birmingham's redeveloped canal

MULTICULTURAL BRITAIN

Figure 30. 'Kathleen', c. 1968. Photograph by Janet Mendelsohn, © Janet Mendelsohn/Cadbury Research Library, University of Birmingham.

district. It was the first time Mendelsohn's work had been seen in public since 1970. And despite her poor health, Mendelsohn came from the US with her husband Marc for the opening. While she was in town, I showed her around Balsall Heath, hoping that seeing some of the same streets, though much-changed from the 1960s, might help bring back memories of that time in her life. This never happened; her amnesia persisted. But it was still poignant to see this warm, now-frail woman—basking in the glow of an unexpected late-career bloom—in Balsall Heath for the first time in forty years. At the same time, however, I could not help noticing how out of place these two white, middle-aged American visitors seemed—Janet in a wheelchair with a cocked fedora hat, Marc with his tanned skin and carefully maintained goatee—as they toured Balsall Heath's nondescript backstreets on a chilly, overcast day in January.[38]

After Mendelsohn returned to Massachusetts, I received an email from one of the invigilators at the Ikon Gallery, where the

RED LIGHTS: 1960s BALSALL HEATH

exhibition of Mendelsohn's photographs had by now been underway for almost two months. The email suggested that Kathleen herself had been to see the exhibition. She was, the invigilator explained, unhappy with the way her life in Balsall Heath had been represented by Mendelsohn. She left the contact details of a friend with the gallery, and suggested she would be keen to meet. A few days later, on a crisp, late-winter morning and with some trepidation, I made my way to meet with Kathleen in the Ikon Gallery's ground-floor café where, two floors above our heads, the exhibition about her life almost forty years earlier was in the last few weeks of its run.

There were four of us there that day: myself and the historian Matthew Hilton, with whom I had collaborated on the exhibition, and Kathleen and her friend Sarah, a friendly woman who was perhaps ten years younger than Kathleen and who, I later realised, acted as Kathleen's effective gatekeeper; whenever I wanted to get in touch with Kathleen, I would always have to go through Sarah. There was an uncomfortable dynamic to this meeting between two male academics and two older women. Kathleen was now in her early-70s, and had let her hair return to its natural blonde colouring; in the 1960s, she explained, she had died it black because that was the way Salim liked it. Kathleen had long since left Balsall Heath, and was now living in a suburban, largely white town on the edge of Birmingham's city limits—a couple of miles away from the secondary school I attended. We ordered our drinks and skirted around the issue for a while. I was nervous and found it difficult to talk in coherent sentences. I remember thinking: if I am this nervous, how must Kathleen feel? I tried to break the ice by talking about my own connection to Balsall Heath. Finally, I asked Kathleen how she felt about Mendelsohn's exhibition.

Kathleen responded by emphasising the poverty she and her family had endured, particularly in the context of the single room she shared with Salim and their children on Lincoln Street, a few stops on from what is now the Aziz supermarket. She explained that she first met Salim while working in a local café, and that he would regularly pursue her by following her home from work. She emphasised that he was a good father to their children, but that his personality changed when he was drunk, at which point he could become violent. He was also what Kathleen called a "womaniser" who would regularly disappear from their flat for days on end. But he was not, so far as Kathleen knew, a pimp, and certainly had never been *her* pimp. Somewhere along the line—in spite of the closeness between the two women—Kathleen explained that Mendelsohn must have gotten confused. Kathleen had never worked as a prostitute.

The rest of the meeting went by quickly. Of course, Kathleen sometimes seemed upset and angry, but there was also a warmth to the way she talked about both Mendelsohn and her time in Balsall Heath. She told me that, like the character of Mary in *Émigré Journeys*, she learnt how to cook Pakistani food for Salim. After a while we went upstairs to look around the exhibition, and Kathleen promised that if she could, she would help me with my research for what has become this book. She pointed out the names of people she knew, and asked for copies of Mendelsohn's photos. We stayed in sporadic contact for years after that initial meeting (though always through her friend Sarah). Once, Kathleen even attended a talk I gave about Mendelsohn's work, in a café a few doors down from DFC chicken.

The exact status of Kathleen's relationship with Salim remains private to her. But as a social historian whose work has been to put forward the voices of marginalised people like Kathleen who are too often missing from mainstream history, it is impossible to contest Kathleen's version of the past. In practice there may well have been many blurred lines between categories like "pimp", "ponce" and "womaniser"; any outsider—no matter how embedded they seemingly were—would have struggled to comprehend them.

To the extent that there is a truth to be found in the story of Kathleen and Salim, it surely lies within its ambiguity. The power balance in Salim and Kathleen's relationship is perhaps emphasised in Mendelsohn's photography by the fact that it is Salim, rather than Kathleen, who often returned the gaze of Mendelsohn's camera. More broadly, the violence of this world was alluded to by many of Mendelsohn's interviewees, particularly Paven, who at the very least was an associate of Salim's. But I was also struck by the brief interview Mendelsohn conducted with Salim, and the extent to which she seemed to catch Salim at a time when—having migrated to Britain from Kenya, embarked on a relationship with Kathleen and become a father to two mixed-race children—his identity seemed to be shifting in a particularly intense way. There was a telling sense of discomfort in his interview, alluded to by the way he seemed to be asking Mendelsohn for a kind of affirmation to his attempts at explaining away his lifestyle. Salim saw himself as having "spoiled" what had initially been a good start to life in Kenya. "I used to listen to my father", he stated. "I didn't smoke...I didn't drink", but "then I started going out, you know what I mean? You know, out to meet girls....you understand? I spoiled [it] didn't I?" Salim contrasted the disillusionment he felt at his own life with the aspirations he had for his new-born son, something that was perhaps wrapped up with the hopes he himself may have harboured on his own journey from East Africa to Britain. "When he is older", Salim reflected in broken-English, "I'll tell him—'look, my life is no good. I don't know no reading, no nothings. I'm an engineer but I can't read, so what's the use to be an engineer?'" In Britain, however, there were opportunities. If his son "learns properly he could be a doctor...a pilot or anything"; people will say, "'there is [Salim's] son' and I will be proud".[39]

Towards the end of Mendelsohn's time in Birmingham, after several failed attempts, Kathleen left Salim by taking her children away to live with a cousin. In her mind, the most poignant photograph that Mendelsohn took of her was Fig. 31, the moment she was about to leave Salim with their two children; her packed suitcase is visible on the bed beside her. Shortly after that photograph was taken, on 10 December 1968, Salim died of a stab wound to the neck, inflicted at an unnamed Balsall Heath café.[40]

Janet Mendelsohn's archive dramatises how the making of multicultural Britain has been defined by the coming together of contradictory, oppositional and sometimes difficult forces. It was a dialectical process, something we've encountered from various vantage points throughout this chapter: the "Blacks go home" graffiti that adorned the same urban topographies that were being altered by ethnic minorities as they established businesses

Figure 31: 'Kathleen at Home With Newborn Baby', Balsall Heath, c. 1968. Photograph by Janet Mendelsohn, © Janet Mendelsohn/Cadbury Research Library, University of Birmingham.

RED LIGHTS: 1960s BALSALL HEATH

like the Kashmir Coffee Bar and the Pyar Ka Sagar; the way children, at one end of the spectrum, and those who were involved in Britain's sex industries, at the other, were in very different ways at the forefront of Britain's emergence as a multicultural society at street level. Looking through Mendelsohn's viewfinder, the sight of the Wallace Inn pub as seen through the window of the halal butcher's opposite, or the portrait of an Asian man posing beneath a poster advertising an event to mark the forthcoming anniversary of Jamaican independence; the ambiguous story of Salim and Kathleen, and Kathleen's later pathway out of the inner city and into suburbia.

Nowadays, when I travel to Birmingham to visit my mother in Moseley (where she continues to live, surrounded by coffee shops) I get off the bus a few stops early at DFC Chicken. Due to my musophobia (of rats), I cross the road to avoid the piles of rubbish on the road outside, and instead pick up a bag of samosas from the Shereen Kadah restaurant opposite. It's usually disappointingly quiet when I go in, but I still find myself bringing to mind the sociability evoked by Mendelsohn's photographs of similar establishments in the 1960s, or Abdullah Hussein's description of them as places where—to a soundtrack of *ghazals* and *qawwalis*—"all our people gathered, passed the time and collected information about making a living".[41]

It is characteristic of the dialectics of multiculturalism that the need for places like the Kashmir and the Pyar Ka Sagar came about as a result of the growing number of people who were beginning to imagine what a permanent life in Britain would be like for themselves, at the very moment that, spurred on by the impact of Powellism, governments of both left and right introduced increasingly stringent measures designed to restrict immigration from citizens of its one-time empire (and black and Asian citizens especially). In 1968, Harold Wilson's Labour Government did pass the updated Race Relations Act, which belatedly extended the 1965 legislation that outlawed discrimination in public places to areas such as employment, the housing sector and trade unions. But in the same year, following on from the 1962 Commonwealth Immigrants Act—and in spite of Labour's firm opposition to what the party initially decried as a "shameful" change in the law—the party also rushed through its own Commonwealth Immigrants Act. This Act was designed with one group of people in mind: the 100,000 strong Asian population in the former British colony of Kenya—people from Salim's background who, following Kenyan independence in 1963, were denied the ability to apply for Kenyan citizenship and effectively expelled from the country. In spite of the fact this population were British passport holders who had hitherto enjoyed the same rights as anyone who had been born in the UK, the new legislation decreed that, while the Kenyan Asians remained British citizens, they no longer had the automatic right to live and work in their own country. Planes carrying Asians from Kenya were turned away from British airports, though a specially inserted clause in the legislation ensured that white citizens of the former empire would not be affected. Like the "anti-tinker ditch" that was installed by Birmingham City Council following the forcible removal of the Traveller community in Balsall Heath in the same year, the 1968 Act was a naked attempt to placate the growing hostility towards ethnic minorities among the British electorate; *The Times* described it as "probably the most shameful measure that Labour members have ever been asked by their whips to support". In effect, the Government was attempting to outlaw racism with one hand while simultaneously enshrining it into law with the other. According to one survey, more than 60 per cent of the British electorate believed that the 1968 restrictions on immigration did not go far enough; emboldened by the Act's unconcealed discrimination, in the same year Birmingham City Council passed a motion that declared no further immigrants should be allowed into the city.[42]

RED LIGHTS: 1960s BALSALL HEATH

With the Powellian tail wagging the dog, in the 1960s it continued to be left to the inhabitants of neighbourhoods like Balsall Heath to work out—haphazardly, ambiguously, and not always successfully—how street-level multiculturalism would take shape. As we shall see in Bradford, the next stop in my journey, by the 1970s and 80s ethnic minority communities had again begun to seriously mobilise to address the impact of structural racism across British society—picking up from where activists like the Guyanese Communist Harry O'Connell had left off in 1930s and 40s Cardiff. What we have encountered in this chapter is the much more organic, rough and ready process of people beginning to put down roots in Britain and learning to live together. In this milieu, it was white women like Chrissy, Laura and Kathleen who were perhaps most ahead of their time. Whatever the precise nature of their own circumstances, and in spite of the ongoing impact of male violence, their marginalised status and position within an increasingly-diverse community had seemingly given them an intuitive understanding of the issues faced by ethnic minorities—one that those who were in positions of power in Britain seemed unable (or unwilling) to obtain.

As I have tried to make sense of these themes, I keep thinking back to the racism expressed by the Balsall Heath shopkeeper in his television interview in 1965 ("I don't hold with coloured people coming into this country and taking jobs off our own countrypeople"), and comparing it with the character of Mary in Abdullah Hussein's *Émigré Journeys*. Having begun a relationship with one of the Asian men in the household, Mary takes two of his friends on a shopping trip in the neighbourhood. It was, the story's narrator explains, "the first time that we picked up things and read the prices, then put them back again and picked up others". In one shop, the two men are introduced to a shopkeeper by Mary as "my friends"; the shopkeeper in turn greets them by saying, "welcome gentleman". Further down the street the group encounter a police officer. The men walk in single-file and try to hide behind Mary; their hearts pound and blood pumps in their ears; they are afraid that their illegal status will be discovered. But the police officer shares a joke with Mary: "what kind of friends are these that won't carry your bags?" By the time the men returned to their house, having by now insisted on carrying Mary's shopping, "the pressure of the old haste had lifted from our hearts". As they stepped inside with Mary, "we felt for the first time that yes, we really lived here, that it was *our* house".[43]

4

BLACK POWERS

1980s BRADFORD

Of all the cities that I visited on my journey through multicultural Britain, it was Bradford that was least familiar. Leeds, a 20-minute train journey away, I knew because one of my best friends—whose Indian father had decided that naming his firstborn child after the Hollywood actor James Coburn might give him a useful head-start in Britain—had attended university there. The many weekends I spent getting drunk with James in the kind of indie bars where your feet stick to the floor and sweat drips off the ceiling had given me a misleading impression of Yorkshire as a generally friendly, but predominately white place; a bit like my transition from junior school in Balsall Heath to a whiter secondary school, visiting James in Leeds had brought me into contact with a muscular, white sensibility that in this instance, to my untrained eye, seemed to be symbolised by the clichéd peculiarities of rugby league, gravy on chips and pints that were substantially cheaper even than in Birmingham a hundred miles down the road.[1]

Of course, I was wrong. Leeds itself has a historic ethnic-minority presence, largely based in Chapeltown in the north of the city which, because of the relative affordability of housing in the area, was the site of a large Eastern European Jewish population in the 1930s and then a growing African-Caribbean community from the 1950s onwards. In May 1969 the discrimination that ensnared the city's burgeoning black population made national headlines when the body of David Oluwale, a Nigerian man who twenty years earlier had migrated to Britain as a stowaway, was recovered from the city's River Aire not far from Chapeltown; prior to his death, Oluwale had been severely beaten and chased by two white police officers. Chapeltown was also one of the neighbourhoods that—like St Pauls in Bristol, Brixton in London, Handsworth in Birmingham and Toxteth in Liverpool—erupted into civil unrest in the 1980s to a backdrop of ascending unemployment, enduring poverty and ongoing tensions between ethnic-minority communities and the police.[2]

Yet Bradford has an even more pronounced history as a key site in the making of multicultural Britain. There, large numbers of immigrants had been arriving since the nineteenth century, something bound up with the dramatic rise of Bradford's textile industry. By 1851, the city was home to almost 10,000 Irish immigrants who had been attracted by the prospect of work in one of the hundreds of spinning mills, textile warehouses and dyeing shops that constituted the city's economic lifeblood. By the end of the 1800s there was also a substantial European Jewish population, members of which played a key role in the development of an export industry that took the fruits of Bradford's mills around the world. And in the years after the Second World War, Bradford also witnessed a more immediately visible kind of immigration from Britain's former colonies—largely from the Indian sub-continent, and especially from rural villages in regions like the Punjab.

Like the earlier arrival of European immigrants, this was a process initially powered by the economic magnet that was the

BLACK POWERS: 1980s BRADFORD

textile industry. "It was a village tradition", one South Asian immigrant explained, "to go out and earn some money. In the village there was no other job besides helping your parents on the farm, so I thought of going abroad". Rural villages in places like the Punjab were subsistence economies—you grew or hunted only enough to live off, and wages were a rarity. The *biradari* system of networks that were orientated around family and village ties and were a central feature of life in rural Pakistan, helped spread the word that Bradford was a place where paid work could be easily found. By 1961, there were over 3,000 Pakistanis in Bradford, the vast majority of whom worked in textiles mills and factories, often taking the unpopular twelve-hour night shifts that had become widespread in an effort to maximise productivity. Three years later, driven by the desire to pre-empt the restrictions to immigration introduced with the 1962 Commonwealth Immigrants Act, the number had grown to 12,000. By the mid-1980s, there was an estimated South-Asian, predominately Muslim, population of 52,000 people in Bradford. This was 11 per cent of the city's total population, though the jobs that had initially attracted immigrants to Bradford had by this point gone. As the process of deindustrialisation was accelerated by Margaret Thatcher's Conservative Party, an estimated 50,000 textiles jobs were lost in the region. The growth in Asian-run businesses went a small way towards filling this gap for Bradford's Asian population—from halal butchers and curry houses to jewellers and specialist VHS rental shops. As in Cardiff, Nottingham and Birmingham, these businesses emerged in particular areas of Bradford: neighbourhoods with large ethnic minority communities like Manningham in the north of the city, a few miles from Bradford University and my main focus for this chapter. By the 1980s South-Asian residents had already become a significant majority. As the writer Hanif Kureishi observed on a visit to the area in 1986, having made the three-hour train journey up from London, "I was yet to see a white face". For Kureishi, whose own father had moved to Pakistan following the 1947 partition of India, if it hadn't been for Bradford's old-fashioned-looking British topography, "I could imagine that everyone was back in their village in Pakistan".³

The size of Bradford's South-Asian community was itself a symbol of the extent of Britain's drift towards the multicultural. But there was also substantial ethnic diversity *within* this community—something that outsiders, to this day, often fail to see. Most Asians in Bradford have family ties to the Mirpur district of Kashmir in Pakistan, but there are also substantial groups who originated from Rawalpindi, 70 miles away in the Punjab, for instance, or from Attock, almost 150 miles away in Chhachh, as well as—even further afield—places like Sylhet in west Bangladesh and Surat in northwest India. This meant that, in a little over thirty years since the end of the Second World War, an unprecedented patchwork of ethnic diversity had become a commonplace feature of Bradford life. This not only included ethnic distinctions between Muslims, Sikhs and Hindus, or the parallel growth of religious denominations such as the *Barelwi* or *Deobandi* Islamic sects. Arguably the most important development, by the time Kureishi visited the city, was the fact that this diversity also included a growing number of British Asians who had been born and gone to school in Bradford and were reaching political maturity.⁴

By 1989, 45 schools in Bradford had Asian intakes of over 70 per cent. But the experiences of ethnic minority communities in the education system could often be brutal. In *Hand on the Sun*, for example, the writer and activist Tariq Mehmood's 1983 novel based on his childhood experiences in Bradford, a near-dystopian picture emerges of life at a Bradford school dominated by the casual racism of both white pupils and staff. The head-teacher in the novel expresses his contempt for the determination

BLACK POWERS: 1980s BRADFORD

of his Asian pupils to cling to what he sees as their "backward" ideals. After a scuffle with a white bully an Asian pupil is told to "move, boy! Don't stand there, like a monkey". *Hand on the Sun* is a work of fiction. Indeed, as the literary critic Claire Chambers has pointed out, it is likely the first novel written in English by a British Muslim writer with the experiences of Muslim-heritage characters as the primary subject. But it also reflected what was actually going on in Bradford. The year after the novel was published it was revealed that Stanley Garnett, the recently retired head-teacher of Delf Hill Middle School in the Low Moor district of the city (and member of the far-right British Movement) had agreed to speak in favour of racial segregation in education at a meeting staged by an organisation calling itself the Bradford Apartheid Group. One report revealed that the British National Party's periodical, *The British Nationalist*, had been found at schools across Bradford, along with racist stickers, graffiti and an outpouring of verbal and physical abuse that had left some ethnic minority children too scared to attend class. Racism in the Bradford school system was thus far from an isolated issue. Rather, as one observer put it, it seemed to "exist permanently, like a pan of water at simmer".[5]

With these experiences being repeated in different ways in cities up and down the country, it is no surprise that, as the number of British-born ethnic minorities increased and reached school-going age, education became a crucial battleground in the politics of multicultural Britain. For the African-Caribbean community, the turning point came with the publication in 1971 of *How the West Indian Child Is Made Educationally Sub-Normal*. This report, authored by the Grenadian teacher Bernard Coard, demonstrated how institutional racism within the British education system had led to a significant over-representation of black pupils in specialist schools for children who were deemed to be educationally "sub-normal". By the time Coard published his report, most of the British Empire had crumbled away. But any serious engagement with the cultures and histories of ethnic minority pupils was largely missing from school curricula—never mind an accurate representation of the racial violence that underpinned the imperial project. Given the more general problem of racism in British schooling, many black parents responded to this situation with the establishment of "supplementary" schools at evenings or weekends that aimed to rectify the damage being done to their children by mainstream institutions. By 1981, there were more than forty such schools in London alone. South-Asian immigration began to increase at a later period and, as we saw in the previous chapter, in the first instance was largely male-orientated compared with the large numbers of women who emigrated from the Caribbean. This meant it took longer for the institutional racism of British schooling to become apparent at first hand, as Asian children began to make their way through the education system. The right of Sikh pupils to wear turbans in school, for instance, was not formally established until 1983. In Bradford, the key flashpoint came in the mid-1980s, with a campaign that was waged against Ray Honeyford, the white head of Drummond Middle School in Manningham, where 75 per cent of pupils were of South Asian descent.[6]

Honeyford was appointed to Drummond in 1980. The controversy around the school was sparked by Honeyford's subsequent opposition to the decision by Bradford Metropolitan Council to try to address the problem of racism in schooling with the introduction of a programme of reforms that included a belated end to the policy of "bussing" ethnic minority children to different parts of the city, the provision of halal meat in certain schools and a policy that would allow Muslim girls to take separate PE classes from boys. From the vantage-point of my own experiences at school in 1990s Birmingham, it is hard to see what Honeyford could have found so contentious in the council's proposals. But

BLACK POWERS: 1980s BRADFORD

in a series of articles it became obvious that Honeyford not only objected to the practicalities of multicultural schooling; he was also opposed to the foundational premise of multiculturalism itself—namely, that the diversity of cultures should be treated with an equality of respect. As a result, and especially when his articles were picked up by the local press and translated into Urdu, both Honeyford and Drummond Middle School became the focal points of a crisis that dominated the news both locally and nationally for the best part of two years.[7]

What became known as the Honeyford Affair is in keeping with some of the better-known flashpoints of the 1980s, a period that I sometimes think about as Britain's decade of divergence. The controversy began in March 1984, while the National Union of Mineworkers embarked on what would turn into its year-long strike in opposition to the Conservative Government's programme of pit-closures (with Yorkshire being a key battleground). And it was reaching its *dénouement* in the autumn of 1985, just as Handsworth in Birmingham—six miles north of Balsall Heath, on the other side of the Bull Ring shopping centre—witnessed two days of rioting in the context of a local unemployment rate that was four times the national average. The Honeyford Affair was shaped by the convergence of an increasingly wide range of voices. There was an older South-Asian generation in Bradford connected to the scores of mosques that were active in the 1980s, as well as a younger cohort of activists who had been born in Britain and were responsible for the establishment of largely secular anti-racist groups like the Asian Youth Movement. But there was also a substantial number of supporters of Honeyford, whose case was taken up as a *cause célèbre* by those who, across the country, seemed pathologically opposed to making any concessions whatsoever to the reality of Britain's multicultural drift.[8]

Although Enoch Powell had long since left his Wolverhampton constituency, where his neighbour had reportedly been an Indian immigrant, for the near-monolithically white seat of South Down in Northern Ireland, what remained of Britain's oldest colony, the support Honeyford attracted showed how strongly the Powellian narrative of white victimhood continued to resonate. And in among all this was the confusing role played by the state—an often-muddled attempt by Bradford Council to bring about multicultural reforms at the local level, at the very moment that, nationally, one of the first acts of Margaret Thatcher's Government was to pass a new British Nationality Act, which formally revoked the 1948 legislation that gave citizens in Britain's colonies and former colonies the right to live and work in the one-time mother country. The Honeyford case crystallises the way that the history of multicultural Britain can sometimes seem as though it is caught in an apparently endless cycle of racism and reaction. On one level, the campaign against Honeyford was eventually a success—after months of protests, Honeyford was removed from his position at Drummond in December 1985. But the affair also helped widen divisions in the city and was a key stop-off in an increasingly polarised debate over the issues of race and the politics of multiculturalism—both in Bradford and across the country.[9]

Manningham, Bradford

The topographical landscape of Manningham was by the 1980s an embodiment of the sense of rootedness ethnic minority communities had arrived at in Britain. Britain's inner cities had been restructured in the decades since the end of the Second World War. As we saw in the previous chapter on Balsall Heath, this was a process driven not only by slum clearance programmes. Just as significant was the sense of confidence communicated by the establishment of immigrant-run establishments like cafés and cinemas and by artistic statements like Kafait Shah's mural depicting the Bombay-born "queen of tragedy" Meena Kumari. By the 1980s, this process had become unmissable. It had, in many ways, become one of the defining features of Britain's urban landscapes.

What we might think of as the "diaspora-ization" of urban Britain—as immigrant communities asserted their own particular diasporic connections as a poised presence in what had become *their* locales—was commonplace by the 1980s. Certainly, having been born in 1985 and spent the first decade of my life in inner-city Birmingham, it seemed that way to me. But what was normal to the inhabitants of inner-city neighbourhoods continued to be the source of fascination for outsiders that oscillated between the kind of nihilistic anxiety exemplified by Powell and a quasi-anthropological desire to gawp at inner-cities as if their residents were like zoo animals. Even Hanif Kureishi, who was the product of his own diasporic formation having been born in Greater London to a Pakistani father and a white-British mother, was disarmed by the hybridised Yorkshire-Pakistani accent of the taxi driver who picked him up from Forster Square Station.[10]

Other writers who visited Manningham in the 1980s regaled their readers with descriptions of Lumb Lane, White Abbey Road and Manningham Lane, which were lined with Asian grocers whose shopkeepers each morning laid out displays made up of fruit, vegetables, fresh coriander, pulses and other produce on tables outside their premises. Next to these, and adjacent to Bradford City Football Club's Valley Parade stadium, were the neighbourhood's Asian-run travel agencies, newsagents, tailors, tobacconists, barbers and *chai-khanas* or tea-houses—places that, to Kureishi's mind, were just like the traditional English greasy spoon apart from the fact the food was Pakistani, there was a jug of water on each table and you ate with your fingers. Foremost among these was the Sweet Centre at 110 Lumb Lane, which was established by two former textile workers, Abdul Rehman and Mohammed Bashir, in December 1964.

Outside the terraced houses, children dressed in *salwars* (trousers) and *kurtas* (shirts) could be seen dotted about playing *gulli danda*—a stick-based variation of cricket. Shops like the Video Palace on the White Abbey Road sold both audio cassettes of Pakistani artists like Master Sajjad and Alamgir as well as VHS tapes of Bollywood movies like *Qayamat Se Qayamat Tak* (1988), the Romeo-and-Juliet-inspired tragedy that helped to make Juhi Chawla, the Ambala-born model and 1984 Miss India, a household name. Film posters hung from corner shops, and parents named their children after the stars of hit movies like *Armaan* (1966), the first film to run for 75 consecutive weeks in Pakistani cinemas. According to one observer, it was impossible to spend any length of time in Manningham and not hear phrases like *Insh'Allah* (God willing), *Maash'Allah* (praise be to God) and *As-Salamu Alaykum* (peace be upon you). For the Irish travel writer Dervla Murphy, meanwhile, who made her name with a series of dispatches from South Asia and who in the mid-1980s embarked on a travel project of a different kind in Bradford, waking to the sound of a neighbour crushing spices on her first morning in Manningham momentarily made her think she was actually back in the Indian sub-continent.[11]

Bradford's Asian communities had anchored themselves in Britain. But this did not mean the spectre of racism was ever far away. Indeed, one of the paradoxes at the heart of the making of multicultural Britain is the way in which ethnic diversity became more established and commonplace over the course of the second half of the twentieth century, at the very same time that racism became an increasingly mainstream feature of both popular and political discourse. As in Birmingham, this was something that also manifested itself in Manningham's built environment with the presence of graffiti spray-painted on bus stops, underpasses, sheds and even in school playgrounds: "Wogs go home", "wogs out, death to the blacks" and "NF Keep Britain Tidy—kill a wog or a Jew a day".[12]

BLACK POWERS: 1980s BRADFORD

If such sentiments were extreme, visiting writers like Murphy found that they were the thin end of the wedge when it came to the casual way that white residents attempted to introduce her to what they understood to be the true nature of race relations in Bradford. This was particularly the case when Murphy was interacting with people away from the geographic confines of Manningham, which had long since been understood as the beating heart of "Bradistan". The very first interaction Murphy had in the city was with a white couple with whom she shared a taxi from the train station. They detailed how in their view immigrants had "messed up" the city at the taxpayer's expense, and expressed a charged fixation on what they understood to be the high birth-rate of Asian communities that meant that "once you've got them, you can't get rid of them". In so doing, they ticked off many of the key Powellite tropes that couched the indigenous white population as the victims of an unwarranted (and taxpayer funded) invasion by an alien force. Later on, seeking shelter on a typically wet spring day in a city centre hotel, Murphy witnessed a waitress refuse two Sikh men service before confiding in Murphy: "think they own the place, that lot!" For another of Murphy's acquaintances, who engaged her in conversation at a bus stop, the simple fact was that Powell was right. It was Powell who best "understood why we shouldn't endure it [immigration], why we should take England back for the English…If you gave me an armoured car and some ammo", Murphy's acquaintance concluded, "I'd clean this place up overnight".[13]

It was no surprise that these sentiments were a mainstay of popular discourse in 1980s Bradford, given that for well over a decade various local figures had worked hard to give the Powell message a distinctively West Yorkshire hue. Key in this respect was Jim Merrick, a one-time Conservative councillor, Bradford dye-house worker and founder of the Yorkshire Campaign to Stop Immigration (YCSI) who cast himself as "the Bradford man's

Powell". In his opposition to a decision to allow Sikh busmen to wear turbans while on duty, focus on the supposed connection between immigration and diseases like typhoid and leprosy, and his conspiratorial notion that the Government was hiding the true levels of black and Asian immigration, Merrick followed the Powell playbook almost to the letter. But his embeddedness in white Bradford also allowed him to tie these narratives to local issues such as the decision by the council to stop distributing free sweets and tobacco to municipal-run homes for pensioners, which Merrick blamed (without evidence) on a council shortfall caused by rising immigration. By 1971, and while still a member of the Conservative Party, Merrick was championing the NF's call for the forcible repatriation of all "coloured" immigrants back to their countries of origin, and YCSI candidates at local elections were attracting an average of 15 per cent of the Bradford vote. Four years later—even with the Conservative Government's introduction of the 1971 Immigration Act, which effectively ended the ability of Commonwealth citizens to migrate to Britain unless they had parents with 'territorial ties' to the UK—Merrick himself achieved 28 per cent of the vote in local elections, and had become an open member of the NF.[14]

By the late-1970s, Merrick's electoral influence—like that of the far right more generally—had receded. This was thanks in no small part to the willingness of Margaret Thatcher, who had been elected leader of the Conservative Party in 1975, to engage with the debate around immigration on the terms that had earlier been popularised by Powell and dragged even further to the right by the Front. Yet the appeal of Merrick's YCSI demonstrated a strength of racist feeling locally that would continue to impact the everyday lives of ethnic minority communities in Bradford.

Discrimination in the workplace, for example, was both a reminder of the limitations of Britain's drift towards the multicultural and an exemplar of how narratives peddled by the far-right could bleed into everyday relations. One survey of Bradford workplaces in the late-1970s revealed a fixation on what was perceived to be the unhygienic nature of the food Asian employees brought with them to work—something that recalled the emphasis placed in 1940s Cardiff on the allegedly insanitary nature of Arabic cooking. Alongside this, and in spite of the long history of Asian mobilisation in the workplace—including, most famously, the long-running strike led by the primarily female workforce at the Grunwick Film Processing factory in North West London in the mid-1970s—there remained an assumption by white managers in Bradford that Asian labour was docile in nature and thus easily exploitable (this also echoed stereotypes about Arabs in Cardiff and other port cities in 1940s Britain). On being asked for a promotion by an Asian employee, one manager explained to a researcher in the early-1980s that he had told the employee in question to go back to India. Other managers explained that they were reluctant to hire Asians because they saw them as having criminal tendencies, or that they preferred Indian rather than Pakistani labour because the former had been subject to British rule (never mind the fact the whole region had been part of the British Empire until 1947, when Pakistan was established as a separate state following Indian independence). According to one employer, workplaces in Bradford were often structured as if there was a formal policy of segregation. One or two Asian workers might start to arrive in a workplace, at which point "the whites voted with their feet" and left for other jobs with predominately white workers; pretty soon, the employer continued, the place would be "full of them".[15]

Such in-your-face discrimination was also a feature of schooling in Bradford, especially before the abolition of "bussing" in the city in 1980, a policy that emulated a longstanding practice deployed in the USA as part of efforts to desegregate its schools. In Bradford (along with Bristol, Luton and Leicester, but notably not Birmingham or most of London) bussing was introduced in January 1965 as a way of ensuring that no more than ten per cent of a given school's intake each year were from ethnic-minority backgrounds (this later rose to 33 per cent). The idea was to prevent the kind of school that I attended in 1990s Birmingham, where white pupils were in the clear minority, from ever becoming a reality. One Bradford administrator explained the policy using more euphemistic language: bussing was in his view a "system of social engineering" that would help avoid the creation of "ghetto schools" and allow ethnic minority pupils to assimilate into the "majority" culture.[16]

The discriminatory nature of the policy was laid bare by the fact that in Bradford it was always black or Asian pupils who were made to travel to school, and never white pupils. One side-effect of this was that it became difficult for ethnic minority parents to play an active role in their children's schooling, or for children to get involved in extra-curricular activities that took place after school hours. And what bussing meant in practice was that while schools in predominately white areas did become more diverse, this took place in an effective vacuum with little ethnic diversity in the community beyond the school gates. There were very few games of *gulli danda* in Eccleshill, for example, a neighbourhood of council estates in the north-east of Bradford to which Asian pupils were bussed that was also a far-right stronghold. The sight of Asian children being transported on board brightly-coloured buses to largely white neighbourhoods not only made the far-right narrative of an immigrant "invasion" tangible to white parents, pupils and even teachers. It also meant that black and Asian pupils were more visible and, lacking both familiarity with the neighbourhood and the security that comes with numbers, at greater risk of abuse.[17]

This abuse could take different forms. Having been bussed to predominately white parts of Bradford, where teaching staff had little or no familiarity with multicultural schooling, ethnic-minority pupils found that they had to confront Fanon's "fact of blackness". Again, there was a focus on numbers that manifested itself with a fascination with the supposed fecundity of Asian families relative to their white counterparts. In the late-1970s one Bradford headteacher on the outskirts of the city saw this as a positive thing. She lamented her impression that Britain had become a society where the importance of the family unit had been neglected and suggested that, if it was true that the Asian children who were being bussed into her school came from large families, at least that meant they were being well cared for. In terms of the everyday rhythms of school life, though, it was much more common for ethnic minority pupils to have to reckon with the spectrum of racial discrimination that came to the fore both structurally and in personal relationships.[18]

In Liverpool, seventy miles west of Bradford, there had never been a policy of bussing in part because of the city's comparatively large British-born ethnic minority population, and the extent to which the national debate around race relations remained intertwined with the issue of immigration. But the problem of racism in schools was nevertheless significant. Ethnic minority pupils in majority-white classes were often called on by white teachers to explain particular issues in the Caribbean or South Asia, for example, or abused by their peers during breaks or after class. One woman of African descent recalled that it was at school in Liverpool in the 1970s where she "learned the word nigger" when, on her way home one day, a group of pupils followed her and chanted "Nigger nigger pull the trigger bang bang bang". In Bradford, the visibility of bussed Asian pupils was often heightened not only by the colour of their skin, but also by the fact that they had to leave school early each day in order to catch the bus back home. At lunchtimes, in the absence of the *de facto* provision of halal food, they would often have to eat separate vegetarian meals (in some instances, Muslim pupils were even forced to eat pork). The racialised nature of this divide gave rise to the myth that Asian pupils were somehow less educationally able than their white counterparts, and helped perpetuate divisions in other areas—during PE lessons and in the playground, for instance, when football matches would be set up as "whites versus browns". In some ways, then, the calls that were being made by the far-right for segregation in Bradford's schools were a waste of time; some observers argued the implications of Bradford's bussing policy meant that there was already a form of racial segregation in operation in the city.[19]

If by the start of the 1980s the far-right was in electoral freefall, it was on the streets that it nevertheless found ways of making its presence felt. The NF had recruited a swathe of disaffected white men to its ranks, and set them about a campaign of intimidation against Britain's ethnic minority population. One Asian man who had attended school in Bradford remembered that his bus back home at the end of each day sometimes required a police escort to protect it from NF protests. The threat of physical assault was real as Front members—having hijacked the "skinhead" style of closely-cropped hair, button-down shirts and lace-up Dr Martens boots—embarked on a programme of "Paki-bashing" across the country. In 1974 in Ealing in West London, a fifteen-year-old-boy was murdered in one such assault. By 1981, a Home Office report estimated the number of racially-motivated attacks on ethnic minorities had risen to over a thousand a month across the country, and Asian communities were fourteen times more likely to be the victims of racial attacks than the African-Caribbean population. "We go up to them and say, 'Hand over your wallet'", one sixteen-year-old Londoner explained in 1970. "If they don't, we give them a kicking. If they do, we probably give them a kicking anyway. They smell, don't they? It's all that garlic. I mean, they've no right to be ere'". As Jalib, one of the narrators of Tariq Mehmood's novel *Hand on the Sun* put it, "the time when racist obscenities were written, under cover of darkness, in lonely passages of flyovers and subways" had reached its logical conclusion: "attacks on black people". And this had also become a feature of life within Bradford's schools.[20]

It is difficult to know how much Mehmood was exaggerating the violent nature of the racism he depicts in *Hand on the Sun*. But for one South Asian immigrant, who arrived in Bradford in the 1960s, "these were things which had begun to develop". The interviewee remembered "end of term fights between Asian boys and white boys" at Bradford schools, and one occasion where Asian pupils leaving school were forced to band together in a phalanx formation to ensure their own safety. It is in this way that, set against the world I have described so far in this chapter—from the influence of the far-right and everyday racism in Bradford's streets and workplaces to the remarkably misguided policy of school bussing—*Hand on the Sun* captures in technicolour the extent to which young Bradford Asians felt they were under siege in the 1980s. In the novel, Jalib and his fellow Asian pupils are told by their white peers that they are "fucking Pakis" and "wogs" who didn't need to worry about getting a black eye because they already have two. Individual feuds between white and Asian pupils begin over nothing and are settled by fights at break times. As it becomes clear this tension is going to explode into a group battle, the novel's white characters look on at "all the wogs getting together" with a determination to "show these black bastards that they can't come to our school and act as though they are still in the jungle!"[21]

In one scene, the dinner ladies venture out into the playground one lunchtime to determine why there isn't the usual unruly queue of children waiting for their lunch. Once outside, a disturbing sight greets them. The windswept playground has been partitioned. On one side is the school's thousand-strong white population. On the other is its 300 Asian pupils. As some of their number begin to disperse, there is a growing sense of trepidation among the Asian group. Their white opponents charge. One of Jalib's friends throws *mirch* (chilli powder) into the air in the hope it would stun the white pupils, but the wind quickly sweeps it harmlessly away. Someone else is hit by a stone, while Jalib is kicked in the back. With shouts of "fucking *gora*" and "*zindabaad*", Jalib and his friends also land some blows, until eventually the school's headmaster calls on the police to restore order. When the police arrive, the pupils are assembled in the school hall with, once again, the Asian pupils on one side and whites on the other. The lead police officer addresses both groups in turn. He urges the white pupils to "show yourselves as an example to these people" by demonstrating what he described as the "virtues of the British". He then turns to the Asian pupils. Britain is a "civilised country", the police officer explains slowly, as if ordering food in a foreign restaurant. "You lads are no longer in a jungle...you must learn to accept the ways of this country". The police officer continues to talk for some time, but Jalib and his friends have stopped listening. Their wounds are too fresh, and thoughts are already turning to what might await them on their journey home.[22]

Honeyford

It was to Bradford Metropolitan Council's credit that in the early-1980s it took steps to try to solve what it belatedly acknowledged was the acute problem of racism in the city's schools. In 1980 the policy of bussing was abolished. Henceforward schools in areas like Manningham began to be a more accurate reflection of the communities in which they were based. Thus in the same year, when Ray Honeyford was appointed head teacher at Drummond Middle School—just around the corner from Lumb

Lane, and in the shadow cast by Lister's Mill, one of the city's largest textile exporters—49 per cent of Drummond pupils were Asian. By 1982 that figure had risen to almost three-quarters of the school's population. Of the 128 children admitted to Drummond two years later, only three were not from Asian backgrounds. By 1985, the proportion of Asian pupils in the school as a whole had risen to 95 per cent, the majority of whom had been born in Britain.[23]

If the abolition of bussing was one early step, the direction of travel in which the Labour-led local authority was moving was signalled by the 1981 publication of a review into race relations in the city. It was the council's delayed response to the 1976 Race Relations Act, legislation passed by the Labour Government that not only outlawed indirect discrimination in public institutions but also demanded that local authorities take proactive steps towards the promotion of "good race relations"—including in education—and established a watchdog, the Commission for Racial Equality, to help bring this about. There was also the spectre of the urban riots of the early-1980s, the initial trigger for which was a virtual breakdown in the relationship between majority-white police forces across the country and young black men in particular, in the broader context of an unemployment rate in Britain not seen since the 1930s. The riots began in St Pauls in Bristol in 1980, the longstanding red-light district to the northeast of the city centre where unemployment was estimated to be running at more than 35 per cent (and was possibly double that figure for ethnic minorities). However, by summer 1981—with more outbreaks of unrest in Toxteth in Liverpool, where unemployment was estimated to have increased by 100 per cent in a decade, and Moss Side in Manchester, where some residents had taken to presenting bottled cockroaches to the housing authorities to try to convince them to take action to improve living standards—the disorder had come worryingly close to Bradford.[24]

MULTICULTURAL BRITAIN

Bradford Council's race relations review was entitled *Turning Point* and was indeed envisaged as a means of ushering in a new era for the city. In effect, it was an admission that—like the authorities in Nottingham more than two decades earlier—the council had been asleep at the wheel. In spite of the difficulties faced by ethnic minorities, the white officials who ran Bradford had presumed there were good race relations in the city when in actual fact, they now conceded, there was "no race relations at all". The report stressed that as a "multiracial, multicultural city" every community had "an equal right to maintain its own identity, culture, language and customs". It therefore argued that the aim should be to bring about "equality of esteem" between cultures and likewise to ensure that services were relevant to all sections of the community. A Race Relations Advisory Council would be set up, as well as a Bradford Council for Mosques that would bring together the dozens of mosques that were active across the city. The council also left the door open to the establishment of Muslim voluntary-aided schools of the kind that would become increasingly common under the New Labour Governments of the late-1990s and early-2000s. It was high time, the authors of *Turning Point* stressed, that what they called the "isolated pluralism" that had characterised community relations in Bradford in the 1960s and 70s was replaced by state-sponsored multiculturalism. With a boldness in keeping with the short-lived re-emergence of municipal socialism in London, Sheffield, and elsewhere, Bradford Council now committed itself to the complete elimination of racial discrimination in any form.[25]

In effect, *Turning Point* was one of the earliest examples of a local authority explicitly attempting to craft a comprehensive agenda in response to the organic, street-level multiculturalism that, at different points in time, we have encountered in this book. When it came to education, what this meant in practice was set out in a series of memorandums in 1982 and 1983. The council instructed that information about a given school should be made available to parents in their first language, that a wide range of faiths be studied in Religious Education (RE) classes, that pupils could be given permission to be absent during religious holidays and would likewise be permitted to cover up during physical education lessons and wear religious jewellery to class. And there were other reforms that, in the specific context of a Bradford race relations scene that had been polluted by the far right for ten years and more, were always likely to be a source of controversy. The council argued that extended trips to the Indian sub-continent during term time were not to be discouraged and instead seen as an enriching educational activity. Formalising an approach that had been taken by some schools in Bradford in the 1970s, all Muslim pupils were to have the right to take part in Friday prayer sessions during lunchtimes led by a local imam. The newly-created Race Relations Advisory Council would help vet curricula to ensure the absence of stereotyped or prejudicial images. Any school with more than ten Muslim pupils would be obliged to serve halal meat, and all headteachers must participate in compulsory racism awareness classes.[26]

It was unsurprising that, in the broader climate of Britain's decade of divergence, the Bradford reforms became the target of a series of hyperbolic newspaper exposés that barely hid their efforts to fan the flames of community tensions in the city. The *Daily Mail*, for example, finessing the role it would play for years to come as the self-professed arbiters of 'political correctness gone mad', even sent an undercover journalist to one of Bradford's racism awareness classes where, it was reported, he was instructed to perform the part of a white racist, told that only white people could be racist and confronted by a black social worker who berated him for being white—all at a cost to taxpayers of "up to" £600 each. As Dervla Murphy found throughout her time in Bradford, what was also striking was how the council's reforms had touched a nerve with Bradford's white population, demonstrating how much the anxieties about race—articulated by Powell and repackaged locally by far-right politicians like Jim Merrick—continued to be intensely felt. The council's multicultural policies had to Murphy's mind become an obsession for white people in Bradford; they were part of a "white backlash" that manifested itself in heated conversations in cafés and pubs and at bus stops and supermarket queues. For a woman tending her garden in Keighley—a former mill town ten miles from Bradford—all the council seemed to care about was "them Pakis". Amplifying Powell's narrative of white victimhood, the woman complained that Asians seemed to qualify for everything for free—from heat and light to school meals cooked using "their own dirty meat" and specialist teachers. Tellingly, it was education that quickly became the primary focus of the woman's diatribe. Asian parents were simply "too lazy" to teach their children English, the woman declared, "so our kids must hang back waiting for them to catch up". And even then, the woman suggested, referencing the council's new RE curriculum, white children were "taught about all them people like whoever started that Paki religion". The sum total of the situation in Bradford was, in her view, that there was "no one left to stand up for *us*".[27]

This was the immediate context for the beginnings of the scandal around Honeyford at Drummond Middle School in the spring of 1984. For a time, both in Bradford and beyond, Honeyford was positioned as that "someone" standing up for the interests of those who, like Murphy's white gardener in Keighley, were unable to reconcile themselves with the scope of Britain's multicultural drift. Honeyford himself—with his thick, greying beard, square spectacles and brown blazer, a self-made man who claimed never to have holidayed abroad and wasn't shy about professing his admiration for all things British—had, as one commentator put it, become many people's "great white hope".

BLACK POWERS: 1980s BRADFORD

He had been born in Manchester in 1934 as one of twelve children and had left school at the age of fifteen, only later in life re-training to become a teacher by attending night school. It was this salt-of-the-earth background that, coupled with Honeyford's sober appearance, Mancunian accent and self-assured persona, perhaps enabled the stance he took in opposition to Bradford's multicultural reforms to cut through so thoroughly.[28]

Like Powell, who became a Professor of Greek in his mid-twenties, the many journalistic profiles of Honeyford that were published at the height of the controversy around him often foregrounded his intellectual credentials. Honeyford had the look of a 1970s academic and had indeed published two scholarly papers based on the research he undertook for his postgraduate degrees in sociolinguistics and educational psychology. But it was his journalistic opinion-pieces, which appeared in places like the *Salisbury Review*—a journal of the burgeoning "new right" that had been established in 1982 by the Cambridge scholar John Casey, who used its inaugural issue to back the far-right's call for the repatriation of black and Asian communities—which became the fuel for a crisis that engulfed Bradford for two years.[29]

Reading Honeyford now, what stands out is not only the degree to which he paints a picture of an established (white) order under attack from a "race relations lobby" or "multi-ethnic brigade", the influence of which was supposedly growing by the day. It is also Honeyford's own barely-concealed ethnocentricity. This was something that clearly made it impossible for him to see the cultures of the Asian pupils under his tutelage as anything other than inferior to his own monolithic conception of Britishness, which was itself divorced from the implications of what the sociologist Kehinde Andrews has called Britain's "foundation stones" of colonialism and the slave trade. Honeyford's early interventions took the form of a series of letters to the Bradford *Telegraph and Argus* in 1982, in response to reports of council expenditure on a

West Indian community centre and a temporary structure in a local school that would prevent pupils from again having to be bussed to a different part of the city. Honeyford suggested that the council was effectively being bounced into spending money because of the threat of race riots in Bradford and called for a public auditor to be appointed to investigate.[30]

Later that year he published a piece in the *Times Educational Supplement* that set out his position more substantively. Most teachers, he argued, regarded Bradford's multicultural agenda with both scepticism and resentment. With its aim to reconstitute the British curriculum so that it made room both for an engagement with the diverse cultures of minority communities and a critical understanding of British imperialism, the multicultural approach was not only patronising ethnic minority children but also confusing education with propaganda. Where there were issues with ethnic-minority pupils, Honeyford placed the blame squarely with their parents, who as immigrants bore sole responsibility for any adaptations involved in settling in a new country. When it came to education, the commitment of immigrants to the British curriculum was "implicit in their decision to become British citizens", Honeyford claimed, ignoring the fact that it was the British Government who had bestowed full citizenship rights on those living in its colonies and former colonies with the passing of the 1948 British Nationality Act. The maintenance and transmission of minority cultures was in Honeyford's view nothing to do with schooling in Britain. Instead, Honeyford suggested, the aim should be for the children of immigrants—a growing number of whom were of course by now born in Britain—to master the "British traditions of civilised discourse and respect for reason" in order that they could compete in what Honeyford understood to be Britain's "ruthless meritocracy".[31]

The inappropriate nature of these comments should have been obvious—on their own terms, for sure, and at the very least coming from the head of a school where most pupils were Asian (and in the context of the council's newfound determination to bring about racial equality in the city). In 1983 Honeyford published another article in which he described the father of one his pupils as being "straight out of a Kipling novel" with an English accent that sounded like "Peter Sellers' Indian doctor on an off day". This was a reference to the 1960 film *The Millionairess* in which the role of an Indian physician was played by Sellers and, as Hanif Kureishi has recalled of his own schooldays in 1960s London, Sellers' highly racialised portrayal had become a common mode of abuse across the country. But while Honeyford's views became the subject of discussions in the letter-pages of local newspapers, they were yet to penetrate more generally, and Honeyford received little more than a slap on the wrist from his employers—for writing to the *Telegraph and Argus* on school notepaper. It took another article, published in early-1984 in the *Salisbury Review* and reprinted by the *Telegraph and Argus* in March, for the implications of Honeyford's positions to become apparent.[32]

By now, Honeyford's narrative of white victimhood had reached new levels. The race relations lobby had become so powerful, he suggested, that the situation was best compared to the witch-hunt against Communists in McCarthyite America. Right-minded people had in effect been forced into silence; they were afraid not only of saying the wrong thing, but also of thinking the wrong thoughts. Honeyford also sought to bring into his rapidly-expanding definition of white victims those who (like me) had been white pupils in largely black and Asian schools. Where white children were in a clear minority it was in his view inevitable that academic standards would suffer. Yet the issue was barely discussed, and there was no lobby or quango along the lines of the newly established Commission for Racial Equality to speak up for white minorities. Instead, "multicultural zealots" who were blinded by post-imperial guilt bandied around the word racism, a term which in Honeyford's view did not provide any real insight but rather had become a mere slogan the aim of which was to supress constructive thought.³³

Even worse, in the mind of Honeyford, was the implications of Bradford Council's determination to bring about equality of esteem between cultures. What this meant in practice, he wrote, was a formalisation of "the West Indian's right to create an ear-splitting cacophony for most of the night", the requirement to teach the dub-poetry of the Jamaican poet Linton Kwesi Johnson alongside the works of Shakespeare, or the Muslim parent's ability to withdraw a daughter from dance or swimming classes, which in Honeyford's eyes in effect meant the imposition of "a purdah mentality" in schools. Honeyford found it ironic that the same people supposedly pushing this agenda—"aggressive black intellectuals", a "half-educated Sikh", those with the "hysterical political temperament of the Indian subcontinent"—enjoyed in Britain rights and privileges that were "unheard of" in their countries of origin. To illustrate the point he used Pakistan, a country that in spite of Honeyford's own avowed lack of overseas travel he nevertheless felt confident enough to describe as corrupt, full of "obstinately backward people", undemocratic and "the heroin capital of the world". Little surprise, then, Honeyford claimed, that Pakistan "loses more of its citizens voluntarily to other countries than any state on earth".³⁴

Honeyford had formalised many of the racialised anxieties of the wider Bradford milieu. After all, what is a call for a quango to speak for the rights of white minorities if not a reified version of the arguments made by Dervla Murphy's Keighley acquaintance, who suggested that there was "no one left to stand up for *us*"? It did not seem to matter that Honeyford's arguments were not born out by the facts. At the same time Honeyford was expanding his journalistic profile, for example, a headmaster at another Bradford school with a large Asian population found that white children actually out-performed the national average in such environments. Alex Fellowes, the headteacher of a nearby language centre for children with limited English, pointed out that children from south Asian backgrounds also performed better at school than the national average. But such findings failed to resonate. Instead, aided by the pro-Honeyford stance of the local press, Honeyford's arguments were often repackaged by white Bradfordonians. "We've needed someone to speak for us for a long time", a white dinner lady explained to a visiting journalist in 1984, and "now Mr Honeyford's done it". In the suburban pubs Murphy frequented in Bradford's 'white highlands', the well-to-do neighbourhoods in the hills that surround the city, Murphy noticed how the phrase "Powell was right" had been replaced by "Honeyford was right", and that the familiar fixation on stereotypes like a lack of hygiene in Asian cuisine had been joined by a notion that Asian immigrants made their money by importing into Bradford heroin from Pakistan. And of course, this was woven together by the idea that Honeyford had become a victim in his own country. As another of Murphy's acquaintances in Bradford reflected indignantly, "why shouldn't a man say what he thinks? This used to be a free country till all them buggers arrived—now people are afraid to speak their mind".[35]

Honeyford claimed to have personally received more than 100 messages of support, and there were reports that headteachers across the city were threatening to resign in protest at the council's new multicultural agenda. The letter pages of local newspapers likewise quickly filled up with outraged correspondents declaring their support for Honeyford. "What kind of a free society are we supposed to be living in when we read that Bradford headteachers are obliged to attend a course on how to recruit and select ethnic staff, run by race officers of whom five out of seven are coloured?", one correspondent wondered. "Mr Honeyford spoke the truth and is now being pilloried by militant ethnic minorities."[36]

With the publication of extracts of Honeyford's *Salisbury* article in the press, however, along with translations in Urdu that were widely distributed in Manningham and elsewhere, Honeyford quickly became the target of widespread opposition. Both the local Labour Party and Max Madden, the Labour MP for Bradford West, called for him to be sacked. Reports circulated that Honeyford was putting his rhetoric into practice at Drummond by refusing to provide the signature required for pupils' passport applications and by denying pupils who had taken extended trips to the Indian sub-continent readmission to school when they returned. The Bradford Council for Mosques—which had been established by the Council in 1981—also condemned Honeyford. In early March 1984 it organised a demonstration in defence of the principles of Bradford's multicultural reforms that was attended by 3,000 protesters. It was in many ways a signal of what was to come. By the middle of March, just a week after extracts from Honeyford's article was republished locally, the Drummond Parents Action Committee had been formed. Its ultimate aim was to bring about Honeyford's removal from Drummond Middle School.[37]

Racism and Reaction

The growth in influence of the far-right in Bradford had already contributed to increased political mobilisation among the city's ethnic minority communities by the time Honeyford arrived on the scene in 1980. The watershed moment came with the protests that were organised against the decision by the NF to stage a march that would culminate with a campaign meeting at Manningham Middle School—barely a ten minute walk from Drummond School on the other side of Lumb Lane. On a mild Saturday in April 1976—the day after St George's Day—600 Front supporters paraded past Manningham's Asian take-out joints, sweet centres and grocers with chants of "send them back" and placards calling on the Government to "put Britons first". The drum-band leading the parade and sea of Union Jack flags made it look like a scene straight out of sectarian Belfast. In one news-clip, a young man dressed in an oversized V-neck and flares can be seen performing a Nazi salute for the camera.[38]

The protest against the Front was organised by the Bradford Trades Council and attended by some 4,000 people. But it culminated in central Bradford, and there was a growing realisation among the younger activists—particularly those who were Asian and from Manningham—that if they were going to protect their community from the Front, they were in the wrong place. A group of them broke through the police cordon and headed back through town to Manningham, where they countered the Front's slogans with chants of "death to fascism". There was a major confrontation between the protestors, Front members and the mostly white police officers protecting the Front meeting—which was being addressed by John Tyndall, the National Front chairman who had earlier spent six months in prison for training neo-Nazis and had a penchant for wearing full Nazi regalia.

The violence in Manningham was so severe, one local resident remembered, that people who lived nearby turned their homes into makeshift hospitals. The significance of this event was that it helped establish the principle of the need to take direct action in defence of the rights of ethnic minority communities. It followed on from the campaigns waged by British Black Power groups in the late-1960s and 1970s which, inspired by the radicalism of American-based activists like Malcolm X and Stokely Carmichael, adopted the principle that "self-defence is no offence" in their campaign to defend institutions like the Mangrove restaurant—a prominent African-Caribbean meeting point in Notting Hill—from police harassment. It was an ethos that was solidified in the response by the Asian community to the murder of the eighteen-year-old student Gurdip Singh Chaggar by a gang of white youths in West London in June 1976, and again in Bradford five years later when twelve young Asian activists—including the writer Tariq Mehmood—were charged by the police with conspiracy to endanger lives for having made thirty-eight petrol bombs.[39]

In the latter case, the activists involved freely admitted to having made the bombs. Yet they argued they had done so because they believed there was an imminent threat to their community posed by the far right. The bombs were there to be used only in extreme circumstances and were part of a range of actions taken by the activists to defend Bradford's Asian population that also included nightly patrols of the streets of Manningham. As Saeed Hussain, one of the activists arrested later reflected: "we would not let fascists walk in and actually destroy a part of Bradford where Black communities lived". Against the odds, at what *Race Today* magazine dubbed the "trial of the decade", the argument worked. All twelve men were acquitted and, in the immediate aftermath of the trial, celebrated in front of the waiting press with their hands clenched in the Black Power salute.[40]

Tariq Mehmood was at the 1976 protest against the NF and was also a key player in the subsequent establishment of organisations like the Asian Youth Movement and the United Black Youth League. Indeed, in his novel *Hand on the Sun*, which culminates with the events at Manningham Middle School, you can feel how intoxicating the need to act had become—against the immediate activities of an organisation that wanted you and your family deported, yes; but also in the broader context of everything the novel's protagonist, Jalib, is having to come to terms with at school and beyond. At the protest Jalib and his friends jump up and down in harmony with their chanting, and Jalib feels a surge of hatred as he catches a glimpse of the NF parade protected by an army of police officers; there are so many of them present, one could be forgiven for mistaking it as a police parade. As the protest reaches town, Jalib becomes increasingly agitated. In the familiar, run-down streets of Manningham he finds it empowering as he recognises friends shouting their support from the side-lines. In central Bradford, however, Jalib becomes worried about those he and his fellow protestors have left behind. "What are we doing here?" Jalib exclaims. "The Front's in our streets! That's where we ought to be!"[41]

This spirit of direct action was infused in the campaign against Honeyford from the start. The parents involved in the group that led the protests—the Drummond Parents' Action Committee— were largely Asian, though they made the conscious decision to elect a white woman, Jenny Woodward, a former law student and Manningham resident whose daughter was one of the few white children at Drummond, as chairperson. It was a tactical manoeuvre based on the assumption that a white advocate would in the climate of 1980s Bradford be able to carry a greater number of people with them. The Committee's rationale was laid out for a visiting journalist by one of its Pakistani members: "we send our children to school for a decent education, but if he [Honeyford] is a racist, what will the children be like?" A Lahore-born merchant regarded the whole affair as having "killed good race relations in our city". After all, he continued, "we started out from Pakistan but now we *do* feel Bradford is our city".[42]

What bound the Committee members together was not only the fact their children attended the same school. They also regarded themselves as being the primary objects of Honeyford's ire in what had already become his infamous *Salisbury Review* article. With her commitment to multicultural education policies Woodward herself was no doubt an embodiment of what Honeyford derided as Britain's multicultural "thought police". As the campaign against Honeyford wore on, she also became the focus of a tabloid smear campaign that characterised her as a feminist "virago" whose tendency to wear Pakistani clothes and socialise with black friends immediately positioned her outside the realms of established social norms. But Woodward also proved to be a shrewd operator who was able to marshal a wide range of constituents in support of the campaign. Within months of the establishment of the Committee, this included the local branch of the Asian Youth Movement, the Bradford University Students' Union, the West Indian Parents' Association, the London-based *Race Today* collective, the Bangladeshi People's Association and *Al Falah*—the Islamic Youth Mission.[43]

The Committee's activities started modestly. A meeting of 100 Drummond parents was convened at which a vote of no confidence was passed in Honeyford. What is striking is how the language of multiculturalism, set out by the Council in 1981 in its *Turning Point* report—and the source of considerable anxiety among many of Bradford's white residents Dervla Murphy encountered—had been taken up as a core part of the group's platform. Honeyford had not only insulted black and Asian parents, the Committee emphasised, he was also openly contradicting the council's stated commitment to fostering equality of esteem between cultures and the eradication of racial discrimination. The Committee put the crux of the issue as it saw it with a question: "Are we, as consumers of the educational services, paid for by public funds, bound to accept the attitude of one headteacher who finds himself in conflict with the policies he is under contract to follow?" Emboldened by the support of a growing number of organisations—in April, for example, members of the Asian Youth Movement staged the first ever occupation of Bradford City Hall in protest against Norman Free, Bradford's Lord Mayor and a prominent supporter of Honeyford—the Committee presented a petition to the council calling for Honeyford's immediate removal. Out of the 500 signatories, more than half were from parents of children at Drummond.[44]

BLACK POWERS: 1980s BRADFORD

By July 1984, it had become difficult to see how Honeyford could survive. The council gave him a formal warning and commissioned a special inspection of conditions at the school that was due to report back on its findings later that summer. On 11 June, to coincide with the start of the inspection (and by coincidence the start of the second week of Ramadan), the Action Committee organised a one-day strike at Drummond where parents would refuse to send their children to school. It was a strategy in keeping with the broader political conjuncture of 1980s Britain. For more than three months strikes by members of the National Union of Mineworkers at pits across Yorkshire had dominated newspaper headlines and TV news reports; on 18 June one of the most violent confrontations of the entire strike took place between picketers and the police at the Orgreave Coking Plant in South Yorkshire, a little under an hour's drive from Manningham.

But in striking, the Action Committee was also embracing a tactic that had been successfully used by ethnic minority communities in the field of education. In the summer of 1973, for example, a group of black parents responded to what they saw as the sub-standard education their children were receiving at a school in Chapeltown in Leeds by calling a day's strike. The action shocked the local authority and the school in question was almost immediately allocated a raft of extra resources. Even more pertinently, in 1983 an increasingly-independent Bradford Council for Mosques had called its own day-long strike in response to concerns that, in the face of mounting criticism, the Metropolitan Council was preparing to row back on its commitment to the provision of halal meat in schools. The withdrawal of thousands of Muslim children from schools across Bradford was a major factor in the Council's ultimate decision to maintain halal options for Muslim schoolchildren.[45]

The focused nature of the strike at Drummond meant that it was nothing like as large. But the Council estimated that

70 per cent of Drummond pupils abstained from school on the day of action. And this inevitably influenced the tenor of the council's special inspection of Drummond. When the report was published in August 1984 it praised what was identified as the "caring attitude" exhibited by many staff at the school, and likewise observed there were "firm inter-ethnic friendships" across the student body. But it also pointedly highlighted how far Drummond had to go if it were to fall in line with the council's commitment to multicultural schooling. There was little in the curriculum to which a child from an ethnic minority background could relate, the report noted, and it urged the school management to do more to "openly acknowledge the value of different cultures and belief systems". There was too much emphasis placed on the deficiencies of pupils, which was having a knock-on impact on the ability of children to reach their potential. In an implicit rejoinder to the arguments made by Honeyford, the report stressed the need for management to recognise that British identity is a developing concept that should allow room for a plurality of definitions. Whether or not Drummond would function effectively in the future, the report concluded, would depend on Honeyford's own ability to regain the trust of the majority of parents.[46]

Given Honeyford's own reluctance to cede ground—it was reported that he had refused to take part in the council's now-compulsory racism awareness classes, and had instructed his lawyers to appeal the formal warning he had received from his employers—the report seemed to make his position at Drummond untenable. Yet the council dragged its feet, caught between the boldness it had laid out in *Turning Point* and what had become clear was a substantial white constituency that had been marshalled in Bradford first by Jim Merrick and now Honeyford. There was a hiatus in activity over the summer holidays. Then, at a specially-convened meeting held by the council in October 1984,

Honeyford survived a no-confidence motion and was given six months to repair relations with the community. But meanwhile the Action Committee endeavoured to keep up the pressure—by guiding the parents of 238 Drummond pupils through the process of requesting that their children be transferred to different schools, for instance, and with a formal complaint against Honeyford made to Bradford's Educational Directorate.

As the dispute dragged on into 1985 it became clear that Honeyford had become a vessel for a much wider ideological schism that had been amplified in the discordant context of Thatcher's Britain. In his column for *The Times*, Roger Scruton, a lecturer in philosophy and Honeyford's editor at the *Salisbury Review*, used the furore at Drummond to expand the theory that anti-racists in Britain had become a bigoted "totalitarian elite" that had effectively silenced critics of the multicultural agenda (Scruton didn't explain how his own journal and weekly column in a national newspaper, both of which he regularly used to echo Honeyford's attacks on the "anti-racist lobby", fitted into this thesis). In the spring of 1985, another special meeting was held by Bradford Metropolitan Council to discuss the situation at Drummond. This time, Honeyford lost a no-confidence motion and was placed on gardening leave. But with the support of the National Association of Headteachers, he immediately announced that he would the appeal the decision in the courts. And it wasn't long before Marcus Fox, the backbench Conservative MP for the affluent (and mostly white) town of Shipley four miles north of Bradford, announced that he would be raising the Honeyford case in parliament, armed with a petition containing the signatures of 6,000 Honeyford supporters.[47]

Fox amplified the arguments made by both Scruton and Honeyford himself. Immigrant communities had come to Britain of their own free will, he argued, and having been granted British citizenship, were simply obliged to accept the education system on offer—whatever the effect it was having on their children. In fact, the events at Drummond were in Fox's view no longer about education or race relations; rather, they struck "at the very root of our democracy" by threatening the principle of freedom of speech. But this was clearly a privilege Fox did not believe extended to the concerned parents of ethnic minority children. He dismissed the members of the Drummond Action Committee as Marxists and Trotskyists, a "rent-a-mob" conducting a smear campaign against an honourable and competent man. "If Mr Honeyford is ultimately dismissed, where will it all stop?" Fox wondered. "The withdrawal of the right to free speech from this one man could have enormous consequences" if the forces against Honeyford were ultimately allowed to succeed. "The race relations bullies may have got their way so far", Fox warned, "but the silent majority of decent people have had enough". By the autumn of 1985, Honeyford was again back at his desk at Drummond having successfully appealed against his suspension in the High Court. And Fox's standpoint was given Government approval when Honeyford was invited to take part in a two-hour education seminar at 10 Downing Street, chaired by Margaret Thatcher and her Education Secretary, Sir Keith Joseph.[48]

In the end, it took a pincer movement conducted at local level to force Bradford Council into taking further, and ultimately decisive action. An important moment came with the Action Committee's decision to run an alternative school for Drummond pupils at the Pakistani Community Centre on the White Abbey Road—just down the street from Video Palace, specialists in Bollywood cinema. The school was attended by an estimated 250 pupils, who received lessons from twenty-five teachers from nearby schools on Arabic and Asian languages, African-Caribbean culture and "antiracist maths" that drew on examples such as salary discrepancies across the racial divide in apartheid South Africa. Free school meals were provided by local Pakistani restaurants.[49]

BLACK POWERS: 1980s BRADFORD

The initiative only lasted a week, but it built on the supplementary school movement that had earlier been developed by African-Caribbean communities in response to the findings by Bernard Coard on black children in "educationally-subnormal" schools. More importantly, though, the Committee's alternative school also capitalised on anxieties in the local authority about the status of education within Muslim communities. On the one hand, this was bound up with longstanding concerns about the Islamic supplementary schools that were commonly attached to mosques and, according to reports, often utilised outdated educational methods that included corporal punishment. On the other hand, even more significantly, by bypassing the local authority altogether the Committee's alternative school dramatised worries among council members that it would be unable to resist longstanding calls on the part of some campaigners for the establishment of mainstream, voluntary-aided Muslim schools in the city.[50]

The council's concessions over issues like halal meat and the RE curriculum was envisaged as a way of staving off Muslim schools and what was regarded, by implication, as the inevitable "destruction of a common education system". While the Action Committee's alternative school was not pitched as a "Muslim School", it stoked fears that Muslim communities might continue to act outside the reach of the council if their demands in education—including with respect to Honeyford—were not met. And the situation was made even more uncomfortable for the council by the Bradford Council for Mosques (BCM). The BCM had hitherto been a key ally for the local authority in its attempts to circumvent calls for Muslim schools. But as the scandal over Honeyford wore on, the BCM asserted its independence by not only backing the campaign against Honeyford, but also by positioning itself as a vocal critic of the rollout of the council's wider multicultural strategy.[51]

In September 1985 the BCM issued a statement describing Honeyford's reinstating as a "slap in the face" that represented severe setback to multicultural education in Bradford. It questioned whether the Council was actually serious about implementing its multicultural reforms and warned that "there is a limit to patience". By October, the BCM announced that it had lost confidence in the council. It withdrew from the Race Relations Advisory Group—also set up as part of the Metropolitan Council's *Turning Point* vision—and declared that, no matter the attempts to present him as the honourable victim of a McCarthyite witch-hunt, the reality was that Honeyford had "abused, insulted and degenerated the religion, culture, [and] countries of origin of Muslims and other minorities". If the issue was not resolved by the politicians imminently, the BCM declared it would be "left with no option but to ask our Muslim community and other communities to pursue all possible and peaceful means of action to ensure the removal of Mr Honeyford".[52]

By this point, the saga was finally reaching its climax. Following Honeyford's return to Drummond in time for the start of a new school year in September 1985, the Action Committee had taken to picketing the school gates on a daily basis. Dozens of parents refused to send their children to school, and instead camped out outside sporting badges with slogans like "Ray-cist", "I Hate Honeyford" and "Bradford is Not South Africa"; school children held aloft letters that spelled out "H-O-N-E-Y-F-O-R-D O-U-T". At times, the atmosphere turned nasty. By this point, Jenny Woodward was already receiving hate mail from supporters of Honeyford, as well as threatening phone calls. On the picket line, meanwhile, a banner appeared that read: "Honeyford writes in the blood of blacks". An Asian parent who supported Honeyford was physically attacked by protestors as he attempted to take his children across the picket line. A photographer for *The Yorkshire Post* was hit in the face.

BLACK POWERS: 1980s BRADFORD

Those pupils still attending school were given an Action Committee leaflet reminding them that Honeyford had insulted their religion and culture, and urging them not to be intimidated; "if he attempts to punish you", the leaflet read, "report it to your parents or someone from the Action Committee. We will prosecute him".[53]

Backed by the BCM, the 15 October was billed by the Committee as a "day of action". Parents of children at Drummond were urged not to send their children to school and instead to assemble at the picket line at 7:45am before marching on Bradford City Hall. That morning, more than 250 protestors congregated outside the school gates, ready for Honeyford's arrival. As his car pulled in, the chanting began—led by a thirteen-year-old boy—and Honeyford seemed to look less self-assured than usual; one onlooker even thought his face betrayed a hint of fear.

It was an unseasonably mild, dry autumnal day—perfect protest weather. By the time picketers began their march into town, there were more than 500 people present. They were accompanied by police on motorbikes, a swarm of journalists and an Asian boy shouting "Honeyford out" through a loudspeaker; children carried banners and climbed on railings, while a group of elderly Asian men with white beards and skullcaps followed behind. Less than one in five pupils attended Drummond that day, and the parents of some 4,400 Muslim pupils across Bradford heeded the BCM's call for solidarity with the campaign against Honeyford by also refusing to send their children to school. Yet still there was stasis. Then, two weeks after the "day of action", the Council was successful in its appeal against the High Court's initial decision that Honeyford should be allowed to return to his duties at Drummond. Finally, on 14 December, and after a long round of negotiations, Honeyford accepted a proposal by the council for him to take early retirement.

Honeyford's last day at Drummond would be 31 December 1985, and he would receive a lump sum of £70,900, as well as an annual pension of £6,500. The total value of the payoff was estimated to be more than £160,000. It was the most substantial settlement any teacher in Britain had ever received.[54]

In some ways, it is testament to the multicultural reforms introduced by Bradford Metropolitan Council in the early-1980s—which were the source of so much contention both locally and nationally, from Manningham to 10 Downing Street—that, by the time I started school in Birmingham a decade later, they had become part of the educational mainstream. There is no doubt that authorities across Britain had been at best ignorant, and at worst negligent when it came to addressing the situation faced by ethnic minority schoolchildren in the post-war decades. They were often forced into action by grassroots activism like Bernard Coard's exposure of the overrepresentation of black pupils in special-needs schools, or by the outbreak in the early-1980s of violence in the inner-areas of Britain's major cities. As one Bradford administrator admitted at the height of the Honeyford controversy, for more than twenty years there had been an assumption on the part of the council that it could "get away with letting sleeping Asians lie. Racism was a taboo subject. At the time of the 1981 riots in Toxteth, there was panic, fear, and ignorance in Bradford. No one knew what was going on".[55]

Although the Thatcher Government's sympathies were with Honeyford, in the year of his retirement the results of a Government-sponsored inquiry into the performance of ethnic-minority children at school—commissioned in 1979 in the last days of the Labour Government—were published, and effectively ratified the approach that had been set out in Bradford. The Swann Report called for the development of an "inclusive multiculturalism" in British schools, something that would enable all ethnic groups to "participate fully" in society. It argued that a "multicultural understanding" should be present in every element of a child's schooling, rather than being envisaged as something that could be tacked onto existing practices. It recommended that how effectively a given school was at combatting racism and developing its curriculum along "multiracial" lines be made a formal part of school inspections. All schools should be required to take practical steps to cater for children who did not speak English as a first language, and (echoing one of the recommendations made by Bernard Coard fifteen years earlier) there should be a concerted effort to recruit more teachers from ethnic minority backgrounds. Where there was demand from local communities, there should be the option for certain elements of the curriculum to be designated single-sex activities, the report suggested, and more should be done by schools to meet the needs of Muslim pupils specifically.[56]

When I think back to my own schooling in Birmingham, I'd be hard pushed to see it as having fully embraced this vision. Despite attending schools in one of the most ethnically-diverse cities in the country, and despite being in classes where at least half of pupils were ethnic minorities, our history curriculum rarely encompassed the experiences of black or Asian people, whether in Britain or around the world. There was an almost fetishised focus on the Nazis, and a one-dimensional examination of Britain's Industrial Revolution that was somehow completely divorced from the integral role slavery and colonial conquest played in western industrialisation—for example, with the mass production and exportation of sugar from the Caribbean that was the essential ingredient in the huge expansion of the Cadbury chocolate factory in south Birmingham. And as late as 2020 ethnocentricity in the school curricula remained an acute issue across the country. At this time, it was estimated that just eleven per cent of GCSE students in British history studied courses that focused on black people.[57]

In other ways, however, it is possible to see in my schooling the legacies of the battles that had earlier been fought with such intensity in Bradford. RE was never my thing—two avowedly atheist parents and a teacher who used to disappear each lesson for long cigarette breaks made it tough to get into—but our curriculum was structured around the belief-systems laid out in the Quran, the Torah and the Guru Granth Sahib, alongside the Bible. Even before RE classes began, though, I already knew about Eid and Diwali because friends took part in such festivals every year. I wouldn't say our English curriculum took "full account of the multiracial nature of society". It would have been nice, contrary to Honeyford's warnings about the implications of doing so, to have studied the dub-poetry of Linton Kwesi Johnson alongside the works of Shakespeare, rather than have to wait for my dad to give me a copy of *Bass Culture* (1980) as a birthday present in my late-teens. But we did look at the poetry of the Guyanese playwright John Agard, and spent a lot of time dissecting his performance, in patois, of his poem "Half Caste". It is only now that I am able to grasp the significance of looking at a poem like that—"explain yuself/wha u mean/when yu say half-caste"—fifty years on from Britain's wartime moral panic around "brown babies", in a room full of young people many of whom were themselves of mixed ethnicity.[58]

Those who mobilised against Honeyford in mid-1980s Bradford had arguably won the battle. Honeyford had not only gone, but the multicultural reforms that the protestors also saw themselves as defending had in the shape of the Swann Report been given state-sponsored approval. Yet it was always doubtful that the forces tapped into by Honeyford would simply accept defeat. They were dormant and, in keeping with the dialectical nature of the history of multicultural Britain, re-emerged powerfully in later years—at the same time that ethnic diversity was becoming more and more embedded in everyday life. In his retirement, for example, Honeyford helped establish the campaign group Majority Rights, which called on people to defend the British "national heritage" and advocated the abolition of the Commission for Racial Equality. The initiative had little impact, but the issues raised by the Honeyford saga re-emerged in Bradford spectacularly in January 1989 following the decision of a group of demonstrators—led by the Bradford Council for Mosques—to publicly burn a copy of Salman Rushdie's *The Satanic Verses* (1988) in protest against what they saw as the book's blasphemous depiction of the Prophet Mohammed. While the aim was to draw attention to what the protestors regarded as Britain's outdated blasphemy laws, the optics of a staged book-burning were never likely to draw sympathy. And in the predictable outcry that followed, many of the same arguments that had earlier been set out by Honeyford were revived.[59]

The former Labour MP and chat-show host Robert Kilroy-Silk, following on from Honeyford, Roger Scruton and others, derided the fact that ethnic minorities seemed to have been given a special status that had somehow placed them beyond scrutiny, with the net result that "British traditions, culture and laws have had to be amended to meet the needs of those with values and mores fashioned in less civilised times and places". Other commentators declared that "multiculturalism is dead" and made the contradictory argument that the Bradford protestors should be "made to respect and obey the rules of our generously tolerant Christian democracy". A generation later, in the context of concerns over false reports of an attempt by Islamic fundamentalists to take over the running of a school in Birmingham in the 2010s, Scruton himself was back summoning the ghost of the now-deceased Honeyford. He argued that it had become impossible to ignore Honeyford's earlier warnings, and questioned whether the primary loyalty of Muslims would ever be to a British identity rather than a religious one (the two categories were apparently mutually exclusive). Honeyford even crept into the years-long schisms over Brexit, and the familiar arguments made by Nigel Farage that immigration to Britain had long since gotten way out of control. In response to a typical tweet by Farage that "Government policy has totally failed to integrate people into our society", one user responded: "didn't poor Ray Honeyford warn about this in 1984? Was dismissed as a racist and lost his job—the creed of multiculturalism needs to end".[60]

While the protestors against Honeyford had won the battle, then, it is hard to avoid the impression of an ongoing war in which the arguments fashioned and re-fashioned by Powell, Honeyford, Scruton, Farage and many others continue to resonate. In relation to Bradford and Manningham specifically, when Hanif Kureishi visited the area in the aftermath of the Honeyford Affair, he found it to be an overwhelmingly political place. He was accosted in pubs and accused of being a reactionary, and wherever he went in the city there was talk of spies and police informants; to Kureishi's mind, the only place that came close to matching the intensity of politics in Bradford was Karachi in Pakistan.[61]

On my last day in Bradford, I went to visit what had once been Drummond Middle School but, following a series of major educational reforms in the 2000s and 2010s, was now called Iqra Academy. The school is not a state-funded faith school of the kind that the Bradford authorities were keen to prevent in the 1980s, and which the New Labour Government actively encouraged from the late-1990s onwards. But nevertheless, it was not hard to imagine what Honeyford himself would have made of his old school having been renamed after the Arabic word for "read".[62]

On my way to Iqra I passed discount furniture outlets, a shop "specialising" in Turkish, Iranian, Pakistani and English foodstuffs and, just around the corner from the school, a unisex tailors called Kashmir. Iqra was up a steep hill. By the time I arrived, the t-shirt beneath my backpack was damp with sweat.

BLACK POWERS: 1980s BRADFORD

The school had a newly-built, wood-panelled annexe next to the original Victorian building; the latter still had "Drummond Road Board School" carved into the sandstone in imposing capital letters. In the park opposite some kids were playing football; a little further down, in among Manningham's terraced houses, there was a halal butchers and Bismilla Banqueting Hall, one of the many venues to have been established in the area to cater for the demand for large Muslim weddings.

As I made my way back down the White Abbey Road, I could hear some fireworks being prematurely set off. It was almost *Eid al-Adha* (Feast of Sacrifice). As I walked, I couldn't help feeling a twinge of disappointment that in researching this chapter I had followed Kureishi, Dervla Murphy and other visiting writers towards Bradford's stifling political divisions over the issue of multiculturalism—something that has arguably become a central flashpoint in a much wider culture war that, much like the political climate in the United States, continues to play out in Britain. The intensity of the battles in 1980s Bradford seemed to leave little room for an exploration of the kind of organic, ambiguous street-level multiculturalism that I have focused on elsewhere in this book—the "actually existing multiculturalism" that, whatever one's political views, has indisputably become a central part of Britain's social and cultural fabric.[63]

As Kureishi recognised, it was not hard to see where the force of Bradford's politics came from. The nature of the socio-economic disadvantage that has affected ethnic minority communities in the city is difficult to overstate. In the year that Honeyford was appointed at Drummond, for example, three-quarters of Asian school-leavers had been without a job for at least twelve months. At the peak of the scandal at Drummond Middle School, 60 per cent of all Asian households were officially classified as overcrowded, and Manningham had the highest infant mortality rate in the county. By 1991, with the full impact of deindustrialisation on the city having become apparent, the Asian unemployment rate as a whole had reached 30 per cent—more than three times the rate for white communities. 58 per cent of houses in Manningham still had no central heating, and the issue of overcrowding persisted well into the 1990s. The numbers of recorded racist incidents had mushroomed rather than receded in Bradford in the post-Honeyford climate. In July 2001, fuelled by the ongoing problem of socio-economic inequality, racial discrimination and the re-emergence of the far-right, Bradford erupted into two nights of major rioting. It was the worst unrest seen in Britain for more than fifteen years.[64]

My trip to Yorkshire was a reminder that, whether it takes the form of a dance organised to pay tribute to a mixed-race rugby player in 1940s Cardiff, a black man talking to white woman in a pub in 1950s Nottingham, the assertive presence of establishments like the Pyar Ka Sagar in 1960s Birmingham, or the protests that were organised against a racist head-teacher in 1980s Bradford, there is nearly always a political dimension to the story of how Britain became multicultural. I wanted to try to tease out the nature of this politics and its relationship to everyday life at the turn of the twentieth century—more than fifty years on from the docking of the *Windrush* at Tilbury Docks, the imaginary starting point in Britain's slow, uneven but undeniable drift towards the multicultural. In order to do that I had to return to a city I knew much more intimately; I was going back to the Birmingham of my youth.

5

WHITE FLIGHTS

1990s BALSALL HEATH

By the start of the 1990s, I had two routes to school. My parents had separated, though they hadn't moved far from one another. To begin with, my father stayed on in Newton Road in the house where my brother and I had spent the first years of our lives; my mother moved to a place just a few streets away on Adria Road. This meant that the journey we made to school each day was similar no matter in whose house we were staying. We would head along Stoney Lane, past the halal butchers outside of which you would often see giant meat carcasses being unloaded from the back of a van. We'd pass Milan's Sweet Centre, which was established in the mid-1970s by Dhiren Patel, who had moved to Britain from the former British colony of Kenya before the introduction of the 1968 Commonwealth Immigrants Act, the legislation designed to prevent Kenyan Asians like Patel—almost all of whom were British passport holders—from entering the country. We would cross the Ladypool Road, barely a mile away from the epicentre of Balsall Heath's still prominent sex industry, and pass the balti restaurants out of which, on any given Friday or

Saturday evening, the smell of fresh coriander, cardamom, clove, nutmeg and *hari mirch* (green chillies) would emanate. At the end of the day, if we were heading back to Mum's house, we would often walk home with my friend Sufyaan, his younger brother Eshan and their mother Shameem, who lived at the bottom of our street. Later on, Shameem would sometimes send Sufyaan up to give us a batch of freshly made pakoras.[1]

It is only a two-mile walk from Balsall Heath to Birmingham city centre; on the bus, the journey barely takes fifteen minutes. But in the 1990s the topographical contrast between the two areas was vast—and widening, thanks to the city council's decision to respond to the damage wreaked by deindustrialisation (370,000 manufacturing jobs were lost in the city between 1965 and 1981) by embracing a service-based economy and, by selling off land to the private sector, establishing the city centre as a capital of retail and leisure. What this meant in practice was the erection of upscale architectural projects like the International Convention Centre (which opened just off Broad Street in 1991), the futuristic Hyatt Hotel (which opened in the same year, replete with an airborne walkway into the Convention Centre opposite), as well as the wholesale redevelopment of Birmingham's central canal area into a pseudo-public "festival marketplace" consisting of offices blocks, restaurants, bars, and a seawater aquarium.[2]

Such buildings stood as shiny monuments to the council's imagined future for the city as a "meeting place of Europe"—a place that, according to the council's marketing tagline, "more than meets the eye". In 1991, the council moved an estimated £64 million out of its education budget to help cover the cost of loans the city had taken out to pay for projects like the Convention Centre. The capital expenditure the council allocated to the Convention Centre and related projects between 1987 and 1991 was more than three times the amount it had allocated to school buildings in the same period. In Balsall Heath, mean-

WHITE FLIGHTS: 1990s BALSALL HEATH

while, pupils at my school on Clifton Road were regularly sent home due to problems with the heating, and we were often taught in temporary, prefabricated huts in the corner of the playground. As the foundations were being laid for the Convention Centre and the Hyatt, in Balsall Heath the proportion of households that still lacked the exclusive use of a bath or toilet, with residents forced to share such facilities with other households, was eleven times the rate in affluent (and predominately white) districts like Four Oaks in the north of the city. Balsall Heath was estimated to be in the fifteen per cent most deprived neighbourhoods in Britain. The local authorities hoped that the gap that had been left behind by the collapse of Birmingham's once-dominant motor industry, which had been a key employer of black and Asian labour but which had seen 40 per cent of jobs lost by the start of the 1990s, would be filled with jobs cleaning hotels, waiting on upmarket tables and selling tourists tickets to the new aquarium. But in 1992, just eight per cent of jobs at the new Convention Centre had been filled by people from ethnic minority backgrounds. The arrival of a "festival marketplace" had not solved the longstanding problem of joblessness in Balsall Heath. In 1994, unemployment in the area stood at 37 per cent, the highest rate in the city and one which, at various points throughout the 1990s, included my own father.[3]

There are two key events that took place just months apart in Balsall Heath that allow us to dramatise how the dialectics of multiculturalism played out in Britain at the tail-end of the twentieth century. The first is the July 1994 campaign to remove the area's longstanding sex industry. This had similarities to the earlier protests against Ray Honeyford in Bradford and was in part the result of the increased centrality of organised religion and family structures within Balsall Heath's South Asian community, which now constituted three-quarters of the local population. For months, Muslim residents in particular took to picketing the key areas of solicitation around the terraced houses of Cheddar Road, just off Clevedon Road. Between 10am and 4am they congregated on street corners and recorded the number plates of passing vehicles to try to force prostitution out of the neighbourhood. The campaign was attempting to drive out local sex workers, a section of the Balsall Heath population that remained mostly white. It was therefore part of a broader demographic shift that witnessed the number of local white residents shrinking from three in four in the late-1960s to two in ten by the start of the 1990s—the very kind of transformation that was grist to the mill for those politicians who continued to subscribe to Enoch Powell's dystopian vision of Britain's multicultural future. Yet the media portrayal of the Balsall Heath campaign was initially favourable—even in the same right-wing newspapers that, in other contexts, were doing their best to maintain the Powellian brand of British nationalism as a central feature of the political landscape.[4]

The second key event is the release in September 1994 of *Bollywood Flashback*, a landmark album of bhangra-infused remixes by the DJ and producer Bally Sagoo. Sagoo was born in India, moved to Britain as a baby, grew up in Balsall Heath and went to the school I would later attend on Clifton Road. His music mixed the kind of Punjabi bhangra that provided the soundtrack to the classic Indian movies of the 1970s and 80s with the reggae, funk and hip-hop that was heard in Birmingham's party and club scenes. It was thus indicative of the extent to which inner-city neighbourhoods like Balsall Heath had, as result of Britain's decades long drift towards the multicultural, become pluralistic sites of artistic and especially musical creativity. *Bollywood Flashback* made Sagoo the first Indian-born artist to be playlisted on Radio One.[5]

Sagoo's commercial success was part of a broader shift in 1990s Britain, where ethnic diversity was belatedly becoming more vis-

WHITE FLIGHTS: 1990s BALSALL HEATH

ible in mainstream cultural life. But the music that was emanating from Britain's increasingly syncretic inner cities had a particular ability to penetrate the cultural mainstream. This was signposted by the success of "Two-Tone" acts like UB40, the reggae band whose ethnically-diverse members grew up in Balsall Heath and who had major hits across the 1980s and 90s. Of course, the commercial success of such acts did little to alleviate the effects of institutional racism and economic inequality on the lives of those who lived in such areas. But their success showed that, by the 1990s, ethnic diversity was becoming unexpectedly fashionable; it was in the process of becoming an increasingly uncontentious feature of social and cultural life.[6]

As the 1990s wore on a string of leading politicians began to take an interest in what was happening in Balsall Heath. This was prompted not by the popularity of Sagoo and UB40, however, but by the ability of those Asian leaders of the campaign against prostitution to declare victory in their battle against the sex industry (no one mentioned the inconvenient fact that Balsall Heath's sex industry had expanded thirty years earlier partly due to the presence of large numbers of single Asian men). Politicians who visited the neighbourhood included the Conservative Secretary for Employment Michael Portillo, the leader of the Liberal Democrats Paddy Ashdown and, in 2001, the newly-installed Labour Home Secretary David Blunkett. By this time, the story of how Balsall Heath had been "cleaned up" by local residents had come to occupy a near-mythical status in New Labour circles. But Blunkett had arrived in Balsall Heath with a message for other inner-city areas elsewhere in the country—places he regarded as being much more problematic. Despite the evidence of Britain's drift towards the multicultural—in the streets around Blunkett in Balsall Heath, in similar inner-city areas elsewhere in the country and increasingly also in popular culture—there were too many neighbourhoods that in Blunkett's view were characterised by an absence of "shared values" and "community cohesion". In 2002 he embraced the language of Powellism by lamenting his impression that there were too many schools in Britain that were being "swamped" by immigrants. Balsall Heath had become caught in the crosshairs of a nationwide panic about the supposed presence of racially segregated communities along American lines and a growing concern that, as one commentator put it, "white flight is here too".[7]

Welcome to the oscillating story of 1990s Balsall Heath. A community campaign consisting of mostly Muslim residents to remove prostitution from the neighbourhood was widely praised in the media and feted by politicians—despite the fact the campaign was responsible for driving out a predominately white section of the population. Meanwhile the ethnic diversity that was by now a defining feature of inner-city life was increasingly influencing Britain's cultural mainstream, even as inner-city neighbourhoods remained topographically and economically cut-off from more prosperous parts of the country. In the context of the subsequent "War on Terror", and with heightened concerns about Islamist terrorism across Europe, Balsall Heath began to be used by politicians as a means of railing against other parts of Britain that were understood to be lacking in cohesiveness. The community cohesion agenda increasingly stressed the need for adherence to and respect for a top-down definition of "Britishness", even as artists like Sagoo were testament to the presence of an alternative reality rooted in the heterogenous cultures and evolving traditions of places like Balsall Heath. 1990s Balsall Heath is a reminder that the making of multicultural Britain cannot be thought about as something that has progressed in linear fashion. Instead, it continues to be an inconveniently messy, unpredictable thing born out of collisions between a complex, often contradictory set of processes.[8]

WHITE FLIGHTS: 1990s BALSALL HEATH

The "Cleansing" of Balsall Heath

On a warm day in July 1994, Raja Amin, a smartly dressed British Rail employee and former policeman in his mid-30s, made his way to join a picket line that had sprung up not far from his house near Balsall Heath's red-light district. It was unusually hot. Earlier in the summer temperatures in England had reached their highest levels for five years, and the city council had introduced a temporary hosepipe ban. When Amin arrived at the picket on Cheddar Road, most of his fellow protestors were in short sleeves. The younger men wore baggy trousers and flip-flops, while older protestors had white beards, carried walking sticks and wore skullcaps and *kurtas*. The men sat around on empty milk crates, playing cards and drinking tea, all the while keeping an eye on the traffic around them. Next to them was a placard with a slogan painted in bold capital letters: "KERB CRAWLERS BEWARE: THE WIFE WILL FIND OUT". By the end of the month, protestors at dozens of pickets across the neighbourhood claimed to have logged the registrations of some 5,000 cars, and were threatening to leak this information to the press.[9]

Over the years there had been various attempts to move prostitution out of Balsall Heath. In July 1967 two Labour councillors suggested that the issue could be solved by the introduction of legalised, municipal-run brothels in a less residential part of the city. The solution town planners offered at the end of the decade was to turn the previous epicentre of the sex industry, Varna Road, into two separate cul-de-sacs in the hope this might prevent the return of kerb crawlers (predictably, the industry just moved onto adjacent streets). In the mid-1980s, the St Paul's community group—which had been established in 1971 by Dick Atkinson, a former sociology lecturer, contemporary of Stuart Hall's at Birmingham University and key player in the 1968 student protest movement—turned its attentions to prostitution. In April 1984, the group declared that it had had enough of the damage being done to Balsall Heath by sex work; the time had come for it to be permanently removed. In its magazine, *The Balsall Heathen*, St Paul's published a series of covertly taken photographs of women dressed in negligees under fur coats, standing on the kerb-crawlers' route between Belgrave Road and Woodbridge Road. "How would you like your daughter to have to walk to and from school past that little lot?", one resident was quoted as asking, next to a photograph of two women leaning on a street sign, smoking cigarettes. The focus was on the effect the sex industry was having on residents—the noise at night, the traffic and the condoms and needles that could often be found in gardens and stairwells. The accompanying focus on the decline of a once-respectable community, and the purported inability of residents to sell up and move out, was an echo of the way Balsall Heath had often been portrayed in the media in the late-1960s, when Enoch Powell was also weaving such sentiment into his anti-immigrant platform. It was also a precursor to the later popularity in Britain of television programmes such as "Neighbours from Hell", the focus of which was the supposed damage caused to communities by those who were positioned as being undesirable and illegitimate members of a particular locale. In *The Balsall Heathen*, the views of the women who had been surreptitiously photographed were conspicuously absent.[10]

The detrimental effect the sex industry had on some residents was real. One woman, a white mother of three who was interviewed in the early-1980s, explained that she couldn't bear living in Balsall Heath because whenever her husband was away her Asian neighbours would accuse her of being a prostitute. The trigger for the 1994 campaign, meanwhile, for which Raja Amin quickly emerged as a key spokesperson, was reportedly the site of a woman soliciting close by to the mosque on Willows

WHITE FLIGHTS: 1990s BALSALL HEATH

Crescent, half a mile south from Cheddar Road (and a five minute walk from where, fifty years earlier, one of Birmingham's earliest mosques was established on Edward Road). Zulfiqar Ali, the 43-year-old proprietor of a nearby shop, claimed to regularly see prostitutes and their clients doing business in the cars that were parked nearby his home. But it was the apparent encroachment of the sex industry onto a site of religious worship that provided the impetus for action. As a young man the fashion designer Osman Yousefzada—whose parents came from Pakistan and Afghanistan and who grew up in Balsall Heath in the 1980s and 90s—remembered the imam at his mosque on Edward Road imploring worshippers to gain *sawab* (spiritual reward) by driving the prostitutes and the kerb crawlers out. For Amin, meanwhile, those who worked in the sex industry had brought shame on Balsall Heath; now, the time had come to "bring shame on them".[11]

In contrast to the media coverage of Balsall Heath in the 1960s, where the newly arrived presence of an ethnically-diverse population was portrayed as the primary reason for the area's descent into urban decay and sexual impropriety, Amin and his fellow protestors were generally positioned by the press as respectable citizens who had been moved to attempt to rescue their community from the consequences of criminality and moral waywardness. To a degree, this was because the tactics deployed by the Balsall Heath picketers, while extreme, were also familiar to millions of would-be community watchers across the country. The Neighbourhood Watch initiative had emerged in Britain in the early-1980s, for example, and encouraged residents to survey their neighbours and passers-by with the idea that they would act as the police's "eyes and ears"; by the mid-1990s, the scheme was in use in 130,000 neighbourhoods, and a national hotline had been established that allowed people to anonymously report potential crimes to the police. In Balsall Heath, newspapers often communicated the perceived respectability of the picketers by juxtaposing images of semi-nude sex workers with representations of the local Asian community that evoked a sense of traditional, family-orientated decency: a white, middle-aged sex worker was shown sitting in the window of a house on Chedder Road, for instance, her right nipple pointing in the direction of Calthorpe Park, where a Muslim woman in a chador was pushing a pram; elsewhere, another white woman was pictured on the same street, again framed by a windowsill and wearing nothing but underwear while outside two Asian girls could be seen skipping along the pavement in floral dresses.[12]

The image of respectability was one that Amin was himself keen to project. He and his fellow protestors were not vigilantes, he emphasised in one interview: they were simply "respectable citizens standing on our street". What gave the campaign further credibility in the eyes of some was that, although its makeup was dominated by Muslim and other South Asian residents (and was thus in keeping with the broader demographics of 1990s Balsall Heath), it also had the support of white figures. This included Dick Atkinson, who through his work with St Paul's had made a name for himself as a formidable player in local politics and acted as the campaign's *de facto* secretary, John Ward, a former vicar of St Ambrose's Church in neighbouring Edgbaston, as well as the Irish owner of a corner shop, Rita, a local retiree, and her friend Kathy, who reportedly attended the picket line every night. This again was meant to stand in contrast to the alleged behaviour of sex workers, some of whom were reported to have called on the NF for assistance. "Dirty Paki bastards", a journalist overheard one woman scream at the picket line. "Go home and clean up your own country!"[13]

There was defiance on the part of those sex workers who were willing to speak to the media. As one woman put it, "we are not cattle". To her mind, what was required was the full legalisation of prostitution so that she would be able work undisturbed in a nice building somewhere in town, a bit like an office block. For sex workers, the threat of violence was acute. Just six months earlier, for example, a twenty-year-old sex worker of Indian origin had been found strangled to death in Leicestershire having last been seen getting into a car in Balsall Heath. By May 1994 four prostitutes had been murdered in the Midlands within a six month period. And although it wasn't always immediately apparent, the campaign to "clean up" Balsall Heath did have a dangerous underbelly. This was particularly the case at night, when the older men with white beards and walking sticks who generally manned the picket lines by day were replaced by younger participants who were seemingly much more willing to move from protest to direct action. This shift was often signalled by a change in the tone of the slogans that were held aloft on picket lines, from semi-ironic proclamations that targeted male kerb crawlers to overt threats against women: from "THE WIFE WILL FIND OUT" to "YOU'RE DEAD, PROSTITUTE".[14]

At evenings during the campaign, young men cruised around Balsall Heath in vans and co-ordinated foot-patrols via prototype mobile phones in an attempt to harass women off the streets. According to some estimates, these patrols could consist of more than 500 Asian men at a time, some of whom had apparently come from other parts of the city and were armed with baseball bats and hockey sticks and accompanied by rottweiler dogs. Notes were posted through the letterboxes of women who were suspected of running brothels, threatening that they would be "burnt out" if they did not sell up quickly. One woman, a 44-year-old sex worker who had been operating in Balsall Heath for six years, told how she had been set upon on her way back from the chip shop and ordered to "clear out". A 26-year old woman who also worked in the area was almost dragged from the street into a car by a group of protestors. "I have never been so scared", she told the press. "The people who live here moved into the area because it's cheap housing. They knew damn well it was a red light area, so why are they up in arms?"[15]

It is hard not to be reminded of the actions of those white Teddy Boys in Nottingham in summer 1958, thousands of whom roamed the streets of St Ann's using broken bottles, knives and razors as weapons with the intention of "getting at the blacks". The Teddy Boys involved in the Nottingham unrest were clear that they wanted their black neighbours to "go back to their own country"; for the mostly Asian protestors in the 1990s, it was about permanently expelling the proponents of the sex industry from the neighbourhood. And although Amin and other protestors were careful to insist that their primary targets were male pimps and kerb crawlers, it was perhaps inevitable that women faced the worst of the campaign.

Women were the most visible symbols of the sex industry and were often the most vulnerable actors within it. And it was not only sex workers who found themselves targeted by the protests. As the campaign wore on there were also instances of other women being attacked. One mother of five reflected that she got on well with most sex workers and generally felt comfortable around them. They would greet her with a "hello, chuck" and ask how she was doing. But once the street patrols began the same woman now felt as though she couldn't go out at night. A support group for sex workers that was run by local nuns was verbally abused and physically prevented from doing its work. Glady Halwell, who lived around the corner from Cheddar Road, recalled having a party on a Saturday night with a few girlfriends in the first weeks of the campaign. "We were a bit pissed and wearing grass skirts"; they were about to head into town for a night out. But as Halwell made her way through Balsall Heath she was confronted by a group of protestors who screamed at her to "Go home, slut". Halwell had lived in Balsall Heath for thirty

WHITE FLIGHTS: 1990s BALSALL HEATH

years without ever encountering such problems. Did they really think, Halwell wondered, that just because she had had a few drinks that gave them license to shout at her?[16]

As there had been in the late-1960s, when Janet Mendelsohn was photographing residents of Balsall Heath's red-light district, the scene in 1994 was characterised by contradictions the implications of which were not always immediately obvious. So while many journalists fixated on the notion that some women had apparently enlisted the NF to fight back against the protestors, no one seemed to recognise the significance of the fact that, while most of the women working in the area were white, almost all of them had black or Asian partners or had daily interactions with clients from a wide range of backgrounds. Similarly, one of the most common methods of solicitation in the early-1990s (as it had been thirty years earlier on Varna Road) was through the windows of the terraced houses that lined Cheddar Road and the surrounding streets. But most of the women working in this way did not own or even occupy these houses on a full-time basis. Rather, they rented out rooms on particular days from local landlords. In the 1960s and 70s, in the face of widespread discrimination from mortgage brokers, many Asian immigrants borrowed money from contacts in the Indian sub-continent to purchase houses in inner-city neighbourhoods, generally the only parts of town where they could afford to buy. They often repaid the loan by sub-letting rooms out, and in Balsall Heath a significant market for such rooms was local sex workers and their pimps. This was a mutually beneficial relationship that continued throughout the 1980s and into the early-1990s. Finally, there was also the persistent rumour that some of the men involved in the campaign against prostitution—including some of its leading spokespeople—were also clients of the same sex workers they were ostensibly so keen to see driven out. During an interview with a journalist, for instance, one woman noticed an Asian man in a turban, carrying a sofa towards the picket line. She broke off her conversation to shout at the man. "You're not going up there to sit with your mates, are you?" the woman yelled across the street. "You hypocrite. You were with me on Monday".[17]

One sex worker was moved to make a hyperbolic comparison between what was happening in Balsall Heath and the ethnic cleansing that was taking place in the former Yugoslavia. But among right-wing commentators, and especially when the Balsall Heath campaign was beginning to show signs of success, the optics of a British Muslim group taking action to defend the moral sanctity of a community were simply too rich with irony to allow room for any complicating factors. "In a suburb of middle England, decent citizens who have had enough of the vice blighting their streets have decided to fight back", a journalist for the *Daily Mail* proclaimed, before hitting readers with the kicker: "the people taking this moral stand are the local Asians, while the prostitutes are mostly white". The journalist explained that men like the shopkeeper Zulfiqar Ali were still prepared to teach their children about shame, unlike white parents in their "host" nation (it was unclear who the journalist thought Britain was "hosting", given many of the younger protestors were born in Britain and their parents and grandparents were British passport holders who had resided in Britain for decades). It was a "reversal of history", the journalist claimed, but nevertheless a lesson the rest of the country would do well to learn. A similar line was taken by the journalist Melanie Phillips, who was in the midst of a political journey that in 2019 would lead her to deride Islamophobia as something that had been bogusly "invented". Why, Phillips asked her readers, were there so few white people on Balsall Heath's pickets? The answer, she suggested, was that white people had been overly-conditioned by "social liberalism", which meant they had been hoodwinked into thinking sex workers had the right not to be deprived of their livelihoods. What was admirable about the Muslims who manned the Balsall Heath picket lines was that they were *not* liberal. They were outraged by the "depravity" around them and were not prepared to accept it. If what was going on in Balsall Heath was any kind of signpost, Phillips concluded, it was one that was pointing in a healthier direction for Britain.[18]

In other areas of the country, in this period, there was a growing moral panic over the activities of "Asian gangs", who were often portrayed by the media in ways that recalled the stereotypes around young black men during the inner-city riots of 1981 and 1985—particularly in the aftermath of the 1989 protests against the publication of Salman Rushdie's *The Satanic Verses*. In Balsall Heath, however, any lingering doubts about the activities of the protestors had been overridden by what most commentators agreed was the stunning success of the campaign. Raja Amin (who reportedly had ambitions to become Birmingham's first Asian MP) announced victory the previous year when he painted a picture of a neighbourhood where, as a result of his campaign, people could now take their dogs for walks, children could play on swings and women could go about their everyday lives without being propositioned. "Decent people" had come out again, Amin proclaimed, adopting the language of the *Daily Mail*; "for the first time in years they feel safe". By 1995, the statistics backed Amin up.[19]

In the space of a year, prostitution had been all but eradicated in Balsall Heath. In the early 1990s, it was estimated that half of the houses on Cheddar Road were being used for prostitution, and there were as many as 450 women working as sex workers in Balsall Heath. By 1995, the number of sex workers had shrunk to five, while kerb crawling had gone down by eighty per cent. Crime more generally had also been reduced. According to analysts, burglary in the area had dropped by 23 per cent, violent crime by 20 per cent, and criminal damage by 18 per cent. The campaign had achieved what thousands of pounds worth of traditional policing had been unable to do. Cast in this light, any initial reservations on the part of the authorities quickly subsided.

In September 1995, eighty members of the original campaign against prostitution were enrolled in a Government backed scheme called "Streetwatch". They were vetted and trained by Home Office officials and given formal responsibilities for tackling crime in the area. Plans were put in place for the "Balsall Heath model" to be rolled out across the country, including Bradford. In Balsall Heath, in an effort to ensure that the gains made by the campaign were not lost, a £200,000 CCTV network was to be installed in the area, strategically placed around Cheddar Road and other streets that previously made up the

Figure 32: Balsall Heath, c. mid-1990s. Photograph by Birmingham Mail, © Trinity Mirror.

red-light district. As politicians began to take notice of what had happened in Balsall Heath, little thought seemed to be given to the fortunes of those women who had hitherto been able to work in the sex industry—the initial growth of which was aided by the presence in Balsall Heath of large numbers of single immigrant men. But in March 1996 a small hut was installed in the area to give street watchers some respite from the cold nights. Outside the hut was a banner with a slogan that read: "every move you make, every step you take, we'll be watching you".[20]

The sounds of the inner city

With its mix of sex, allegations of violence and the idea that, in the excitable narrative of some reporters, the involvement of Muslim activists had somehow turned Britain's established moral order on its head, the campaign against prostitution was prime journalistic copy. But what is strange about this episode is how much it was out of sync with other elements of 1990s Balsall Heath—what we might call, following the literary critic Raymond Williams, its "structures of feeling". It was clear by the mid-1990s that, if measured on its own terms, the campaign had been a success. But in other ways, Balsall Heath had been anything but "cleansed". What often characterised its structures of feeling—what Williams defined as "impulses, restraints and tones", the raw stuff of everyday life—was the messy confluence of cultures that had, by the 1990s, been a developing feature of life in the area for more than thirty years.[21]

As we have seen throughout this book, the increasing diversity of modern Britain was often signposted in the first instance by changes to the geographic landscape. By the 1990s the Kashmir and the Pyar Ka Sagar cafés on Clevedon Road—photographed by Janet Mendelsohn in the late-1960s—were long gone. But the Shereen Kadah was still open on Moseley Road, and had been joined opposite by Zaff's "halal diner", purveyors of Tandoori dishes, Southern Fried Chicken and "Taste Max Pizzas". A golden-domed mosque had opened on Clifton Road (one of the few Shia mosques in the city), not far from World of Fabric on Ladypool Road (specialists in *lehenga* wedding dresses) and the Nelson Mandela primary school on Colville Road, which had been opened by Archbishop Desmond Tutu in April 1988 and visited by Mandela himself in October 1993. These landmarks were mirrors that reflected what was going on around them. It was in social and increasingly cultural life that, for young people especially, the hybridised nature of Balsall Heath often revealed itself most fully.[22]

In the late-1980s, Simon Jones, a sociologist and one-time student at Stuart Hall's Centre for Contemporary Cultural Studies, described the scene around him as he made his way to a youth club on Balsall Heath Road on a gloomy December evening. As he passed by the council houses that had eventually replaced Balsall Heath's slum housing, Jones could just about make out the sound of reggae music emanating from a side-street further up the road. He turned the corner and bumped into two Asian boys carrying a boombox. They were blasting out "Police Officer" by Smiley Culture, the reggae MC born in London to a Jamaican father and Guyanese mother who in 1984 made his name with "Cockney Translation", a song which moved between cockney rhyming slang and Jamaican patois to translate the former to an imagined Jamaican audience. The Asian boys were accompanied by a white girl singing along to "Police Officer", Smiley's follow up single that satirised the issue of the police harassment of black youth and had been a feature on the UK Top 40 for thirteen successive weeks. Inside the youth club, Jones observed it was mostly Asian, black, mixed race and white boys present, decked out in the adolescent style of the day: Gabicci tops or ski jumpers, baseball caps, baggy trousers and

WHITE FLIGHTS: 1990s BALSALL HEATH

moccasin shoes. The sound system in the corner was being operated by two older, dreadlocked Rastafarians. Jones watched a white boy playfully steal a pair of glasses off the face of his black friend. He perched them on his nose, goading his friend by skanking along to the music; eventually, the matter was settled by a friendly wrestling match on the floor.[23]

At our school on Clifton Road, a particular way of speaking had emerged from this milieu, a kind of multicultural slang or "remixed English" that fused Punjabi exclamations and insults such as *teri maa di* ("your mother's...") and *kutti* (bitch) with snippets of Jamaican patois like "slack", "wicked", "dutty", "whagwan" and "laters", the currency of which was ensured by the ongoing influence of reggae music. Racism remained a feature of this setting, not least on the part of the white teachers who continued to dominate Britain's schools. At a school in nearby Edgbaston, for example, one teacher declared that wherever there was a large influx of people of a "different culture" coming into a community, it was inevitable that sections of the white population would be prepared to act on their "antagonistic feelings" (this was almost the exact language Margaret Thatcher chose to deploy in 1978 when, as leader of the Conservative Party, she sought to reach out to voters apparently gravitating towards the NF by sympathising with those who felt "swamped" by immigrants and were understandably "rather hostile" towards people with a "different culture"). Yet for Simon Jones, among the young people he encountered in Birmingham (if not their teachers) what was most noticeable was how white children in largely black and Asian areas looked for interactive strategies, ways of trying to become accepted in ethnically diverse friendship circles or emphasising an affinity towards black culture more generally. One such strategy was dance and the practising of styles like skanking at home, in preparation for the next disco. But for Jones, it was multicultural slang that was the approach most commonly adopted by young people in everyday Balsall Heath life.[24]

For Jo-Jo, one of Jones' Balsall Heath-based interviewees, there were "no racial fuckries round this way". Jo-Jo had been brought up by his Irish father and Scottish mother on Durham Road—the next street down from what had been my family's house on Newton Road—and he positioned his use of patois in relation to what he saw as his identity as a "black boy/white boy" who was also regularly cared for by a black neighbour and had mixed with black friends from a young age. At school, friends would regale Jo-Jo with stories about their parents' homes in Spanish Town, Trenchtown or Montego Bay; "I mean, it's like, I never met many English people, you know what I mean?" Some white teenagers explained that they used multicultural slang because they saw it as a more appropriate way of communicating in the inner city. If you were to use a thick Brummie accent, one white teenager reflected, people might think, "Oh God, what's this guy?" My cod-Punjabi was mostly just a reliable way of making my friends laugh. But as Jones observed, there were rules to be followed. The use of multicultural slang by white people was a recognition of difference as well as a means of expressing cultural affinity. As a result, it was not something that could necessarily be used by white people around black or Asian strangers, when there could be a danger of it being taken the wrong way. But it was widely employed at school jokingly, or as a symbol of disobedience, particularly when talking back to teachers. It was an organic idiom that functioned most effectively in the inner-city environment from which it emerged. Words like "slack" and "extra" just came out of you, another of Jones' white interviewees declared, simply because they were so common. "If they're our friends, we teach them", an Asian teenager explained regarding his willingness to teach white or black people Punjabi; "it's impressive, ain't it, if they learn it...if they can talk it right, they're obviously interested in us".[25]

WHITE FLIGHTS: 1990s BALSALL HEATH

If there was a soundtrack to the emergence of multicultural slang in Britain, it was embodied by bands like the Specials and the Selecter, Coventry-based Two-Tone groups that in the early-1980s developed a distinctive fusion of Jamaican ska and British post-punk, and UB40. The context was not just the global popularity of Jamaican reggae, and Bob Marley above all else. By this time a growing number of black British bands had also become a fixture of the British reggae scene, including Steel Pulse, who formed in the same year as UB40 in the Handsworth district of Birmingham.[26]

If Steel Pulse marked the moment when the Rastafarian ethos of Jamaican reggae began to be applied to the experiences of a black British generation, UB40 were further evidence of the cross-cultural appeal reggae had. The band's founding members included Terance Wilson (AKA Astro), the group's percussionist and occasional toaster whose parents came from Jamaica; the trombonist Norman Hassan, who was of Welsh-Yemeni descent; and the brothers Robin and Ali Campbell, who would provide guitar and vocals for the band's biggest hits and whose father was the Scottish folk singer Ian Campbell. The massive commercial success of UB40 throughout the 1980s and 90s—their 1993 album *Promises and Lies*, for example, which also contributed to the soundtrack for the Hollywood movie *Sliver*, sold nine million copies—has certainly been detrimental to the group's credibility. Yet the band's early work is in its own way just as political as Steel Pulse's Rasta-infused oeuvre. Both the band and their 1980 album, *Signing Off*, are named after the bureaucracies involved in attempting to access unemployment benefit. But the group tend to be dismissed as a covers band, thanks largely to the popularity of their 1983 cover of Tony Tribe's version of "Red Red Wine", which ensured the song was destined to be sung by legions of drunk white people at weddings for years to come. The visibility of the Campbell brothers in the band's publicity has also meant that UB40 have often been seen as part of the long history of white acts achieving major commercial success by sanitising and commodifying black music. For the Birmingham-born poet Benjamin Zephaniah, for example, who cut his teeth toasting on reggae sound systems alongside Steel Pulse in 1970s Handsworth, UB40 were "a whitewashed imitation" of reggae. "You came, you saw, you copied", Zephaniah wrote in a 2001 collection of poetry. "The record company loved you, / but you can't swing it... U.B. robbing we".[27]

UB40 were certainly marketed to white audiences: the video for "Red Red Wine" basically consists of Ali Campbell wandering through a crowd of white people drinking pints of Ansell's bitter at the Eagle and Tun pub in Birmingham city centre. But then so was Bob Marley, whose producer Chris Blackwell toned down the basslines on Marley's early work and added extra guitar riffs so that it would have maximum "crossover" appeal to white consumers. The strategy worked. When the geographer Anoop Nayak conducted fieldwork in Tyneside in the North East of England in the 1990s, for example—an area where 96 per cent of the local population identified as white and where, according to surveys, well over half of the city's ethnic minority population had experienced some form of racist abuse—he encountered white youths who claimed to have learnt Jamaican patois by listening to Bob Marley records, and others who explained that they were planning to braid their hair as a way of expressing their appreciation for "black culture". Many of Nayak's Tyneside subjects were clearly fetishising the sense of exoticness they associated with symbols of "blackness"; the limitations of their position were made clear by the fact that very few seemed to have much contact with the local South Asian population, the region's largest and most visible minority group. But the rise of bands like UB40—indeed, the whole notion of an ethnically-diverse British reggae band fronted by a white, working class Brummie

WHITE FLIGHTS: 1990s BALSALL HEATH

singing in a faux-Jamaican accent, itself a version of the kind of syncretic slang that was being spoken in schools like my own—would surely have been inconceivable without the organic diversity that was a feature of everyday life in neighbourhoods like Balsall Heath, and was itself a product of Britain's decades-long drift towards the multicultural.[28]

In their joint autobiography, the brothers Campbell describe their early life at 25 Speedwell Road, the other side of the River Rea from Clevedon Road and adjacent to Calthorpe Park, a stone's throw from the core of Balsall Heath's red-light district on Chedder Road. They played with the children of their next-door neighbours, whose parents were Caribbean and Arab respectively. Their father would return home with takeout from Bhutt's or Imran's on the Ladypool Road, two pioneers of Birmingham's balti scene. The traditional Scottish folk music played by their father at home—and the lessons he would provide on the *bodhrán* (Irish frame drum)—contrasted with the growing popularity in Balsall Heath of first Jamaican ska and then the "roots" reggae that had been sold to British audiences by Blackwell's Island Records. The brothers began to sneak into to local "blues" parties, semi-formal house parties generally run by Caribbean immigrants which remained the primary venues at which the widest selection of reggae could be heard, and at the best quality ("an assault on your senses", as Ali Campbell remembered it). They made trips to specialist reggae shops like Don Christie's on the Ladypool Road, whose proprietor was a white mod whose real name was David McGynn. Reggae tracks were played all day long and you had to request to buy a particular song while the vinyl was still spinning, before you missed the boat.[29]

By the mid-1990s, reggae's appeal was beginning to subside among younger audiences. In London especially, jungle—an amalgamation of the dancehall, house and rave scenes—was coalescing around the capital's pirate radio stations and independent record labels. And it was joined by the growth of bhangra, the Punjabi folk music originally associated with the harvest festival of Vaisakhi but which, in the late-1980s and 1990s, had been re-imagined by British-Asian acts and mixed with genres including reggae, jazz, funk, soul and hip-hop. Like the emergence of northern soul in the northwest of England a generation earlier, bhangra was a displaced musical movement. Its initial arrival in Britain went hand-in-hand with the popularity of classic Indian films which, as we saw in Chapter Three, were used by South Asian immigrants as vehicles for reconnecting emotionally with life back home. The earliest bhangra performances in Britain consisted of impromptu recitals of songs from such films in cafés and in pubs like the Blue Gates in Smethwick, near to the foundries where many South Asian men initially found work. Then shops like Oriental Star Records—co-founded in 1966 on the Moseley Road (just across the street from the Shereen Kadah curry house) by Muhammad Ayub, who migrated from Pakistan to Britain in 1961—began to import EPs on ships directly from Calcutta to monetise the evident demand for such music. Oriental Star also played an important role in popularising traditional acts like the Pakistani qawwali singer Nusrat Fateh Ali Khan, widely regarded of as one of the most important Sufi singers in the world. By the mid-1980s, however, alongside Nachural Records in Smethwick and Roma Music Bank in Handsworth, the company had transformed into a recording studio-*cum*-distributor that represented many of the growing number of British bhangra acts.[30]

Such acts fused the traditional, percussion-orientated core of "old school" bhangra (powered by the *dhol*, *dholki*, and *tabla* drums) with more established commercially-successful genres—particularly reggae, where the deep, heavy basslines were understood to chime with the sound of the *dhol*. As the emphasis increasingly shifted from live performances by bands to the work of DJs and producers, acts often incorporated methods associated with hip-hop like sampling, scratching and mixing; "putting it all together in a mix", as one Birmingham bhangra fan put it. The lyrics could intersperse English with Punjabi and often referenced the contemporary socio-political climate in Britain—and never more than with the Birmingham-based band Achanak's 1990 song "*Dhol* Tax". The song was a riff on the nationwide protests that had suddenly emerged in the spring of that year against the Conservative Government's introduction of a Community Charge or "Poll Tax", a compulsory, flat-rate tax that every adult over the age of eighteen was obliged to pay. "*Dhol* Tax" included ironic impersonations of Margaret Thatcher, the Queen and an immigration officer, and revolved around the oft-repeated chorus *Dhol tax lion dehna lokho*/Poll tax *nahin dehna mil*—Pay the *Dhol* tax people/Don't pay the Poll Tax![31]

Birmingham had become a focal point for British bhangra. To the mind of Suky Sohal, Achanak's keyboardist, it was the proximity of different cultures in the city as much as its large south Asian population that was the key reason for this. Sohal went to a mostly white school, was brought up in an Indian household in a predominately black area and played in a bhangra band; as a result, he felt able to take inspiration from the music he was exposed to in each setting. In Britain, the demand for bhangra performances was orientated around the South-Asian hubs of Birmingham, London, Bradford, and Leicester. On the Asian wedding circuit in these cities, the popularity of live bhangra was such that, in summer especially, bands could be booked up for consecutive weekends over a two-month period (and often pocketed more than £1,000 for each four-hour performance). Because the genre originated in the Punjab it was often Punjabi Indians and Pakistanis who were the dominant demographic at bhangra events. But aided by the growth of south Asian magazines like *Ghazal and Beat* and *The Asian Weekly*—as well as specialist radio stations like the Birmingham-based Radio XL ("night and day, the Asian way")—British bhangra was also popular with young people from Sikh, Muslim and Hindu backgrounds with family ties across the Indian sub-continent. And the breadth of bhangra's appeal was in many ways exemplified by the growing popularity of "daytime parties" or "daytimers".[32]

These were essentially bhangra club nights that were held during the day. In part, this was because accommodating venues like the New Inns pub in Handsworth or the Hummingbird and Dome nightclubs in Birmingham City Centre were much more affordable to hire for events that did not take place at night. And the daytime slots also had the additional advantage of enabling Asian youths to circumvent the anxieties about such events that were beginning to emerge among older, more conservative elements in Asian communities. In Bradford, for instance, the president of the local Council for Mosques declared that the kind of dancing that could take place at bhangra events was "suggestive" and therefore *haram* (forbidden). The advantage of a daytimer was that, in theory, you could attend without your parents knowing. You would buy your tickets in advance from the Roma Music Bank on Soho Road. You would finish college at lunchtime on a Wednesday when, unbeknownst to many parents, colleges would often run half days. You would get the bus into town and head to the Dome on Bristol Street. Upon arrival, you'd head straight to the toilets to apply makeup and change out of your day clothes and into the *desi* dresses with gold-embroidered scarfs that almost looked as if they could be wedding outfits. Then, illuminated by "projection power strobes" and powered by the "mega bass sound system", you would dance until 5pm at which point, one attendee remembered, the music would stop, you'd change back into your day clothes and head on home to help make chapattis.[33]

The importance of daytimers was twofold. First, while the media portrayed the willingness of some attendees to smoke and

WHITE FLIGHTS: 1990s BALSALL HEATH

drink as evidence young British Asians were embracing "Western depravity", the events acted as vehicles for a British-born generation to engage with their South-Asian identities. This was manifest through the perfection of dance moves (which themselves often originated in Bollywood movies), as well as through the interplay between audiences and live performers, often expressed through the communal chanting of phrases like *dhol wajjha* ("play the *dhol*") and *chak de phattey* ("lift the floorboards" or "mash-up the dancefloor"). Second, the events were also crucial in that they gave DJs a large platform—the biggest daytimers could be attended by thousands of people—to be able to test and finesse new mixes. The true popularity of bhangra in Britain had long been obscured by its informal distributive networks, often in the shape of *nakali* (pirated) cassettes sold at grocery shops like Abdullah's on the Ladypool Road, where albums could be sold for as little as 50p alongside racks of East End spices. But the increased visibility of what was diagnosed as Britain's "bhangra fever" meant that it wasn't long before mainstream record labels belatedly recognised that there was money to be made.[34]

With his aviator shades, pierced ears, Rolex watch and trademark pencil goatee, Bally Sagoo was the poster-boy for commercial bhangra. He was born in New Delhi in 1964 and had been taken to Balsall Heath by his parents as a six-month-old baby. At Clifton School, Sagoo was exposed to reggae, electro and disco by his predominately black friendship circle. He learnt how to swear in Jamaican patois, suck his teeth and, along with his best friend, Horace, began to study the basslines of Chic, Bob Marley and Steel Pulse. They practised the beats with pencils on the desk they shared at school. By his teens, Sagoo was already attracting a following for the mixtapes he was making by recording vinyl and songs off the radio onto cassettes and literally mixing the music up—taking the beats, guitar riffs or vocals from one song, and fusing them with snippets of the instrumental or acapella versions that were often found on the B-sides of records. Having left school, Sagoo acquired a job as a salesman at the Curry's electronics shop in Birmingham City Centre. By day, he hawked electronic equipment in the city; by night he cut and mixed in his Balsall Heath bedroom and, under the stage name GMB (Grand Mixer Bally), sold cassettes at the number 74 bus stop that connected central Birmingham to the black and Asian communities who lived in the north of the city.[35]

Sagoo began incorporating into his *oeuvre* the classic bhangra tracks that surrounded him at home. The originality of his mixes meant he was increasingly in-demand as a DJ on the inner-city circuit—at house parties, weddings and daytimers, where he could earn as much for a single session as he was taking home from a week working at Curry's. Sagoo's father had worked at Oriental Star Records as a driver transporting the label's releases from the company's base on Moseley Road to specialist Asian music shops in other cities. This connection, coupled with Sagoo's growing reputation in Birmingham, encouraged Oriental Star to recruit Sagoo. In 1989 they employed him as their in-house producer and gave him free range with the Oriental Star back catalogue. Sagoo's position as a major player on the hybridised bhangra scene was confirmed. His 1991 song with Oriental Star, "Mera Laung Gawacha", mixed a traditional Punjabi folk song, sung by the British-based Indian folksinger Rama, with a heavy bassline and interjections from Cheshire Cat (Stephen Cheshire), a white dancehall toaster from the predominately white neighbourhood of Bartley Green in Birmingham who performed in Jamaican patois. The album on which "Mera Laung Gawacha" featured was entitled *Essential Ragga*, a nod to the influence of reggae on Sagoo's sound. It sold 100,000 copies. Aided by this success—as well as that of Apache Indian (Steven Kapur), whose distinctive "Bhangragga" style had emerged from his time as a reggae sound system toaster in Handsworth—in 1994 Sagoo signed with Columbia Records.[36]

WHITE FLIGHTS: 1990s BALSALL HEATH

Sagoo's first album with Columbia, *Bollywood Flashback*, was released in September 1994. The sleeve notes proclaimed that this was "the most modern Hindi album ever". Indeed, the album took the approach that Sagoo had finessed, first in his Balsall Heath bedroom and then in his role as an Oriental Star producer and ran with it. It consisted of remixes of songs from the Bollywood movies of the 1980s that were stocked in specialist VHS rental shops in inner cities across the country and, by the 1990s, beamed directly into the houses of South-Asian households via satellite TV channels like Zee TV. In "Chura Liya Hai Tumne", for instance, Sagoo took a song from the movie *Yaadon Ki Baraat* (1973) and reworked and incorporated it into what had by this point become the staples of the British bhangra sound: the punchy, dancehall-inspired bassline, the powerful (usually female) vocals in Punjabi or Hindi, the (male) MCs toasting in patois, the sampling from other musical genres. "*Chura Liya*" became the first song by an Indian-born artist to gain regular airplay on Radio One, and was estimated to have been pirated by more than forty companies across the Indian sub-continent.[37]

With *nakalis* included, Sagoo was already one of the most commercially successful British Asian acts even before he signed with Columbia. When a journalist visited the Sargom Cassette Shop on London's Brick Lane, for example, one of the largest Asian music shops in the country, the staff reported that it was Sagoo who was consistently the shop's best seller. My friend James had grown up around his parents' extensive collection of traditional bhangra. He remembered being in the family car one day and hearing Sagoo's remix of the classic Indian song "Hey! Jamalo" on Radio XL. "I knew it was different", James remembered; "it had an energy, it was loud and proud". What Columbia gave Sagoo was the kind of mainstream recognition that eluded those artists who were primarily reliant on Asian distribution networks. What Sagoo gave James was access to a broader range of cultural influences, beyond those that dominated his everyday life at home. Sagoo's music was "my bridge into the society I lived in. A metaphorical bridge from South Asia to England. His music was modern, it was British and Indian—just like me".[38]

Bollywood Flashback became the biggest-selling Indian remix album of all time. In October 1996, following in the footsteps of the Specials, UB40, Smiley Culture, Apache Indian and other sounds from Britain's inner cities, Sagoo's single, "Dil Cheez", entered the UK charts at number twelve. It was a cross between a Punjabi *ghazal*—the traditional poems that had once been heard in inner-city cafés like the Pyar Ka Sagar—and "lovers' rock", the melodic, ballad-orientated sub-genre of reggae that had emerged in Britain in the 1980s. Alongside vocals by the Pakistani singer Shabnam Majid, the song featured the *dholak* (Indian barrel drum) and a solo played on an Afghan *rabab* or lute. It was the first Hindi language single ever to make the UK top 40.[39]

The dialectics of multiculturalism

There were just months between the start of the picketing against prostitution in Balsall Heath and the release of *Bollywood Flashback*. If the latter showed how the creativity of the multicultural inner city was increasingly journeying into the mainstream in the 1990s, it was the former that rendered Balsall Heath a popular destination for those politicians who, following another dispiriting election defeat at the hands of the Conservative Party in April 1992, were seeking to triangulate a way beyond the Conservative electoral leviathan. And while newly-erected landmarks like the Convention Centre and the Hyatt Hotel in Birmingham city centre were much more in keeping with the New Labour vision for British cities as spaces characterised

WHITE FLIGHTS: 1990s BALSALL HEATH

by glass-fronted, private-finance-initiative-funded Barcelona-style piazzas, it was Balsall Heath that became ensnared in the web of think tanks that fed into the New Labour project and provided intellectual cover for the party's broad acceptance of the post-Thatcher neoliberal landscape. And this was something initiated by Dick Atkinson and his rapidly-expanding St Paul's Community Group.[40]

By the 1990s, operations that fell under the St Paul's banner included a playgroup, a private community school for pupils who had been expelled from mainstream institutions, an inner-city farm, and *The Balsall Heathen* (the neighbourhood magazine that had earlier published voyeuristic photographs of sex workers in an attempt to intimidate them off the streets). In 1994, and with the support of Melanie Phillips, Atkinson wrote a pamphlet that sought to summarise the key lessons he had drawn from twenty-five years of community activism. The pamphlet was published by the think-tank Demos, which had a close relationship with many of the key architects of New Labour. It was emblematic of how far Atkinson's politics had moved since his days as a radical lecturer closer to the counter-cultural student movement than to the stuffy staff common rooms on university campus. Atkinson called for individuals to take greater responsibility for their neighbourhoods, and for "social entrepreneurs" to be empowered to take the necessary action to mend Britain's fractured communities. It is also noteworthy that, in spite of having spent most of his working life in multicultural Balsall Heath, Atkinson had embraced what in the 1990s had become the American obsession with the policing of social boundaries. In his Demos pamphlet Atkinson emphasised what he underlined as the importance of enclosed communities, places with figuratively "clear entry and exit points" where "visitors" would be welcomed as long as they were committed to facilitating "the right atmosphere" (it was presumably the task of "social entrepreneurs" like Atkinson to decide what the "right" atmosphere was, and who would or would not be welcomed).[41]

The story of Balsall Heath as told by Atkinson, and especially the story of the 1994 campaign against the sex industry, resonated in the incestuous world of New Labour policymaking. What made the campaign appealing to Geoff Mulgan (the first Demos director and a former advisor to the Shadow Chancellor Gordon Brown), Tom Bentley (Mulgan's successor at Demos and a former advisor to the Shadow Health Secretary David Blunkett) and Charles Leadbeater (a research associate at Demos and a future advisor to Prime Minister Tony Blair) was that it apparently provided a concrete example of what could be achieved if the left accepted the notion that, in the post-Thatcher climate, the central political questions were about how to give people greater autonomy, choice and responsibility in a way that reflected the market-orientated society Britain had become. Where Atkinson saw the Balsall Heath campaign as "one of the most developed neighbourhood watch schemes in the country"—one that had, in the space of a few short months, supposedly enabled residents to leave their cars and front doors unlocked—Leadbeater and his colleagues saw a case study in "progressive individualism", "active citizenship", and something called the "self-policing society".[42]

Influenced by his young, fresh-out-of-Oxford advisor Tom Bentley, it was Blunkett who paid attention to Balsall Heath most consistently. He made a low-key visit to the area as Shadow Health Secretary in 1994—the spring before Bally Sagoo signed with Columbia Records. Blunkett returned six years later as Education Secretary to announce the establishment of a community "champions" fund that would seek to replicate Atkinson's role as a "social entrepreneur" in neighbourhoods across the country. By this time, Atkinson's influence was such that he was able to win a personal intervention from Blunkett to distribute emergency funds to his Balsall Heath community school. But it was in Blunkett's role as Home Secretary following Labour's second successive general election victory in June 2001 that, seven years after dozens of picketers took to the streets to drive sex work out of the community, re-established Balsall Heath in the national limelight. And in the context of a changing domestic and geopolitical climate, the questions of what constituted "healthy" communities, and how those that were deemed to be "unhealthy" could be cured, had emerged as lightning rods that once more electrified long-standing anxieties about Britain's emergence as a multicultural society.[43]

Blunkett arrived in Balsall Heath on a Tuesday morning in mid-December 2001. And this time the event was stage-managed to ensure there was maximum potential for photo-ops. Blunkett met with Raja Amin and other members of Street Watch to hear at first-hand how they had been able to transform the neighbourhood from "blight to beauty". He posed in front of a Union Jack flag with Amin, who was decked out in what had become the Street Watch uniform of a green bomber-jacket with "Neighbourhood Warden" emblazoned in yellow stitching over the breast pocket. He visited the expensive network of CCTV cameras that had been installed in Balsall Heath to ensure that the gains won by the campaign against prostitution were not lost, and was presented with a flowered garland by two local schoolchildren. Finally, in the community centre Dick Atkinson had established at the bottom of St Paul's Road, Blunkett addressed a crowd of some 400 residents and activists.[44]

Praise for the campaign to clean up Balsall Heath had by this point become *de rigueur* in New Labour circles. In his remarks, Blunkett duly doffed his cap to Balsall Heath's transformation from a "run-down, prostitute-ridden" part of town into a "beacon" for "what can be done when the drive and initiative of local people is harnessed". But there was a marked change in tone in

Blunkett's speech. He called for a debate about why other inner-city areas across the country had apparently become such difficult places to live and argued that it was not possible to tip-toe around issues like race and the question of national belonging. If certain things could not be said by politicians without accusations of racism being made, Blunkett warned, before departing the stage to the sound of "Pass it On" by Bob Marley and the Wailers, then democracy was dead.[45]

If Blunkett was diplomatically vague in front of his Balsall Heath audience, the meaning of his remarks was clarified in the quotes he gave to the press in the days before and after his Birmingham outing. For Blunkett, in the face of what he understood to be the presence in Britain of "ghettos" that had become dangerously fragmented along ethnic lines, the time had come to talk about "British values". In inner-city areas across Britain there was a need to follow the example that had been set in Balsall Heath and rebuild a sense of "social cohesion" and "common citizenship". Making his target explicit, Blunkett stated that ethnic minorities needed to understand that there were "norms of acceptability" in Britain, including the expectation that people would speak English (six years later free English classes for asylum seekers were abolished in England by one of Blunkett's successors as Home Secretary, John Reid). "Those who come into our home", Blunkett declared, echoing the emphasis that Atkinson had earlier placed on enclosed communities, "should accept those norms just as we would have to if we went elsewhere". Britain had "core values", Blunkett asserted, knowledge of which could and should be used as a test for whether prospective immigrants would be admitted into the country. Blunkett made no apology for the bluntness of his words; the only group who would benefit from a retreat into relativism, he declared, was the neo-Nazi British National Party (BNP).[46]

WHITE FLIGHTS: 1990s BALSALL HEATH

There were three factors that contributed to Blunkett's move from his early interest in Balsall Heath as a model for empowering communities to his willingness, by the winter of 2001, to use the area as a stick with which to beat inner-city neighbourhoods elsewhere in the country. First, there was a heightening of alarm around immigration and asylum seekers in the run-up to the June 2001 election. The number of asylum applications in Britain did increase in this period—from 32,500 in 1997 to 84,000 by 2002, at the height of the conflict in the Balkans. But this was only the sixth highest rate among EU member states. The sense of hysteria around the asylum issue was largely driven by the hyperbolic coverage of the subject in the tabloid press. An editorial in the *Sun*, for example, declared that when Enoch Powell spoke out against Britain's immigration policies in the late-1960s, most people called him a racist. However, in light of a situation where "bogus" asylum seekers were apparently costing British taxpayers "zillions" of pounds, the paper wondered whether it was time to recognise that maybe Powell "had a point". One study estimated that between them the *Sun*, the *Daily Mail* and the *Daily Express* ran four stories a day on asylum seekers in this period. And the Conservative leader at the 2001 election, William Hague, only fanned the flames of Britain's "asylum panic" by positioning the party's offer to voters in explicitly nationalistic terms. He not only pledged to save the pound in the face of the spectre of European integration and usher in a system of immediate deportations for "bogus" asylum seekers; he also promised to bring an end to the age of "political correctness" where, to the mind of Hague, if you talked about asylum seekers you were called a racist and if you talked about the nation you were called a "Little Englander". 11,000 people voted for the BNP at the 2001 election and its leader, Nick Griffin, came third in the Oldham West constituency with a 16 per cent share of the vote. It was the largest share of the vote a far-right party had received at a general election in Britain since the Second World War.[47]

Second, in the summer of 2001 the presence of a re-energised far right—particularly in deindustrialised, multicultural parts of the north of England like Oldham, Burnley and Bradford—had led to the worst rioting seen in Britain since the 1980s. As had been the case in Nottingham and London in 1958, as well as in Bradford in 1976, the unrest was stoked by the far right. Both the BNP and the NF were active in Northern England. The propaganda of these groups aped the jingoistic language of the tabloid newspapers and increasingly sought to capitalise on concerns about asylum seekers. And at the same time, in cahoots with local "firms" of football hooligans, in the north of England especially far-right members repeatedly attempted to march through areas with large Asian populations and attacked Asian-owned businesses.[48]

The official reports that followed the unrest painted a depressingly familiar picture of overt racism, disproportionate levels of unemployment for ethnic minorities and inner-city areas that, like Balsall Heath, continued to be blighted by poor-quality housing stock. Yet, crucially, they also ushered into the political mainstream ideas about racial segregation and the need for cohesive communities, as well as what quickly became an obsessive focus on neighbourhoods with large Muslim populations (also like Balsall Heath). In a report that coincided with the 2001 unrest (but was authored prior to it), Herman Ousley, the former head of the Commission for Racial Equality, suggested many schools in Bradford existed in a state of "virtual apartheid". Paradoxically, Ousley understood that certain inner-city areas were "ghettos" characterised by acute deprivation and simultaneously "comfort zones" to which Muslim residents had apparently chosen to retreat so that they would only mix with people from the same background. Ted Cantle, the former chief executive of

WHITE FLIGHTS: 1990s BALSALL HEATH

Nottingham City Council who was tasked by the Government with investigating the riots in Oldham, Burnley and Bradford, similarly evoked the image of racial segregation on an endemic scale and suggested that, like ships in a foggy night, white and Asian populations in northwest England were effectively living "parallel lives". In the absence of greater community cohesion—which Cantle defined as ways of encouraging different groups to "gel or mesh into an integrated whole"—further violence was deemed not only possible but likely.[49]

Finally, sandwiched between the Labour election victory of June 2001 and the publication of the Cantle Report in December of that year came the terrorist attacks on the World Trade Centre in New York City on 11 September 2001. When David Blunkett took to his feet to address his Balsall Heath audience just three months later, it was already obvious that the attack on America would have profound geopolitical implications, even if the exact nature of those implications remained unclear. The keenness of New Labour to stand with the United States in the "War on Terror"—and the extent to which Muslim communities by now found themselves firmly established as Britain's primary racialised folk-devil—helps explain why Blunkett was so quick to accept both the tenor of the Cantle Report and some of its more eye-catching proposals. These included the promotion of a "meaningful" concept of citizenship and the establishment, along North American lines, of a statement of national allegiance for all prospective immigrants. It was a long way from New Labour's earlier dalliance with what was understood as the progressive potential of individualised communities, never mind the diverse cultural influences that helped launch the careers of artists like Bally Sagoo. Blunkett was criticised by liberal commentators, many of whom drew comparisons with the suggestion, made in 1990 by the former chair of the Conservative Party Norman Tebbit, that the true test of loyalty for immigrants in Britain was whether they supported the English cricket team. But his stance also attracted widespread support, especially from commentators in the right-wing press many of whom showed themselves to be fully on board with the newly-fashionable, Orientalist notion that the "War on Terror" was part of a much larger, existential "clash of civilisations" between east and west.[50]

This included the columnist Melanie Phillips, who in 1994 had been a cheerleader for the campaign against prostitution in Balsall Heath and the leading role that had been played by those Muslim protestors Phillips then regarded as being admirably illiberal in their refusal to accept the pervasiveness of the local sex industry. Now, though, in her new role as a columnist for the *Daily Mail*—and rehearsing the theories she would propagate in a 2006 book on Britain's "terror state within"—Phillips thought there was a clear problem of alienation among those same Muslim communities. There was a reason why so many young Muslim men in Britain were, she claimed, professing their support for Osama bin Laden and Al-Qaeda in the wake of 9/11. The key issue, Phillips wrote, was that Islam taught "hostility towards modernity", and that as a result many Muslims conceive of "western values" as an attack on Islamic life. This problem had in Phillips's view been exacerbated by Britain's "multiculturalist agenda" which had apparently deprived both "indigenous" and "minority" children of any common culture (it was unclear where British-born ethnic minorities fitted into this thesis, which in 2001 included 800,000 British-born Muslims). Phillips was clear that Blunkett deserved credit for his refusal to sink even further into the "multicultural mire". Finally, Phillips predicted, echoing the narrative that in the 1980s had been put forward by Ray Honeyford in the pages of the *Salisbury Review*, Britain's schools would once again be able to function as places that transmitted "British identity" through a focus on the "Christian values on which western democracy is based".[51]

WHITE FLIGHTS: 1990s BALSALL HEATH

By now, it had become impossible to misconstrue where Blunkett and New Labour's sympathies lay. In 2000, the Government did implement the findings of the MacPherson Report which, in its investigation of the Metropolitan Police's handling of the racist murder of the black teenager Stephen Lawrence in 1993, belatedly provided official recognition of the police's endemic problem with institutional racism. An amendment to the Race Relations Act was subsequently introduced that required the police and other public authorities to eliminate racial discrimination and promote equality of opportunity. But in the aftermath of the riots in the northwest, Blunkett openly re-allocated funds that had originally been earmarked for deprived neighbourhoods with large Asian populations to those constituencies that had voted heavily for the BNP. Later, he described the 200 mostly Muslim men who had been convicted for their part in the unrest as "maniacs" who were victims of their own destruction (54 per cent of families from Pakistani or Bangladeshi backgrounds relied on some form of income support in 2001). In September 2002 he warned Asian families that they risked "schizophrenic" divisions between different generations unless they spoke English at home, and proclaimed he had no sympathy with refugees because in his view they would be better off going back home to rebuild their own countries; that same month, Blunkett was found to have acted unlawfully when, the previous summer, he ordered the forcible removal of an Afghan couple and their two young children from a Stourbridge Mosque and deported them to Germany. As one commentator observed, it was as if Blunkett was determined to stretch New Labour's "big tent" all the way to the far right.[52]

Blunkett's hard-line approach was soon backed up by new legislation. In November 2002 the Nationality, Immigration and Asylum Act came into law and toughened the Government's approach in various ways. New Labour had already introduced measures that restricted asylum seekers to just 70 per cent of the income support otherwise available to the general population—a rate which was deemed to be significantly below the poverty line. The 2002 legislation sought to placate Britain's asylum panic through the establishment of "reception centres" for asylum seekers, which would house up to 400 people away from the major conurbations and contain in-built health and education facilities to prevent doctors' surgeries, hospitals and schools from becoming "swamped". Second, it turned immigration officials into *de facto* police officers, giving them new powers to search people's homes, seize evidence, use reasonable force and arrest and detain people who were suspected of being in the country illegally. Third, it enacted the Cantle Report's recommendation that a statement of allegiance should be introduced for prospective immigrants by establishing that all new applicants for British citizenship would have to take a "Citizenship Oath and Pledge". This required anyone seeking to gain British citizenship to pledge that they would uphold Britain's "democratic values" and its "rights and freedoms" (white Britons who were members of neo-fascist groups like the BNP were not required to prove their commitment to democratic freedoms). Finally, the Act stated that housing, food and support for other living costs could be withdrawn if asylum seekers were found not to have followed the correct procedures at any point. It was estimated that up to 700 people a week would face destitution by the change in the law, including vulnerable adults, women, and people with special needs.[53]

The 2002 Act was, in effect, a precursor to what would become the Conservative-Liberal Democrat Government's "Hostile Environment" policy a decade later. As one Government minister put it in 2007, "living here illegally should become ever more uncomfortable and ever more constrained". Like the Hostile Environment, the approach New Labour adopted in the

WHITE FLIGHTS: 1990s BALSALL HEATH

2000s would have far-reaching implications for immigrants, the descendants of immigrants, asylum seekers and anyone who happened to be living in Britain's ethnically-diverse inner cities. And this included Balsall Heath.[54]

Within a matter of years from David Blunkett's December 2001 speech in Balsall Heath, and as the community cohesion agenda became indistinguishable from the post-9/11 focus on preventing "homegrown" terrorism, local residents began noticing the appearance of new CCTV cameras in the neighbourhood. The cameras were mounted on top of intimidating, fifteen-foot tall platforms; they looked like they had been borrowed from the set of a bad science fiction movie. Residents of other-inner city areas in Birmingham began to notice the cameras, too. Stranger still, the cameras only ever appeared in districts with large Muslim populations—Balsall Heath, neighbouring Sparkhill and Alum Rock in the north-east of the city. The cameras, it subsequently transpired, were paid for with anti-terrorist funds and were able to record and register the number plates of all passing cars; the intention was for these panopticon surveillance towers to form a "ring of steel" that would prevent people in these neighbourhoods from being able to move about the city undetected. The installation of the cameras effectively meant the establishment in Balsall Heath of an enclosed community with "clear entry and exit points", though presumably not the kind that Dick Atkinson originally had in mind. Many of the new cameras were just minutes away from those that had earlier been installed on the streets of Balsall Heath to prevent the return of the sex industry.[55]

By 2002, I had embarked on my own journey away from Balsall Heath. After my parents separated, my father eventually left the house on Newton Road where my brother and I spent our earliest years and moved into a place in Hall Green, a fifteen-minute bus journey from my junior school on Clifton Road. At the top end of the street, where Dad lived, there was a noticeably different feel to the area. The houses all had front gardens, rather than the brick walls and concrete yards the council had erected in Balsall Heath and Sparkhill; a few doors down there was an allotment that Dad spent many Saturday afternoons tending in battered, maroon-coloured Doc Martens boots. Just around the corner from Dad's new place—south from Balsall Heath, towards Hall Green Secondary School, was a house that had once been lived in by J. R. R. Tolkien.

Hall Green was a hinterland. The top end of Springfield Road, where Dad lived, felt more suburban and whiter than the inner-city topographies of our youth. Hall Green was one of the neighbourhoods to which Irish families often moved when they left the inner city in search of more aspirational lifestyles. But at the bottom end of the street there were sights that were much more familiar: a newly-erected *masjid*, for example, a halal butchers and the *roti-handi* on the Stratford Road from which we would, on rare occasions, be allowed to get takeout on a Saturday night. On either side of Dad was Subash, an East-African immigrant who would give us a hamper each year for Christmas, and Chris, the son of Polish immigrants who every summer would play cricket and football with us in the industrial yard that backed onto our houses.[56]

Hall Green Secondary School was different from Clifton in certain ways, especially the presence of what had hitherto been the largely alien white, working-class sensibility that was especially present in spaces like the school football team. But there were other features of school life that were more recognisable. Half of all pupils came from ethnic minority backgrounds, and it was here that I met my two oldest friends: James, who had discovered Bally Sagoo via Radio XL, and Pete, whose dad had come to Britain from Jamaica. To a soundtrack of UK garage—another musical fusion that had emerged from Britain's multicultural

WHITE FLIGHTS: 1990s BALSALL HEATH

inner cities—and especially the compilation album *Pure Garage: Volume I*, we killed the time between lessons by discussing England's chances at the next World Cup, bartering for Hubba-Bubba chewing gum and marvelling at Sunil's new girlfriend, Mariella (whose father was Italian). When the time came for us to leave school, my friends and I headed even further south to take our A Levels at a college in Solihull, the town on the outskirts of Birmingham where the local MP, more than forty years earlier, had been a vocal critic of Britain's immigration policies (see Chapter Two). We had begun drinking, and I funded my nights out by working a few shifts a week at K2, one of well over a hundred balti restaurants that were now open in Birmingham.[57]

The whole notion of a balti was originally intended as a joke. The term's meaning in Urdu refers to the buckets that were often used to carry water (or flush the toilet) across the Indian sub-continent. *Balti* was trialled in Britain because the original South Asian restaurateurs felt it would be easier for white people to pronounce than *karahi*, the wok-like cooking pot widely used in South Asian cooking. As one Balsall Heath restaurateur put it, balti was an "invention for the *goras*"; it was a way to "civilise the natives by introducing different kinds of cuisine". K2 was based in Moseley, the neighbouring, more affluent part of town to Balsall Heath—just across the road from Luker's, a Jewish bakery. It was owned by Naim, a jazz fan who had hit on the idea of offering his predominately white clientele baltis combined with live performances from local musicians like Steve Ajao, the saxophonist and blues guitarist whose father had emigrated to Britain from Ghana after the Second World War. After a night waiting tables Naim and I would drink half-pints of Cobra lager and devour a not-on-the-menu "special" that our Punjabi chef had been simmering all evening.[58]

Even if my family had wanted to, it would have been difficult for us to have taken flight from the everyday consequences of

Britain's drift towards the multicultural. Multicultural Britain was all around us. Even as David Blunkett and New Labour increasingly obsessed over what was understood to be the urgent need to create "cohesive" communities in Britain, the syncretic milieu that surrounded me in 1990s Balsall Heath—and which was exemplified by the diverse sounds of Britain's inner cities, from the multicultural slang spoken in local schools to the rise of British bhangra and acts like UB40 and Smiley Culture—was becoming an increasingly unavoidable feature of everyday life.[59]

The campaign against prostitution that began in the summer of 1994 was just one more example of the complicated, often-contradictory nature of this historical process. It also illustrates the extent to which, fifty years on from Britain's "brown babies" panic, sex remained a key battleground in the making of multicultural Britain. On the one hand, you could read the 1994 campaign as another instance of an immigrant community mobilising itself as a forceful presence in Britain. Like the bold signage that accompanied the cafés, cinemas and other immigrant-run establishments of the 1960s, or the protests against Ray Honeyford in Bradford in the 1980s, the 1994 campaign showed how immigrant communities and their descendants were continuing to assert themselves as a forceful presence in British society.

But on the other hand, the harassment of sex workers and other women in Balsall Heath was not just uncomfortable on its own terms. There were not only barely acknowledged ambiguities about the relationships between the mostly white sex workers and some of the mostly Asian protestors, or the changing demographics of the neighbourhood that meant sex workers were often renting premises from Asian landlords, some of whom were apparently also supporting the campaign against prostitution. As I was examining the newspaper coverage of the campaign, I thought of Janet Mendelsohn's subjects in Balsall Heath thirty years earlier, and the way in which the sex industry

WHITE FLIGHTS: 1990s BALSALL HEATH

had been an incubator for the emergence of street level multiculturalism in the 1960s. By the mid-1990s, however, it had been all but eradicated from those same streets thanks to those mostly South-Asian campaigners, many of whom had themselves been immigrants and were old enough to remember a very different social climate.

It is testament to how successfully Dick Atkinson and the New Labour intelligentsia were able to flatten out these contradictions that the story of Balsall Heath's transformation continued to capture the imagination of politicians in the years that

Figure 33: Raja Brothers Supermarket, Balsall Heath, c. 2010. Photograph © Balsall Heath Local History Society.

followed David Blunkett's decision to use the neighbourhood as a vehicle for his championing of the politics of community cohesion. Less than six years had passed between Blunkett's 2001 speech in Balsall Heath and David Cameron's arrival in the area as the newly elected leader of the Conservative Party. And Cameron went to even greater lengths to ally himself with what had purportedly happened in the area—despite the uncomfortable reality that Balsall Heath remained one of the most deprived neighbourhoods in the country, with almost a quarter of residents living in overcrowded conditions and an unemployment rate in the area that remained above thirty per cent. Cameron not only visited the projects that continued to fall under the banner of St Paul's, the group that had been established by Atkinson in 1971. With a smile "as wide as a balti bowl", as one journalist put it, he also posed for the cameras at the Raja Brothers supermarket (Fig. 33), attended a meeting at a local mosque, and drank a pint of John Smith's bitter with Pravin Gohil, the landlord of the nearby George Pub. And having been introduced by Atkinson, Cameron also stayed the night at the home of Abdullah Rehman, one of the original picketers in the campaign against prostitution who had subsequently become, like Raja Amin, a Balsall Heath "Neighbourhood Warden". Cameron wanted to understand "how Balsall Heath transformed itself from a run down, crime-ridden area to what it is today", Rehman later told reporters, as well as find out more about the importance placed on family values in South Asian communities. Before leaving, Abdullah and his wife Shaheeda gifted Cameron a traditional robe that would, the Rehmans explained, be perfect if he ever decided to visit Pakistan.[60]

In some ways, it is not surprising that Cameron was able to switch so quickly from eulogising the sense of "civic responsibility" he saw as being present in Asian families—something which he argued put "the rest of us to shame"—to his decision, within

WHITE FLIGHTS: 1990s BALSALL HEATH

a year becoming Prime Minister in 2010, to use a speech at a major conference on global security to rail against what he called "the doctrine of state multiculturalism" that had purportedly allowed "different cultures to live separate lives, apart from each other and apart from the mainstream". As his Government's Hostile Environment policy took shape from 2012 onwards, what was most striking was how familiar Cameron's *volte-face* felt.[61]

The policies of the Hostile Environment—the emphasis on deporting immigrants first and hearing appeals later, the advertisements that were placed in ethnically-diverse neighbourhoods with the message "Go home or face arrest", the introduction of identity checks to be carried out by landlords and NHS workers—were devised by a Conservative Party alarmed by the electoral implications of growing support for the anti-European Union, anti-immigrant UKIP. They were expanded upon in 2014, in the wake of allegations about a plot to "Islamicise" schools in Birmingham, with the policy that schools across the country would be required to "promote British values". But what helped enable Cameron to stress that a "muscular" approach was now required to prevent "segregated communities" from fostering Islamic terrorists was the rightward turn that had earlier been taken by New Labour in the context of growing support for the BNP and the prolonged tabloid campaign against "bogus" asylum seekers.[62]

In returning to the Balsall Heath of my youth, and while writing this book, I have often wondered how the making of multicultural Britain might have been different for people in the cities I have visited if those in power at Westminster had been willing to take a more principled stance. Would things have been any easier if, for example, the Labour Party had kept its promise to rescind the 1962 Commonwealth Immigrants Act—which in opposition it decried as the effective institutionalisation of Britain's "colour bar"? How would things have played out if racial discrimination in the workplace and in the housing sector had been made illegal earlier than 1968? What would have happened if, rather than embracing the community cohesion agenda, the Labour Government of the early-2000s had taken seriously the suggestion made by Stuart Hall and others in a report published in October 2000, that post-colonial Britain needed to rethink its national story so that it could embrace what was becoming its multicultural essence? To put these questions another way: is national pride in multiculturalism really such a difficult political project?[63]

EPILOGUE

This book is partly the product of my childhood. But it has also been shaped by the histories of my parents, something that has revealed itself to me only gradually, and over a long period of time. With my father it was inseparable from the strange contrast between the Nuneaton my brother and I encountered on our monthly trips to see Grandma Dorothy, and our everyday lives in inner-city Birmingham. Nuneaton meant afternoon tea, Nice biscuits and stodgy Mr Kipling cake, trips to see Nuneaton Borough play in the Southern League Midland Division, and outings to "Woolies" in Nuneaton town centre. Dad was no didact, but his actions and interests back home told us he had left this world far behind. When I remember that time, the images that emerge most readily are of him learning how to make chapati on the gas hob, of his daily cigarette runs to Akbar's at the bottom of our road, or the birthday presents that, I can now see, amounted to the creation of a library of the canonical music of multicultural Britain: *Exodus*, *Handsworth Revolution*, *Making History*, and the Two-Tone sounds of The Specials, The Selecter and The Beat.[1]

My mother's family story is longer and more complicated, and was therefore more difficult for my younger self to grasp. My Grandma Hanna was German, though growing up her Germanness was only apparent with the copies of *Der Spiegel* she kept on a footrest, or in the *pumpernickel* she sometimes served for lunch. It was much later in life that I learnt how Hanna's father, Wilhelm Schumer, had brought his wife, Amalia, and eleven-year-old daughter from Solingen in Dusseldorf to the seaside town of Morcambe in Lancashire in 1926. He had secured a job as an engineer with Souplex, a newly established plastics company that would make its name manufacturing "double-six" disposable razors. With Germany's engulfing economic and political crises and the prospect of a steady wage of £7 a week at Souplex (plus the cost of the family's relocation from Germany), the offer was too good to refuse.[2]

1920s Britain was a difficult place for Germans. The Germanophobia of the First World War—which led to the internment and repatriation of thousands of German citizens in Britain, the winding-up of German businesses, anti-German rioting as well as the confiscation of German-owned property—retained a presence that would re-emerge again during the Second World War. There were rumours German shopkeepers in Britain spiked their goods with poison, and that German barbers were undercover spies who slit the throats of their customers. Wilhelm anglicised his name to Willy, and Amalia threw herself into housekeeping—pillowcases filled with down, eiderdown covers and matching spreads made with coarse silk, lampshades in shell-coloured satin, curtains made from velvet. It amounted to the careful cultivation of an image of respectability, something used by Amalia to shield her family from attacks on its foreignness. But the attacks still came. Hanna was nicknamed "the little foreigner" at school, and on summer evenings taxi-drivers would bring cargos of tourists to the family house so they could gawp at the neighbourhood "Huns". As I was finishing this book, my mother showed me the rough notes of a memoir my grandmother had intended to write about her childhood experiences.

EPILOGUE

This only amounted to a few pages, but her words testified to how much the pain of being an outsider in Britain had remained with Hanna throughout her life. "No one knows better than I the grinding ache of homesickness", Hanna wrote, "of alienation from a society in which one has at all costs to make one's way in order to survive".[3]

At the end of the Second World War, Hanna moved to Liverpool. Anti-German sentiment was still strong—it remained illegal for British women to marry German prisoners of war until 1947—but it was Liverpool where Hanna met her future husband, Kenneth, where they were both working at the university. He was the eldest son of James and Susanna Connell, who had left their home in Kilkerranmore, County Cork prior to the First World War and had settled in Southampton. With his tall, wiry frame, large eyes and witty conversation, Kenneth was charming. As the children of immigrants, the couple found they had a similarly detached perspective on life in Britain; it was as if they were spectators looking through a window. Kenneth became a Communist, embraced the revolutionary spirit of Irish nationalism and liked to talk about his own family's "Irish peasant stock". He dreamt of one day settling in Cork to build a house in a part of Ireland where many Connells still lived. In 1952 Kenneth accepted a job in Belfast. It was about as far away from Cork as you can get on the island, but still one step closer than being in Britain. With his young family—Hanna (who gave up her job in Liverpool), my mother and her younger sister, both of whom were under the age of three—Kenneth crossed the Irish Sea, set up home in Belfast and became an Irish citizen. He never made it to Cork. But thanks to a strange turn of history, over the past ten years Belfast has also become my home. It is here in the north of Ireland that my own children were born, a hundred years after their ancestors embarked on their respective journeys to Britain from Solingen and Kilkerranmore.[4]

MULTICULTURAL BRITAIN

In Britain, the question "Where are you from?" is a loaded one. It is often posed to people who are identified as looking or sounding different with the underlying assumption that the person asking the question has some higher authority bestowed on them by a supposedly more solid, authentic grounding in "Britishness". Indeed, with the implementation of the Hostile Environment policies of the 2010s, it became a legal requirement for officials to ask what the journalist Afua Hirsch has characterised as "The Question" to anyone who was suspected of being in the country illegally (in practice, this meant anyone who looked or sounded "foreign"). It was this that led to thousands of black British citizens being wrongly classified as illegal immigrants, denied access to urgent healthcare and benefits and, in the cases that made up the "Windrush scandal", being removed from their homes and deported to countries they had not known since childhood.[5]

Given the potential consequences of giving the "wrong" answer to The Question in Britain—from the Germanophobia of the two World Wars to the state-sponsored racism of the 2000s and 2010s—it is not hard to see how it has retained such potency. But the more I travelled around Britain researching this book, the more convinced I became that the time has come to reclaim The Question, or at least reformulate it in such a way that would allow us to reckon with the historic nature of the social, cultural and political changes I have described in the preceding pages. In the space of seventy years, ethnic diversity has become a central feature of everyday life in Britain. And we can begin to acknowledge this, as Stuart Hall once argued, by trying to register how commonplace it has become for people to have to tell complicated stories about their family ties and cultural roots. For Afua Hirsch, this means her Germanic-Jewish-Ghanaian heritage, Norwegian place of birth and London upbringing; for Hall, it meant his Jamaican childhood, African, Scottish and Portuguese-Jewish roots, and intellectual engagement with

EPILOGUE

Oxford, London and Birmingham; for me, it means my upbringing in Balsall Heath, family ties to Nuneaton and Germany and my "Irish peasant stock".[6]

In light of this, our focus needs to shift away from The Question, with all the racialised prejudices and power dynamics that this connotates, and towards a proper engagement with the question "Where are *we* from?" This question feeds into the ongoing political project—spearheaded by the Black Lives Matter movement—for an overdue reckoning with the legacies of Britain's colonial past and the driving role Britain played in the genocidal atrocity of the slave trade. Seriously engaging with the question of where we are from is also the necessary starting point for finally overcoming the longstanding potency of the nationalistic narrative of white victimhood that has emerged so often in the story of the making of multicultural Britain, one that is in turn rooted in Britain's melancholic inability to adequately to process the trauma caused by the loss of empire. Finally, the question "Where are we from?" also serves as a way of beginning to acknowledge just how far, over the twentieth century and into the first quarter of the new millennium, Britain has become multicultural. It has ceased to be possible for the diasporic traditions of people with "elsewhere in their blood" to be boxed off from mainstream Britain. As Hall put it, "after cultural diversity, Britishness cannot be what it was before". Or as one respondent from Birmingham explained in the early 2000s when she was asked to describe the nature of her own identity: "frig me, I live in England, Mom's from Ireland, my grandad's from Ireland, my bleedin' Dad's from Jamaica...in my family, you've got everybody".[7]

This is one side of the dialectic I have described in *Multicultural Britain*. The other side is the persistent and pernicious presence of racism. And looking out at Britain's social, economic and political landscapes in the first decades of our century, it's not hard to find evidence of the entrenched nature of British racism, and to see how profoundly this continues to alienate ethnic minorities in multifaceted ways.

Institutionally, we can see this in the massive over-representation of black men in prison, for example, to the point where in 2007 there were more black men in prison than there were in higher education; in the 2010 Ethnic Minority Election Study, which found that six in ten respondents believed black and Asian people were stopped and searched by the police for no reason; in the damning statistic that, during the first months of the 2020–23 pandemic, black people were more than four times more likely to die from Covid-19 than white people; in the 2021 scandal over the treatment of ethnic minority cricketers in England, and the way clubs were willing to dismiss racial abuse aimed at players like Azeem Rafiq as "just banter"; and in the 2022 report that found that black, Asian and mixed-race women were far more likely to die in pregnancy and childbirth than white women due to discrimination in the NHS. The corollary of institutional racism is physical and interpersonal abuse, something that remains a potent possibility for ethnic minorities whether on the street or, even more commonly—especially for high-profile black or Asian figures—online via social media. In the polarised climate that followed the 2016 Brexit vote, for instance, there was a 41 per cent increase in racially and religiously motivated crimes including verbal abuse and physical assault, while at the 2017 general election it was estimated that the Labour MP Diane Abbott, Britain's first black shadow Home Secretary, received almost half of all abusive tweets aimed at female politicians. And then there is political racism, and the familiar spectacle of mainstream political parties—cheered on by the tabloid press—seeking to amplify hostility to racialised folk devils for their own short-term political gain.[8]

It is in this light that the Conservative Government's 2022 policy of sending British-based asylum seekers to the former

EPILOGUE

German and Belgian colony of Rwanda in East Africa should be seen. The proposal was an extreme example of a pathological desire in Britain to remove what is understood to constitute an alien presence with the absurd fantasy of restoring a mythical sense of British homogeneity. It was only a step away from the NF's policy, articulated in the pages of magazines like *Bulldog* and *Spearhead* in the 1970s, of forcibly repatriating Caribbean immigrants to the former British colony of Guyana, as well as that of the British National Party in the 1990s, which stressed that immigrants should be "resettled" in unspecified "third world" countries. Crafted as the policy was by the leading lights of the campaign for Britain to leave the European Union, the Rwanda initiative was certainly connected to the possessive nationalism that was a key element of the Brexit vote, alongside the corresponding fetishisation of the need to "take back control" of Britain's borders with a view to curtailing the presence of those unwanted immigrants who acted as unwitting symbols of Britain's lost empire. But the policy of exporting people who had risked their lives to escape famine, war and persecution— or, as one commentator put it, "offshoring Britain's responsibilities onto Europe's former colonies instead of doing our fair share to help some of the most vulnerable people on the planet"— should more accurately be seen as an apogee of the historic willingness of British governments of all stripes to legislate on issues around race, immigration and ethnic diversity on terms dictated by the far right.[9]

The Rwanda policy was in effect an extension of Theresa May's stated ambition—in the face of growing support for Nigel Farage's UKIP—to give illegal immigrants in Britain "a really hostile reception". As we saw in Chapter Five, May's Hostile Environment was in turn built on the foundations of the policies of the New Labour Government, which passed an unprecedented six Acts of Parliament that focused on immigration in thirteen years of government. The New Labour approach was crafted with one eye on growing support for the BNP. And this not only meant the establishment of British "reception" centres in order to prevent asylum seekers from "swamping" the rest of the country (the notion of a "reception" centre was in fact a means of allowing the Government to get around the fact the British Government's use of detention centres for asylum seekers had been declared illegal). In spring 2003 it also included the expressed ambition to deal with the claims of asylum seekers in overseas "transit zones".[10]

This is a political process, aided by the remarkable durability of Powellism, that has been a near-constant feature of the history of multicultural Britain. As Ambalavaner Sivanandan observed in 1981, "what Powell says today, the Tories say tomorrow and Labour legislates on the day after". Or as the spokesperson for Oswald Mosley's fascist Union Movement presciently put it in the aftermath of the 1958 riots in Nottingham and London—which paradoxically led to the first legislation of the post-war era explicitly designed to restrict the ability of black and Asian immigrants to settle in Britain—anyone calling for restrictions on immigration or the deportation of "undesirables" was simply repeating, parrot-like, what the far-right had demanded years earlier.[11]

It's a grim thought that, if the past is any guide, it is almost certain that policies like these will periodically re-emerge in the years to come. And of course, it should be reiterated that government initiatives are not abstract things. They not only have a profound impact on their primary targets—black and Asian immigrants (and their families) with the 1962 Commonwealth Immigrants Act, Kenyan Asians (and their families) with the 1968 Commonwealth Immigrants Act, asylum seekers (and their families) with the 2002 Nationality, Immigration and Asylum Act. The kind of language and tone that are deemed acceptable by lawmakers seeps into the cultural ether in a way that can

EPILOGUE

severely pollute everyday social relations. In the aftermath of Enoch Powell's 1968 speech, for example, the London-born DJ Don Letts recalled that overnight he went from being called "Lettsie" in the school playground to "black bastard", "golliwog" and "Brillo bonce". Similarly, over half a century later the Rwanda policy paved the way for a modification of the familiar racist trope "go back to your own country". "If you hate this country so much, why do you stay?", one social media user asked a British Asian journalist, as the Rwanda policy dominated the news-cycles in summer 2022. "We don't want you, don't need you and like millions of the indigenous people of this country would like you to avail yourself of a flight to Rwanda."[12]

The kind of contradictions that have been a recurring feature of the preceding chapters are also likely to remain a defining force in the ongoing story of multicultural Britain. This is something also writ large in the Rwanda policy, which was announced by only the second ethnic minority MP to serve as Home Secretary, Priti Patel, whose own parents had fled Uganda in the years that followed Ugandan independence from Britain in 1962. A decade later tens of thousands of people who, like Patel, were from South Asian families were forced to leave Uganda when the president, Idi Amin, emulated the approach that had earlier been taken in Kenya by expelling Asians and seizing their property. Patel's Rwanda policy—which was also enthusiastically backed by individuals like Alex Davis, the founding member of the banned neo-Nazi group National Action—was cheered by the same elements of the British political class who ushered in the 1968 Commonwealth Immigrants Act, designed explicitly to keep East African Asians like Patel's parents (most of whom were also British passport holders) out of the country. And the policy was supported by Rishi Sunak, whose own father had also left East Africa in the mid-1960s and who, in October 2022, was elected by Conservative MPs to become Britain's first ethnic minority Prime Minister.[13]

MULTICULTURAL BRITAIN

Sunak is a multimillionaire former public schoolboy whose hard-line positions on everything from immigration to Brexit in many ways made him a natural fit in the modern Conservative Party. It was this background, coupled with Sunak's own politics and reluctance to highlight the significance of his arrival as Prime Minister in racial terms, that meant there were few commentators bold enough to characterise his election as Britain's "Obama moment". Symbols are important, as the journalist Gary Younge has emphasised. But they should not be mistaken for substance. Indeed, in March 2023, Sunak launched his Government's Illegal Migration Bill by boasting that the proposals would mean that asylum seekers entering into Britain "illegally" would be immediately detained, deported, banned from claiming asylum in the future and prevented from seeking assistance under UK modern slavery laws, which were portrayed as acting as an "incentive" for people to enter into the country. The United Nations described the proposals as a "clear breach" of the 1951 UN Refugee Convention. The Bill was brought before parliament within five months of Sunak's first audience with the new King Charles III at Buckingham Palace which, it had recently been revealed, a generation earlier maintained a policy of not appointing people like Sunak's parents to clerical positions in the royal household.[14]

Multicultural Britain is likely to remain a maddeningly contradictory thing for years to come. Yet we can also be sure that the broader processes I have described in this book will continue apace. Having become multicultural in the twentieth-century, ethnic diversity will only become more commonplace in the twenty-first; like other formerly imperial countries across Europe, British society will continue to be re-shaped by cultural hybridity, "diasporaization" and the dialectics of multiculturalism.[15]

One way of recognising the direction of travel in Britain is to think in terms of generation. In 1942, for instance, five years

EPILOGUE

before St Clair Drake arrived in Cardiff's Tiger Bay, one sociologist estimated that fewer than five per cent of the population had experienced any direct contact with someone from an ethnic minority background. At the end of the Second World War there were an estimated 2,000 mixed-race "brown babies" in Britain—0.004 per cent of the total population. A person born at that time grew up in a period where fewer than one in a hundred British residents had been born outside of Europe or were from an ethnic minority background. By contrast, more than thirty per cent of all babies born in England and Wales in 2015 had at least one foreign-born parent, and twenty per cent of people identified with an ethnicity other than white British (this proportion masks the significant number of people who would likely have ticked the "white British" box while also having family connections to places like Greece, Germany and Malta). By 2021, more than a third of the population of England were either migrants themselves or else had parents or grandparents born outside of the UK, and ten million people—almost 17 per cent of the population as a whole—had been born overseas.[16]

In 1958, when even in so-called "coloured quarters" like Balsall Heath and St Ann's most residents were white, polls suggested that more than 70 per cent of the population disapproved of the idea of mixed-race relationships—often on the grounds that they believed such relationships would lead to a loss of social standing and the "contamination" of the "white race". At this time, one survey found that seven in ten men agreed with the views of one father whose daughter was in a relationship with a West Indian immigrant: "rather than see her married to a nigger", he declared, "I'd watch her die having a kid". In 2000, however, it was estimated that 40 per cent of children with one black parent also had a white parent; in 2011, six per cent of all children under the age of ten were mixed race, while ten years later Britain's mixed-race population was approaching two million people. Children attending school in 2020 were the most ethnically diverse cohort in British history, while in 2021 both Birmingham and Leicester became the first cities in Britain to have majority ethnic minority populations; by the 2040s, there will likely be no one left with any memory of Britain before the twin post-war processes of growing immigration and widespread ethnic diversity.[17]

We can also think about Britain's future trajectory geographically and the extent to which, although the major cities continue to be the primary crucibles for "street-level multiculturalism", ethnic diversity is becoming an ordinary feature of new parts of the United Kingdom. Between 2001 and 2011, the largest growth in ethnic diversity was in suburban and rural areas of England like East Anglia, driven primarily by the increase in immigration from Poland, Lithuania and those other Eastern European states that made up the 2004 expansion of the European Union. Other places that are rarely, if ever, included in the story of how Britain became multicultural are now more ethnically diverse than cities like Birmingham were in the 1980s. Milton Keynes, for example, the Buckinghamshire "new town" designated by the Labour Government in 1967, saw its ethnic minority population double from 13 per cent to 26 per cent between 2001 and 2011 (as late as 1991 Birmingham's ethnic minority population stood at 22 per cent).[18]

Similarly, over the same period in the well-to-do town of Oadby—four miles from Leicester—the number of people from ethnic minority backgrounds grew by more than fifty per cent, largely because of affluent Asian families moving out of the city in search of more recognisably middle-class lifestyles. In my father's home-town of Nuneaton, the number of ethnic minority residents increased by 58 per cent between 2001 and 2011, and the town became home to the prominent Pakistani *pir* (holy man) Abdul Wahhab Siddiqi, whose body now rests in a mauso-

EPILOGUE

leum in Nuneaton that has become one of the most important sites of Muslim pilgrimage in Western Europe. And even in Belfast, the city to which my maternal grandparents moved in the 1950s and where I now live, ethnic diversity is also increasing. Although there has been an Indian and Chinese presence across Northern Ireland for generations, by 2022 more than six per cent of residents were born outside the UK and Ireland, and more than three per cent were from an ethnic minority background. This represented a doubling of the number of ethnic minority residents in ten years. And in parallel with the tense politics of language more generally in Northern Ireland, where a key flashpoint centres on the campaign for the Irish language to be given formal recognition, an often-overlooked fact is that, after English, the second most-spoken language is Polish.[19]

But this kind of analysis can only take us so far. The most vivid exemplar of Britain's multicultural future is a less quantifiable sensibility, but one which both illuminates the changes I have tried to capture in this book, as well as signposts the path that Britain is on. It is something that is there in what has become the everyday multiplicity of life outside Britain's school gates, in its parks, college canteens, hospital wards, cafés and on its buses, trains and streets. It's there in the topographical make-up of our cities and towns: in Lycamobile sim card shops, Pentecostal churches, Cypriot bakers, Irish boxing clubs, Palestinian falafel takeouts, African-Caribbean "beauty palaces", Western Union money transfer outlets and the tens of thousands of restaurants and fast-food joints that often serve tandoori chicken and samosas alongside doner kebabs, pies and fish and chips. It's there in Selfridge's department stores extending their opening hours for Eid, in the provision of *wudu* (washing) facilities at airports, in specialist second-hand reggae stalls at town markets, in photographs of Air Max 90s paired with saris shared to WhatsApp groups, in TV dinners of *sulu yemek* (Turkish stew) or Homepride cook-in "curry sauce", as well as the Birmingham post-club speciality of chips-in-naan bread with chilli sauce. Musically, it's there in the transformation of Notting Hill carnival from an attempt to raise the morale of black immigrants following the 1958 white riots to its status, by the turn of the century, as the largest event of its kind in western Europe. It's there in the emergence—via the pirate radio aerials that began to spring up on council estates like the Crossways in East London in the early-2000s—of new hybridised sounds like grime. Drawing on elements of reggae, jungle and garage, grime was performed in new iterations of multicultural slang by black, mixed-race and white artists evoking a heterogeneous sense of Britishness that, as the novelist Guy Gunaratne put it, "owes as much to elsewhere as to here".[20]

It's there in sport and particularly football, and not just in what has become the remarkable cosmopolitanism of the English professional game but also the way in which, notwithstanding the ongoing fascination of sections of England supporters with "two World Wars and one World Cup", this cosmopolitanism is reflected in amateur football as, across the country—and often to a soundtrack of Kano, Stormzy, The Streets and Little Simz—people enter the park, football cage or five-a-side pitch in the hope of emulating teams which quite literally would not exist without historic and contemporary immigration. It's there in the commonplace sight of Muslim players reciting prayers before kick-off and celebrating goals by performing the *Sujud* (bow to God). It's there in the visibility of Naz Premji, Bernardine Evaristo, Ozwald Boateng, Jaz Dheol, Sarah Maple, Moeen Ali, Alex Scott, Romesh Ranganathan, Motsi Mabuse, Dermot O'Leary, Fatima Manji and, yes, Rishi Sunak alongside the many other public figures who—belatedly, despite the ongoing presence of structural discrimination—have become mainstays of Britain's cultural and political landscapes.[21]

EPILOGUE

It should not be seen as Whiggish, naively "metropolitan" or elitist to call for a political project that takes pride in what has become the irreversible, if enduringly ambiguous fact of British multiculturalism—as well as one that finally addresses its underlying inequalities. After all, what unites most of the characters in *Multicultural Britain* is that, in four cities across the second half of the twentieth century, they lived in some of the most impoverished neighbourhoods in the country. Thinking seriously about that question 'Where are we from?'—and considering our family histories, the histories of our friends, or our children and grandchildren's friends, or the team we support, the music we listen to, the food we eat, our doctors, nurses, taxi drivers, childminders, builders, next-door neighbours, and teachers—is not just about Britain's past and present. It's also about the society we can become.[22]

On one of my trips back to Birmingham from Belfast, I decided to walk from Birmingham city centre to Balsall Heath. On an overcast Saturday afternoon I left the shoppers and hen parties in Birmingham city centre behind and made my way past an upmarket Korean grill, an adult bookshop, an Ethiopian restaurant and the 40-foot Chinese pagoda that had been donated to the city by the Chinese proprietors of the local Wing Yip supermarket in 1998. The traffic was bumper-to-bumper, and made a mockery of the "clean air zone" signs that had recently been installed by the city council. I had to cross over eight lanes of it to get to the Perhsore Road, which would eventually take me back to Balsall Heath. As I waited for the green man, I was so close to the crawling cars I could touch them.

Eventually, I made it onto the Balsall Heath Road and headed north. Here were the maisonettes that came following the slum clearances of the late-1960s, plus one or two bigger, more modern houses; the tidy front gardens had deckchairs and children's scooters folded away in the corners. I crossed the River Rea, where the white minaret of Birmingham Central Mosque was visible in the skyline, and went east along Clevedon Road, where the Kashmir Coffee House and the Pyar Ka Sagar had once symbolised a transition that had taken place among south Asian immigrants in Britain—a move towards a sense of permanence that was the necessary precursor to the political campaigns against Ray Honeyford in 1980s Bradford and against the sex industry in 1990s Balsall Heath. There were no cafés here today, but there was the Apna Ghar multi-faith care home and a group of young children playing football in high-vis vests in the park opposite, overseen by two chunky Asian men in their 30s, wrapped up warm against the autumn chill.

Adjacent to the park is Cheddar Road, the one-time focal point for Balsall Heath's sex industry and thus for the campaign against it. A Palestinian flag was hanging from one of the windows; further on a young Asian girl with pigtails was sorting out her family's recycling. I decided to do a loop back north, so I could take a look at my old school. On Edward Road I passed Al Noor Bakery and the old Coach and Horses pub which in more recent times had been a Yemeni food outlet; at the crossroads, not far from the Victorian public toilet, I noticed that the half-dozen permanent bollards by the side of the road had been painted in Islamic green and gold, and had the image of a minaret carved into them. A little further on, I stopped off for a pint in the Clock, not far from where the Wallace Inn pub used to be—where Janet Mendelsohn had once photographed Kathleen and her lover Salim. Curtis Mayfield was on the radio, there were cheese and ham cobs behind the bar and a Pukka Pie menu with a choice of steak and kidney, beef and onion and chicken balti fillings. A group of middle-aged white men were speculating about how the rise in gas prices would affect the cost of beer. An elderly black man with a thick Jamaican accent sat in the corner, watching cricket on the TV with the sound turned down.

EPILOGUE

By the time I got to my old school, dusk seemed to have come early. It was almost dark. The old school building was abandoned, with boarded-up windows and an unkempt bush making its way up the front wall. The school itself had long since moved to a modern premises around the corner and, in spite of the efforts of local community groups, no one was sure what to do with this once-grandiose, now decaying and expensive-to-run shell. I lingered for a moment, thinking about what the future might hold for my own children when they begin going to school. But the pint had made me feel sleepy, and my legs were beginning to hurt. I decided to head on home to visit my mother up in yuppie Moseley. I walked along the Ladypool Road, now dominated by Afghan, Pakhtoon and Turkish establishments. I passed Balsall Heath park and watched for a while the gaggle of Asian and Somalian boys playing football and basketball at either end of the concrete pitch.

It was here, as I was playing on the same unforgiving surface on another Saturday afternoon twenty-five years earlier, that it somehow transpired that I wanted to kiss Bushra, the girl with the sparkling hazelnut eyes. I retraced what must have been my route that day: out of the park, across the Ladypool Road and onto Brighton Road, where Bushra had lived. I found what I thought was the right spot. The identikit front walls were still there—dark blue at the top and bottom, clay red in the middle. There were blue balloons attached to the front door of the house in question, and a banner that read: "It's a boy!". Someone was having a baby.

NOTES

INTRODUCTION

1. Enoch Powell, speech to the Conservative Association, Midland Hotel, Birmingham, 20 April 1968 (https://www.telegraph.co.uk/comment/3643823/Enoch-Powells-Rivers-of-Blood-speech.html). Opinion poll data from Jed Fazakarley, *Muslim Communities in England, 1962–90: multiculturalism and political identity* (Cham, Switzerland: Palgrave, 2017), p. 48. See also Bill Schwarz, "'The Only White Man in There': the re-racialization of England, 1956–1968", *Race and Class* 38: 1 (1996), pp. 65–78 & Camilla Schofield, *Enoch Powell and the Making of Post-Colonial Britain* (Cambridge: Cambridge University Press, 2013).
2. Paul Gilroy, *After Empire: melancholia or convivial culture?* (London: Routledge, 2004), p. 2 & Paul Gilroy, "Multiculture, Double Consciousness and the 'War on Terror'", *Patterns of Prejudice* 39: 4 (2005), pp. 431–443. See also Beryl Gilroy, *Black Teacher* (London: Faber, 2022 [1976]).
3. Party for Freedom manifesto, quoted in Koen Damhuis, "'The biggest problem in the Netherlands': Understanding the Party for Freedom's politicization of Islam", *Brookings*, 24 July 2019 (https://www.brookings.edu/research/the-biggest-problem-in-the-netherlands-understanding-the-party-for-freedoms-politicization-of-islam/); Baukje Prins & Sawitri Saharso, 'From Toleration to Repression: the Dutch backlash against multiculturalism', in Steven Vertovec & Susanne Wessendorf (eds.), *The Multiculturalism Backlash: European discourses, policies and practices* (Abingdon; New York: Routledge, 2010), pp. 72–91; David Cameron, speech at 2011 Munich Security Conference, 5 Feb 2011 (https://www.gov.uk/government/speeches/pms-speech-at-munich-security-conference);
4. Nigel Farage, quoted in Maya Oppenheim, "Nigel Farage Blames Multiculturalism for London Terror Attack", *The Independent*, 23 March 2017 (https://www.independent.co.uk/news/uk/home-news/nigel-farage-london-terror-attack-multiculturalism-blame-immigration-lbc-radio-ukip-mep-leader-a7645586.html).

5. Tariq Modood, *Multiculturalism* (Cambridge: Polity, 2007), p. 3; Stuart Hall, "The Multicultural Question", in Barnor Hesse (eds), *Un/Settled Multiculturalisms: diasporas, entanglements, transruptions* (London/New York: Zed Books, 2000), pp. 209; Elizabeth Buettner, *Europe after Empire: decolonization, society, and culture* (Cambridge: Cambridge University Press, 2016); Rita Chin, *The Crisis of Multiculturalism in Europe: a history* (Princeton, NJ: Princeton University Press, 2017), p. 18; Paul Gilroy, "Multiculture, Double Consciousness and the 'War on Terror'", p. 438. On "actually existing" multiculturalism, see Ralph Grillo, 'An Excess of Alterity? Debating difference in a multicultural society', in Steven Vertovec (ed.), *Anthropology of Migration and Multiculturalism* (London: Routledge, 2010), pp. 19–38.
6. Enda Delaney, *The Irish in Post-War Britain* (Oxford: Oxford University Press, 2007), p. 119.
7. Reni Eddo-Lodge, *Why I'm No Longer Talking to White People About Race* (London: Bloomsbury, 2018), p. 85.
8. Homi K. Bhabha, *The Location of Culture* (London; New York: Routledge, 1994), p. 3.
9. Stuart Hall, "From Scarman to Stephen Lawrence", *History Workshop Journal* 48 (autumn 1999), p. 188; Johny Pitts, *Afropean: notes from Black Europe* (London: Penguin, 2020), p. 1.
10. Trevor & Mike Phillips, *Windrush: the irresistible rise of multi-racial Britain* (London: HarperCollins, 1998), p. 6; Matthew Mead, '*Empire Windrush*: The cultural memory of an imaginary arrival', *Journal of Postcolonial Writing* 45: 2 (2009), p. 142–3; Panikos Panayi, *Migrant City: a new history of London* (New Haven; London: Yale University Press, 2022), p. 33; Clair Wills, *Lovers and Strangers: an immigrant history of post-war Britain* (London: Allen Lane, 2017), p. 23.
11. Caribbean immigrant quoted in *Windrush* episode 1 (BBC television, May 1998).
12. Jed Fazakarley, *Muslim Communities in England*, pp. 22–23.
13. Immigration statistics quoted in Kennetta Hammond Perry, *London Is the Place for Me: Black Britons, citizenship and the politics of race* (Oxford: Oxford University Press, 2015), p. 7. All other testimony quoted in Daniel Lawrence, *Black Migrants: White Natives—A Study of Race Relations in Nottingham* (Cambridge: Cambridge University Press, 1974), p. 40.
14. On the evolution of Powell's British nationalism, see Camilla Schofield, *Enoch Powell and the Making of Post-Colonial Britain* & Shirin Hirsch, *In the Shadow of Enoch Powell: race, locality and resistance* (Manchester: Manchester University Press, 2018); on the styles of the skinheads, see Dick Hebdige, *Subculture: the meaning of style* (London; New York: Methuen, 1979) & Timothy S. Brown,

"Subcultures, Pop Music and Politics: Skinheads and 'Nazi Rock' in England and Germany", *Journal of Social History* 38: 1 (2004), pp. 157–178.
15. See Amelia Gentleman, *The Windrush Betrayal* (London: Faber, 2019). The Immigration Act 2014 required private landlords to check the immigration status of potential tenants, and restricted NHS care to people who are "ordinarily resident" in the UK; the Immigration Act 2016 required banks to also perform immigration checks on potential customers. See Hannah Jones, Yasmin Gunaratnam, Gargi Bhattacharyya *et al*, *Go Home? The politics of immigration controversies* (Manchester: Manchester University Press, 2017).
16. Anon, "Cameron Sprinkles His Magic in Birmingham", *Business Live*, 11 May 2007 (https://www.business-live.co.uk/economic-development/cameron-sprinkles-magic-birmingham-3970084); David Cameron, "What I Learnt From My Stay With a Muslim Family", *The Guardian*, 13 May 2007 (https://www.theguardian.com/commentisfree/2007/may/13/comment.communities); Stuart Hall, "From Scarman to Stephen Lawrence", p. 197.
17. For a further discussion of the uniqueness of London, see Panikos Panayi, *Migrant City*, pp. xvi & 1–3.
18. Samuel Selvon, *The Lonely Londoners* (Harlow: Longman, 1991 [1956]), p. 74. West Indian immigrant quoted in Kenneth L. Little, 'Loudoun Square: a community survey—I (an aspect of race relations in an English society), *The Sociological Review* 34: 1–2 (1942), p. 23, n. 2. For London-centric histories of race and immigration, see (as an indicative example) Mica Nava, *Visceral Cosmopolitanism: gender, culture and the normalisation of difference* (Oxford; New York: Berg, 2007), Kennetta Hammond Perry, *London Is the Place for Me*; Clair Wills, *Lovers and Strangers*, Rob Waters, *Thinking Black: Britain, 1964–1985* (Oakland: University of California Press, 2019) & Rob Waters, *Colonized by Humanity: Caribbean London and the politics of integration at the end of empire* (Oxford: Oxford University Press, 2023).
19. The phrase "Brixtonization" is from Johny Pitts'. See Johny Pitts, *Afropean*, p. 8.
20. On the geographic distinction between 'space' and 'place' see, for example, Yi-Fu Tuan, *Space and Place: the perspective of experience* (Minneapolis: University of Minnesota Press, 1977).
21. The exact number of African American troops that were based in the UK during the conflict is not known. Lucy Bland estimates that it could be as many as 240,000 based on the fact three million American troops passed through Britain between 1942 and 1945, and 8 per cent of these soldiers were black. Several thousand West Indian troops were also stationed in Britain during the war. See Lucy Bland *Britain's "Brown" Babies: the stories of children born to black GIs and white women in the Second World War* (Manchester: Manchester

University Press, 2019), p. 14. Anonymous observer quoted in Sonya O. Rose, 'Girls and GIs: Race, Sex, and Diplomacy in Second World War Britain', *The International History Review* 19: 1 (1997), p. 154.

22. Women in Balsall Heath from unpublished transcript, Janet Mendelsohn Archive, Cadbury Research Library, University of Birmingham [hereafter JMA], USS100/3.

23. Chamion Caballero & Peter J. Aspinall, *Mixed Race Britain in The Twentieth Century* (London: Palgrave Macmillan, 2018), pp. 334, 481 & 483. For histories of the 1958 riots in London, see Kennetta Hammond Perry, *London Is the Place for Me*, pp. 89–90 and Ashley Dawson, *Mongrel Nation: diasporic culture and the making of postcolonial Britain* (Ann Arbor: University of Michigan Press, 2007), pp. 27–28.

24. Didier Eribon, *Returning to Reims* (London: Allen Lane, 2018), pp. 11–12. For recent examples of historians introducing their own lives and family histories to their stories, see Hazel Carby, *Imperial Intimacies: a tale of two islands* (London; New York: Verso, 2019), Jon Lawrence, *Me, Me, Me? The search for community in post-war England* (Oxford: Oxford University Press, 2019), Sarah Knott, *Mother: an unconventional history* (London: Penguin, 2019) & Shabna Begum, *From Sylhet to Spitalfields: Bengali squatters in 1970s East London* (London: Lawrence and Wishart, 2023).

25. Anon., 'Women Tramps Menace Social Life in Wales', *Western Mail and South Wales News*, 12 September 1945, p. 3; anon., "White Women and Coloured Troops 'Disgrace to Everyone Concerned'—Lord Mayor", *Western Mail and South Wales News*, 13 September 1945; anon., "Girls Saw Coloured Men Off", *Cardiff Times*, 3 November 1945, p. 4; St Clair Drake, "The Rainbow Homes Fiasco, 1946–1947", unpublished typescript, c. 1948, the St Clair Drake Papers, Schomburg Center for Research in Black Culture, Harlem, New York Public Library [hereafter Drake Papers], 61/1–2.

26. In terms of my analysis of the dialectical relationship between the entrenched nature of British racism, on the one hand, and the growing familiarity with—and centrality of—ethnic diversity in Britain, on the other, I'm indebted to Mike Davis's analysis of class consciousness in the USA. See Mike Davis, *Prisoners of the American Dream: politics and economy in the history of the US working class* (London: Verso, 2018 [1986]), pp. 17–18.

1. BROWN BABIES: 1940s CARDIFF

1. Ross Cameron, '"The Most Colourful Extravaganza in the World": images of Tiger Bay, 1845–1970', *Patterns of Prejudice* 31: 2 (2010), pp. 67 & 78. For a fuller account of Drake's work in Cardiff and his influences, see my article on the subject: Kieran Connell, 'An African American Anthropologist in Wales:

St. Clair Drake and the transatlantic ecologies of race relations', *Journal of British Studies* (advanced access, Feb 2024), pp. 1–32.
2. See St. Clair Drake & Horace R. Cayton, *Black Metropolis: a study of Negro life in a Northern City* (Chicago: University of Chicago Press, 2015 [1945]), pp. 177–179, 204, 208, 210 & 219. See also Henri Peretz, 'The Making of *Black Metropolis*', *The Annals of the American Academy of Political and Social Science* 595 (2004), p. 169 & Kevin Gaines, 'Scholar-Activist St. Clair Drake and the Transatlantic World of Black Radicalism', in D.G. Kelley & Stephen Tuck (eds.), *The Other Special Relationship: race, rights, and riots in Britain and the United States* (New York: Palgrave Macmillan, 2015), pp. 75–76. For a fictional depiction of the mechanisations of the colour line in 1930s Chicago, see Richard Wright's classic *Native Son* (New York: HarperCollins, 2003 [1940]).
3. Kenneth Little, 'Race Relations in English Society. Preliminary report on a community survey', *Man* 42 (1942), p. 90; Drake Papers, Drake draft Ph.D, 8–11/60, n.p.; Stanley Bishop, 'Clean Up at "Tiger Bay"', *John Bull*, 29 January 1938, p. 30.
4. St. Clair Drake & Horace R. Cayton, *Black Metropolis*, pp. 101–104; Wendy Webster, *Mixing It: diversity in World War Two Britain* (Oxford: Oxford University Press, 2018), p. 6
5. Frantz Fanon, *Black Skins, White Masks* (New York: Grove Press, 2008 [1952]), pp. 109 & 111.
6. St. Clair Drake & Horace R. Cayton, *Black Metropolis*, p. 383. See also Mary Patillo's foreword to the same edition, p. xvii.
7. Drake, draft Ph.D, p. 180, 202 & 328. Estimate of the number of cafés is from Kenneth Little, *Negroes in Britain: a study of racial relations in an English society* (London; Kegan Paul, 1948), p. 42. Estimate of the number of pubs is from Sydney Collins, *Coloured Minorities in Britain: studies in British race relation based on African, West Indian and Asiatic immigrants* (London: Lutterworth Press, 1957), p. 118.
8. Lucy Bland, *Britain's "Brown" Babies*, p. 14. For memories of black GIs visiting Tiger Bay, see Neil M.C. Sinclair, *The Tiger Bay Story* (Cardiff: Dragon and Tiger Enterprises, 2003), p. 63. On the hostility that could face black troops stationed in Britain during the war, see Wendy Webster, *Mixing It*, p. 197.
9. Henry Lee Moon, 'Little Negro Community in Britain Faces Same Race Bias as US Coloured', *Chicago Defender*, 5 May 1945, p. 11; anon., 'Plain People: "is there anywhere…?"', *Time* Magazine, 11 March 1946, p. 27; anon., quoted in Drake Papers, Blacks in England—misc. mss and notes, 7/62.
10. Lawrence Reddick, interview with Wilbur Young, 9 August 1946, in Lawrence Reddick African Americans in WWII project, Schomburg Centre for Research in Black Culture, Harlem, New York [hereafter Reddick papers], Box 1,

Interviews with Servicemen, W-Z. See also Lucy Bland, 'Interracial Relationships and the "Brown Baby Question": Black GIs, white British women, and their mixed-race offspring in World War II', *Journal of the History of Sexuality* 26: 3 (2017), p. 428 & Mica Nava, *Visceral Cosmopolitanism*, pp. 10 & 80.

11. Anon., 'Girls Saw Coloured Men Off', *Cardiff Times*, 3 November 1945, p. 4. On the popular association of African American troops with a modish urbanism, see Mica Nava, *Visceral Cosmopolitanism*, p. 10 & Lucy Bland, 'Defying racial prejudice: Second World War relationships between British women and black GIs and the raising of their offspring', *Women's History Review* 28: 6 (2019), p. 856.

12. Sonya O. Rose, 'Sex, Citizenship, and the Nation in World War II Britain', *The American Historical Review* 103: 4 (1998), pp. 1147–1176; Neil A. Wynn, "Race War": Black American GIs and West Indians in Britain during the Second World War', *Immigrants and Minorities* 24: 3 (2006), pp. 324–346.

13. Anon., 'Women Tramps Menace Social Life in Wales', *Western Mail and South Wales News*, 12 September 1945, p. 3; anon., 'Scenes on Cardiff's Burma Road', *Cardiff Times*, 15 September 1945, p. 1; anon., 'Shock and Shame of Disclosures', *Western Mail and South Wales News*, 17 September 1945, p. 3. On imagery of 'Burma Road', see Simon Jenkins, 'Prostitution in Cardiff, 1900–1959', unpublished Ph.D thesis (Cardiff University, 2017), p. 171 & Radhika Natarajan, 'The "Bogus Child" and the "Big Uncle": the impossible South-Asian family in post-imperial Britain', *Twentieth Century British History* 34: 3 (2023), p. 459.

14. Drake Papers, Blacks in England—misc. mss and notes, 7/62. See also anon., 'Chief Says "I Have Done All I Can"', *South Wales Echo and Express*, 12 September 1945, p. 3 & anon., 'Police Say J.P.s Too Lenient', *Western Mail and South Wales News*, 13 September 1945, p. 3.

15. Quoted in anon., 'A Soldier Replies', *Western Mail and South Wales News*, 15 September 1945, p. 3 & Drake Papers, Blacks in England—misc. mss and notes, 7/62.

16. Neil Evans, 'The South Wales Race Riots of 1919', *Llafur*, 3:1 (1980), pp. 5–29 & Peter Fryer, *Staying Power: the history of black people in Britain* (London: Pluto, 2018 [1984]), p. 309. Estimate of the equivalent value of the damage to property in 1919 is based on Retail Price Index data provided by the Bank of England (https://www.bankofengland.co.uk/monetary-policy/inflation/inflation-calculator). See also Jacqueline Jenkinson, *Black 1919: riots, racism and resistance in imperial Britain* (Liverpool: Liverpool University Press, 2009).

17. Chief Constable James Wilson, quoted in Ross Cameron, "The Most Colourful Extravaganza in the World", p. 74; David Featherstone, 'Harry O'Connell, Maritime Labour and the Racialised Politics of Place', *Race & Class* 57: 3 (2016), p. 72. The most infamous of the Aliens Orders was the 1925 Special Restriction

(Coloured Seamen) Order though, as Laura Tabili and others have shown, the authorities also used earlier orders like the 1920 Aliens Order to target ethnic minority seamen. See Laura Tabili, 'The Construction of Racial Difference in Twentieth Century Britain: The Special Restriction (Coloured Seamen) Order, 1925', *Journal of British Studies* 33: 1 (1994), pp. 54–94. For a discussion of the discrimination of the trade unions in this area, see Khizar Humayun Ansari, *The Infidel Within: Muslims in Britain since 1800* (London: Hurst, 2004), p. 43.

18. Survey on the Mercantile Marine, conducted by F.A. Richardson on behalf of the British Social Hygiene Council and the British Council for the Welfare of the Mercantile Marine, 1935, quoted in Kenneth Little, *Negroes in Britain*, p. 82.

19. Survey on the Mercantile Marine, conducted by F.A. Richardson, 1935, quoted in anon., 'Cardiff's Coloured Population', *Cardiff Times*, 13 July 1935, p. 7; editorial, 'The Coloured Man in Our Midst', *Western Mail and South Wales News*, 8 July 1935, p. 8; Allister Smith, 'Among Cardiff's Coloured Seamen', *World Dominican* 12: 3 (July 1934), p. 222. For more on the enduring persistence of racial hierarchies in post-colonial Britain, see Paul B. Rich, *Race and Empire in British Politics*, (Cambridge: Cambridge University Press, 1990), p. 208.

20. Chris Waters, '"Dark Strangers" in our Midst: discourses of race and nation in Britain, 1947–1963', *Journal of British Studies* 36: 2 (1997), pp. 224–225; K.L. Little, 'Loudoun Square: a community survey I', p. 16; K.L. Little, 'Loudoun Square: a community survey II', *The Sociological Review* 34: 3–4 (1942), pp. 119–146; K.L. Little, *Negroes in Britain*, pp. 43 & 108–109.

21. Alan Sheppard, quoted in Marika Sherwood, 'Racism and Resistance: Cardiff in the 1930s and 40s', *Llafur: the journal of the Society of Welsh Labour History* 5: 4 (1991), p. 62; Leslie James and Daniel Whittall, 'Ambiguity and Imprint: British racial logics, colonial commissions of enquiry and the creolization of Britain in the 1930s and 40s', *Callaloo* 39: 1 (2016), p. 180; Drake, 'The Cardiff Race Relations Situation', Drake Papers, Summary of Dissertation, 6/60. See also James G. Cantres, *Blackening Britain: Caribbean radicalism from Windrush to decolonization* (London: Rowman & Littlefield International, 2020), p. 27. Drake published an account of his time in Cardiff in *The Crisis*, the journal of the National Association for the Advancement of Colored People. See St. Clair Drake, "A Report on the Brown Britishers," *The Crisis* 56: 6 (June 1949), pp. 174 & 188–89.

22. St Clair Drake, 'The Cardiff Race Relations Situation', in Drake Papers, Summary of Dissertation, 6/60; Lucy Bland, *Britain's "Brown" Babies*, pp. 97–102; John Belchem, *Before Windrush: race relations in twentieth-century Liverpool* (Liverpool: Liverpool University Press, 2014), pp. 2, 5 & 65.

23. White woman, quoted in Little, 'Loudoun Square: a community survey II', p. 141; Roger Burnham, quoted in profile of Roger Burnham, in Drake Papers, Blacks in England, notes and interviews with local figures, 5/62; anonymous testimony, quoted in Drake, draft PhD, p. 26. For more on the supposed "superiority" of the white wives of Arab men, see Sydney Collins, *Coloured Minorities in Britain*, p. 218. See also anon., 'Down the Bay', *Picture Post*, 22 April 1950, p. 16 & Glenn Jordan, *'Down the Bay': Picture Post, humanist photography and images of 1950s Cardiff* (Cardiff: Butetown History & Arts Centre, 2001).
24. St. Clair Drake, notes of an interview with the Edwards Family, in Drake Papers, Blacks in England—notes and interviews with local figures, 5/62. Between 1946 and 1948 the annual average of stowaways entering into Britain was estimated to be 407. See Sheila Patterson, *Dark Strangers: a sociological study of the absorption of a recent West Indian migrant group in Brixton, South London* (London: Tavistock, 1963), p. 414.
25. St. Clair Drake, notes of an interview with the Edwards Family, in Drake Papers, Blacks in England—notes and interviews with local figures, 5/62. On the ethnic segregation of pre-war Cardiff boarding houses, see Neil Evans, 'Regulating the Reserve Army: Arabs, blacks and the local state in Cardiff, 1919–45', *Immigrants and Minorities* 4: 2 (1985), p. 71; on the importance of geography to black or mixed ethnicity experiences of cities, see Chamion Caballero & Peter J. Aspinall, *Mixed Race Britain*, p. 182.
26. St. Clair Drake, notes of an interview with the Edwards Family, in Drake Papers, Blacks in England—notes and interviews with local figures, 5/62.
27. Descriptions of Africans and Arabs quoted in Drake, draft PhD, pp. 360 & 375; description of 'half castes' quoted in Drake Papers, Blacks in England—notes and interviews with local figures, 5/62.
28. St Clair Drake & Horace R. Cayton, *Black Metropolis*, p. 115.
29. Anonymous activist quoted in Drake, draft PhD, pp. 374–375.
30. Description of O'Connell quoted in Mr Elliott, letter to Marika Sherwood, c. 1990 (shared with the author by Marika Sherwood); Harry O'Connell, quoted in Drake Papers, Blacks in England, Diary and Notes, 3/62. See also David Featherstone, 'Harry O'Connell, Maritime Labour and the Racialised Politics of Place', pp. 71–87. The Colonial Defence Association was formerly called the Colonial Defence League.
31. Statistics quoted in Drake, draft PhD, p. 330 & 340; Fred Halliday, *Britain's First Muslims: portrait of an Arab community* (London; New York: I.B. Tauris, 2010), p. 31.
32. Drake, draft PhD, p. 336; Humayun Ansari, *The Infidel Within*, p. 37. Descriptions of the opening of the mosque quoted in Drake, draft PhD, p. 336 & anon., 'Britain's Moslems Get a Handsome New Mosque', *Picture Post*,

25 September 1943, pp. 17–19. For more background on al-Hakimi, see Humayun Ansari, *The Infidel Within*, pp. 137–138.

33. Abdullah Ali al-Hakimi, quoted in Drake, draft PhD, p. 342–343; anonymous, quoted in Drake, draft PhD, p. 336. On the Islamization of seafaring communities in this period, see Sophie Gilliat-Ray, *Muslims in Britain: an introduction* (Cambridge: Cambridge University Press, 2010), p. 35.
34. Statistics on Arab community quoted in Drake, draft PhD, pp. 330 & 347; Drake Papers, Blacks in England—Drake Notes, 1/63; Islamic scholar quoted in Drake, draft PhD, p. 346; Al-Hakimi, quoted in Drake, draft PhD, p. 345; Humayun Ansari, *The Infidel Within*, p. 100; Sydney Collins, *Coloured Minorities in Britain*, p. 219. Tualla Mohammed is referred to by the historian Marika Sherwood as 'Dualla'. Here I follow Drake's lead in using the former name.
35. Sydney Collins, *Coloured Minorities in Britain*, p. 220; Drake, draft PhD, p. 348; Al Hakimi, quoted in Drake, draft PhD, pp. 342–343; Somali activist, quoted in Marika Sherwood, 'Racism and Resistance', p. 64; Somalian political slogans, quoted in Drake Papers, Blacks in England—Drake notes, 1/63. For a summary of the geopolitical context in the run up to the partition of Palestine, see Rashid Khalidi, *The Hundred Years' War on Palestine: a history of settler colonial conquest and resistance* (London: Profile Books, 2020), pp. 58, 62 & 72.
36. Drake, draft PhD, p. 334.
37. Harry O'Connell, quoted in Drake Papers, Blacks in England—notes and interviews with local figures, 5/62 & Drake Papers, Blacks in England—Drake Notes, 1/63.
38. Drake, draft PhD, pp. 342–343, 367 & 475; Drake, notes on the International Coloured Athletic Club, in Drake Papers, Blacks in England—notes and interviews with local figures, 5/62. See also Peter Fryer, *Staying Power*, pp. 342–357.
39. Anonymous local resident, quoted in Drake, Draft PhD, p. 378. For sailors institutes, see Drake Papers, Drake MSS—negro seaman, 61/7, p. 14; for descriptions of Bute Town Social and Welfare Club, see Drake draft PhD, pp. 482–484 and Drake Papers, Blacks in England—The Brown Baby Problem, 1/61. For a superb fictional depiction of this Cardiff milieu, see Nadifa Mohamed, *The Fortune Men* (London: Viking, 2021), p. 11.
40. Claude McKay, *Romance in Marseilles* (London: Penguin, 2020 [1929].
41. Fred Halliday, *Britain's First Muslims*, p. 42.
42. Descriptions of Tiger Bay cafés taken from Sinclair, *The Tiger Bay Story*, p. 15; Kenneth L. Little, 'Loudoun Square: a community survey I', p. 16; Chamion Caballero & Peter J. Aspinall, *Mixed Race Britain in The Twentieth Century*, p. 265; Kenneth L. Little, 'Loudoun Square: a community survey II', pp. 132–

133; Kenneth L. Little, *Negroes in Britain*, pp. 48–49; Drake, draft survey, in Drake Papers, Drake MSS—Negro Seamen, p. 15. On the moral panic over Maltese cafés in the interwar period, see Simon Jenkins, 'Inherent Vice? Maltese Men and the Organization of Prostitution in Interwar Cardiff', *Journal of Social History* 49: 4 (2016), pp. 928–958. On growing anxieties around late-night cafés in London, see Clair Wills, *Lovers and Strangers*, pp. 78–79.

43. Alan Sheppard, quoted in Drake Papers, Blacks in England—Cardiff, notes and interviews with local figures, 5/62 & Blacks in England—Cardiff, misc. mss and notes, 7/62. On the connection between perceptions of gambling and colonial 'depravity', see Carl Chinn, *Better Betting With A Decent Feller: a social history of bookmaking* (London: Aarum Press, 2004), pp. 188–189.

44. Anonymous observer, quoted in Drake, draft PhD, p. 416; descriptions of the CIAC quoted in draft PhD, p. 471 and 473.

45. Drake, profile of Bill Douglas, Drake Papers, Blacks in England—the brown baby problem, 1/61. For a discussion of the multicultural nature of sports teams more generally in Cardiff at this time, see Sydney Collins, *Coloured Minorities in Britain*, p. 119.

46. Alan Sheppard, quoted in Drake Papers, Blacks in England—notes and interviews with local figures, 5/62 & Drake draft PhD, p. 479.

47. Member of the CIAC quoted in Drake, draft PhD., p. 384; Observations of Sheppard quoted in Marika Sherwood, 'Racism and Resistance: Cardiff in the 1930s and 40s', p. 63.

48. Drake Papers, Blacks in England—notes and interviews with local figures, 5/62. My thanks to Simon Baker at the Cardiff Rugby Museum for the information on Douglas.

49. Ibid.

50. Ibid.

51. See Alida Payson, 'Feeling Together: emotion, heritage, conviviality and politics in a changing city', unpublished Ph.D thesis (Cardiff University, 2018), pp. 9, 16–17 & 37.

52. Neil M.C. Sinclair, *The Tiger Bay Story*, p. 125; Leonard Bloom, introduction to Kenneth Little, *Negroes in Britain: a study of racial relations in English society* (London; Boston: Routledge & Kegan Paul, 1972 [1948]), p. 10

53. Ana Gonçalves & Huw Thomas, 'Waterfront Tourism and Public Art in Cardiff Bay and Lisbon's Park of Nations', *Journal of Policy Research in Tourism, Leisure & Events* 4: 3 (2012), pp. 327–352; David Hilling, 'Socio-economic Change in the Maritime Quarter: the demise of sailortown', in B.S. Hoyle, D.A. Pinder & M.S. Husain (eds.), *Revitalising the Waterfront* (London: Belhaven Press, 1988), p. 31; Ferdinand Dennis, *Behind the Frontlines: journey into Afro-Britain* (London: Victor Gollancz, 1988).

2. COLOUR BARS: 1950s NOTTINGHAM

1. Jerry White, *London in the Nineteenth Century: a human awful wonder of God* (London: Vintage, 2007), p. 131; anon.; 'What Went Wrong at Nottingham', *Manchester Guardian*, 26 August 1958, p. 3; Patrick Murphy, 'Irish Settlement in Nottingham in the Early-Nineteenth Century', *Transactions of the Thoroton Society of Nottinghamshire*, vol. XCVIII (1994), p. 83; John Giggs, 'Housing, Population and Transport', in John Beckett (ed.), *A Centenary History of Nottingham* (Manchester: Manchester University Press, 1997), p. 454; Colin Griffin, 'The Identity of a Twentieth Century City', in John Beckett (ed.), *A Centenary History of Nottingham*, p. 436; Laura Elizabeth Sinclair Odelius, 'Bringing the Empire Home: narratives of empire and the shaping of racial identity in Nottingham, 1945–1962', unpublished Ph.D thesis (Northwestern University, Illinois, 2001), pp. 148–149. For my descriptions of Nottingham, I am drawing on Alan Sillitoe, *Saturday Night and Sunday Morning* (London: Pan Books, 1960 [1958]) & Peter Richardson, *St Ann's, the End of an Era* (Nottingham: Five Leaves, 2020), as well as the memories of Nottingham shared by former residents on community websites (https://sistino.weebly.com/edits.html) and Facebook (https://www.facebook.com/groups/StAnnsWellRdPreDemolition 1970/). See also Jon Lawrence, *Me, Me, Me?*, pp. 41–56 & Camilla Schofield, 'In Defence of White Freedom: working men's clubs and the politics of sociability in late industrial England', *Twentieth Century British History* 34: 3 (2023), pp. 515–551.
2. For more on the suspicion of 'out groups' in working-class communities, see Richard Hoggart's classic, *The Uses of Literacy: aspects of working-class life with special reference to publications and entertainments* (Harmondsworth: Penguin, 1957).
3. Ron Ramdin, *The Making of the Black Working Class in Britain* (London; New York: Verso, 2017 [1987]), p. 204.
4. Stuart Hall (with Bill Schwarz), *Familiar Stranger: a life between two islands* (London: Allen Lane, 2017), p. 185; David Kynaston, *Modernity Britain, 1957–62* (London: Bloomsbury, 2015), p. 175; Trevor & Mike Phillips, *Windrush*, pp. 139–140. At the start of the 1950s, the ethnic minority population across Britain was estimated to be 74,500; by the middle of the decade, more than 40,000 black and Asian immigrants were arriving into Britain each year. See Chris Waters, "Dark Strangers", p. 209.
5. Ken Coates and Richard Silburn, *Poverty: the forgotten Englishman* (Harmondsworth: Penguin, 1970), p. 64; Paul Rock and Stanley Cohen, 'The Teddy Boy', in Verdon Bogdanor and Robert Skidelsky (eds.), *The Age of Affluence 1951–1964* (London; Basingstoke: Macmillan, 1970), pp. 288–320; George

Melly, *Revolt into Style: the pop arts in the 50s and 60s* (Oxford: Oxford University Press, 1989), pp. 33–34; Arthur Koestler, 1963, quoted in Ian Sanjay Patel, *We're Here Because You Were There: immigration and the end of Empire* (London: Verso, 2021), p. 110; Stuart Hall, *Familiar Stranger*, p. 185.

6. George Powe, *Don't Blame the Blacks* (Nottingham: Five Leaves, 2022 [1956]), p. 17; Shrin Hirsch, *In the Shadow of Enoch Powell*, p. 16; Eric George Irons, *Papaman* (unpublished memoir, c. 2005), pp. 65 & 71; anon., 'Coloured Customers', *Guardian Journal*, 25 August 1958, n.p, Nottingham Local Studies Library, newspaper clippings relating to the St Ann's Riots [hereafter NLSL], L/30/32; Oscar Robinson, quoted in Norma Gregory, *Jamaicans in Nottingham: narratives and reflections* (Hertford: Hansib Publications, 2015), p. 51; Stuart Hall, *Familiar Stranger*, p. 184.

7. Anon., 'Prison Sentence for Five Nottingham "Rowdies"', *The Times*, 2 September 1958, p. 6; Peter Fryer, *Staying Power*, pp. 383–394; Ron Ramdin, *The Making of the Black Working Class in Britain*, p. 205; David Kynaston, *Modernity Britain*, p. 170; Clair Wills, *Lovers and Strangers*, p. 160; anon., 'What Went Wrong at Nottingham', *Manchester Guardian*, 26 August 1958, p. 3; anon., 'Dozens Hurt in Racial Clash', *The Times*, 25 August 1958, p. 8. In this period, immigrants from British colonies in the Caribbean increasingly thought of themselves as 'West Indian' as a means of referencing their shared experiences. The term became less popular as the independence movement played out in the Caribbean along national lines. For a discussion of this process, see Catherine Hall, 'What is a West Indian?', in Bill Schwarz (ed.), *West Indian Intellectuals in Britain* (Manchester: Manchester University Press, 2003), pp. 31–50.

8. Donald Hinds, *Journey to an Allusion: the West Indian immigrant in Britain* (London: Heinemann, 1966), pp. 133–134; Peter Fryer, *Staying Power*, p. 388. See also Trevor & Mike Phillips, *Windrush*, p. 166.

9. Eric Irons, *Papaman*, p. 37; Daniel Lawrence, *Black Migrants*, p. 15. On 'mento' music, see Robert Witmer, '"Local" and "Foreign": the popular music culture of Kingston, Jamaica, before ska, rock steady, and reggae', *Latin American Music Review* 8: 1 (1987), pp. 1–25 & Stuart Hall, *Familiar Stranger*, pp. 125–126.

10. Eric Irons, *Papaman*, pp. 4–8, 20, 27 & 44–48; Stuart Hall, *Familiar Stranger*, p. 150. I've also drawn on other Caribbean immigrants' first impressions of Britain in this paragraph. These are Arthur Curling, Cy Grant and Vince Reid, quoted in Trevor & Mike Phillips, *Windrush*, pp. 12–14; George Lamming, *The Emigrants* (Ann Arbor: University of Michigan Press, 1994 [1954]), pp. 75 & 237; Donald Hinds, *Journey to an Illusion*, p. 17 & Bernice Smith, quoted in Colin Grant, *Homecoming: voices of the Windrush generation* (London: Jonathan Cape, 2019), p. 82.

11. Descriptions taken from Norma Gregory, *Jamaicans in Nottingham*, pp. 15, 45, 53, 67, George Lamming, *The Emigrants*, p. 36, 40–41, 78, 96, 99, 103, 107–109, 111, 120 & Ruth Glass, *Newcomers: the West Indians in London* (London: George Allen & Unwin, 1960), p. 45. See also Colin Grant, *Homecoming*, p. 43. The 1952 McCarran-Walter Act served to provide separate immigration quotas for each individual UK colony.
12. Eric Irons, *Papaman*, pp. 42–45. For comparable examples, see James G. Cantres, *Blackening Britain*, p. 39. On 'pigmentocracies' see Kennetta Hammond Perry, *London is the Place for Me*, p. 81.
13. Rozina Visram, *Asians in Britain: 400 years of history* (London: Pluto Press, 2002), p. 260–262; June Evans, 'African/Caribbeans in Scotland: a socio-geographical study', unpublished Ph.D thesis (Edinburgh University, 1987), p. 126; Donald Hinds, *Journey to an Allusion*, p. 49; Clair Wills, *Lovers and Strangers*, p. 166; Richard Hoggart, *The Uses of Literacy*, pp. 93–94. See also Jon Lawrence, *Me, Me, Me?*, p. 64. For a book length study of black Scotland, see Francesca Sobande & layla-roxanne hill, *Black Oot Here: Black lives in Scotland* (London: Bloomsbury, 2022).
14. Alan Sillitoe, *Saturday Night and Sunday Morning*, pp. 70–72 & 166–176.
15. George Lamming, *The Pleasures of Exile* (London: Michael Joseph, 1960), p. 81; ethnic minority immigrant quoted in Daniel Lawrence, *Black Migrants: White Natives*, p. 42.
16. Eric Irons, *Papaman*, pp. 49–51. See also testimony from Laurie Philpots, a Jamaican volunteer with the RAF who was also based for a time in Filey and later lived in Nottingham, in Trevor & Mike Phillips, *Windrush*, p. 36. For more on inter-racial sex in this period, see George Lamming, *The Pleasures of Exile*, pp. 77–78.
17. *Radio Times*, 12 December 1958, quoted in Ruth Glass, *Newcomers*, p. 1; hostels manager, quoted in Edward Pilkington, *Beyond the Mother Country: West Indians and the Notting Hill white riots* (London: IB Tauris, 1988), p. 50. See also Learie Constantine, *Colour Bar* (London: Kegan Paul, 1954).
18. Grant quoted in Donald Hinds, *Journey to an Allusion*, pp. 133–134; George Lamming, *The Emigrants*, p. 67. See also Matthew Whittle, 'Hosts and Hostages: mass immigration and the power of hospitality in post-war British and Caribbean literature', *Comparative Critical Studies* 11 (2014), p. 85.
19. West Indian immigrant quoted in Robert N. Murray, *Lest We Forget: the experiences of World War II West Indian ex-service personnel* (Nottingham: Nottinghamshire West Indian Combined Ex-Services Association, 1996), p. 153; Ainsley Grant, quoted in Donald Hinds, *Journey to an Allusion*, p. 66; Eric Irons, *Papaman*, p. 80. The tendency for landlords and other gatekeepers to blame neighbours, lodgers and others for their unwillingness to accept eth-

nic minority patrons was a longstanding feature of how the colour bar operated. See, for instance, Rozina Visram, *Asians in Britain*, p. 276.
20. Eric Irons, *Papaman*, pp. 12 & 69; Radhika Anita Natarajan, 'Organizing Community: commonwealth citizens and social activism in Britain, 1948–1982', unpublished Ph.D thesis (UC Berkeley, California, 2013), p. 36; Eric Irons & L. Philpotts, 'To the Coloured People of Nottingham', 18 Jan 1952, in Nottinghamshire Archives [hereafter NA], Community Relations papers, DD/CR22/1; Colin Grant, *Homecoming*, p. 100. For a discussion of comparable social clubs in Brixton and Handsworth respectively, see Sheila Patterson, *Dark Strangers*, pp. 364–373 & Kieran Connell, *Black Handsworth: race in 1980s Britain* (Oakland: University of California Press, 2019), pp. 134–136.
21. Sheila Patterson, *Dark Strangers*, pp. 183–194; Elizabeth Burney, *Housing on Trial: a study of immigrants and local government* (Oxford: Oxford University Press, 1967), p. 200; Edward Pilkington, *Beyond the Mother Country*, p. 23 & 28; Radhika Anita Natarajan, 'Organizing Community', p. 33; Donald Hinds, *Journey to an Allusion*, p. 33; Colin Grant, *Homecoming*, p. 120.
22. Nottingham Irish Studies Group, *Making it Home: experiences of being Irish* (Nottingham: Nottingham Irish Studies Group, 2001), p. 184; Kaja Irene Ziesler, 'The Irish in Birmingham, 1830–1970', unpublished Ph.D thesis (University of Birmingham, 1989). p. 318; John Corbally, 'The Othered Irish: shades of difference in post-war Britain, 1948–71', *Contemporary European History* 24: 1 (2015), p. 117; Joan Reid, Marjorie Norris, Bill Stanton & Paul Curtis, interviewed by Kieran Connell, 16 June 2021. See also Clair Wills, *Lovers and Strangers*, pp. 49–50.
23. Wendy Webster, *Mixing It*, p. 232; anon., 'Colour Divides Hosiery Workers', *Guardian Journal*, 12 September 1956, n.p., NLSL, L/30/32; the Ghulam case is detailed in Ruth Glass, *Newcomers*, pp. 82–83. On the discrimination encountered by Irish immigrants in Britain, and the relationship between this and the colour bar, see Louise Ryan, 'Family Matters: (e)migration, familial networks and Irish women in Britain', *Sociological Review* 52: 3 (2004), pp. 351–370, Enda Delaney, *The Irish in Post-War Britain*, pp. 122–125 & Erika Hanna, *Snapshot Stories: visuality, photography, and the social history of Ireland, 1922–2000* (Oxford: Oxford University Press, 2020), p. 210.
24. S. Fazl Imam, letter to the editor, *Manchester Guardian*, 29 August 1958, p. 6. On the Teddy Boys, see Bill Osgerby, 'Youth Culture', in Paul Addison and Harriet Jones, *A Companion to Contemporary Britain, 1939–2000* (Oxford: Blackwell, 2005), p. 130; Dick Hebdige, *Subculture*, p. 51; Tony Jefferson, 'The Teds: a political resurrection', Centre for Contemporary Cultural Studies Stencilled Occasional Paper (September 1973) & T.R. Fyvel, *The Insecure Offenders: rebellious youth in the welfare state* (London: Chatto and Windus,

1961), p. 44. See also Richard Griswold del Castillo, 'The Los Angeles "Zoot Suit Riots" Revisited: Mexican and Latin American perspectives', *Mexican Studies/Estudios Mexicanos* 16: 2 (2000), pp. 367–391 & Paul Gilroy & Errol Lawrence, 'Two-Tone Britain: white and Black youth and the politics of anti-racism', in Phillip Cohen & Harwant S. Bains (eds.), *Multi-Racist Britain* (Basingstoke: Macmillan, 1988), pp. 127–128.

25. Edward Scobie, 'A New Scar on the Face of Britain', *The Tribune*, 5 September 1958, pp. 6–7; Sheila Patterson, *Dark Strangers*, p. 271. For background on Scobie, see James G. Cantres, *Blackening Britain*, pp. 36–37.
26. Samuel Roberts, quoted in Edward Pilkington, *Beyond the Mother Country*, pp. 106–107; Eric Irons, *Papaman*, p. 88; David Kynaston, *Modernity Britain*, p. 170.
27. Edward Pilkington, *Beyond the Mother Country*, pp. 106–107; anon., 'Dozens Hurt in Racial Clash', *The Times*, 25 August 1958, p. 8; anon., 'Coloured Customers', *Guardian Journal*, 25 August 1958, n.p., NLSL, L/30/32; Radhika Anita Natarajan, 'Organizing Community', p. 60.
28. *Nottingham Evening News*, 25 August 1958, n.p., NLSL, L/30/32.
29. Anon., 'Dozens Hurt in Racial Clash', *The Times*, 25 August 1958, p. 8; anon., 'Coloured Customers', *Guardian Journal*, 25 August 1958, n.p, NLSL, L/30/32; Radhika Anita Natarajan, 'Organizing Community', pp. 59–60.
30. Vernon Ringrose, quoted in Edward Scobie, 'A New Scar on the Face of Britain', *The Tribune*, 5 September 1958, pp. 6–7
31. Anon.; 'What Went Wrong at Nottingham', *Manchester Guardian*, 26 August 1958, p. 3; anon., 'Trouble Brewing for Weeks', *Evening Post*, 25 August 1958, n.p, NLSL, L/30/32; George Clay, 'Menace Behind the Brawl', *The Observer* 31 August 1958, p. 11; Edward Pilkington, *Beyond the Mother Country*, p. 39. For an overview of the changing laws around prostitution at this time, see Julia Laite, *Common Prostitutes and Ordinary Citizens: commercial sex in London, 1885–1960* (Basingstoke: Palgrave, 2012).
32. Joseph A. Hunte, *Nigger Hunting in England?* (London: West Indian Standing Conference, 1966); Eric Irons, quoted in anon., 'Race Clash in Nottingham "Alarming"', *The Times*, 26 August 1958, p. 4; Peter Fryer, *Staying Power*, p. 383. The figure of 4,000 is given by Edward Pilkington in *Beyond the Mother Country*, p. 112 and Ron Ramdin in *The Making of the Black Working Class in Britain*, p. 205.
33. Driver of car, as told to Eric Irons, quoted in Trevor & Mike Phillips, *Windrush*, p. 169; Peter Fryer, *Staying Power*, pp. 383–394; Ron Ramdin, *The Making of the Black Working Class in Britain*, p. 205; anon., 'No Coloured Folk Involved in New Disturbances', *Guardian Journal*, 1 September 1958, n.p., NLSL, L/30/32.

34. Captain Popkess, quoted in Ron Ramdin, *The Making of the Black Working Class in Britain*, p. 205; anon., 'Prison Sentence for Five Nottingham "Rowdies"', *The Times*, 2 September 1958, p. 6;
35. Editorial, *The Times*, 3 September 1958, p. 11; Laura Elizabeth Sinclair Odelius, 'Bringing the Empire Home', p. 49.
36. John Wray, quoted in Edward Pilkington, *Beyond the Mother Country*, p. 108; Eric Irons, *Papaman*, p. 89; statement on the Committee for the Welfare of Coloured People's work, 13 October 1958, NA, DD/CR/36; M. Amosu, letter to the editor, *The Manchester Guardian*, 1 September 1958, p. 6. The remarks about seeking refuge in France come from George Lamming, *The Pleasures of Exile*, p. 80.
37. Christopher Hilliard, 'Mapping the Notting Hill Riots: racism and the streets of post-war Britain', *History Workshop Journal* 93: 1 (2022), pp. 47–68; Edward Pilkington, *Beyond the Mother Country*, pp. 113–120; Clair Wills, *Lovers and Strangers*, pp. 160–170; Peter Fryer, *Staying Power*, pp. 384–386; Ron Ramdin, *The Making of the Black Working Class*, p. 206; Paul Stocker, *English Uprising: Brexit and the mainstreaming of the far right* (London: Melville House UK, 2017), p. 28. For Morrison's own story of her relationship with Raymond and work as a prostitute, see Majbritt Morrison, *Jungle West 11* (London: Tandem Books, 1964).
38. On the emergence of the inner city as a focal point of racialised anxieties in Britain, see James Rhodes & Lawrence Brown, 'The Rise and Fall of the "Inner City": race, space and urban policy in postwar England', *Journal of Ethnic and Migration Studies* 45: 17 (2019), pp. 3243–3259.
39. Clair Wills, *Lovers and Strangers*, p. 171; Ann Dummett, *A Portrait of English Racism* (Harmondsworth: Penguin, 1973), p. 188; anon, 'A Dangerous Portent', *The Observer*, 31 August 1958, p. 4; Don Iddon, 'Dear Governor Faubus', 6 September 1958, quoted in Stephen Tuck, 'Malcolm X's Visit to Oxford University: US civil rights, Black Britain and the special relationship on race', *The American Historical Review* 118: 1 (2013), p. 97; Nuala Sanderson, 'The Impact of the Struggle for Racial Equality in the United States on British Racialised Relations from 1958–1968', unpublished PhD thesis (University of Southampton, 1999), pp. 39 & 137; Kennetta Hammond Perry, '"Little Rock" in Britain: Jim Crow's transatlantic topographies', *Journal of British Studies* 51: 1 (2012), pp. 155–177.
40. Ruth Glass, *Newcomers*, p. 130; Cyril Osborne quoted in quoted in Nuala Sanderson, 'The Impact of the Struggle for Racial Equality in the United States on British Racialised Relations from 1958–1968', p. 36; Bow campaign group quoted in Ruth Glass, *Newcomers*, p. 148.
41. Manley, quoted in Kennetta Hammond Perry, '"Little Rock" in Britain', p. 168.

42. Anon., '"Colour Problem Does Not Solve Itself"', *The Times*, 16 September 1958, p. 4 & anon., 'Nottingham Coloured People "Will Be Attacked Again"', *The Times*, 12 September 1958, p. 5. Jackson, quoted in anon., 'Nottingham Coloured People "Will Be Attacked Again"', *The Times*, 12 September 1958, p. 5.
43. Manley, quoted in in anon., 'Nottingham Coloured People "Will Be Attacked Again"', *The Times*, 12 September 1958, p. 5 & anon., 'Colour Problem Does Not Solve Itself', *The Times*, 16 September 1958, p. 4. See also anon., 'Don't Fence Yourself In, Says Manley', *Daily Mail* 12 September 1958, p. 2.
44. Kennetta Hammond Perry, *London is the Place for Me*, pp. 132–133; Colin Grant, *Homecoming*, p. 160; Claudia Jones, quoted in Clair Wills, *Lovers and Strangers*, p. 169; Miss D.M. Woods, to Mrs P. Jennings, 6 September 1960, NA, DD/CR/22/1; Colonial and Sports Club memo, c. 1958, NA, DD/CR/22/1; Commonwealth Citizens Association, internal memo, c. 1959, NA, DD/CR/22/1; constitution of the CCSP, c. 1957, NA, DD/CR/22/1. On local politics in Notting Hill, see Edward Pikington, *Beyond the Mother Country*, pp. 142–143 & Camilla Schofield and Ben Jones, '"Whatever Community Is, This Is Not It": Notting Hill and the reconstruction of "race" in Britain after 1958', *Journal of British Studies* 58: 1 (2019), pp. 142–173.
45. Spokesperson quoted in Ira Katznelson, 'The Politics of Racial Buffering in Nottingham, 1954–1968', *Race* XI: 4 (1970), p. 435.
46. Laura Elizabeth Sinclair Odelius, 'Bringing the Empire Home', pp. 312–313 & 355; Radhika Anita Natarajan, 'Organizing Community', pp. 74–75; Ira Katznelson, 'The Politics of Racial Buffering', p. 433. On the politics of community leaders, see Ambalavaner Sivanandan, *A Different Hunger: writings on black resistance* (London: Pluto Press, 1982)—especially part three, 'The Black Experience in Britain', pp. 99–140.
47. Cecil Palmer, to Miss Wood, 26 April 1959, NA, DD/CR22/1; Miss Wood, to Mrs Davis, 7 October 1959, NA, DD/CR22/1; DM Wood, to Mrs V. Martlew, 26 Nov 1958, NA, DD/CR/47; Statement on the Committee for the Welfare of Coloured People's work, 13 October 1958, NA, DD/CR/36; DM Wood, to Mrs Hayman, 3 December 1962; Present Work of the CCCC, c. 1962, NA, DD/CR/36. Unemployment rate for Nottingham's black population in 1958 taken from Edward Pilkington, *Beyond the Mother Country*, p. 39.
48. James Harrison MP, letter to the editor, *The Manchester Guardian*, 29 August 1958, p. 6; J.K. Cordeaux, quoted in anon., 'Nottingham MPs Urge Curb on Entry of Immigrants', *The Times*, 27 August 1958, p. 4; *Daily Mirror* editorial, 2 September 1958, & *The People* editorial, 7 September 1958, both quoted in Edward Pilkington, *Beyond the Mother Country*, p. 130. Statistics on emi-

gration from Pat Thane, 'Population and the Family', in Paul Addison and Harriet Jones (eds.), *A Companion to Contemporary Britain*, p. 48
49. Union Movement spokesperson, quoted in Edward Pilkington, *Beyond the Mother County*, p. 131
50. Walter Terry, 'Premier Hints at Checks in the Flow of Coloureds', *Daily Mail*, 4 September 1958, p. 1; Tom Driberg, quoted in Peter Fryer, *Staying Power*, pp. 386–387. For the notion of the immigrant 'scrounger' in letters to Enoch Powell, see Camilla Schofield, *Enoch Powell and the Making of Postcolonial Britain*, p 230.
51. Immigration (Control), HC Deb 05 December 1958 vol 596 cc1552–97; anon., 'Renewed Call for Changes in Immigration Law', *The Times*, 28 August 1958, p. 4; Driberg, quoted in Peter Fryer, *Staying Power*, pp. 386–387; Cyril Osborne, 'The Facts on Immigration', *The Times*, 21 October 1961, p. 9; Osborne, quoted in Ann Dummett, *A Portrait of English Racism*, p. 184. On the perceived threat of dispossession in this period, see Stuart Hall, *Familiar Stranger*, p. 182.
52. J.W. Green, letter to the editor, *The Times*, 27 October 1961, p. 13; anon., 'Quota System of Entry into Britain', *The Times*, 2 November 1961, p. 12.
53. Civil servant quoted in David Feldman, 'Why the English Like Turbans: multicultural politics in British history', in David Felman & Jon Lawrence (eds.), *Structures and Transformations in Modern British History: essays for Gareth Stedman Jones* (Cambridge: Cambridge University Press, 2011), p. 285; R. A. Butler, quoted in Ian Sanjay Patel, *We're Here Because You Were There*, p. 79; Commonwealth Immigrants Bill, HC Deb 16 November 1961 vol 649 cc687–819; Ambalavaner Sivanandan, *A Different Hunger*, p. 108. See also Ron Ramdin, *The Making of the Black Working Class in Britain*, p. 228 & Peter Fryer, *Staying Power*, p. 388.
54. Peter Fryer, *Staying Power*, p. 389; Gavin Schaffer, 'Legislating Against Hatred: meaning and motive in Section Six of the Race Relations Act of 1965', *Twentieth Century British History* 25: 2 (2014), pp. 251–275; Rachel Yemm, 'Immigration, Race and Local Media: Smethwick and the 1964 general election', *Contemporary British History* 33: 1 (2019), pp. 98–122; Daniel Renshaw, *The Discourse of Repatriation in Britain, 1845–2016: a political and social history* (London; New York: Routledge, 2021), p. 167; Christopher Hilliard, 'Words That Disturb the State: hate speech and the lessons of fascism in Britain, c. 1930s-1960s', *The Journal of Modern History* 88 (2016), p. 766, n. 8. Opinion Poll data taken from Donley T. Studlar, 'Policy Voting in Britain: the colored immigration issue in the 1964, 1966, and 1970 General Elections', *The American Political Science Review* 72: 1 (1978), p. 53.
55. Kennetta Hammond Perry, *London is the Place for Me*, pp. 146–152 & Clair Wills, *Lovers and Strangers*, p. 160; Ann Dummett, *A Portrait of English Racism*,

p. 49. For accounts of events in Middlesborough, see Peter Fryer, *Staying Power*, p. 386 & Panikos Panayi, 'Middlesbrough 1961: a British race riot of the 1960s?', *Social History* 16: 2 (1991), pp. 139–153.
56. Paul Gilroy, *Black Britain: a photographic history* (London: Saqi, 2007), p. 100; Ira Katznelson, 'The Politics of Racial Buffering', p. 439.
57. Eric Irons, *Papaman*, pp. 49–51.
58. Erica Irons, Paul Irons and Ben Irons, interviewed by Kieran Connell, 29 July 2020.

3. RED LIGHTS: 1960s BALSALL HEATH

1. The Mendelsohn archive is now part of the wider Centre for Contemporary Cultural Studies archive at the Cadbury Research Archive at Birmingham University. See Kieran Connell & Matthew Hilton (eds.), *Cultural Studies 50 Years On: history, practice and politics* (London: Rowman & Littlefield International, 2016).
2. Following Mendelsohn in her published photo-essay, I am using pseudonyms here to protect the identity of those concerned. Where I am drawing on Mendelsohn's unpublished work and I have not been able to obtain permission to use names, I have added my own pseudonyms.
3. CCCS, *Annual Report 1966–67*, pp. 9–10, Centre for Contemporary Cultural Studies Archive, Cadbury Research Library, University of Birmingham, UB/CCCS/A/3. For the Asian population in Kenya, see also Randall Hansen, 'The Kenyan Asians, British Politics, and the Commonwealth Immigrants Act, 1968', *The Historical Journal* 42: 3 (1999), p. 816.
4. Johny Pitts, *Afropean*, p. 15.
5. Ian Sanjay Patel, *We're Here Because You Were There*, p. 75; Humayun Ansari, *The Infidel Within*, pp. 152–153; Richard Vinen, *Second City: Birmingham and the forging of modern Britain* (London: Allen Lane, 2022), p. 324; Olivier Esteves, *The "Desegregation" of English Schools: bussing, race and urban Space, 1960s-90s* (Manchester: Manchester University Press, 2018), p. 81. For more on the impact of the 1962 Commonwealth Immigrants Act on South-Asian communities in particular, see Philip Lewis, *Islamic Britain: religion, politics and identity among British Muslims* (London; New York: IB Tauris, 1994), p. 17 and Clair Wills, *Lovers and Strangers*, p. 235.
6. Frank Mort, *Capital Affairs: London and the making of the permissive society* (New Haven; London: Yale University Press, 2010), pp. 309–313. For more on the extent to which men from black and Asian backgrounds were stereotyped as potential pimps, see Maureen E. Cain, *Society and the Policeman's Role* (London: Routledge & Kegan Paul, 1973), p. 117.

7. Description of Varna Road in Kate Paul, *Journal* (Hay-on-Wye: Carrington Press, 2000), p. 154; Kaja Irene Ziesler, 'The Irish in Birmingham', p. 184. Ian Sanjay Patel, *We're Here Because You Were There*, p. 105. For statists relating to immigration to Balsall Heath and Birmingham, see Phillip N. Jones, 'Some Aspects of the Changing Distribution of Coloured Immigrants in Birmingham, 1961–66', *Transactions of the Institute of British Geographers* 50 (1970), pp. 202 & 215; John R. Lambert, *Crime, Police and Race Relations: a study in Birmingham* (Oxford: Oxford University Press, 1970), p. 77 & 103; Anthony Sutcliffe & Roger Smith, *History of Birmingham Volume III: Birmingham 1939–1970* (Oxford: Oxford University Press, 1974), p. 207. Exact statistics for Balsall Heath at this time are hard to come by because of changes to ward and electoral boundaries. Calthorpe Park and Balsall Heath are often listed as two distinct areas, though the former would—certainly in popular understandings of the city's geography—generally be understood as constituting part of Balsall Heath, and contains many of the prime streets photographed by Mendelsohn.
8. For the emergence of the "inner city" as an object of political intervention see Aaron Andrews, 'Decline and the City: the urban crisis in Liverpool c. 1968 to 1986,' unpublished Ph.D thesis (University of Leicester, 2018); Otto Saumarez Smith, 'Action for Cities: The Thatcher Government and inner-city policy,' *Urban History* 47: 2 (2020), 274–291.
9. Balsall Heath statistics quoted in John R. Lambert, *Crime, Police and Race Relations* pp. 75–76, 103 & 107; Hazel Flett, Jeff Henderson & Bill Browns, 'The Practice of Racial Dispersal in Birmingham, 1969–75', *Journal of Social Policy* 8: 3 (1979), p. 289. Description of housing in Birmingham quoted in Abdullah Hussein, *Émigré Journeys* (London: Serpent's Tail, 2000), p. 59. On the extensive list of crimes associated with the word 'vice', see Frank Mort, *Capital Affairs*, p. 41. On the importation of American labels to the British context, see Stuart Hall *et al*, *Policing the Crisis: mugging, the state and law and order* (Basingstoke: Macmillan, 1978), pp. 18–28 & Mark Clapson, *Anglo-American Crossroads: urban planning and research in Britain, 1940–2010* (London; New York: Bloomsbury, 2013).
10. Anon., 'Where They Sleep on the Landings', *Evening Mail & Dispatch*, 24 January 1963 (From Birmingham Newspaper Cuttings, Library of Birmingham [hereafter BNC], Balsall Heath & Highgate, 24 Jan 1963–13 July 2006, (KQ SEQ); Harry Hawkes, 'The Problem Beneath the Surface in Balsall Heath', *Evening Mail & Dispatch*, 29 January 1963, BNC; Ministry of Social Security, quoted in unpublished transcript, JMA, USS100/3; John R. Lambert, *Crime, Police and Race Relations*, p. 76; Frank Griffin, in anon, 'Vice Areas: police pledge to the city', *Evening Mail & Dispatch*, 7 July 1967, p. 12; Frank Price, in anon, 'Call for Vice Area Inquiry', *Evening Mail & Dispatch*, 6 July 1967, p. 12.

11. John Rex & Robert Moore, *Race, Community and Conflict: a study of Sparkbrook* (London: Oxford University Press, 1967), p. 19; Terrance Morris, quoted in John R. Lambert, *Crime, Police and Race Relations*, p. vii. All other testimony quoted in *The Colony* (d. Phillip Donnellan, 1964).
12. Kaja Irene Ziesler, 'The Irish in Birmingham', pp. 173 & 175; James Moran, *Irish Birmingham: a history* (Liverpool: Liverpool University Press, 2010), pp. 2, 165, 176 & 179; Clair Wills, *Lovers and Strangers*, p. 302; Richard Vinen, *Second City*, pp. 287–290; John Corbally, 'The Othered Irish', p. 111 & Phillip A. McCarvill, 'An Examination of Ethnic Identity: a case study of "second generation" Irish people in Birmingham', unpublished Ph.D thesis (Warwick University, 2002), p. 191. On Irish ballads being sung in Birmingham pubs, see Kit De Wall's memoir, *Without Warning and Only Sometimes: scenes from an unpredictable childhood* (London: Tinder Press, 2022), p. 96. The anecdote about the Mermaid pub functioning as a quasi-labour exchange for the Irish in Birmingham is originally in Richard Vinen, *Second City*, p. 294. For more on the St Patrick's Day parade in Birmingham, see Angela Moran, 'Hail Ambiguous St Patrick: sounds of Ireland on parade in Birmingham', *Irish Studies Review* 20: 2 (2012), pp. 157–178.
13. James Moran, *Irish Birmingham*, p. 180; Clair Wills, *Lovers and Strangers*, pp. 50, 129 & 302; Phillip A. McCarvill, 'An Examination of Ethnic Identity', p. 188; Sparkbrook resident quoted in Rex and Moore, *Race, Community and Conflict*, p. 204. For more on the 1965 emphasis on those with 'Irish names' receiving drunk and disorderly charges, as well as the impact of the Troubles on Irish immigrants in Birmingham, see Sarah O'Brien, 'Negotiations of Irish identity in the Wake of Terrorism: the case of the Irish in Birmingham 1973–74', *Irish Studies Review* 25: 3 (2017), p. 375. On stereotypes about the Irish in Britain, see John Corbally, 'The Jarring Irish: postwar immigration to the heart of empire', *Radical History Review* 104 (2009), pp. 103–125.
14. Simon Prince & Geoffrey Warner, *Belfast and Derry in Revolt: a new history of the start of the troubles* (Newbridge: Irish Academic Press, 2012), pp. 114–115; Myra Connell, 'K', unpublished story, c. 1980s, p. 3; Phillip A. McCarvill, 'An Examination of Ethnic Identity', p. 201; Richard Vinen, *Second City*, pp. 299–301 & 413; Tom Kew, *The Multicultural Midlands: multicultural textualities* (Manchester: Manchester University Press, 2023), p. 137. See also Gavin Schaffer & Saima Nasar, 'The White Essential Subject: race, ethnicity, and the Irish in post-war Britain', *Contemporary British History* 32: 2 (2018), pp. 209–230.
15. On Irish perceptions of Irish travellers, see Jim Mac Laughlan, 'Nation Building, Social Closure and Anti-Traveller Racism in Ireland', *Sociology* 33: 1 (1999), pp. 129–151; Dennis Howell, quoted in Keith Collins, 'Minister Backs Mothers in School Boycott Over Tinkers', *Daily Mail*, 10 September 1968, p. 3; public

health inspector quoted in anon., 'Twenty Tinker Families Are Evicted From Camp', *The Times*, 16 September 1968, p. 3; members of the Balsall Heath traveller settlement quoted in Ian Francis, *This Way To the Revolution: art, activism and upheaval in Birmingham 1968* (Birmingham: Flatpack, 2019), p. 53. On the use of *shelta* see Sean J. Connolly (ed.), *The Oxford Companion to Irish History* (Oxford: Oxford University Press, 1998), p. 542. For perceptions of travellers in Britain and Birmingham, see Becky Taylor, *A Minority and the State: travellers in Britain in the twentieth century* (Manchester: Manchester University Press, 2008), p. 114; See also John Rex & Robert Moore, *Race, Community and Conflict*, pp. 98–99.

16. Anon., 'Tinkers Evicted Without Incident', *Irish Times*, 16 September 1968, p. 1; Albert Shaw, quoted in Ian Francis, *This Way To the Revolution*, p. 53.
17. Anonymous, 'Where They Sleep on the Landings', *Evening Mail & Dispatch*, 24 January 1963, BNC; Ian Sanjay Patel, *We're Here Because You Were There*, p. 105. On the 'perceptual prison' faced by the Irish, see Richard Ned Lebow, *White Britain and Black Ireland: the influence of stereotypes on colonial policy* (Philadelphia: Institute for the Study of Human Issues, 1976), pp. 73–74.
18. ATV Balsall Heath Documentary Interviews Reels 1 & 2, 1965, Media Archive of Central England, Lincoln University; Wendy Webster, *Mixing It*, pp. 19, 240 & 242.
19. ATV Balsall Heath Documentary Interviews Reels 1 & 2, 1965.
20. Enoch Powell, speech to the Conservative Association, Midland Hotel, Birmingham, 20 April 1968; Harold Macmillan, quoted in David Kynaston, *Modernity Britain*, p. 56. On the centrality of children in documentary photography in Britain, see Stephen Brooke, 'Revisiting Southam Street: class, generation, gender and race in the photography of Roger Mayne', *Journal of British Studies* 53: 2 (2014), p. 471.
21. Thanks to Ian Francis, who has done so much in the way of detective work around Mendelsohn's images, for pointing out the location of many of Mendelsohn's photos to me. For Bhabha's idea of 'hybridization', see Homi K. Bhabha, *The Location of Culture*, pp. 169 & 212–235. See also Robert J. C. Young, *Colonial Desire: hybridity in theory, culture and race* (London; New York: 1995).
22. On the routinization of touch in a different context, see Simeon Koole, 'How We Came to Mind the Gap: time, tactility, and the Tube', *Twentieth Century British History* 27: 4 (2016), pp. 524–554.
23. On slum clearance, tower blocks and housing estates, see Lynsey Hanley, *Estates: an intimate history* (London: Granta, 2007) & John Boughton, *Municipal Dreams: the rise and fall of council housing* (London: Verso, 2018); on the 'slow violence' associated with urban renewal, see Rachel Pain, 'Chronic Urban

Trauma: the slow violence of housing dispossession', *Urban Studies* 56: 2 (2019), pp. 385–400. See also Rob Nixon, *Slow Violence and the Environmentalism of the Poor* (Cambridge, MA: Harvard University Press, 2011).

24. On Asian-run cinemas in Britain, see Rajinder Dudrah, 'Vilayati Bollywood: popular Hindi cinema-going and diasporic south Asian identity in Birmingham (UK)', *Javnost—the public: Journal of the European Institute for Communication and Culture* 9: 1 (2014), p. 24. On the decline of cinema going more generally, see Sam Manning, *Cinemas and Cinema-Going in the United Kingdom: decades of decline, 1945–65* (London: University of London Press, 2020). On the pioneering Indian-run shops in inter-war London, see Rozina Visram, *Asians in Britain*, p. 279. According to some estimates, the first South Asian shop in Birmingham was opened in 1949. See Panikos Panayi, *Spicing Up Britain: the multicultural history of British food* (London: Reaktion Books, 2008), p. 142. For a discussion of similar processes at play in Leicester, see Sue Zeleny Bishop, 'Inner-City Possibilities: using place and space to facilitate inter-ethnic dating and romance in 1960s-80s Leicester', *Urban History* 50 (2023), pp. 232–247.

25. Elizabeth Buettner, '"Going for an Indian": South Asian restaurants and the limits of multiculturalism in Britain', *The Journal of Modern History* 80: 4 (2008), pp. 874–875; Rehana Ahmed, 'Equality of Citizenship', in Ruvani Ranasinha (ed.), *South Asians and the Shaping of Britain, 1870–1950* (Manchester; New York: Manchester University Press, 2012), p. 40; Panikos Panayi, *Migrant City*, pp. 240–241; Abdullah Hussein, *Émigré Journeys* pp. 24 & 43. For a discussion of Hussein's work, see Claire Chambers, *Britain Through Muslim Eyes: literary representations, 1780–1988* (Basingstoke: Macmillan, 2015), p. 192.

26. Abdullah Hussein, *Émigré Journeys* pp. 43–45; Guy Gunaratne, *In Our Mad and Furious City* (London: Tinder Press, 2018), p. 114. On the multicultural nature of cinema-going in Britain in this period, see Ziauddin Sardar, *A Person of Pakistani Origins* (London: C. Hurst & Co, 2018), p. 91.

27. Statistics from Dilip Hiro, *Black British, White British* (Bristol: Eyre & Spottiswoode, 1971), p. 136; anonymous testimony, quoted in Bradford Heritage Recording Unit, *Here to Stay: Bradford's South Asian communities* (Bradford: Bradford Heritage Recording Unit, 1994), p. 73.

28. Shah, quoted in Ian Francis, *This Way To the Revolution*, p. 51. For an analysis of women in this period of Indian cinema, see Saswati Sengupta, Shampa Roy & Sharmila Purkayastha, *'Bad' Women of Bombay Films: studies in desire and anxiety* (Basingstoke: Palgrave Macmillan, 2019). For more on the reliance of Black Country foundries on South Asian labour, see Clair Wills, *Lovers and Strangers*, p. 199.

29. Anon, 'Rush Hour at Midnight', *Evening Mail & Dispatch*, 10 July 1967, p. 8;

John R. Lambert, *Crime, Police, and Race Relations*, p. 75. See also Lauren Elkin, *Flaneuse* (London: Vintage, 2016).

30. Joseph Connolly, 'Mission Preached to Irish Emigrants, St John's Parish, Balsall Heath, Birmingham', 24 September to 15 October 1961, McQuaid Papers, Irish Diocese, Dublin, Emigrants' Welfare 1, 1939–1961, General Correspondence, AB8/B/XXIX, DDA.
31. Statistics on arrests for solicitation and proportion of Asian male immigrants from John R. Lambert, *Crime, Police, and Race Relations*, pp. 78–80; statistics on immigration to Birmingham and male-female immigrants from Anthony Sutcliffe & Roger Smith, *History of Birmingham Volume III*, pp. 202 & 209. See also Jed Fazakarley, *Muslim Communities in England*, p. 27. The phrase 'enclosed landscape' is from Clair Wills, *Lovers and Strangers*, p. 267.
32. Anonymous interviewee, 5 March 1984, Bradford Heritage Recording Unit Papers, Bradford Industrial Museum, C0012; Abdullah Hussein, *Émigré Journeys*, pp. 46–47. For a discussion of the red-light district in Bradford, see Phil Hubbard, 'Community Action and the Displacement of Street Prostitution: evidence from British cities', *Geoforum* 29: 3 (1998), pp. 278–280.
33. Abdullah Hussein, *Émigré Journeys*, pp. 84, 87, 105, 107, 165, 169 & 238.
34. 'L', cited in unpublished transcript, JMA, USS100/3; 'C', cited in unpublished transcript, JMA, USS100/3.
35. Colin MacInnes, quoted in Clair Wills, *Lovers and Strangers*, p. 181.
36. Paven, cited in unpublished transcript, JMA, USS100/3; Daniella Dyer, interviewed by Kieran Connell, 1 July 2016. For more on MacInnes, his sexuality and his relationship to Notting Hill specifically, see Ed Vulliamy, 'Absolute MacInnes', *The Observer*, 15 April 2007 (https://www.theguardian.com/uk/2007/apr/15/britishidentity.fiction). For a discussion of the gendered nature of MacInnes's work, see Martha Robinson Rhodes, 'Bisexuality, Multiple-Gender-Attraction, and Gay Liberation Politics in the 1970s', *Twentieth Century British History* 32: 1 (2021), pp. 119–142.
37. Paven, cited in unpublished transcript, JMA, USS100/3; Kathleen's mother, quoted in *Alta: the University of Birmingham review* (spring 1969), pp. 67–71.
38. The exhibition catalogue was published in 2016. See Kieran Connell, Matthew Hilton & Jonathan Watkins, *Janet Mendelsohn: Varna Road* (Birmingham: Ikon Gallery, 2016).
39. 'Salim', cited in unpublished transcript, JMA, USS100/3.
40. Certified death certificate, 10 April 1969, BBE771275.
41. Abdullah Hussein, *Emigre Journeys*, p. 25.
42. Ian Sanjay Patel, *We're Here Because You Were There*, pp. 84–85 & 174; Shirin Hirsch, *In the Shadow of Enoch Powell*, p. 18; Paul Stocker, *English Uprising*, p. 55: Ann Dummett, *A Portrait of English Racism*, p. 188. For more on the

anti-immigrant sentiment in Birmingham, see E.J.B. Rose, *Colour and Citizenship: a report on British race relations* (London; New York: Oxford University Press, 1969), p. 217. See also Randall Hansen, 'The Kenyan Asians, British Politics, and the Commonwealth Immigrants Act, 1968', pp. 809–834 & Camilla Schofield, *Enoch Powell and the Making of Postcolonial Britain*, pp. 192 & 200.
43. Abdullah Hussein, *Émigré Journeys*, pp. 105–106.

4. BLACK POWERS: 1980s BRADFORD

1. For a discussion of the politics of names in multicultural Britain, see Chimene Suleyman, 'My Name is My Name', in Nikesh Shukla (ed.), *The Good Immigrant* (London: Unbound, 2017), pp. 22–32.
2. In Chapeltown, by 1991 approximately 21 per cent the area's 14,000 residents were black, and 26 per cent were South Asian. For an exploration of the history of multicultural Chapeltown, see Max Farrar, *The Struggle for "Community" in a British Multi-Ethnic Area: paradise in the making* (Lewiston: The Edwin Mellen Press, 2002) & Colin Grant, *Homecoming*, pp. 163–76. For histories of the Oluwale affair, see Kester Aspden, *The Hounding of David Oluwale* (London: Vintage, 2007) & Kennetta Hammond Perry, 'The Sights and Sounds of State Violence: encounters with the archive of David Oluwale', *Twentieth Century British History* 34: 3 (2023), pp. 467–490.
3. South Asian immigrant quoted in Bradford Heritage Recording Unit, *Here to Stay*, p. 34; Clair Wills, *Lovers and Strangers*, p. 55; Kenan Malik, *From Fatwa to Jihad: the Rushdie Affair and its legacy* (London: Atlantic Books, 2009), p. 44; Roger Ballard, 'The Emergence of Desh Pardesh', in Roger Ballard (ed.), *Desh Pardesh: the South Asian presence in Britain* (London: Hurst, 1994), p. 11; statistics from Bradford Heritage Recording Unit, *Destination Bradford* (Bradford: Bradford Heritage Recording Unit, 1987), pp. 8–12; Philip Lewis, *Islamic Britain*, pp. 15–17, 62; Mark Halstead, *Education, Justice and Cultural Diversity: an examination of the Honeyford Affair, 1984–85* (Barcombe: The Falmer Press, 1988), p. 10; Badr Dahya, 'The Nature of Pakistani Ethnicity in Industrial Cities in Britain', in Abner Cohen (ed.), *Urban Ethnicity* (London: Tavistock, 1974), pp. 80–81; David Selbourne, 'The Culture Clash in Bradford', *New Society*, 26 April 1984, p. 135; Ramindar Singh, *Indians in Bradford: the development of a community* (Bradford: Bradford and Ilkley Community College, 1986), p. 3. See also Hanif Kureishi, 'Bradford', 1986, in Hanif Kureishi, *Collected Essays* (London: Faber and Faber, 2011), p. 38.
4. Philip Lewis, *Islamic Britain*, pp. 56–57; Badr Dahya, 'The Nature of Pakistani Ethnicity in Industrial Cities in Britain', p. 80.

5. Philip Lewis, *Islamic Britain*, p. 71; Tariq Mehmood, *Hand on the Sun* (Harmondsworth: Penguin, 1983), pp. 9 & 16; Claire Chambers, *Britain Through Muslim Eyes*, p. 192; anon., 'Racism "Rife in Schools"', *Telegraph & Argus*, 5 January 1984, n.p; Stanley Garnett, 'Force-Feeding with White Guilt', *Telegraph & Argus*, 4 April 1984, n.p.; Alex Fellowes, 'A Divisive View Which Can Only Hurt Children', *Telegraph & Argus*, 22 March 1984, n.p., all in West Yorkshire Archives, Bradford [hereafter WYA], Race Relations in Bradford, Papers and Reports, WYB644/2/5.
6. In 1971, almost three-quarters of Pakistani women in Bradford had arrived after 1967. See Philp Lewis, *Islamic Britain*, p. 55. For a further discussion of the gendered nature of South Asian immigration to Britain, see Jed Fazakarley, *Muslim Communities in England*, p. 28. See also Bernard Coard, *How the West Indian Child is Made Educationally Sub-Normal: the scandal of the black child in schools in Britain* (London: New Beacon Books, 1971); Max Farrar, 'Racism, Education and Black Self-Organisation', *Critical Social Policy* 12: 36 (1993), p. 56; David Feldman, 'Why the English Like Turbans', pp. 281–302. For a discussion of Coard and supplementary schools in London, see Rob Waters, *Thinking Black*, p. 130. See also Ann Dummett, *A Portrait of English Racism*, p. 146.
7. Anon., 'Metro Scraps "Bussing" of Schoolchildren', *Telegraph & Argus*, 23 January 1980, n.p. in WYA, newspaper cuttings relating to halal meat debate, WYB644/2/2; Local Administrative Memorandum, Schools 13+ and 13-division, no 2/82, pp. 1–5, WYA, Newspaper cuttings and papers relating to education and Asian children, WYB644/2/8.
8. Robert Gildea, *Backbone of a Nation: mining communities and the Great Strike of 1984–85* (Oxford: Oxford University Press, 2023); Kieran Connell, *Black Handsworth*, p. 137.
9. Shirin Hirsch, *In the Shadow of Enoch Powell*, p. 29. As has been shown, Ulster Unionist politicians—which Powell himself became following his election as MP for South Down in 1974—have often understood their status in Northern Ireland as that of "besieged settlers" at risk of being abandoned by the one-time British imperial power. See, for example, John Doyle, 'Irish Nationalism and the Israel-Palestine Conflict', in Rory Miller (ed.), *Ireland and the Middle East: trade, society and peace* (Dublin: Irish Academic Press, 2007), pp. 88–89 & Brenda O'Leary & John McGarry, *The Politics of Antagonism: understanding Northern Ireland* (London: The Athlone Press, 1997), pp. 101–102. For more on the 1981 British Nationality Act, see Ian Sanjay Patel, *We're Here Because You Were There*, pp. 93–94.
10. Stuart Hall, 'New Ethnicities', 1989, in David Morley and Kuan-Hsing Chen (eds.), *Critical Dialogues in Cultural Studies* (London: Routledge, 1995), p. 448; Hanif Kureishi, 'Bradford', p. 37.

11. Dervla Murphy, *Tales From Two Cities: travel of another sort* (London: Penguin, 1989), pp. 6–8; Tariq Mehmood, *Hand on the Sun*, pp. 43 & 68–77; Philip Lewis, *Islamic Britain*, p. 67. See also Zaiba Malik, *We are Muslim, Please* (London: Windmill Books, 2011), pp. 32–33, 206 & Charles Husband, Yunis Alam & Jorg Huttereman et al, *Lived Diversities: space, place, and identities in the multi-ethnic city* (Bristol: Policy Press, 2016), p. 51.
12. Dervla Murphy, *Tales From Two Cities*, p. 132.
13. Dervla Murphy, *Tales From Two Cities*, pp. 5–6, 79, 87, 132; Tariq Mehmood, *Hand on the Sun*, pp. 15 & 96.
14. Stuart Bentley, 'Merrick and the British Campaign to Stop Immigration: populist racism and political influence', *Race & Class* 36 (1995), pp. 57–72; David Feldman, 'Why the English Like Turbans', pp. 281–302; Paul Stocker, *English Uprising*, p. 54 & 58; Ian Sanjay Patel, *We're Here Because You Were There*, pp. 87–89.
15. David Swift, 'Competition or Culture? Anti-Migrant Hostility and Industrial Decline: the case of West Yorkshire, 1962–81', *Journal of Ethnic & Migration Studies* 47:11 (2019), pp. 1–17; Ralph Fevre, *Cheap Labour and Racial Discrimination* (Aldershot: Gower Publishing, 1984), pp. 110–116. See Ambalavaner Sivanandan, *A Different Hunger*, p. 37 & *Race Today*, 'Grunwick Gates: the entry to unionisation', 1977, in Paul Field et al (eds.), *Here To Stay, Here To Fight: a 'Race Today' Anthology* (London: Pluto Press, 2019), pp. 131–135, for more on the Grunwick dispute specifically.
16. Local official quoted in Barry Troyna and Jenny Williams, *Racism, Education and the State* (Beckenham: Croom Helm, 1986), pp. 18–19; Stanley Arthur, 'Why We Bus', *Telegraph & Argus*, 22 March 1979, n.p., anon., 'Metro Scraps "Bussing"', n.p., WYA, Newspaper cuttings and papers relating to education and Asian children, WYB644/2/8. See also Farrukh Dhondy, 'The Black Explosion in British Schools', *Race Today*, Feb 1974, in Paul Field et al (eds.), *Here to Stay, Here to Fight*, pp. 40–41 & Olivier Esteves, *The "Desegregation" of English Schools*, pp. 51 & 71. The policy that was adopted in Birmingham was one of "friendly persuasion" with the aim of encouraging black and Asian parents to send their children to mostly white schools. See Richard Vinen, *Second City*, p. 347.
17. Garry Morris, Ali Hussain and Tarlochan Gata Aura, 'Racism and the Schooling Crisis in Bradford', *Critical Social Policy* 4: 12 (1984), p. 71 & Olivier Esteves, 'Babylon by Bus? The dispersal of immigrant children in England, race and urban space (1960s–1980s)', *Paedagogica Historica* 54: 6 (2018), pp. 750–765; Dave Hamilton, 'Schools of Racism', *New Statesman*, 13 January 1984, p. 13. For a description of Eccleshill, see Dervla Murphy, *Tales From Two Cities*, p. 74. Bussing was ultimately abolished by the Bradford authority because of a warn-

ing from the Commission for Racial Equality that the policy was in breach of the 1976 Race Relations Act. See Helen Carr, 'Muslims and the State Education System: England c.1965–1997', unpublished Ph.D thesis (Birkbeck College, University of London, 2018), p. 175.
18. Head teacher quoted in David Swift, 'Competition or Culture?', p. 10. This perspective contrasted with earlier anxieties around South Asian families in Britain which, as Radhika Natarajan has shown, often focused on what was understood to be the problem of absent mothers. See Radhika Natarajan, 'The "Bogus Child" and the "Big Uncle"', pp. 440–466.
19. Sue Mackay, quoted in Joe Hopkinson, 'Racism in Memories of British Schooling, 1960–1989', unpublished Ph.D thesis (University of Huddersfield, 2022), p. 223; Dervla Murphy, *Tales From Two Cities*, p, 79; formerly bussed pupil quoted in Olivier Esteves, 'Babylon by Bus?', p. 759. On the alleged force-feeding of Muslim pupils, see Jed Fazakarley, *Muslim Communities in England*, p. 74.
20. Richard Thurlow, *Fascism in Britain: from Oswald Mosley's Blackshirts to the National Front* (London: I.B. Tauris, 1998), p. 252; Olivier Esteves, 'Babylon by Bus?', p. 759; Rob Waters, *Thinking Black*, pp. 129–130; anon., 'An Unremitting Campaign of Hate', *The Times*, 18 November 1981, p. 4; Ann Dummett, *A Portrait of English Racism*, p. 11; sixteen-year-old quoted in Panikos Panayi, *Migrant City*, pp. 153–154; Tariq Mehmood, *Hand on the Sun*, pp. 90–91. For an overview of the origins of the skinhead subculture, see Dick Hebdige, *Subculture*, pp. 54–59. For a fictional depiction, see Richard Allen, *Skinhead* (London: Dean Street Press, 2015 [1970]).
21. Asian immigrant, quoted in Bradford Heritage Recording Unit, *Here to Stay*, p. 83; Tariq Mehmood, *Hand on the Sun*, p. 13, 26.
22. Tariq Mehmood, *Hand on the Sun*, pp. 12–13, 26–31.
23. Directorate of Educational Services, *Drummond Middle School Advisors Inspection* (Bradford: City of Bradford Metropolitan Council,1984), p. 5.
24. Simon Peplow, *Race and Riots in Thatcher's Britain* (Manchester: Manchester University Press, 2019), pp. 1, 50–51, 152 & 158.
25. Mark Halstead, *Education, Justice and Cultural Diversity*, pp. 45–49 & 237; Seán McLoughlin, 'Writing "Bradistan" Across the Domains of Social Reality', in Seán McLoughlin et al (eds.), *Writing the City in British Asian Diasporas* (Abingdon: Routledge, 2014), p. 30; Dervla Murphy, *Tales From Two Cities*, p. 94; Kenan Malik, *From Fatwa to Jihad*, p. 73. On the re-emergence of municipal socialism, see Daisy Payling, 'Socialist Republic of South Yorkshire': grassroots activism and left-wing solidarity in 1980s Sheffield', *Twentieth Century British History* 25: 4 (2014), pp. 602–627. As Helen Carr's research has shown, some of the changes that *Turning Point* introduced had been in operation in

some Bradford schools in an earlier period, albeit in an ad hoc basis. See Helen Carr, 'Muslims and the State Education System', pp. 151–194.
26. Local Administrative Memorandum, Schools 13+ and 13-division, no 2/82, pp. 1–5, WYA, Newspaper cuttings and papers relating to education and Asian children, WYB644/2/8; Mark Halstead, *Education, Justice and Cultural Diversity*, pp. 21–54 & Kevin Myers, *Struggles for a Past: Irish and Afro-Caribbean histories in England, 1951–2000* (Manchester: Manchester University Press, 2015), p. 162. On the provision of Islamic prayer in Bradford schools in the 1970s, see Helen Carr, '"I Think You are Ignoring the Relevant Provisions of the 1944 Education Act": Muslims, the state and education in England, c. 1966-c. 1985', *Contemporary British History* 35: 1 (2021), pp. 59–63.
27. Anthony Doran, 'Inside the Race "School" Ripping This City Apart', *Daily Mail*, 15 March 1984, n.p., WYA, Honeyford Affair, WYB644/2/5; Dervla Murphy, *Tales From Two Cities*, pp. 72–73. For more on the potential of a 'white backlash' as a result of the reforms of the early-1980s, see Barry Troyna and Jenny Williams, *Racism, Education and the State*, p. 97.
28. Dervla Murphy, *Tales From Two Cities*, p. 110–111.
29. Ian Jack, 'A Severed Head?', *Sunday Times Magazine*, 15 December 1985, pp. 30–31; Dervla Murphy, *Tales From Two Cities*, p. 110; Jim Greenhalf, 'The Head who Spoke His Mind', *Telegraph & Argus*, 15 November 1984, n.p.; Jim Greenhalf, 'The Life, Times and Turmoil of Ray Honeyford', *Telegraph & Argus*, 29 March 1985, n.p., all in WYA, Honeyford Affair, WYB644/2/5; Casey, quoted in Murphy, *Tales from Two Cities*, p. 107. On the New Right, see John Solomos, *Race and Racism in Contemporary Britain* (Basingstoke: Macmillan, 1989), p. 126. See also Aled Davies, Ben Jackson & Florence Sutcliffe Braithwaite, *The Neoliberal Age? Britain since the 1970s* (London: UCL Press, 2021).
30. Ray Honeyford, 'Multi-Ethnic Intolerance', *The Salisbury Review* 4 (summer 1983), pp. 12–13; Kehinde Andrews, *The New Age of Empire: how racism and colonialism still rule the world* (London: Allen Lane, 2021), p. xiii.
31. Ray Honeyford, 'Multiracial Myths?', *The Times Educational Supplement*, 19 November 1982, pp. 20–21; Ian Jack, 'A Severed Head?', *Sunday Times Magazine*, 15 December 1985, p. 34 & Mark Halstead, *Education, Justice and Cultural Diversity*, pp. 56–58.
32. Ray Honeyford, 'When East is West', *The Times Educational Supplement*, 2 September 1983, p. 19. See also Hanif Kureishi, 'London and Karachi', in Raphael Samuel (ed.), *Patriotism: the making and unmaking of British national identity*, vol. 2 (London: Routledge, 1989), p. 129 & Rob Waters, *Thinking Black*, p. 129.
33. Ray Honeyford, 'Education and Race—an alternative view', *The Salisbury Review*

6 (winter 1984), pp. 30–32. The reference to post-imperial guilt comes from Ray Honeyford, 'Multiracial Myths?', *The Times Educational Supplement*, 19 November 1982, pp. 20–21.

34. Ray Honeyford, 'Education and Race—an alternative view', pp. 30–32.
35. David Selbourne, *Left Behind: journeys into British politics* (London: Jonathan Cape, 1987), p. 107; Dervla Murphy, *Tales From Two Cities*, pp. 67 & 137; Bert Lodge, 'Home Truths Jar Racial Harmony', *Times Educational Supplement*, 13 March 1984, p. 11; John Mahoney and Jim Greenhalf, 'Head Hits Out at City's Policy on Race', *Telegraph & Argus*, 8 March 1984, n.p.; Andrew Brown, 'Whoever Wins in Court the Battle Goes On, *The Times*, 3 September 1985, p. 12; DPAC newsletter, no. 1 (October 1984), p. 1; Alex Fellowes, 'A Divisive View Which Can Only Harm Our Children', *Telegraph & Argus*, 22 March 1985, n.p., in WYA, Honeyford Affair, WYB644/2/5. The reference to the report detailing the performance of white pupils in ethnically diverse schools is from Glyn Middleton, 'School Where White Children are Brighter', *Telegraph & Argus*, 7 October 1985, p. 7.
36. F. Brian Breton, letter to the editor, *The Yorkshire Post*, 2 April 1985, in WYA, Bishop of Bradford Papers, 64D94/1/9/1.
37. Mark Halstead, *Education, Justice and Cultural Diversity*, p. 247; Michael Nally, 'Bradford Torn By Racial Tensions as Asians Speak Out', *The Observer*, 11 March 1984, p. 4.
38. Anon., 'Race Brawls: 55 Held', *The Observer*, 25 April 1976, p. 1; anon., 'Inquiry Sought on Front March', *The Guardian*, 26 April 1976, p. 1.
39. Interview with Junior Rashid, 21 April 1986, Bradford Heritage Recording Unit Papers, Bradford Industrial Museum, C0055; Rob Waters, *Thinking Black*, pp. 165–207; Anandi Ramamurthy, *Black Star: Britain's Asian Youth Movements* (London: Pluto Press, 2013), p. 26.
40. Activist quoted in Anandi Ramamurthy, *Black Star*, p. 123. See also *Race Today* Collective, 'Reflecting on the Trial of the Decade: The Bradford 12', 1982, in Paul Field *et al* (eds.), *Here To Stay, Here To Fight*, pp. 157–167.
41. Tariq Mehmood, *Hand on the Sun*, pp. 112–125.
42. DPAC member quoted in Andrew Brown, 'Whoever Wins in Court the Battle Goes On', *The Times*, 3 September 1985, p. 12; merchant quoted in Murphy, *Tales from Two Cities*, p. 136; Jenny Woodward, interviewed by Kieran Connell, 6 July 2022.
43. Dervla Murphy, *Tales from Two Cities*, pp. 103 & 114, Jenny Woodward *et al*, 'Racism in Bradford', *Times Educational Supplement*, 4 May 1984, p. 20; DPAC newsletter, no. 1 (October 1984), p. 1 & David Selbourne, *Left Behind*, p. 99; Olivia Foster-Carter, 'The Honeyford Affair: political and policy implications', in Barry Troyna (ed.), *Racial Inequality in Education* (London: Routledge, 1989), p. 51; anon., 'Schooling Crisis in Bradford', *Race Today*, pp. 8–10.

44. DPAC statement, quoted in Murphy, *Tales from Two Cities*, pp. 114–115.
45. Max Farrar, 'Racism, Education and Black Self-Organisation', pp. 53–72; anon., 'Thousands in "Keep Halal Meat" Demo', *Telegraph & Argus*, 6 March 1984, n.p., in WYA, Newspaper Reports Relating to Halal Meat, WYB644/2/2. See also Philip Lewis, *Islamic Britain*, p. 149.
46. Directorate of Educational Services, *Drummond Middle School Advisors Inspection*, pp. 5, 7, 10, 13, 25, 27, 29. See also DPAC newsletter, no. 1 (October 1984), p. 1 & anon., 'Pupils Play Truant as Protest', *The Times*, 12 June 1984, p. 1.
47. Roger Scruton, 'Punish the Real School Bullies', *The Times*, 4 December 1984, p. 14; anon., '6,000 Backers for "Race Row" Head', *Telegraph & Argus*, 11 April 1985, n.p., in WYA, Honeyford Affair, WYB644/2/5.
48. Marcus Fox, HC Deb 16 April 1985 vol 77 cc235–44; anon., 'Maggie's Invitation', *Telegraph & Argus*, 28 September 1985, n.p., in WYA, Honeyford Affair, WYB644/2/5. See also Margaret Thatcher engagement diary, 2 October 1985, from the Margaret Thatcher Foundation Archive, THCR 6/1/2/7. The perverse idea that anti-racist initiatives are totalitarian in nature has become a core element of the present-day culture wars over issues such as how best to diversify university curricula. See, for just one of many examples, Zoe Strimpel, 'Cambridge Should be a Bastion of Excellence—Not Social Engineering', *The Daily Telegraph* 7 May 2022 (https://www.telegraph.co.uk/news/2022/05/07/toopes-early-departure-cambridge-blessing-hope-no-damage-done/).
49. Anon., 'Rebels Set Up Own School', *Telegraph & Argus*, 4 March 1985, n.p., in WYA, Honeyford Affair, WYB644/2/5; Jenny Woodward, interviewed by Kieran Connell, 6 July 2022.
50. On the campaign for Muslim schools in the early-1980s, see H.H. Barrick, to R. Shahid, 31 October 1983, in WYA, Muslim Parents Association, WYB644/2/7; John Salmon, 'A Boring Farce in Bad Taste', *Telegraph & Argus*, 5 July 1983, p. 6. See also Mark Halstead *Education, Justice and Cultural Diversity*, pp. 94–95; Olivia Foster-Carter, 'The Honeyford Affair', p. 53; Philip Lewis, *Islamic Britain*, p. 140–148. For an analysis of the roots of the campaign for Muslim schools in Britain, see Helen Carr, "I Think You are Ignoring the Relevant Provisions of the 1944 Education Act", pp. 52–71. For an overview of a similar campaign in Birmingham, see Humayun Ansari, *The Infidel Within*, p. 325.
51. Mike Whittaker, quoted in David Selbourne, 'The Culture Clash in Bradford', p. 136. By 1994, the Bradford Local Education authority was supporting the idea of Voluntary Aided Muslim Schools with the application of Faversham College to be the first such school in the country. See Sean McLoughlin, '"A Part of the Community"? The politics of representation and a Muslim school's application for state funding', *Innovation* 11: 4 (1998), pp. 451–470.

52. Statement from Bradford Council for Mosques, 11 September 1985; statement from the Council for Mosques, 17 September 1985; statement from the Council for Mosques, 13 October 1985, in WYA, Honeyford Affair, WYB644/2/5.
53. Dervla Murphy, *Tales from Two Cities*, pp. 135–141; Michael Clarke and Jill Parkin, 'Honeyford Triumph', *The Yorkshire Post*, 16 October 1985, p. 1; Glyn Middleton, 'Dad Beaten Taking Children to School', *Telegraph & Argus*, 18 September 1985, p. 1, in WYA, Honeyford Affair, WYB644/2/5; Jenny Woodward, interviewed by Kieran Connell, 6 July 2022.
54. Dervla Murphy, *Tales from Two Cities*, pp. 135–141; anon., 'Parent Attacked at Bradford Protest School', the *Times*, 19 September 1985, p. 1; anon., 'Honeyford to Go for £71,000', *Telegraph & Argus*, 14 December 1985, p. 1; Peter Davenport, '"Cooling Off" Time After Honeyford's Departure', *The Times*, 16 December 1985, p. 2.
55. Bradford administrator quoted in David Selbourne, *Left Behind*, p. 97.
56. Lord Michael Swann, *Education for All: Report of the Committee of Enquiry into the Education of Children from Ethnic Minority Groups* (London: HMSO, 1985). See also Kevin Myers, *Struggles for a Past*, p. 10 & Jed Fazakarley, *Muslim Communities in England*, p. 42.
57. Sathnam Sanghera, *Empireland: how Imperialism has shaped Modern Britain* (London: Penguin Random House, 2021), p. 192; Kehinde Andrews, *The New Age of Empire*, p. 86.
58. John Agard, *Half-Caste* (London: Hodder Children's Books, 2005), pp. 11–13. For the background to Agard's inclusion in the national curriculum, see Asha Rogers, *State Sponsored Literature: Britain and cultural diversity after 1945* (Oxford: Oxford University Press, 2020), pp. 165–166.
59. Majority Rights campaign leaflet, c. 1988, in WYA, Honeyford Affair, WYB644/2/5. Not all the recommendations of the Swann Report were put into practice, and the government did introduce the 1988 Education Act, which formally required that the majority of religious activity in schools (e.g. during assemblies) be Anglican in nature. In practice, however, the Act contained a degree of flexibility that allowed teachers to adapt to the religious and cultural beliefs of the school more generally. See David Feldman, 'Why the English Like Turbans', p. 297.
60. Robert Kilroy-Silk, 'Defending Ethnic Majorities', *The Times*, 17 Feb 1989, p. 14; Fay Weldon, 1989, quoted in Philip Lewis, *Islamic Britain*, p. 4; Michael Nicholson, letter to the editor, *The Times*, 20 Jan 1989, p. 13; Roger Scruton, 'Let's Face It—Honeyford Got it Right on Islam and Education', *The Spectator*, 5 July 2014 (https://www.spectator.co.uk/article/let-s-face-it-ray-honeyford-got-it-right-on-islam-and-education/); Nigel Farage Twitter feed, 18 September 2018 (https://twitter.com/NorthernGuru/status/909745360742047745?s=20).

61. Hanif Kureishi, 'Bradford', pp. 41 & 43.
62. Sean McLoughlin, '"A Part of the Community"?', pp. 541–470; Denise Cush, 'The Faith Schools Debate', *British Journal of Sociology of Education* 26: 3 (2005), pp. 435–442 & Roy Gardner, 'Faith Schools Now: an overview', in Roy Gardner, Jo Cairns and Denis Lawton (eds.), *Faith Schools: consensus or conflict?* (Oxonbridge: RoutledgeFalmer, 2005), pp. 7–13.
63. On 'actually existing multiculturalism' see Ralph Grillo, 'An Excess of Alterity?', pp. 19–38 & Thomas E. Hodgson, 'Multicultural Harmony? Mirpuris and Music in Bradford', unpublished Ph.D thesis (Oxford University, 2012), pp. 3 & 71. The key text on culture wars in a US context is James Davison Hunter, *Culture Wars: the struggle to define America* (New York: Basic Books, 1991).
64. Hanif Kureishi, 'Bradford', p. 57; Ralph Fevre, *Cheap Labour and Racial Discrimination* p. 137; David Selbourne, *Left Behind*, p. 110; Bradford Heritage Recording Unit, *Here to Stay*, p. 11; Dervla Murphy, *Tales From Two Cities*, p. 7; Phil Hubbard, 'Community Action and the Displacement of Street Prostitution', p. 278; Humayun Ansari, *The Infidel Within*, p. 180.

5. WHITE FLIGHTS: 1990s BALSALL HEATH

1. Information about Milan's Sweet Centre from Four Fathers project (https://www.fourfathers.org.uk/stories/dhiren-patel/); description of Ladypool Road from Ziauddin Sardar, *Balti Britain: a provocative journey through Asian Britain* (London: Granta, 2008), p. 13.
2. Andrew Coulson & Geoff Wright, 'Brindleyplace, Birmingham: creating an inner city mixed-use development in times of recession', *Planning Practice & Research* 28:2 (2013), pp. 256–274; Michael Keith, *After the Cosmopolitan? Multicultural cities and the future of racism* (Abingdon, Oxon: Routledge, 2005), p. 23; Nick Henry et al, 'Globalisation From Below: Birmingham—postcolonial workshop of the world?' *Area* 34: 2 (2002), pp. 117–127. For a discussion of similar processes in a US context, see Mike Davis, *City of Quartz: excavating the future in Los Angeles* (London; New York: Verso, 2018 [1990]), pp. 199–201.
3. Austin Barber & Stephen Hall, 'Birmingham: Whose Urban Renaissance? Regeneration as a response to economic restructuring', *Policy Studies* 29: 3 (2008), pp. 281–292; Patrick Loftman & Alan Middleton, 'Emasculating Public Debate and Eroding Local Accountability: city promotion of urban development projects in Birmingham', *Geographische Zeitschrift* 89: 2/3 (2001), pp. 86 & 92; anon., 'Bad News and Good News', *The Balsall Heathen* 157 (November 1994), p. 2; Birmingham Area Studies Group, *Sparkbrook Ward* (Birmingham: Birmingham Development Dept, 1988), pp. 8 & 26; Mike Beazley, Patrick Loftman & Brenden Nevin, 'Downtown Redevelopment and Community Resistance: an

international perspective', in Nick Jewson and Susanne MacGregor (eds.), *Transforming Cities: contested governance and new spatial dimensions* (London and New York: Routledge, 1997), p. 189; T.R. Slater, 'Birmingham's Black and South Asian Population', in J. Gerrard and T.R. Slater (eds.), *Managing a Conurbation: Birmingham and its region* (Studley: Brewin Books, 1996), p. 153; Mary Lean, 'The Red Lights Go Green in Birmingham', *For a Change* 9: 3, 1996 (https://forachange.co.uk//browse/1504.html).

4. David Ward, 'Angry Muslims Picket City's Red Light Streets', *The Guardian*, 20 July 1994, p. 4; Melanie Phillips, 'When a Community Stands Up For Itself', *The Observer*, 17 July 1994, p. 25; Jessica Davies, 'Streets Free From Shame', *Daily Mail*, 23 July 1994, pp. 16–17; Phil Hubbard, 'Community Action and the Displacement of Street Prostitution', pp. 275–277; T.R. Slater, 'Birmingham's Black and South-Asian Population', p. 152.

5. For a discussion of the cultural and political implications of this plurality, see Homi K. Bhabha, *The Location of Culture*, p. 224.

6. Michael Keith, *After the Cosmopolitan?*, p. 130; Mica Nava, *Visceral Cosmopolitanism*, pp. 126–127; Stuart Hall, 'Aspiration and Attitude... Reflections on Black Britain in the Nineties', *New Formations* 33 (1997), p. 43; Stuart Hall, 'From Scarman to Stephen Lawrence', pp. 188 & 191; Paul Gilroy, *Black Britain*, p. 297; Claire Alexander, *The Art of Being Black: the creation of black British youth identities* (Oxford: Oxford University Press, 1996), p. 1; Rupa Huq, 'From the Margins to Mainstream? Representations of British Asian youth musical cultural expression from bhangra to Asian underground music', *Young: Nordic Journal of Youth Research* 11: 1 (2003), p. 32.

7. David Blunkett, quoted in Alan Travis, 'Citizenship Classes for Immigrants', *The Guardian*, 26 October 2001, p. 1; David Blunkett, 'It's Not About Cricket Tests', *The Guardian*, 14 December 2001, p. 1; anon., 'Row Erupts Over Blunkett's "Swamped" Comment', *The Guardian* 24 April 2002 (https://www.theguardian.com/politics/2002/apr/24/immigrationpolicy.immigrationandpublicservices); David Hughes, 'Blunkett: Speak English in Your Homes', *Daily Mail*, 16 September 2002 (https://www.dailymail.co.uk/news/article-138409/Blunkett-Speak-English-homes.html); Anthony Browne, 'We Can't Run Away From It: White Flight is Here Too', *The Times*, 5 May 2004, p. 5.

8. Paul Gilroy, *After Empire*, p. 105; Raymond Williams, *Marxism and Literature* (Oxford: Oxford University Press, 1977), p. 108.

9. Jessica Davies, 'Streets Free From Shame', *Daily Mail*, 23 July 1994, pp. 16–17.

10. Roger Silver, 'Councillors Call for City Brothels', *The Guardian*, 1 July 1967, p. 3; anon., 'Kerb-Crawling and Prostitution', *The Balsall Heathen* 69 (September 1984), p. 2; Hilary Kinnell, *Violence and Sex Work in Britain* (Uffculme: Willian, 2007), p. 94; David Ward, 'Angry Muslims Picket City's Red Light Streets',

The Guardian, 20 July 1994, p. 4. Weather forecasts for July 1994 available on YouTube (https://www.youtube.com/ watch?v=vkt4U-umz_w). *The Balsall Heathen* 69 (September 1984), pp. 9–11; Nick Cohen, 'When Self-Help is Not Enough', *New Statesman*, 3 April 2000, p. 8; Osman Yousefzada, *The Go-Between: a portrait of growing up between different worlds* (Edinburgh: Canongate, 2022), p. 7; Shirin Hirsch, *In the Shadow of Enoch Powell*, p. 30. For a discussion of programmes such as *Neighbours From Hell*, see Sara Ahmed, *Strange Encounters: embodied others in post-coloniality* (London; New York: Routledge, 2000), pp. 26–31.

11. Interview with 36-year-old woman, from C. Bagley & E. Cashmore, 'Ethnic Relations on West Midland Housing Estates, 1983–1984', Interview 037, UK Data Service. SN: 4846, DOI: 10.5255/UKDA-SN-4846-1; Jessica Davies, 'Streets Free From Shame', *Daily Mail*, 23 July 1994, pp. 16–17; Osman Yousefzada, *The Go-Between*, p. 196. Amin, quoted in Ian Murray, 'Pavement Pickets Banish Prostitutes', *The Times*, 21 July 1994, p. 8; Phil Hubbard, 'Community Action and the Displacement of Street Prostitution', p. 277; T.R. Slater, 'Birmingham's Black and South-Asian Population', p. 152. One of the earliest known mosques in Birmingham was opened in 1944 on Speedwell Road. See Carl Chinn, *Birmingham: the great working city* (Birmingham: Birmingham City Council, 1994), p. 101. For a fictional depiction of the hostility toward sex workers among some young British Muslims at this time, see Hanif Kureishi, 'My Son the Fanatic', in Hanif Kureishi, *The Black Album & My Son the Fanatic* (New York: Simon & Schuster, 1996), pp. 285–298.

12. James Vernon, *Modern Britain: 1750 to the present* (Cambridge: Cambridge University Press, 2017), p. 500; Chris Moores, 'Thatcher's troops? Neighbourhood Watch schemes and the search for 'ordinary' Thatcherism in 1980s Britain', *Contemporary British History* 31: 2 (2017), pp. 230–255.

13. Maggie O'Kane, 'Cruising, Abusing, or on the Game', *The Guardian*, 23 July 1994, p. 25; Jessica Davies, 'Streets Free From Shame', *Daily Mail*, 23 July 1994, pp. 16–17; Amin quoted in David Ward, 'Angry Muslims Picket City's Red Light Streets', *The Guardian*, 20 July 1994, p. 4; Mary Lean, 'The Red Lights Go Green in Birmingham', *For a Change* 9: 3, 1996; John Torode, 'How an Asian Vigilante Group Took the Law into Their Own Hands—and cleaned up a city's sordid red-light area', *Daily Mail*, 20 March 1996, pp. 32–33; Nick Cohen, 'When Self-Help is Not Enough', *New Statesman*, 3 April 2000, pp. 8–9; Abdullah Rehman, interviewed by Kieran Connell, 21 September 2021.

14. David Ward, 'Angry Muslims Picket City's Red Light Streets', *The Guardian*, 20 July 1994, p. 4.

15. David Ward, 'Angry Muslims Picket City's Red Light Streets', *The Guardian*,

20 July 1994, p. 4; Karen Bibby, 'Evil Worse Than Prostitution', *The Observer*, 24 July 1994, p. 24; Maggie O'Kane, 'Cruising, Abusing, or on the Game', *The Guardian*, 23 July 1994, p. 25; Nick Cohen, 'When Self-Help is Not Enough', *New Statesman*, 3 April 2000, p. 9; anonymous woman quoted in Kinnell, *Violence and Sex Work in Britain*, p. 99. For the death of the 20-year-old sex worker in December 1994, see Duncan Campbell, 'Police Join Forces as Fourth Prostitute is Strangled', *The Guardian*, 24 May 1994, p. 9 & Sally Weale, 'Death Links Raise Serial Killer Fears', *The Guardian*, 21 July 1994, p. 7.

16. Ian Murray, 'Pavement Pickets Banish Prostitutes', p. 8; Osman Yousefzada, *The Go-Between*, p. 8; Hillary Kinnell, *Violence and Sex Work in Britain*, pp. 101–102 & 104; Halwell quoted in Maggie O'Kane, 'Cruising, Abusing, or on the Game', *The Guardian*, 23 July 1994, p. 25.

17. Hillary Kinnell, *Violence and Sex Work in Britain*, p. 99–100; Richard Vinen, *Second City*, p. 326; Phil Hubbard, 'Community Action and the Displacement of Street Prostitution', p. 275; Maggie O'Kane, 'Cruising, Abusing, or on the Game', *The Guardian*, 23 July 1994, p. 25.

18. Jessica Davies, 'Streets Free From Shame', *Daily Mail*, 23 July 1994, pp. 16–17; Melanie Phillips, 'Bye Hooker, Bye Crook', *The Observer*, 4 February 1996, p. 7; Melanie Phillips, 'Don't Fall for Bogus Claims of "Islamophobia"', *The Jewish Chronicle*, 16 December 2019 (https://www.thejc.com/lets-talk/dont-fall-for-bogus-claims-of-islamophobia-qsvwxvnt).

19. For more on the construction of the Asian 'folk devil' in the mid-1990s, see Claire Alexander, '(Dis)Entangling the "Asian Gang": ethnicity, identity, masculinity', in Barnor Hesse (ed.), *Un/settled Multiculturalisms*, pp. 123–147 & Claire Alexander, *The Asian Gang: ethnicity, identity, masculinity* (Oxford: Berg, 2000); Jessica Davies, 'Streets Free From Shame', *Daily Mail*, 23 July 1994, pp. 16–17.

20. Jessica Davies, 'Streets Free From Shame', *Daily Mail*, 23 July 1994, pp. 16–17; Anne Shooter, 'The Street Cleaners', *Daily Mail*, 18 March 1996, p. 15; John Torode, 'How an Asian Vigilante Group Took the Law into Their Own Hands', *Daily Mail*, 20 March 1996, pp. 32–33; Phil Hubbard, 'Community Action and the Displacement of Street Prostitution', pp. 276–277. In 1988, police estimated £500,000 had been spent on attempting to curb prostitution in Balsall Heath. See Hillary Kinnell, *Violence and Sex Work in Britain*, p. 96. For a discussion of the Bradford campaign against sex work, see Stacey Burlet & Helen Reid, 'A Gendered Uprising: political representation and minority ethnic communities', *Ethnic & Racial Studies* 21: 2 (1998), p. 276.

21. Raymond Williams, *Politics and Letters: interviews with the New Left Review* (London: New Left Books, 1979), p. 159.

22. Nick Cohen, 'When Self-Help is Not Enough', *New Statesman*, 3 April 2000,

p. 9; anon., 'Forgotten Victims', *The Heathen* 137 (July 1991), p. 8; Daniele Joly, *Britannia's Crescent: making a place for Muslims in British society* (Aldershot: Avebury, 1995), pp. 27–28; anon., 'Nelson Mandela Visits Balsall Heath!', *The Balsall Heathen* 152 (October/November 1993), p. 1.

23. Simon Jones, *Black Culture, White Youth: the reggae tradition from JA to UK* (Birmingham: Bassline Books, 2016 [1988]), p. 1. For a discussion of 'Cockney Translation' & Smiley Culture, see Dick Hebdige, *Cut 'n' Mix: culture, identity and Caribbean music* (London; New York: Routledge, 1987), pp. 149–151 & Lucy Robinson, 'Smiley Culture: a hybrid voice for the Commonwealth', in William 'Lez' Henry & Matthew Worley (eds.), *Narratives from Beyond the UK Reggae Bassline* (Cham: Palgrave, 2021), pp. 101–123.

24. Nikesh Shukla, 'Namaste', in Nikesh Shukla (ed.), *The Good Immigrant*, p. 5; interview with teacher from Edgbaston High School for Girls, from C. Bagley & E. Cashmore, 'Ethnic Relations on West Midland Housing Estates, 1983–1984', Interview 126, UK Data Service. SN: 4846, DOI: 10.5255/UKDA-SN-4846-1; Margaret Thatcher, TV interview for Granada *World in Action*, 27 January 1978, Margaret Thatcher Foundation (https://www.margaretthatcher.org/document/103485); Simon Jones, 'Music and Symbolic Creativity', in Paul Willis (ed.), *Common Culture: symbolic work at play in the everyday cultures of the young* (Milton Keynes: Open University Press, 1990), p. 66; Paul Gilroy & Errol Lawrence, 'Two-Tone Britain', p. 138. On the centrality of swearing within the use of Punjabi by non-native speakers in Britain, see Ben Rampton, 'Interracial Panjabi in a British Adolescent Peer Group', *Language in Society* 20 (1991), p. 395–398. On the importance of dancing in this milieu, see Claire Alexander, *The Art of Being Black*, p. 122.

25. Simon Jones, *Black Culture, White Youth*, pp. 1, 3, 122, 135–6; Ben Rampton, 'Interracial Panjabi', p. 404. Asian teenager quoted in Ben Rampton, *Crossing: language and ethnicity among adolescents* (Manchester: St Jerome Publishing, 2005), p. 58; Paul Gilroy & Errol Lawrence, 'Two-Tone Britain', pp. 138–139. For a foundational analysis of this kind of slang, see Roger Hewitt, *White Talk Black Talk* (Cambridge: Cambridge University Press, 1986). For more on the rules of multicultural slang, see Les Back, *New Ethnicities and Urban Cultures: racisms and multiculture in young lives* (London: Routledge, 1996), pp. 133–134. See also Robert J.C. Young, *Colonial Desire*, p. 5. For a study of the use of slang in a predominately white school setting, see Paul Willis, *Learning to Labour: how working class kids get working class jobs* (Farnborough: Saxon House, 1977), pp. 32–34.

26. For a discussion of the Coventry milieu that gave birth to both the Specials and the Selecter, see Pauline Black's memoir, *Black By Design: a 2-Tone memoir* (London: Serpent's Tail, 2012).

27. Kieran Connell, *Black Handsworth*, pp. 91–118; Benjamin Zephaniah, 'The Approved School of Reggae', in Benjamin Zephaniah, *Too Black, Too Strong* (Northumberland: Bloodaxe Books, 2001), pp. 80–81. See also Mike Alleyne, 'White Reggae: cultural dilution in the record industry', *Popular Music and Society* 24: 1 (2000), pp. 15–30.
28. Dick Hebdige, *Cut 'N' Mix*, p. 79 & Simon Jones, *Black Culture, White Youth*, pp. 67–69; Anoop Nayak, *Race, Place and Globalization: youth cultures in a changing world* (Oxford; New York: Berg, 2003), pp. 38, 44, 113, 117–118. For a discussion of the politics of black hair styles, see Kobena Mercer, 'Black Hair/Style Politics', *New Formations* 3 (1987), pp. 33–54.
29. Ali & Robin Campbell, *Blood & Fire: the autobiography of the UB40 Brothers* (London: Arrow Books, 2006), pp. 14, 29–31; Garth Cartwright, 'Birmingham's Lost Reggae Store', *Long Live Vinyl*, 1 April 2020 (https://longlivevinyl.net/2020/04/01/don-christie-birmingham/); 'Don Christie', Birmingham Music Archive (https://longlivevinyl.net/2020/04/01/don-christie-birmingham/).
30. On jungle music, see Les Back, *New Ethnicities and Urban Culture*, pp. 232–233, Andy Wood, 'Jungle', in Alison Donnell (ed.), *Companion to Contemporary Black British Culture* (London: Routledge, 2002), p. 163, Akala, *Natives: race & class in the ruins of Empire* (London: Two Roads, 2018), p. 251 & Two Fingas & James T. Kirk, *Junglist* (London: Repeater Books, 2021), p. 9; on the origins of bhangra, see Amarjit Talwar, introduction to Rajinder Dudrah (ed.), *Bhangra: Birmingham and beyond* (Birmingham: Punch Records, 2007), p. 11; Boy Chana and Rajinder Dudrah, 'The British Bhangra Live Music Scene', in Rajinder Dudrah (ed.), *Bhangra*, p. 27; Boy Chana, 'Bhangra's DJ Culture', in Rajinder Dudrah (ed.), *Bhangra*, p. 62; Ben Rampton, *Crossing*, p. 237, Gayatri Gopinath '"Bombay, U.K., Yuba City": Bhangra music and the engendering of diaspora', *Diaspora: A Journal of Transnational Studies* 4: 3 (1995), pp. 303–321 & Gerd Baumann & Sabita Banerji, 'Bhangra 1984–8: fusion and professionalisation in a genre of South Asian dance music', in Paul Oliver (ed.), *Black Music in Britain* (Milton Keynes: Open University Press, 1990), pp. 137–152; on Oriental Star Records see the Asian Youth Culture website (https://asianyouthculture.co.uk/oral-histories/mohammed-ayub/) & Samina Zahir, 'Oriental Star Agencies', in Alison Donnell (ed.), *Companion to Contemporary Black British Culture*, p. 227; on British bhangra I am indebted to Rajinder Dudrah's work in particular. See Rajinder Kumar Dudrah, 'British South Asian Identities and the Popular Cultures of British Bhangra Music, Bollywood Films and Zee TV in Birmingham', unpublished Ph.D thesis (University of Birmingham, 2001), pp. 160–171. On *Qawwali* music in Britain, see John Baily, '*Qawwali* in Bradford: traditional music in Muslim communities', in P. Oliver (ed.), *Black Music in Britain*, pp. 153–165.

31. Rajinder Kumar Dudrah, 'British South Asian Identities', p. 161–162, 166–168; Gurdeep John Singh Khabra, 'The Heritage of British Bhangra: popular music heritage, cultural memory, and cultural identity', unpublished Ph.D thesis (University of Liverpool, 2014), p. 26.
32. Rajinder Kumar Dudrah, 'British South Asian Identities', pp. 158, 185 & 193; Gerd Baumann & Sabita Banerji, 'Bhangra 1984–8', p. 147–9; Rupa Huq, 'From the Margins to the Mainstream?', p. 33; Gurdeep John Singh Khabra, 'The Heritage of British Bhangra', p. 26; Rajinder Dudrah, 'The Representation of Bhangra in the British Media', in Rajinder Dudrah (ed.), *Bhangra*, p. 44.
33. Bradford Council for Mosques, quoted in Humayun Ansari, *The Infidel Within*, p. 220; Bally Sagoo, interviewed by Kieran Connell, 29 March 2022; Osman Yousefzada, *The Go-Between*, p. 321; Rajinder Dudrah, '"Balle-Balle, Balle-Balle": fashion—British Bhangra style', *Atlantic Studies* 13: 4 (2016), p. 504; Boy Chana and Rajinder Dudrah, 'The British Bhangra Live Music Scene', p. 33; Rajinder Dudrah, 'The Representation of Bhangra in the British Music Scene', p. 48.
34. Rajinder Kumar Dudrah, 'British South Asian Identities', pp. 158 & 185; Gerd Baumann & Sabita Banerji, 'Bhangra 1984–8', p. 147–9; Les Back, *New Ethnicities*, p. 219. See also Ninder Billing, 'Rave of the Secret Rebels', *The Guardian*, 9 November 1990, p. 38. The description of the grocery shop is from Osman Yousefzafa, *The Go-Between*, p. 54. For a discussion of representations of daytimers in the media, see Rupa Huq, 'Asian Kool? Bhangra and Beyond', in Sanjay Sharma, John Hutnyk & Ashwani Sharma (eds.), *Dis-Orientating Rhythms: the politics of the new Asian dance music* (London: Zed Books, 1996), pp. 61–80.
35. Bally Sagoo, interviewed by Kieran Connell, 29 March 2022.
36. Les Back, *New Ethnicities and Urban Culture*, p, 228; Bally Sagoo, interviewed by Kieran Connell, 29 March 2022; Cheshire Cat, on Kiz Manley, *Enter the 36 Chambers* podcast, episode 18, 16 March 2022.
37. Rupa Huq, 'From the Margins to the Mainstream', p. 38; Vivien Goldman, 'Gimme Indi Pop!', *The Village Voice*, 18 February 1997, p. 68. For a discussion of the significance of Zee TV in a British context, see Rajinder Dudrah, 'British South Asian Identities', pp. 268–327.
38. Caroline Sullivan, 'Rock of Asians', *The Guardian* Weekend Supplement, 13 March 1993, pp. 35–36 & 53; James Bagan, interviewed by Kieran Connell, 1 March 2023.
39. Bally Sagoo, interviewed by Kieran Connell, 29 March 2022; Caroline Sullivan, 'Rock of Asians', *The Guardian* Weekend Supplement, 13 March 1993, pp. 35–36 & 53; Alex Bellos, 'Indian Leader to Set Seal on Singer's Success', *The Guardian*, 25 October 1996, p. 4; Shirin Housee & Mukhtar Dar, inter-

view with Bally Sagoo and Radical Sista, in Sanjay Sharma, John Hutnyk and Ashwani Sharma (eds.), *Dis-Orientating Rhythms*, pp. 81–91; Bally Sagoo personal website (https://ballysagoomusic.com/about/); Gayatri Gopinath, '"Bombay, U.K., Yuba City"', p. 303; Ashley Dawson, '"Bollywood Flashback": Hindi film music and the negotiation of identity among British-Asian youths', *South Asian Popular Culture* 3: 2 (2005), p. 166; Rupa Huq, 'Asian Kool? Bhangra and Beyond', p. 65; Martin Cayton, '"You can't fuse yourself": contemporary British-Asian music and the musical expression of identity', *East European Meetings in Ethnomusicology* 5 (1998), pp. 74–75. For a discussion of Lovers' Rock, see Lisa Amanda Palmer, '"Ladies A Your Time Now!" Erotic politics, Lovers' Rock and resistance in the UK', *African and Black Diaspora: an international journal* 4: 2 (2011), pp. 177–192.

40. Stuart Hall, 'The Great Moving Nowhere Show', *Marxism Today* (November/December 1998), pp. 9–14. I am indebted to Sukhdev Sandhu for the descriptions of New Labour's vision for urban space. See Sukhdev Sandhu, *Night Haunts* (London; New York, 2006), p. 12.

41. Dick Atkinson, *The Common Sense of Community* (London: Demos, 1994), pp. 1, 32, 33, 37–38, 45. For an overview of the origins of Demos and its relationship to *Marxism Today*, see Charles Thorpe, 'Participation as Post-Fordist Politics: Demos, New Labour, and science policy', *Minerva* 48 (2010), pp. 389–411. On the role of think tanks in an earlier period, see Ben Jackson, 'The Think Tank Archipelago: Thatcherism and neoliberalism', in Ben Jackson & Robert Saunders (eds.), *Making Thatcher's Britain* (Cambridge: Cambridge University Press, 2012), pp. 43–61. Both Ashdown and Phillips were thanked by Atkinson in *The Common Sense of Community*. See also Melanie Phillips, 'When a Community Stands Up for Itself', *The Observer*, 17 July 1994, p. 25. For an overview of the American emphasis placed on the policing of social boundaries, see Mike Davis, *City of Quartz*, p. 200.

42. Charlie Leadbeater, 'Power to the Person', in Stuart Hall & Martin Jaques (eds.), *New Times: the changing face of politics in the 1990s* (London: Lawrence & Wishart, 1990), p. 137; Charles Leadbeater, *The Self-Policing Society* (London: Demos, 1996); David Blunkett, interviewed by Kieran Connell, 31 March 2022. See also Jonathan Burnett, 'Community, Cohesion and the State', *Race & Class* 45: 3 (2004), p. 13. For other examples of Balsall Heath featuring as a prominent case study in Demos literature, see Charles Leadbeater, *Civic Spirit: the big idea for a new political area* (London: Demos, 1997), Charles Leadbeater & Ian Christie, *To Our Mutual Advantage* (London: Demos, 1999), Amitai Etzioni, *The Third Way to a Good Society* (London: Demos, 2000) & David Blunkett, *Politics and Progress: renewing democracy and civil society* (London: Demos, 2001). For a critique of this 'New Times' thinking, see

NOTES pp. [253–256]

Ambalavaner Sivanandan, 'All That Melts into Air is Solid: the hokum of New Times', *Race & Class* 31: 3 (1990), pp. 1–30.

43. See anon., 'Another MP (and his dog) Visit Balsall Heath', *The Balsall Heathen* 155 (May/June 1994), p. 5; anon., 'Risk Essential in Urban Renewal Communities—Blunkett', *Local Government Chronicle*, 9 May 2000 (https://www.lgcplus.com/archive/risk-essential-in-urban-renewal-of-communities-blunkett-09-05-2000/). For more on Blunkett's intervention in the Balsall Heath private school, see Geoffrey Walford, *Markets and Equity in Education* (London; New York: Continuum, 2006), pp. 180–181. In December 2007 Atkinson was given an OBE for "services to the community in Balsall Heath". He died in May 2023

44. Anon., 'Blunkett Brands Balsall Heath as a Beacon for Britain', *The Balsall Heathen*, December 2002, p. 3.

45. David Blunkett, 'Full Text of David Blunkett Speech', *The Guardian*, 11 December 2001 (https://www.theguardian.com/politics/2001/dec/11/immigrationpolicy.race); anon., 'Blunkett Urges Citizenship Debate', BBC news, 11 December 2001 (http://news.bbc.co.uk/1/hi/uk_politics/1703322.stm); anon., 'Blunkett Brands Balsall Heath as a Beacon for Britain', *The Balsall Heathen*, December 2002, p. 3; David Blunkett, 'It's Not About Cricket Tests', *The Guardian*, 14 December 2001, p. 1.

46. Gaby Hinsliff, 'Riots Fuelled by Envy Over Grants', *The Observer*, 9 December 2001, p. 8; Blunkett, quoted in Colin Brown, 'Blunkett's "British Test" for Immigrants', *The Independent*, 9 December 2001 (https://www.independent.co.uk/news/uk/politics/blunkett-s-british-test-immigrants-9263369.html) & Andrew Grice, 'Blunkett Under Fire For Backing "British Norms"', *The Independent*, 10 December 2001 (https://www.independent.co.uk/news/uk/politics/blunkett-under-fire-for-backing-british-norms-9256806.html); David Blunkett, 'It's Not About Cricket Tests', *The Guardian*, 14 December 2001, p. 1; David Blunkett, 'Full Text of David Blunkett Speech', *The Guardian*, 11 December 2001 (https://www.theguardian.com/politics/2001/dec/11/immigrationpolicy.race). See also Catherine Curran-Vigier, 'From Multiculturalism to Global Values: how New Labour set the agenda', *Observatoire de la Societe Britannique* 5 (2008), p. 69.

47. Sarah Spencer, 'Immigration', in Anthony Seldon (ed.), *Blair's Britain: 1997–2007* (Cambridge: Cambridge University Press, 2007), p. 342; James Vernon, *Modern Britain*, p. 500; the *Sun* editorial quoted in Jeremy Seabrook, 'Racists and Hypocrites', *The Guardian*, 8 February 2000, p. 21; study on tabloid newspapers quoted in Paul Stocker, *English Uprising*, pp. 75–76; Hague, quoted in George Jones, 'Hague Vows to Deport All Bogus Refugees', *The Daily Telegraph*, 5 March 2001, p. 10; Alwyn W. Turner, *A Classless Society*, p. 569; Daniel

Trilling, *Bloody Nasty People: the rise of Britain's far right* (London: Verso, 2012), p. 106 & 121.

48. Paul Stocker, *English Uprising*, p. 70; Arun Kundnani, *The End of Tolerance: racism in 21st Century Britain* (London: Pluto Press, 2007), pp. 53–54; Helen Carter & Paul Kelso, 'BNP Makes Its Mark in Oldham', *The Guardian*, 8 June 2001 (https://www.theguardian.com/politics/2001/jun/08/uk.election200131).

49. Daniel Trilling, *Bloody Nasty People*, p. 106; Herman Ouseley, *Community Pride Not Prejudice* (Bradford: Bradford City Council, 2001), pp. 12–13, 16 & 18; Ted Cantle, *Community Cohesion* (London: HMSO, 2001), pp. 9 & 70; anon., 'Key Points of the Cantle Report', *The Guardian*, 11 December 2001 (https://www.theguardian.com/uk/2001/dec/11/race.world5).

50. James Rhodes & Laurence Brown, 'The Rise and Fall of the "Inner City"', p. 3254; Claire Alexander, 'Imagining the Asian Gang: ethnicity, masculinity and youth after "the riots"', *Critical Social Policy* 24: 4 (2004), p. 532; Home Office/Ted Cantle, *Community Cohesion*, pp. 20; Colin Brown, 'Blunkett's "British Test" For Immigrants', *The Independent*, 9 December 2001; Samuel Huntington, 'The West and the Rest', *Prospect*, 20 Feb 1997 (https://www.prospectmagazine.co.uk/magazine/thewestandtherest). See also Samuel Huntington, *The Clash of Civilizations and the Remaking of World Order* (New York: Simon and Schuster, 1996).

51. Melanie Phillips, 'They Can be both Muslim and British', *Daily Mail*, 10 December 2001, p. 10; Ceri Peach, 'Muslims in the 2001 Census of England and Wales: gender and economic disadvantage', *Ethnic & Racial Studies* 29: 4 (2006), p. 637. See also Melanie Phillips, *Londonistan: How Britain Is Creating a Terror State Within* (London: Gibson Square, 2007).

52. Stewart Field and Pauline Roberts, 'Racism and Police Investigations: individual redress, public interests collective change after the Race Relations (Amendment) Act 2000', *Legal Studies* 22: 4 (2002), p. 494; Jeevan Vasagar, 'Asian Cash Aid to be Diverted to Whites', *The Guardian*, 15 June 2001, p. 5; Alan Travis, 'Anger at Blunkett "Whining Maniacs" Attack', *The Guardian*, 6 September 2002, p. 1; Chris Allen, *Fair Justice: the Bradford Disturbances, the sentences and impact* (London: Forum Against Islamophobia and Racism, 2003), p. 8; Arun Kundnani, *The End of Tolerance*, p. 53; anon., 'Row Erupts Over Blunkett's "Swamped" Comment', *The Guardian*, 24 April 2002, p. 2; Gaby Hinsliff, 'Speak English at Home, Blunkett Tells British Asians', *The Guardian*, 15 September 2002 (https://www.theguardian.com/politics/2002/sep/15/race.immigrationpolicy); Matthew Tempest, 'Blunkett: Refugees Should Rebuild Their Own Countries', *The Guardian*, 18 September 2002 (https://www.theguardian.com/politics/2002/sep/18/immigrationpolicy.immigration); anon., 'Immigrants Evicted From Mosque Face Deportation', *Evening Standard*, 25 July

2002, p. 19; Raekha Prasad, 'Deportation of Afghan Family Was Unlawful', *The Guardian*, 12 September 2002, p. 9; Jonathan Freedland, 'New Labour has Opened its Big Tent to the Far Right', *The Guardian*, 19 September 2002, p. 22. Blunkett's comment about rioters being victims of their own destruction came from my own interview with him. David Blunkett, interviewed by Kieran Connell, 31 March 2022. See also Paul Gilroy, 'A Land of Tea Drinking, Hokey Cokey and Rivers of Blood', *The Guardian*, 18 April 2008 (https://www.theguardian.com/commentisfree/2008/apr/18/britishidentity.race).

53. UK Government, Nationality, Immigration and Asylum Act, 2002 (https://www.legislation.gov.uk/ukpga/2002/41/notes); Gareth Mulvey, 'When Policy Creates Politics: the problematizing of immigration and the consequences for refugee integration in the UK', *Journal of Refugee Studies* 23: 4 (2010), p. 441; Ash Amin, 'Ethnicity and the Multicultural City: living with diversity', *Environment & Planning A* 34 (2002), p. 977; Alan Travis, 'Thousands of Asylum Seekers Face "Destitution"', *The Guardian*, 27 December 2002, p. 1; Dallal Stevens, 'The Nationality, Immigration and Asylum Act 2002: secure borders, safe haven?', *The Modern Law Review* 67: 4 (2004), pp. 616–631 & Vicki Square, '"Integration With Diversity in Modern Britain": New Labour on nationality, immigration and asylum', *Journal of Political Ideologies* 10: 1 (2005), pp. 51–74; Arun Kundnani, *The End of Tolerance*, pp. 86 & 160.

54. John Reid, quoted in Gareth Mulvey, 'When Policy Creates Politics', p. 447.

55. Paul Lewis, 'Surveillance Cameras in Birmingham Track Muslims' Every Move', *The Guardian*, 4 June 2010 (https://www.theguardian.com/uk/2010/jun/04/surveillance-cameras-birmingham-muslims); Paul Lewis, 'Legal Fight Over Spy Cameras in Muslim Suburbs', *The Guardian*, 11 June 2010 (https://www.theguardian.com/uk/2010/jun/11/project-champion-numberplate-recognition-birmingham); Arshad Isakjee & Chris Allen, '"A Catastrophic Lack of Inquisitiveness": a critical study of the impact and narrative of the Project Champion surveillance project in Birmingham', *Ethnicities* 13: 6 (2013), pp. 751–770. For a similar initiative in the US, see Mike Davis, *City of Quartz*, p. 199. The Birmingham anti-terrorism cameras were eventually removed following public outcry and a community campaign.

56. Richard Vinen, *Second City*, p. 297. The novelist Kit De Waal also lived on Springfield Road, albeit more than 20 years earlier. For her recollections of the area, see *Without Warning & Only Sometimes*, p. 35. By the late 2010s Hall Green had largely lost its reputation for upward mobility, and had one of the worst unemployment rates in the country.

57. On garage music see Akala, *Natives*, pp. 251–252.

58. Restauranteur quoted in Ziauddin Sardar, *Balti Britain*, p. 36. For more on the Jewish bakers in Moseley, see Osman Youseffzada, *The Go-Between*, p. 52.

59. Les Back, *New Ethnicities and Urban Culture*, p. 34.
60. Saskia Warren and Phil Jones, 'Local governance, Disadvantaged Communities and Cultural Intermediation in the Creative Urban Economy', *Environment and Planning C: Government & Policy* 33 (2015), p. 1744; Phil Jones *et al*, 'Urban Landscapes and the Atmosphere of Place: exploring subjective experience in the study of urban form', *Urban Morphology* 21: 1 (2017), p. 33; anon, "Cameron sprinkles his magic in Birmingham", *Business Live*, 11 May 2007; Robert Mendick and Nicholas Cecil, 'Tory Leader Spends 2 Days Living in Asian Community', *Evening Standard*, 11 May 2007, p. 18. See also Colm Muphy, *Futures of Socialism: 'Modernisation', the Labour Party, and the British Left* (Cambridge: Cambridge University Press, 2023), 152–190.
61. David Cameron, "What I Learnt From My Stay With a Muslim Family", *The Guardian*, 13 May 2007; David Cameron, speech at 2011 Munich Security Conference, 5 Feb 2011.
62. David Cameron, speech at 2011 Munich Security Conference, 5 Feb 2011; Richard Adams, Patrick Wintour & Steven Morris, 'All Schools Must Promote "British Values", Says Michael Gove', *The Guardian*, 9 June 2014 (https://www.theguardian.com/politics/2014/jun/09/michael-gove-says-all-schools-must-promote-british-values-after-trojan-horse-reports); James Kirkup, 'Theresa May Interview: "we're going to give illegal migrants a really hostile reception"', *The Daily Telegraph*, 25 May 2012 (https://www.telegraph.co.uk/news/0/theresa-may-interview-going-give-illegal-migrants-really-hostile/). Regarding the alleged plot to Islamicise schools in Birmingham, there was in fact "no extremism and no conservative religious ideology promoted at the schools in question". See John Holmwood & Therese O'Toole, *Countering Extremism in British Schools? The truth about the Birmingham Trojan Horse Affair* (Bristol: Policy Press, 2018), p. 20. See also the 2022 *New York Times* podcast, *The Trojan Horse Affair*, researched and presented by the journalists Hamza Syed and Brian Reed.
63. Bhikhu Parekh/The Runnymede Trust, *The Future of Multi-Ethnic Britain* (London: Profile Books, 2000), p. 14. The question on which I end this chapter is originally Ali Rattansi's, quoted in Les Back *et al*, 'New Labour's White Heart: politics, multiculturalism and the return of assimilation', *The Political Quarterly* 73: 4 (2002), p. 452. For a discussion of the New Labour response to the Parekh report, see Stuart Hall, *Familiar Stranger*, p. 196 & Maya Goodfellow, *Hostile Environment: how immigrants became scapegoats* (London: Verso, 2020), p. 92. For an example of the hostile reception the report attracted in the media, see, e.g., Tom Utley, 'They Met at Runnymede—To Boss Us All Around', *The Daily Telegraph*, 11 October 2000, p. 27.

NOTES

EPILOGUE

1. For a discussion of the declining importance of Woolworth's or 'Woolies' in late-twentieth century British towns, see Richard Hoggart, *Townscape With Figures: Farnham—portrait of an English town* (London: Chatto & Windus, 1994), p. 24.
2. Souplex Limited, to Mr Willy Schumer, 22 Jan 1926; Myra Connell, 'Granny Mally', unpublished typescript, c. 1980; Monica Connell, 'The Mother I Loved', unpublished manuscript (2020).
3. Colin Holmes, *John Bull's Island: immigration and British Society, 1871–1971* (Basingstoke: Macmillan Education, 1988), pp. 22, 23 & 119 & Panikos Panayi, *The Enemy in Our Midst: Germans in Britain during the First World War* (Oxford: Berg, 1991); Jacqueline Jenkinson, *Black 1919*, p. 2; Hanna Connell, unpublished typescript, c. 1975.
4. Michael Drake, 'Professor KH Connell', *Irish Historical Studies* 19: 73 (1974), pp. 83–85; R.M. Hartwell, 'Kenneth H. Connell: an appreciation', *Irish Economic & Social History* 1: 1 (1974), pp. 7–13; unattributed article, 'university lecturers' romance', c. 1947. For background on Irish cultural nationalism see, for example, D. George Boyce, *Nationalism in Ireland* (London: Routledge, 1991). On the anti-German sentiment of the immediate post-war period, see Wendy Webster, *Mixing It*, p. 217.
5. Afua Hirsch, *Brit(ish): on race, identity and belonging* (London: Jonathan Cape, 2018), pp. 32–33. See also Nikesh Shukla, 'Namaste', p. 1 & Hazel Carby, *Imperial Intimacies*, pp. 11–12. In late-2022 the politics around the question 'where are you from?' re-emerged spectacularly when it transpired that the black British charity leader Ngozi Fulani was repeatedly asked the question by the 83-year-old Lady Susan Hussey, the former Lady in Waiting to Queen Elizabeth, at an event at Buckingham Palace. See Sean Coughlan, 'Lady Susan Hussey Quits Over Remarks to Charity Boss Ngozi Fulani', BBC Online, 1 December 2022 (https://www.bbc.co.uk/news/uk-63810468).
6. Stuart Hall, quoted in *The Stuart Hall Project* (d. John Akomfrah, 2013); Afua Hirsch, *Brit(ish)*, p. 33; Stuart Hall, *Familiar Stranger*, pp. 15–16; Stuart Hall, 'New Ethnicities', p. 447. Similar arguments are made by Salman Rushdie in *Jospeh Anton: a memoir* (London: Vintage, 2012), p. 54.
7. Guy Gunaratne, *In Our Mad and Furious City*, p. 3; Stuart Hall, "Opens the Discussion", British Council *Reinventing Britain* forum, 1997, in *Wasafiri* 14: 29 (1999), p. 38; Birmingham respondent quoted in Phillip A. McCarvill, 'An Examination of Ethnic Identity', p. 260.
8. Paul Gilroy, *Black Britain*, p. 308; Maria Sobolewska & Robert Ford, *Brexitland: identity, diversity and the reshaping of British politics* (Cambridge: Cambridge University Press, 2020), p. 71; Gary Younge, *Dispatches from the Diaspora: from*

Nelson Mandela to Black Lives Matter (London: Faber, 2023), p. 123; Marc Mayo, 'Azeem Rafiq: Yorkshire players "constantly" made racist comments and county chiefs did nothing about it', *Evening Standard*, 16 November 2021 (https://www.standard.co.uk/sport/cricket/azeem-rafiq-dcms-yorkshire-racist-comments-b966398.html); Hannah Summers, 'Racism in UK Maternity Care Risks Safety of Black, Asian and Mixed Ethnicity women—study', *The Guardian*, 23 May 2022 (https://www.theguardian.com/world/2022/may/23/racism-in-uk-maternity-care-risks-safety-of-black-asian-and-mixed-ethnicity-women-study); Afua Hirsch, *Brit(ish)*, p. 274; Yasmin Khan, 'Refugees, Migrants, Windrush and Brexit', in Stuart Ward & Astrid Rasch, *Embers of Empire in Brexit Britain* (London: Bloomsbury, 2019), p. 102; Tom Peck, 'Diane Abbott Received Almost Half of all Abusive Tweets Sent to Female MPs Before Election, Poll Finds', *The Independent*, 5 September 2017 (https://www.independent.co.uk/news/uk/politics/diane-abbott-abuse-female-mps-trolling-racism-sexism-almost-half-total-amnesty-poll-a7931126.html). On racism in the NHS, see also British Medical Association, *Racism in Medicine*, June 2006 (https://www.bma.org.uk/media/5746/bma-racism-in-medicine-survey-report-15-june-2022.pdf). See also Lisa Amanda Palmer, 'Diane Abbott, Misogynoir and the Politics of Black British Feminism's Anticolonial Imperatives: "In Britain too, it's as if we don't exist"', *The Sociological Review* 68: 3 (2019), pp. 508–523.

9. Paul Gilroy, *After Empire*, p. 95; Paul Gilroy, 'Multiculture in Times of War: an inaugural lecture given at the London School of Economics', *Critical Quarterly* 48: 4 (2006), pp. 31–34; Daniel Renshaw, *The Discourse of Repatriation in Britain*, pp. 167 & 191; Tim Naor Hilton, quoted in Rachel Hall, 'UK Plan to Send Asylum Seekers to Rwanda Sparks Fierce Criticism', *The Guardian*, 14 April 2022 (https://www.theguardian.com/uk-news/2022/apr/14/uk-plan-to-send-asylum-seekers-to-rwanda-sparks-fierce-criticism); Yasmin Khan, 'Refugees, Migrants, Windrush and Brexit', p. 103. For a detailed role of the pivotal role the question of immigration played in the Brexit vote, see Maria Sobolewska & Robert Ford, *Brexitland*. See also Michael Kenny & Nick Pearce, *Shadows of Empire: the Anglosphere in British politics* (Cambridge: Polity Press, 2018) & Jack Shenker, *Now We Have Your Attention: the new politics of the people* (London: Bodley Head, 2019), p. 250.

10. Anon., 'EU "Support" for Migrant Plan', BBC News, 28 March 2003 (http://news.bbc.co.uk/1/hi/uk_politics/2892301.stm); Alan Travis, 'Blunkett Backed on Asylum Plans', *The Guardian*, 22 April 2003 (https://www.theguardian.com/politics/2003/apr/22/immigrationandpublicservices.thinktanks); Gareth Mulvey, 'When Policy Creates Politics', pp. 439–440.

11. Ambalavaner Sivanandan, *A Different Hunger*, p. 24; Union Movement spokesperson, quoted in Edward Pilkington, *Beyond the Mother County*, p. 131.

12. Don Letts, quoted in Colin Grant, *Homecoming*, p. 263. The tweet in question was sent to the journalist Ash Sarkar. See Sarkar's Twitter feed, 14 June 2022 (https://twitter.com/kent_se/status/1536666739328663556?s=20&t=HRAv9Vjx3LZZ0zWA9OX4dA).
13. Palash Ghosh, 'Priti Patel, MP: the New Face of Britain's Conservative Party', *International Business Times*, 1 August 2013 (https://www.ibtimes.com/priti-patel-mp-new-face-britains-conservative-party-1000142); Sara Cosemans, 'The Politics of Dispersal: turning Ugandan colonial subjects into postcolonial refugees (1967–76), *Migration Studies* 6: 1 (2018), pp. 99–119; Ian Sanjay Patel, *We're Here Because You Were There*, pp. 243–278; Rajeev Syal & Jessica Elgot, 'Priti Patel Accused of Misleading MPs Over Ukrainian Refugees', *The Guardian*, 8 March 202 (https://www.theguardian.com/world/2022/mar/08/ukrainian-refugees-uk-ben-wallace); Tom Pyman & Stewart Carr, 'Pictured: Britain's "biggest Nazi" is shown proudly making Hitler salute in Buchenwald death camp as the National Action founder is convicted of being member of banned far right group', *Daily Mail*, 17 May 2022 (https://www.dailymail.co.uk/news/article-10812883/Neo-Nazi-guilty-member-banned-far-right-group-National-Action.html); Ben Judah, 'Inside the World of Rishi Sunak, Our New Prime Minister', *Tatler*, 24 October 2022 (https://www.tatler.com/article/rishi-sunak-chancellor-of-the-exchequer-feature).
14. Aamna Mohdin, 'Rishi Sunak's Arrival as PM is Historic but Britain Still Has Work to do on Racism', *The Guardian*, 25 October 2022 (https://amp.theguardian.com/world/2022/oct/25/rishi-sunaks-appointment-pm-historic-but-britain-still-work-to-do-racism); Lizzie Deardon, Kate Devlin & Adam Forrest, 'Rishi Sunak's Plan to Stop Small-Boat Crossings Breaks International Law, UN Says', *The Independent*, 8 March 2023 (https://www.independent.co.uk/news/uk/home-news/rishi-sunak-channel-crossing-bill-law-un-b2295975.html). Gary Younge's comments were made at an event as part of Belfast International Festival on 18 October 2023 in the context of his book *Dispatches from the Diaspora*.
15. Elizabeth Buettner, *Europe After Empire*, p. 498.
16. Kenneth Little, *Negroes in Britain*, pp. 218 & 234–5; Richard Ford, 'More Than a Third of Babies Born to Foreign Parents', *The Times*, 1 December 2016; Sarah Neal *et al*, *Lived Experiences of Multiculture: the new social and spatial relations of diversity* (London; New York: Routledge, 2018), p. 8; Maria Sobolewska & Robert Ford, *Brexitland*, p. 27; Sunder Katwala, 'Ten Million Stories of Migration to Britain', *Eastern Eye*, 9 November 2022 (https://www.easterneye.biz/ten-million-stories-of-migration-to-britain).
17. Father quoted in Wendy Webster, *Mixing It*, p. 221; Chamion Caballero & Peter J. Aspinall, *Mixed Race Britain*, pp. 334, 481 & 483; Maria Sobolewska

& Robert Ford, *Brexitland*, pp. 30, 50 & 58; David Olusoga, *Black and British*, p. 525; Ian Sanjay Patel, *We're Here Because You Were There*, p. 4; Mica Nava, *Visceral Cosmopolitanism*, p. 161; Jeremy Cliffe, *Britain's Cosmopolitan Future: how the country is changing and why its politicians must respond* (London: Policy Network, 2015), pp. 5 & 10; Robert Booth, Pamela Duncan & Carmen Aguilar Garcia, 'England and Wales Now Minority Christian Countries, Census Reveals', *The Guardian*, 29 November 2022 (https://www.theguardian.com/uk-news/2022/nov/29/leicester-and-birmingham-are-uk-first-minority-majority-cities-census-reveals).

18. Sarah Neal et al, *Lived Experiences of Multiculture*, pp. 8–15; Katherine Tyler, 'The Suburban Paradox of Conviviality and Racism in Postcolonial Britain', *Journal of Ethnic and Migration Studies* 43: 11 (2017), pp. 1890–1906.

19. Sarah Neal et al, *Lived Experiences of Multiculture*, p. 13; Tahir Abbas, 'Muslims in Birmingham, UK', Compass Background Paper (Jan 2006), p. 5; Jeremy Cliffe, *Britain's Cosmopolitan Future*, p. 11; Humayun Ansari, *The Infidel Within*, p. 358; Naomi de Souza, 'Inside Hijaz College, Nuneaton's Islamic University', *Coventry Live*, 6 January 2021 (https://www.coventrytelegraph.net/news/coventry-news/inside-hijaz-college-nuneatons-islamic-19483681); Jack Crangle, '"Left to Fend for Themselves": immigration, race relations and the state in Twentieth Century Northern Ireland', *Immigrants & Minorities* 36: 1 (2018), pp. 20–44; Rozina Visram, *Asians in Britain*, pp. 255 & 260; Sarah McMonagle & Philip McDermott, 'Transitional Politics and Language Rights in a Multi-ethnic Northern Ireland: towards a true linguistic pluralism?', *Ethnopolitics* 13: 3 (2014), p. 250; Mark Simpson & Darran Marshall, 'Census 2021: more from Catholic background in NI than Protestant', BBC News NI, 22 September 2022 (https://www.bbc.com/news/uk-northern-ireland-62980394); Ciaran Dunbar & Mark Bain, 'Revealed: the astonishing range of languages spoken in Northern Ireland schools', *Belfast Telegraph*, 30 March 2021 (https://www.belfasttelegraph.co.uk/news/education/revealed-the-astonishing-range-of-languages-spoken-in-northern-ireland-schools-40254325.html). I explored the issue of increasing ethnic diversity in Belfast in a BBC podcast, *The Crisis Files* (https://www.bbc.co.uk/sounds/series/m001f4bl).

20. Paul Gilroy, *After Empire*, pp. x, xi & 79; Susanne Wessendorf, 'Commonplace Diversity and the "Ethos of Mixing": perceptions of difference in a London neighbourhood', *Identities: global studies in power and culture* 20: 4 (2013), p. 417; Ash Amin, 'Ethnicity and the Multicultural City', p. 970; Johny Pitts and Roger Robinson, *Home is Not a Place* (London: William Collins, 2022); Kieran Yates, 'On Going Home', in Nikesh Shukla (ed.), *The Good Immigrant*, p. 112; Ian Cook, Philip Crang and Mark Thorpe, 'Eating into Britishness:

multicultural imaginaries and the identity politics of food', in Sasha Roseneil & Julie Seymour (eds.), *Practicing Identities: Power and Resistance* (Basingstoke: Palgrave Macmillan, 1999), pp. 226–240; Elizabeth Buettner, '"Going for an Indian", pp. 865 & 877; Panikos Panayi, *Spicing Up Britain*, p. 78; David Bentley, 'Birmingham Selfridges Celebrates Eid With Special Activities and Extended Hours', *Birmingham Live*, 23 July 2014 (https://www.birminghammail.co.uk/whats-on/shopping/birmingham-selfridges-celebrates-eid-special-7489599); Akala, *Natives*, pp. 260–261; Gary Younge, *Dispatches from the Diaspora*, p. 32; Dan Hancox, *Inner City Pressure: the story of grime* (London: William Collins, 2018), pp. 19, 21, 33–54; Guy Gunaratne, *In Our Mad and Furious City*, p. 294. See also Tice Cin's description of Turkish cuisine in *Keeping the House* (Sheffield/London: And Other Stories, 2021), p. 1. Thanks to James Bagan for brining Gunaratne's book to my attention.

21. Paul Gilroy, *After Empire*, pp. 116–118 & 141; Callum Jacobs, introduction to Callum Jacobs (ed.), *A New Formation: how black footballers shaped the modern game* (London: #Merky Books, 2022), p. 11; Sanaa Qureshi, 'A Parallel History of Black Muslim Footballers', in Callum Jacobs (ed.), *A New Formation*, p. 182.

22. For an example of a critic of what is understood to constitute the 'metropolitan' position, see David Goodhart, *The Road to Somewhere: the new tribes shaping British politics* (London: Penguin, 2017).

SELECT BIBLIOGRAPHY

FILM

Armaan, dir. Pervez Malik. Film Arts, 1966.
The Colony, dir. Phillip Donnellan. BBC, 1964.
Hollywood Canteen, dir. Delmer Daves. Warner Bros, 1944.
The Millionairess, dir. Anthony Asquith. 20th Century Fox, 1960.
Pyaar Ka Sagaar, dir. Devendra Goel. Filmrays Productions, 1961.
Qayamat Se Qayamat Tak, dir. Mansoor Khan. Nasir Hussain Films, 1988.
Silver, dir. Philip Noyce. Paramount Pictures, 1993.
The Stuart Hall Project, dir. John Akomfrah. Smoking Dog Films, 2013.
Upkar, dir. Manoj Kumar. Vishal Pictures, 1967.
Yaadon Ki Baraat, dir. Nasir Hussain. Nasir Hussain Films, 1973.

INTERVIEWS

James Bagan, 1 March 2023.
David Blunkett, 31 March 2022.
Paul Curtis, 16 June 2021.
Daniella Dyer, 1 July 2016.
Ben Irons, 29 July 2020.
Erica Irons, 29 July 2020.
Paul Irons, 29 July 2020.
Marjorie Norris, 16 June 2021.
Abdullah Rehman, 21 September 2021.
Joan Reid, 16 June 2021.

SELECT BIBLIOGRAPHY

Bally Sagoo, 29 March 2022.
Bill Stanton, 16 June 2021.
Jenny Woodward, 6 July 2022.

MANUSCRIPTS & ARCHIVES

Archdiocese of Dublin, Ireland
John Charles McQuaid Papers.

Bradford Industrial Museum, Bradford, UK
Bradford Heritage Recording Unit Papers.

Cadbury Research Library, University of Birmingham, Birmingham, UK
Centre for Contemporary Cultural Studies Papers.
Janet Mendelsohn Papers.

Hansard (Online)
Parliamentary Debates and Bills.

Library of Birmingham, Birmingham, UK
Birmingham Newspaper Cuttings, Balsall Heath & Highgate.

Margaret Thatcher Foundation Archive (Online)
Engagement Diaries.
Interview Transcripts.

Media Archive of Central England, University of Lincoln, Lincoln, UK
ATV Documentary Interview Reels.

Nottinghamshire Archives, Nottingham, UK
Community Relations Papers.

Nottingham Local Studies Library, Nottingham, UK
Newspaper clippings relating to the St Ann's Riots, L/30/32.

SELECT BIBLIOGRAPHY

The Schomburg Center for Research in Black Culture, New York Public Library, New York, USA

St Clair Drake Papers.

Lawrence D. Reddick World War II Project Papers.

UK Data Service (Online)

Ethnic Relations on West Midland Housing Estates.

West Yorkshire Archives, Bradford, UK

Bishop of Bradford Papers.
City of Bradford Press Cuttings.
Race Relations in Bradford, Papers and Reports.

MEMOIR

Black, Pauline, *Black By Design: a 2-Tone memoir*. London: Serpent's Tail, 2012.

Cambell, Ali & Robin Campbell, *Blood & Fire: the autobiography of the UB40 Brothers*. London: Arrow Books, 2006.

Carby, Hazel, *Imperial Intimacies: a tale of two islands*. London; New York: Verso, 2019.

Connell, Hanna, untitled, unpublished typescript, c. 1975.

Connell, Monica, 'The Mother I Loved'. Unpublished manuscript, 2020.

Connell, Myra, 'Granny Mally'. Unpublished manuscript, c. 1980s.

———, 'K'. Unpublished manuscript, c. 1980s.

Eribon, Didier, *Returning to Reims*. London: Allen Lane, 2018.

Gilroy, Beryl, *Black Teacher*. London: Faber, 2022 [1976].

Hall, Stuart, *Familiar Stranger: a life between two islands*. London: Allen Lane, 2017.

Irons, Eric George, *Papaman*. Unpublished memoir, c. 2005.

Malik, Zaiba, *We are Muslim, Please*. London: Windmill Books, 2011.

Morrison, Majbritt, *Jungle West 11*. London: Tandem Books, 1964.

Rushdie, Salman, *Jospeh Anton: a memoir*. London: Vintage, 2012.

de Waal, Kit, *Without Warning and Only Sometimes: scenes from an unpredictable childhood*. London: Tinder Press, 2022.

SELECT BIBLIOGRAPHY

Yousefzada, Osman, *The Go-Between: a portrait of growing up between different worlds*. Edinburgh: Canongate, 2022.

MUSIC, TELEVISION & PODCASTS

Achanak, *panACHe*, Multitone, 1990.
The Beat, *I Just Can't Stop It*, Go-Feet, 1980.
Kieran Connell & Colm Heatley, *The Crisis Files*. BBC, 2022.
Smiley Culture, 'Cockney Translation'. Polydor, 1984.
———, 'Police Officer'. Fashion Records, 1984.
EZ, *Pure Garage: Volume 1*. Warner, 2000.
Arthur Godfrey, 'Too Fat Polka'. Columbia, 1947.
Apache Indian, *No Reservations*. Island Records/Mango, 1993.
Linton Kwesi Johnson, *Bass Culture*. Island Records, 1980.
———, *Making History*. Island Records, 1984.
Kiz Manley, *Enter the 36 Chambers*. Arts Council England, 2022.
Bob Marley, *Exodus*. Island Records, 1977.
Bally Sagoo, *Essential Ragga*. Oriental Star Agencies, 1991.
———, *Bollywood Flashback*. Columbia Records, 1994.
———, 'Chura Liya Hai Tumne'. Columbia Records, 1994.
———, 'Dil Cheez'. Columbia Records, 1996.
Hamza Sayed & Brian Reed, *The Trojan Horse Affair*. Serial/*New York Times*, 2022.
The Specials, *The Specials*. 2 Tone, 1979.
Malkit Singh, 'Hey! Jamalo'. Star Records, 1990.
Steel Pulse, *Handsworth Revolution*. Island Records, 1978.
UB40, *Signing Off*. Graduate, 1980.
———, 'Red Red Wine'. DEP, 1982.
———, *Promises and Lies*. DEP, 1993.
Windrush, dir. David Upshal. BBC Television, May 1998.

NEWSPAPERS, PERIODICALS & MAGAZINES

The Balsall Heathen
Belfast Telegraph
Birmingham Live

SELECT BIBLIOGRAPHY

Business Live
Cardiff Times
Chicago Defender
Coventry Live
The Crisis
Daily Mail
Daily Mirror
Daily Telegraph
Eastern Eye
Evening Mail & Dispatch
Evening Standard
The Guardian
Guardian Journal
Headlines & Pictures
Independent
International Business Times
Irish Times
John Bull
Local Government Chronicle
Manchester Guardian
Marxism Today
New Society
New Statesman
Observer
The People
Picture Post
Prospect
South Wales Echo & Express
Sunday Times
Tatler
Telegraph & Argus
Time
The Times
Times Educational Supplement
The Tribune

SELECT BIBLIOGRAPHY

The Village Voice
Western Mail & South Wales News
Yorkshire Post

NOVELS, SHORT STORIES & POETRY

Agard, John, *Half-Caste*. Hodder Children's Books, 2005.
Allen, Richard, *Skinhead*. London: Dean Street Press, 2015 [1970].
Cin, Tice, *Keeping the House*. Sheffield/London: And Other Stories, 2021.
Gunaratne, Guy, *In Our Mad and Furious City*. London: Tinder Press, 2018.
Hussein, Abdullah, *Émigré Journeys*. London: Serpent's Tail, 2000.
Kureishi, Hanif, *The Black Album and My Son the Fanatic*. New York: Simon & Schuster, 1996.
Lamming, George, *The Emigrants*. Ann Arbor: University of Michigan Press, 1994 [1954].
MacInnes, Colin, *Absolute Beginners*. London: Allison & Busby, 1992 [1959].
McKay, Claude, *Home to Harlem*. Boston, MA: Northeastern University Press, 1987 [1928].
———, *Romance in Marseilles*. London: Penguin, 2020 [1929].
Mehmood, Tariq, *Hand on the Sun*. Harmondsworth: Penguin, 1983.
Mohamed, Nadifa, *The Fortune Men*. London: Viking, 2021.
Selvon, Samuel, *The Lonely Londoners*. Harlow: Longman, 1991 [1956].
Sillitoe, Alan, *Saturday Night and Sunday Morning*. London: Pan Books, 1960 [1958].
Two Fingas & James T. Kirk, *Junglist*. London: Repeater Books, 2021.
Wright, Richard, *Native Son*. New York: HarperCollins, 2003 [1940].
Zephaniah, Benjamin, *Too Black, Too Strong*. Northumberland: Bloodaxe Books, 2001.

UNPUBLISHED THESES

Andrews, Aaron, 'Decline and the City: The urban crisis in Liverpool c. 1968 to 1986,' (University of Leicester, 2018).
Carr, Helen, 'Muslims and the state education system: England c. 1965–1997' (Birkbeck College, University of London, 2018).

SELECT BIBLIOGRAPHY

Evans, June, 'African/Caribbeans in Scotland: a socio-geographical study' (Edinburgh University, 1987).

Hodgson, Thomas E., 'Multicultural Harmony? Mirpuris and Music in Bradford' (Oxford University, 2012).

Hopkinson, Joe, 'Racism in Memories of British Schooling, 1960–1989' (University of Huddersfield, 2022).

Jenkins, Simon, 'Prostitution in Cardiff, 1900–1959' (Cardiff University, 2017).

Khabra, Gurdeep John Singh, 'The Heritage of British Bhangra: popular music heritage, cultural memory, and cultural identity' (University of Liverpool, 2014).

McCarvill, Phillip A., 'An Examination of Ethnic Identity: a case study of "Second Generation" Irish people in Birmingham' (Warwick University, 2002).

Natarajan, Radhika Anita, 'Organizing Community: commonwealth citizens and social activism in Britain, 1948–1982' (UC Berkeley, California, 2013).

Odelius, Laura Elizabeth Sinclair, 'Bringing the Empire Home: narratives of empire and the shaping of racial identity in Nottingham, 1945–1962' (Northwestern University, Illinois, 2001).

Payson, Alida, 'Feeling Together: emotion, heritage, conviviality and politics in a changing city' (Cardiff University, 2018).

Sanderson, Nuala, 'The Impact of the Struggle for Racial Equality in the United States on British Racialised Relations from 1958–1968' (University of Southampton, 1999).

Ziesler, Kaja Irene, 'The Irish in Birmingham, 1830–1970' (University of Birmingham, 1989).

BOOKS & ARTICLES

Addison, Paul & Harriet Jones, *A Companion to Contemporary Britain, 1939–2000*. Oxford: Blackwell, 2005.

Ahmed, Rehana, 'Equality of Citizenship', in Ruvani Ranasinha (ed.), *South Asians and the Shaping of Britain, 1870–1950*. Manchester; New York: Manchester University Press, 2012.

Ahmed, Sara, *Strange Encounters: embodied others in post-coloniality*. London; New York: Routledge, 2000.

SELECT BIBLIOGRAPHY

Akala, *Natives: race and class in the ruins of Empire*. London: Two Roads, 2018.

Alexander, Claire, *The Art of Being Black: the creation of black British youth identities*. Oxford: Oxford University Press, 1996.

———, '(Dis)Entangling the "Asian Gang": ethnicity, identity, masculinity', in Barnor Hesse (ed.), *Un/settled Multiculturalisms: diasporas, entanglements, transruptions*. London; New York: Zed Books, 2000, pp. 123–147.

———, *The Asian Gang: ethnicity, identity, masculinity*. Oxford: Berg, 2000.

———, 'Imagining the Asian Gang: ethnicity, masculinity and youth after "the riots"', *Critical Social Policy* 24: 4 (2004), pp. 526–549.

Allen, Chris, *Fair Justice: the Bradford disturbances, the sentences and impact*. London: Forum Against Islamophobia and Racism, 2003.

Alleyne, Mike, 'White Reggae: cultural dilution in the record industry', *Popular Music and Society* 24: 1 (2000), pp. 15–30.

Amin, Ash, 'Ethnicity and the Multicultural City: living with diversity', *Environment and Planning A* 34 (2002), pp. 958–980.

Andrews, Kehinde, *The New Age of Empire: how racism and colonialism still rule the world*. London: Allen Lane, 2021.

Ansari, Khizar Humayun, *The Infidel Within: Muslims in Britain since 1800*. London: Hurst, 2004.

Aspden, Kester, *The Hounding of David Oluwale*. London: Vintage, 2007.

Atkinson, Dick, *The Common Sense of Community*. London: Demos, 1994.

Back, Les, *New Ethnicities and Urban Cultures: racisms and multiculture in young lives*. London: Routledge, 1996.

Back, Les, Michael Keith, Azra Khan *et al*, 'New Labour's White Heart: politics, multiculturalism and the return of assimilation', *The Political Quarterly* 73: 4 (2002), pp. 445–454.

Ballard, Roger (ed.), *Desh Pardesh: the South Asian presence in Britain*. London: Hurst, 1994.

———, 'The Emergence of Desh Pardesh', in Roger Ballard (ed.), *Desh Pardesh: the South Asian presence in Britain*. London: Hurst, 1994, pp. 1–34.

SELECT BIBLIOGRAPHY

Barber, Austin & Stephen Hall, 'Birmingham: Whose Urban Renaissance? Regeneration as a response to economic restructuring', *Policy Studies* 29: 3 (2008), pp. 281–292.

Baumann, Gerd & Sabita Banerji, 'Bhangra 1984–8: fusion and professionalisation in a genre of South Asian dance music', in P. Oliver (ed.), *Black Music in Britain*. Milton Keynes: Open University Press, 1990, pp. 137–152.

Beazley, Mike, Patrick Loftman & Brenden Nevin, 'Downtown Redevelopment and Community Resistance: an international perspective', in Nick Jewson & Susanne MacGregor (eds.), *Transforming Cities: contested governance and new spatial dimensions*. London; New York: Routledge, 1997, pp. 181–192.

Beckett, John (ed.), *A Centenary History of Nottingham*. Manchester: Manchester University Press, 1997.

Begum, Shabna, *From Sylhet to Spitalfields: Bengali squatters in 1970s East London*. London: Lawrence and Wishart, 2023.

Belchem, John, *Before the Windrush: race relations in 20th Century Liverpool*. Liverpool: Liverpool University Press, 2014.

Bentley, Stuart, 'Merrick and the British Campaign to Stop Immigration: populist racism and political influence', *Race & Class* 36 (1995), pp. 57–72.

Bhabha, Homi K., *The Location of Culture*. London; New York: Routledge, 1994.

Birmingham Area Studies Group, *Sparkbrook Ward*. Birmingham: Birmingham Development Dept, 1988.

Bishop, Sue Zeleny, 'Inner-City Possibilities: using place and space to facilitate inter-ethnic dating and romance in 1960s-80s Leicester', *Urban History* 50 (2023), pp. 232–247.

Bland, Lucy, 'Interracial Relationships and the "Brown Baby Question": Black GIs, white British women, and their mixed-race offspring in World War II', *Journal of the History of Sexuality* 26: 3 (2017), pp. 424–453.

———, *Britain's "Brown" Babies: the stories of children born to black GIs and white women in the Second World War*. Manchester: Manchester University Press, 2019.

SELECT BIBLIOGRAPHY

Bloom, Leonard, introduction to Kenneth Little, *Negroes in Britain: a study of racial relations in English society*. London; Boston: Routledge & Kegan Paul, 1972 [1948]), pp. 1–45.

Blunkett, David, *Politics and Progress: renewing democracy and civil society*. London: Demos, 2001.

Bogdanor, Verdon & Robert Skidelsky (eds.), *The Age of Affluence 1951– 1964*. London & Basingstoke: Macmillan, 1970.

Boughton, John, *Municipal Dreams: the rise and fall of council housing*. London: Verso, 2018.

Boyce, D. George, *Nationalism in Ireland*. London: Routledge, 1991.

Bradford Heritage Recording Unit, *Destination Bradford*. Bradford: Bradford Heritage Recording Unit, 1987.

———, *Here to Stay: Bradford's South Asian communities*. Bradford: Bradford Heritage Recording Unit, 1994.

Brooke, Stephen, 'Revisiting Southam Street: class, generation, gender and race in the photography of Roger Mayne', *Journal of British Studies* 53: 2 (2014), pp. 453–496.

Brown, Timothy S., "Subcultures, Pop Music and Politics: Skinheads and 'Nazi Rock' in England and Germany", *Journal of Social History* 38: 1 (2004), pp. 157–178.

Buettner, Elizabeth, '"Going for an Indian": South Asian restaurants and the limits of multiculturalism in Britain', *The Journal of Modern History* 80: 4 (2008), pp. 874–875.

———, *Europe after Empire: Decolonization, Society, and Culture*. Cambridge: Cambridge University Press, 2016.

Burlet, Stacey & Helen Reid, 'A Gendered Uprising: political representation and minority ethnic communities', *Ethnic and Racial Studies* 21: 2 (1998), pp. 270–287.

Burnett, Jonathan, 'Community, Cohesion and the State', *Race & Class* 45: 3 (2004), pp. 1–18.

Burney, Elizabeth, *Housing on Trial: a study of immigrants and local government*. Oxford: Oxford University Press, 1967.

Caballero, Chamion & Peter J. Aspinall, *Mixed Race Britain in The Twentieth Century*. London: Palgrave Macmillan, 2018.

Cain, Maureen E., *Society and the Policeman's Role*. London: Routledge & Kegan Paul, 1973.

SELECT BIBLIOGRAPHY

Cameron, Ross, '"The Most Colourful Extravaganza in the World": images of Tiger Bay, 1845–1970', *Patterns of Prejudice* 31: 2 (2010), pp. 59–90.

Cantle, Ted, *Community Cohesion*. London: HMSO, 2001.

Cantres, James G., *Blackening Britain: Caribbean radicalism from Windrush to decolonization*. London: Rowman & Littlefield International, 2020.

Carr, Helen, '"I Think You are Ignoring the Relevant Provisions of the 1944 Education Act": Muslims, the state and education in England, c. 1966-c. 1985', *Contemporary British History* 35: 1 (2021), pp. 57–71.

del Castillo, Richard Griswold 'The Los Angeles "Zoot Suit Riots" Revisited: Mexican and Latin American perspectives', *Mexican Studies/ Estudios Mexicanos* 16: 2 (2000), pp. 367–391.

Cayton, Martin, '"You can't fuse yourself": contemporary British-Asian music and the musical expression of identity', *East European Meetings in Ethnomusicology* 5 (1998), pp. 73–87.

Chambers, Claire, *Britain Through Muslim Eyes: literary representations, 1780–1988*. Basingstoke: Macmillan, 2015.

Chana, Boy & Rajinder Dudrah, 'The British Bhangra Live Music Scene', in Rajinder Dudrah (ed.), *Bhangra: Birmingham and Beyond*. Birmingham: Punch Records, 2007, pp. 27–33.

———, 'Bhangra's DJ Culture', in Rajinder Dudrah (ed.), *Bhangra: Birmingham and beyond*. Birmingham: Punch Records, 2007, pp. 62–67.

Chin, Rita, *The Crisis of Multiculturalism in Europe: a history*. Princeton, NJ: Princeton University Press, 2017.

Chinn, Carl, *Birmingham: the great working city*. Birmingham: Birmingham City Council, 1994.

———, *Better Betting With A Decent Feller: a social history of bookmaking*. London: Aurum Press, 2004.

Clapson, Mark, *Anglo-American crossroads: urban planning and research in Britain, 1940–2010*, London; New York: Bloomsbury, 2013.

Cliffe, Jerremy, *Britain's Cosmopolitan Future: how the country is changing and why its politicians must respond*. London: Policy Network, 2015.

Coard, Bernard, *How the West Indian Child is Made Educationally Sub-Normal: the scandal of the black child in schools in Britain*. London: New Beacon Books, 1971.

Coates, Ken & Richard Silburn, *Poverty: the forgotten Englishman*. Harmondsworth: Penguin, 1970.

SELECT BIBLIOGRAPHY

Cohen, Abner (ed.), *Urban Ethnicity*. London: Tavistock, 1974.

Cohen, Phillip & Harwant S. Bains (eds.), *Multi-Racist Britain*. Basingstoke: Macmillan, 1988), pp. 121–155.

Collins, Sydney, *Coloured Minorities in Britain: studies in British race relation based on African, West Indian and Asiatic immigrants*. London: Lutterworth Press, 1957.

Connell, Kieran & Matthew Hilton, 'The Working Practices of Birmingham's Centre for Contemporary Cultural Studies', *Social History* 40: 3 (2015), pp. 287–311.

——— (eds.), *Cultural Studies 50 Years On: history, practice and politics* London: Rowman & Littlefield International, 2016.

Connell, Kieran, Matthew Hilton & Jonathan Watkins, *Janet Mendelsohn: Varna Road*. Birmingham: Ikon Gallery, 2016.

Connell, Kieran, 'Race, Prostitution and the New Left: the post-war inner city through Janet Mendelsohn's "social eye"', *History Workshop Journal* 83:1 (2017), pp. 301–340.

———, *Black Handsworth: race in 1980s Britain*. Oakland: University of California Press, 2019.

———, 'An African American Anthropologist in Wales: St. Clair Drake and the transatlantic ecologies of race relations', *Journal of British Studies* (advanced access, Feb 2024), pp. 1–32.

Connolly, Sean J., (ed.), *The Oxford Companion to Irish History*. Oxford: Oxford University Press, 1998.

Constantine, Learie, *Colour Bar*. London: Kegan Paul, 1954.

Cook, Ian, Philip Crang & Mark Thorpe, 'Eating into Britishness: multicultural imaginaries and the identity politics of food', in Sasha Roseneil & Julie Seymour (eds.), *Practicing Identities: power and resistance*. Basingstoke: Palgrave Macmillan, 1999, pp. 226–240.

Corbally, John, 'The Jarring Irish: postwar immigration to the heart of empire', *Radical History Review* 104 (2009), pp. 103–125.

———, 'The Othered Irish: shades of difference in post-war Britain, 1948–71', *Contemporary European History* 24: 1 (2015), pp. 105–125.

Cosemans, Sara, 'The Politics of Dispersal: turning Ugandan colonial subjects into postcolonial refugees (1967–76), *Migration Studies* 6: 1 (2018), pp. 99–119.

SELECT BIBLIOGRAPHY

Coulson Andrew, & Geoff Wright, 'Brindleyplace, Birmingham: creating an inner city mixed-use development in times of recession', *Planning Practice & Research* 28:2 (2013), pp. 256–274.

Crangle, Jack, '"Left to Fend for Themselves": immigration, race relations and the state in Twentieth Century Northern Ireland', *Immigrants & Minorities* 36: 1 (2018), pp. 20–44.

Curran-Vigier, Catherine, 'From Multiculturalism to Global Values: how New Labour set the agenda', *Observatoire de la Societe Britannique* 5 (2008), pp. 65–80.

Cush, Denise, 'The Faith Schools Debate', *British Journal of Sociology of Education* 26: 3 (2005), pp. 435–442

Dahya, Badr, 'The Nature of Pakistani Ethnicity in Industrial Cities in Britain', in Abner Cohen (ed.), *Urban Ethnicity*. London: Tavistock, 1974, pp. 77–113.

Davis, Mike, *Prisoners of the American Dream: politics and economy in the history of the US working class*. London: Verso, 2018 [1986].

———, *City of Quartz: excavating the future in Los Angeles*. London; New York: Verso, 2018 [1990].

Davies, Aled, Ben Jackson & Florence Sutcliffe Braithwaite, *The Neoliberal Age? Britain since the 1970s*. London: UCL Press, 2021.

Dawson, Ashley, '"Bollywood Flashback": Hindi film music and the negotiation of identity among British-Asian youths', *South Asian Popular Culture* 3: 2 (2005), pp. 161–176.

———, *Mongrel Nation: diasporic culture and the making of postcolonial Britain*. Ann Arbor: University of Michigan Press, 2007.

Delaney, Enda, *The Irish in Post-War Britain*. Oxford: Oxford University Press, 2007.

Dennis, Ferdinand, *Behind the Frontlines: journey into Afro-Britain*. London: Victor Gollancz, 1988.

Donnell, Alison (ed.), *Companion to Contemporary Black British Culture*. London: Routledge, 2002.

Doyle, John, 'Irish Nationalism and the Israel-Palestine Conflict', in Rory Miller (ed.), *Ireland and the Middle East: trade, society and peace*. Dublin: Irish Academic Press, 2007, pp. 87–100.

Drake, Michael, 'Professor KH Connell', *Irish Historical Studies* 19: 73 (1974), pp. 83–85.

SELECT BIBLIOGRAPHY

Drake, St. Clair, & Horace R. Cayton, *Black Metropolis: a study of Negro life in a northern city*. Chicago: University of Chicago Press, 2015 [1945].

Drake, St. Clair, "A Report on the Brown Britishers," *The Crisis* 56: 6 (June 1949), pp. 174 & 188–89.

Dudrah, Rajinder (ed.), *Bhangra: Birmingham and beyond*. Birmingham: Punch Records, 2007.

———, 'Vilayati Bollywood: popular Hindi cinema-going and diasporic south Asian identity in Birmingham (UK)', *Javnost–the public: Journal of the European Institute for Communication & Culture* 9: 1 (2014), pp. 19–36.

———, '"Balle-Balle, Balle-Balle": fashion–British Bhangra style', *Atlantic Studies* 13: 4 (2016), pp. 491–511.

Dummett, Ann, *A Portrait of English Racism*. Harmondsworth: Penguin, 1973.

Eddo-Lodge, Reni, *Why I'm No Longer Talking to White People About Race*. London: Bloomsbury, 2018.

Elkin, Lauren, *Flaneuse*. London: Vintage, 2016.

Esteves, Olivier, '*Babylon by Bus*? The dispersal of immigrant children in England, race and urban space (1960s–1980s)', *Paedagogica Historica* 54: 6 (2018), pp. 750–765.

———, *The "Desegregation" of English Schools: bussing, race and urban space, 1960s-90s*. Manchester: Manchester University Press, 2018.

Etzioni, Amitai, *The Third Way to a Good Society*. London: Demos, 2000.

Evans, Neil, 'The South Wales Race Riots of 1919', *Llafur*, 3:1 (1980), pp. 5–29.

———, 'Regulating the Reserve Army: Arabs, blacks and the local state in Cardiff, 1919–45', *Immigrants and Minorities* 4: 2 (1985), pp. 68–115.

Fanon, Frantz, *Black Skins, White Masks*. New York: Grove Press, 2008 [1952].

Farrar, Max, 'Racism, Education and Black Self-Organisation', *Critical Social Policy* 12: 36 (1993), pp. 53–72.

———, *The Struggle for "Community" in a British Multi-Ethnic Area: paradise in the making*. Lewiston: The Edwin Mellen Press, 2002.

Fazakarley, Jed, *Muslim Communities in England, 1962–90: multiculturalism and political identity*. Cham, Switzerland: Palgrave, 2017.

SELECT BIBLIOGRAPHY

Featherstone, David, 'Harry O'Connell, Maritime Labour and the Racialised Politics of Place', *Race & Class* 57: 3 (2016), pp. 71–87.

Feldman, David, 'Why the English Like Turbans: multicultural politics in British history', in David Feldman & Jon Lawrence (eds.), *Structures and Transformations in Modern British History: essays for Gareth Stedman Jones*. Cambridge: Cambridge University Press, 2011.

Feldman, David & Jon Lawrence (eds.), *Structures and Transformations in Modern British History: essays for Gareth Stedman Jones*. Cambridge: Cambridge University Press, 2011.

Fevre, Ralph, *Cheap Labour and Racial Discrimination*. Aldershot: Gower Publishing, 1984.

Field, Paul, Robin Bunce, Leila Hassan *et al* (eds.), *Here To Stay, Here To Fight: a 'Race Today' anthology*. London: Pluto Press, 2019.

Field, Stewart & Pauline Roberts, 'Racism and Police Investigations: individual redress, public interests collective change after the Race Relations (Amendment) Act 2000', *Legal Studies* 22: 4 (2002), pp. 493–526.

Flett, Hazel, Jeff Henderson & Bill Browns, 'The Practice of Racial Dispersal in Birmingham, 1969–75', *Journal of Social Policy* 8: 3 (1979), pp. 289–309.

Foster-Carter, Olivia 'The Honeyford Affair: political and policy implications', in Barry Troyna (ed.), *Racial Inequality in Education*. London: Routledge, 1989, pp. 44–58.

Francis, Ian, *This Way To the Revolution: art, activism and upheaval in Birmingham 1968*. Birmingham: Flatpack, 2019.

Fryer, Peter, *Staying Power: the history of black people in Britain*. London: Pluto, 2018 [1984].

Fyvel, T.R., *The Insecure Offenders: rebellious youth in the welfare state*. London: Chatto & Windus, 1961.

Gaines, Kevin, 'Scholar-Activist St. Clair Drake and the Transatlantic World of Black Radicalism', in D.G. Kelley & Stephen Tuck (eds.), *The Other Special Relationship: race, rights, and riots in Britain and the United States*. New York: Palgrave Macmillan, 2015.

Gardner, Roy, 'Faith Schools Now: an overview', in Roy Gardner, Jo Cairns & Denis Lawton (eds.), *Faith Schools: consensus or conflict?* Oxonbridge: RoutledgeFalmer, 2005, pp. 7–13.

SELECT BIBLIOGRAPHY

Gardner, Roy, Jo Cairns & Denis Lawton (eds.), *Faith Schools: consensus or conflict?* Oxonbridge: RoutledgeFalmer, 2005.

Gentleman, Amelia, *The Windrush Betrayal*. London: Faber, 2019.

Giggs, John, 'Housing, Population and Transport', in John Beckett (ed.), *A Centenary History of Nottingham*. Manchester: Manchester University Press, 1997, p. 435–463.

Gildea, Robert, *Backbone of a Nation: mining communities and the Great Strike of 1984–85*. Oxford: Oxford University Press, 2023.

Gilliat-Ray, Sophie, *Muslims in Britain: an introduction*. Cambridge: Cambridge University Press, 2010.

Gilroy, Paul & Errol Lawrence, 'Two-Tone Britain: white and black youth and the politics of anti-racism', in Phillip Cohen & Harwant S. Bains (eds.), *Multi-Racist Britain*. Basingstoke: Macmillan, 1988, pp. 121–155.

Gilroy, Paul, *After Empire: melancholia or convivial culture?* London: Routledge, 2004.

———, "Multiculture, Double Consciousness and the 'War on Terror'", *Patterns of Prejudice* 39: 4 (2005), pp. 431–443.

———, 'Multiculture in Times of War: an inaugural lecture given at the London School of Economics', *Critical Quarterly* 48: 4 (2006), pp. 27–45.

———, *Black Britain: a photographic history*, London: Saqi, 2007.

Glass, Ruth, *Newcomers: The West Indians in London*. London: George Allen & Unwin, 1960.

Gonçalves Ana & Huw Thomas, 'Waterfront Tourism and Public Art in Cardiff Bay and Lisbon's Park of Nations', *Journal of Policy Research in Tourism, Leisure and Events* 4: 3 (2012), pp. 327–352.

Goodfellow, Maya, *Hostile Environment: how immigrants became scapegoats*. London: Verso, 2020.

Goodhart, David, *The Road to Somewhere: the new tribes shaping British politics*. London: Penguin, 2017.

Gopinath, Gayatri '"Bombay, U.K., Yuba City": Bhangra music and the engendering of diaspora', *Diaspora: A Journal of Transnational Studies* 4: 3 (1995), pp. 303–321.

Grant, Colin, *Homecoming: voices of the Windrush generation*. London: Jonathan Cape, 2019.

SELECT BIBLIOGRAPHY

Gregory, Norma, *Jamaicans in Nottingham: narratives and reflections*. Hertford: Hansib Publications, 2015.

Griffin, Colin, 'The Identity of a Twentieth Century City', in John Beckett (ed.), *A Centenary History of Nottingham*. Manchester: Manchester University Press, 1997, pp. 421–434.

Grillo, Ralph, 'An Excess of Alterity? Debating difference in a multicultural society', in Steven Vertovec (ed.), *Anthropology of Migration & Multiculturalism*. London: Routledge, 2010, pp. 19–38.

Hall, Catherine, 'What is a West Indian?', in Bill Schwarz (ed.), *West Indian Intellectuals in Britain*. Manchester: Manchester University Press, 2003, pp. 31–50.

Hall, Stuart, Chas Critcher & Tony Jefferson *et al*, *Policing the Crisis: mugging, the state and law and order*. Basingstoke: Macmillan, 1978.

Hall, Stuart (with Bill Schwarz), *Familiar Stranger: a life between two islands*. London: Allen Lane, 2017.

Hall, Stuart, 'New Ethnicities', 1989, in David Morley & Kuan-Hsing Chen (eds.), *Critical Dialogues in Cultural Studies*. London: Routledge, 1995, pp. 441–449.

———, 'Aspiration and Attitude... Reflections on Black Britain in the Nineties', *New Formations* 33 (1997), pp. 38–46.

———, 'The Great Moving Nowhere Show', *Marxism Today* (November/December 1998), pp. 9–14.

———, "From Scarman to Stephen Lawrence", *History Workshop Journal* 48 (1999), pp. 71–120.

———, "Opens the Discussion", British Council *Reinventing Britain* forum, 1997, in *Wasafiri* 14: 29 (1999), pp. 37–38.

———, "The Multicultural Question", in Barnor Hesse (eds), *Un/Settled Multiculturalisms: diasporas, entanglements, transruptions*. London; New York: Zed Books, 2000, pp. 209–241.

Halliday, Fred, *Britain's First Muslims: portrait of an Arab community*. London; New York: I.B. Tauris, 2010.

Halstead, Mark, *Education, Justice and Cultural Diversity: an examination of the Honeyford Affair, 1984–85*. Barcombe: The Falmer Press, 1988.

Hancox, Dan, *Inner City Pressure: the story of grime*. London: William Collins, 2018.

SELECT BIBLIOGRAPHY

Hanley, Lynsey, *Estates: an intimate history*, London: Granta, 2007.

Hanna, Erika, *Snapshot Stories: visuality, photography, and the social history of Ireland, 1922–2000*. Oxford: Oxford University Press, 2020.

Hansen, Randall, 'The Kenyan Asians, British Politics, and the Commonwealth Immigrants Act, 1968', *The Historical Journal* 42: 3 (1999), pp. 809–834.

Hartwell, R.M., 'Kenneth H. Connell: an appreciation', *Irish Economic & Social History* 1: 1 (1974), pp. 7–13.

Hebdige, Dick, *Subculture: the meaning of style*. London; New York: Methuen, 1979.

———, *Cut 'n' Mix: culture, identity and Caribbean music*. London and New York: Routledge, 1987.

Henry, Nick, C, McEwan & J.S. Pollard, 'Globalisation From Below: Birmingham–postcolonial workshop of the world?' *Area* 34: 2 (2002), pp. 117–127.

Hesse, Barnor, (eds), *Un/Settled Multiculturalisms: diasporas, entanglements, transruptions*. London; New York: Zed Books, 2000.

Hewitt, Roger, *White Talk Black Talk*. Cambridge: Cambridge University Press, 1986.

Hilliard, Christopher, 'Words That Disturb the State: hate speech and the lessons of fascism in Britain, c. 1930s-1960s', *The Journal of Modern History* 88 (2016), p. 764–796.

———, 'Mapping the Notting Hill Riots: racism and the streets of postwar Britain', *History Workshop Journal* 93: 1 (2022), pp. 47–68

Hilling, David, 'Socio-economic Change in the Maritime Quarter: the demise of sailortown', in B.S. Hoyle, D.A. Pinder & M.S. Husain (eds.), *Revitalising the Waterfront*. London: Belhaven Press, 1988, pp. 20–37.

Hinds, Donald, *Journey to an Allusion: the West Indian immigrant in Britain*. London: Heinemann, 1966.

Hiro, Dilip, *Black British, White British*. Bristol: Eyre & Spottiswoode, 1971.

Hirsch, Afua, *Brit(ish): on race, identity and belonging*. London: Jonathan Cape, 2018.

Hirsch, Shirin, *In the Shadow of Enoch Powell: race, locality and resistance*. Manchester: Manchester University Press, 2018.

SELECT BIBLIOGRAPHY

Hoggart, Richard, *The Uses of Literacy: aspects of working-class life with special reference to publications and entertainments*. Harmondsworth: Penguin, 1957.

———, *Townscape With Figures: Farnham–portrait of an English town*. London: Chatto & Windus, 1994.

Holmes, Colin, *John Bull's Island: immigration and British society, 1871–1971*. Basingstoke: Macmillan Education, 1988.

Holmwood, John & Therese O'Toole, *Countering Extremism in British Schools? The truth about the Birmingham Trojan Horse Affair*. Bristol: Policy Press, 2018.

Hoyle, B.S., D.A. Pinder & M.S. Husain (eds.), *Revitalising the Waterfront*. London: Belhaven Press, 1988.

Hubbard, Phil, 'Community Action and the Displacement of Street Prostitution: evidence from British cities', *Geoforum* 29: 3 (1998), pp. 269–286.

Hunte, Joseph A., *Nigger Hunting in England?* London: West Indian Standing Conference, 1966.

Hunter, James Davison, *Culture Wars: the struggle to define America*. New York: Basic Books, 1991.

Huntington, Samuel, *The Clash of Civilizations and the Remaking of World Order*. New York: Simon & Schuster, 1996.

Huq, Rupa, 'Asian Kool? Bhangra and beyond', in Sanjay Sharma, John Hutnyk and Ashwani Sharma (eds.), *Dis-Orientating Rhythms: the politics of the new Asian dance music*. London: Zed Books, 1996, pp. 61–80.

———, 'From the margins to mainstream? Representations of British Asian youth musical cultural expression from bhangra to Asian underground music', *Young: Nordic Journal of Youth Research* 11: 1 (2003), 29–48.

Husband, Charles, Yunis Alam, Jorg Huttereman *et al*, *Lived Diversities: space, place, and identities in the multi-ethnic city*. Bristol: Policy Press, 2016.

Isakjee, Arshad & Chris Allen, '"A Catastrophic Lack of Inquisitiveness": A critical study of the impact and narrative of the Project Champion surveillance project in Birmingham', *Ethnicities* 13: 6 (2013), pp. 751–770

SELECT BIBLIOGRAPHY

Jackson, Ben, 'The Think Tank Archipelago: Thatcherism and neoliberalism', in Ben Jackson & Robert Saunders (eds.), *Making Thatcher's Britain*. Cambridge: Cambridge University Press, 2012, pp. 43–61.

Jackson, Ben & Robert Saunders (eds.), *Making Thatcher's Britain*. Cambridge: Cambridge University Press, 2012.

Jacobs, Callum (ed.), *A New Formation: how black footballers shaped the modern game*. London: #Merky Books, 2022.

James, Leslie & Daniel Whittall, 'Ambiguity and Imprint: British racial logics, colonial commissions of enquiry and the creolization of Britain in the 1930s and 40s', *Callaloo* 39: 1 (2016), pp. 166–184.

Jefferson, Tony, 'The Teds: a political resurrection', Centre for Contemporary Cultural Studies Stencilled Occasional Paper (September 1973), pp. 1–13.

Jenkins, Simon, 'Inherent Vice? Maltese men and the organization of prostitution in interwar Cardiff', *Journal of Social History* 49: 4 (2016), pp. 928–958.

Jenkinson, Jacqueline, *Black 1919: riots, racism and resistance in imperial Britain*. Liverpool: Liverpool University Press, 2009.

Jewson, Nick & Susanne MacGregor (eds.), *Transforming Cities: contested governance and new spatial dimensions*. London; New York: Routledge, 1997, pp. 181–192.

Joly, Daniele, *Britannia's Crescent: making a place for Muslims in British society*. Aldershot: Avebury, 1995.

Jones, Hannah, Yasmin Gunaratnam, Gargi Bhattacharyya *et al*, *Go Home? The politics of immigration controversies*. Manchester: Manchester University Press, 2017.

Jones, Phil, Arshad Isakjee, Chris Jam *et al*, 'Urban Landscapes and the Atmosphere of Place: exploring subjective experience in the study of urban form', *Urban Morphology* 21: 1 (2017), pp. 29–40.

Jones, Phillip N., 'Some Aspects of the Changing Distribution of Coloured Immigrants in Birmingham, 1961–66', *Transactions of the Institute of British Geographers* 50 (1970), 199–219.

Jones, Simon, *Black Culture, White Youth: the reggae tradition from JA to UK*. Birmingham: Bassline Books, 2016 [1988].

———, 'Music and Symbolic Creativity', in Paul Willis (ed.), *Common*

SELECT BIBLIOGRAPHY

Culture: symbolic work at play in the everyday cultures of the young. Milton Keynes: Open University Press, 1990.

Jordan, Glenn, *'Down the Bay': Picture Post, humanist photography and images of 1950s Cardiff*. Cardiff: Butetown History & Arts Centre, 2001.

Katznelson, Ira, 'The Politics of Racial Buffering in Nottingham, 1954–1968', *Race* XI: 4 (1970), pp. 431–446.

Keith, Michael, *After the Cosmopolitan? Multicultural cities and the future of racism*. Abingdon, Oxon: Routledge, 2005.

Kelley, D.G., & Stephen Tuck (eds.), *The Other Special Relationship: race, rights, and riots in Britain and the United States*. New York: Palgrave Macmillan, 2015.

Kenny, Michael & Nick Pearce, *Shadows of Empire: the Anglosphere in British politics*. Cambridge: Polity Press, 2018.

Kew, Tom, *The Multicultural Midlands: multicultural textualities*. Manchester: Manchester University Press, 2023.

Khalidi, Rashid, *The Hundred Years' War on Palestine: a history of settler colonial conquest and resistance*. London: Profile Books, 2020.

Khan, Yasmin, 'Refugees, Migrants, Windrush and Brexit', in Stuart Ward & Astrid Rasch, *Embers of Empire in Brexit Britain*. London: Bloomsbury, 2019, pp. 101–110.

Kinnell, Hilary, *Violence and Sex Work in Britain*. Uffculme: Willian, 2007.

Knott, Sarah, *Mother: an unconventional history*. London: Penguin, 2019.

Koole, Simeon, 'How We Came to Mind the Gap: time, tactility, and the tube', *Twentieth Century British History* 27: 4 (2016), pp. 524–554.

Kundnani, Arun, *The End of Tolerance: racism in 21st century Britain*. London: Pluto Press, 2007.

Kureishi, Hanif, *Collected Essays*. London: Faber & Faber, 2011.

———, 'Bradford', 1986, in Hanif Kureishi, *Collected Essays*. London: Faber & Faber, 2011, pp. 35–57.

Kynaston, David, *Modernity Britain, 1957–62*. London: Bloomsbury, 2015.

Laite, Julia, *Common Prostitutes and Ordinary citizens: commercial sex in London, 1885–1960*. Basingstoke: Palgrave, 2012.

Lambert, John R., *Crime, Police and Race Relations: a study in Birmingham*. Oxford: Oxford University Press, 1970.

SELECT BIBLIOGRAPHY

Lawrence, Daniel, *Black Migrants: White Natives–a study of race relations in Nottingham*. Cambridge: Cambridge University Press, 1974.

Lawrence, Jon, *Me, Me, Me? The search for community in post-war England*. Oxford: Oxford University Press, 2019.

Leadbeater, Charlie, 'Power to the Person', in Stuart Hall & Martin Jaques (eds.), *New Times: the changing face of politics in the 1990s*. London: Lawrence & Wishart, 1990, pp. 137–149.

———, *The Self-Policing Society*. London: Demos, 1996.

———, *Civic Spirit: the big idea for a new political area*. London: Demos, 1997.

Leadbeater, Charlie & Ian Christie, *To Our Mutual Advantage*. London: Demos, 1999.

Lebow, Richard Ned, *White Britain and Black Ireland: the influence of stereotypes on colonial policy*. Philadelphia: Institute for the Study of Human Issues, 1976.

Lewis, Philip, *Islamic Britain: religion, politics and identity among British Muslims*. London; New York: IB Tauris, 1994.

Little, Kenneth L., 'Loudoun Square: a community survey I (an aspect of race relations in an English society), *The Sociological Review* 34: 1–2 (1942), pp. 12–33.

———, 'Loudoun Square: a community survey II', *The Sociological Review* 34: 3–4 (1942), pp. 119–146.

———, 'Race Relations in English Society. Preliminary report on a community survey', *Man* 42 (1942), pp. 90–91.

———, *Negroes in Britain: a study of racial relations in an English society*. London; Boston: Routledge & Kegan Paul, 1972 [1948].

Loftman, Patrick & Alan Middleton, 'Emasculating Public Debate and Eroding Local Accountability: city promotion of urban development projects in Birmingham', *Geographische Zeitschrift* 89: 2/3 (2001), pp. 85–103.

Mac Laughlan, Jim, 'Nation Building, Social Closure and Anti-Traveller Racism in Ireland', *Sociology* 33: 1 (1999), pp. 129–151

Malik, Kenan, *From Fatwa to Jihad: The Rushdie Affair and its legacy*. London: Atlantic Books, 2009.

Malik, Zaiba, *We are Muslim, Please*. London: Windmill Books, 2011.

SELECT BIBLIOGRAPHY

Manning, Sam, *Cinemas and Cinema-Going in the United Kingdom: decades of decline, 1945–65*. London: University of London Press, 2020.

Matera, Marc, *Black London: the imperial metropolis and decolonization in the twentieth century*. Oakland, CA: University of California Press, 2015.

McLoughlin, Seán, 'Writing "Bradistan" Across the Domains of Social Reality', in Seán McLoughlin, William Gould, Ananya Jahanara Kabir & Emma Tomalin (eds.), *Writing the City in British Asian Diasporas*. Abingdon: Routledge, 2014, pp. 21–48.

———, '"A Part of the Community"? The politics of representation and a Muslim School's application for state funding', *Innovation* 11: 4 (1998), pp. 541–470.

McLoughlin, Seán, William Gould, Ananya Jahanara Kabir & Emma Tomalin (eds.), *Writing the City in British Asian Diasporas*. Abingdon: Routledge, 2014.

McMonagle, Sarah & Philip McDermott, 'Transitional Politics and Language Rights in a Multi-ethnic Northern Ireland: towards a true linguistic pluralism?', *Ethnopolitics* 13: 3 (2014), pp. 245–266.

Mead, Matthew, '*Empire Windrush*: The cultural memory of an imaginary arrival', *Journal of Postcolonial Writing* 45: 2 (2009), pp. 137–149.

Melly, George, *Revolt into Style: the pop arts in the 50s and 60s*. Oxford: Oxford University Press, 1989.

Mercer, Kobena, 'Black Hair/Style Politics', *New Formations* 3 (1987), pp. 33–54.

Modood, Tariq, *Multiculturalism*. Cambridge: Polity, 2007.

Moores, Chris, 'Thatcher's troops? Neighbourhood Watch schemes and the search for 'ordinary' Thatcherism in 1980s Britain', *Contemporary British History* 31: 2 (2017), pp. 230–255.

Moran, Angela, 'Hail Ambiguous St Patrick: sounds of Ireland on parade in Birmingham', *Irish Studies Review* 20: 2 (2012), pp. 157–178.

Moran, James, *Irish Birmingham: a history*. Liverpool: Liverpool University Press, 2010.

Morley, David & Kuan-Hsing Chen (eds.), *Critical Dialogues in Cultural Studies*. London: Routledge, 1995,

Morris, Garry, Ali Hussain & Tarlochan Gata Aura, 'Racism and the Schooling Crisis in Bradford', *Critical Social Policy* 4: 12 (1984), pp. 69–78.

SELECT BIBLIOGRAPHY

Mort, Frank, *Capital Affairs: London and the making of the permissive society*. New Haven; London: Yale University Press, 2010.

Mulvey, Gareth, 'When Policy Creates Politics: the problematizing of immigration and the consequences for refugee integration in the UK', *Journal of Refugee Studies* 23: 4 (2010), pp. 437–462.

Murphy, Colm, *Futures of Socialism: 'modernisation', the Labour Party, and the British Left*. Cambridge: Cambridge University Press, 2023.

Murphy, Dervla, *Tales From Two Cities: travel of another sort*. London: Penguin, 1989.

Murphy, Patrick, 'Irish Immigration in Nottingham in the Early-Nineteenth Century', *Transactions of the Thoroton Society of Nottinghamshire*, vol. XCVIII (1994), pp. 82–91.

Murray, Robert N., *Lest We Forget: the experiences of World War II West Indian ex-service personnel*. Nottingham: Nottinghamshire West Indian Combined Ex-Services Association, 1996.

Myers, Kevin, *Struggles for a Past: Irish and Afro-Caribbean histories in England, 1951–2000*. Manchester: Manchester University Press, 2015.

Natarajan, Radhika, 'The "Bogus Child" and the "Big Uncle": the impossible South-Asian family in post-imperial Britain', *Twentieth Century British History* 34: 3 (2023), pp. 440–466.

Nava, Mica, *Visceral Cosmopolitanism: gender, culture and the normalisation of difference*. Oxford; New York: Berg, 2007.

Nayak, Anoop, *Race, Place and Globalization: youth cultures in a changing world*. Oxford; New York: Berg, 2003.

Neal, Sarah, Katy Bennett, Allan Cochrane *et al*, *Lived Experiences of Multiculture: the new social and spatial relations of diversity*. London; New York: Routledge, 2018.

Nixon, Rob, *Slow Violence and the Environmentalism of the Poor*. Cambridge, MA: Harvard University Press, 2011.

Nottingham Irish Studies Group, *Making it Home: experiences of being Irish*. Nottingham: Nottingham Irish Studies Group, 2001.

O'Brien, Sarah, 'Negotiations of Irish identity in the wake of terrorism: the case of the Irish in Birmingham 1973–74', *Irish Studies Review* 25: 3 (2017), pp. 372–394.

O'Leary, Brenda & John McGarry, *The Politics of Antagonism: understanding Northern Ireland*. London: The Athlone Press, 1997.

SELECT BIBLIOGRAPHY

Oliver, Paul (ed.), *Black Music in Britain*. Milton Keynes: Open University Press, 1990.

Osgerby, Bill, 'Youth Culture', in Paul Addison & Harriet Jones, *A Companion to Contemporary Britain, 1939–2000*. Oxford: Blackwell, 2005, pp. 127–144.

Ouseley, Herman, *Community Pride Not Prejudice*. Bradford: Bradford City Council, 2001.

Pain, Rachel, 'Chronic Urban Trauma: the slow violence of housing dispossession', *Urban Studies* 56: 2 (2019), pp. 385–400.

Palmer, Lisa Amanda, '"Ladies A Your Time Now!" Erotic politics, Lovers' Rock and resistance in the UK', *African and Black Diaspora: an international journal* 4: 2 (2011), pp. 177–192.

———, 'Diane Abbott, Misogynoir and the Politics of Black British Feminism's Anticolonial Imperatives: "In Britain too, it's as if we don't exist"', *The Sociological Review* 68: 3 (2019), pp. 508–523.

Panayi, Panikos, 'Middlesbrough 1961: a British race riot of the 1960s?', *Social History* 16: 2 (1991), pp. 139–153.

———, *The Enemy in Our Midst: Germans in Britain during the First World War*. Oxford: Berg, 1991.

———, *Spicing Up Britain: the multicultural history of British food*. London: Reaktion Books, 2008.

———, *Migrant City: a new history of London*. New Haven; London; Yale University Press, 2022.

Parekh, Bhikhu/The Runnymede Trust, *The Future of Multi-Ethnic Britain*. London: Profile Books, 2000.

Patel, Ian Sanjay, *We're Here Because You Were There: immigration and the end of Empire*. London: Verso, 2021.

Patterson, Sheila, *Dark Strangers: a sociological study of the absorption of a recent West Indian migrant group in Brixton, South London*. London: Tavistock, 1963.

Paul, Kate, *Journal*. Hay-on-Wye: Carrington Press, 2000.

Payling, Daisy, 'Socialist Republic of South Yorkshire': grassroots activism and left-wing solidarity in 1980s Sheffield', *Twentieth Century British History* 25: 4 (2014), pp. 602–627.

Peach, Ceri, 'Muslims in the 2001 Census of England and Wales: gender and economic disadvantage', *Ethnic & Racial Studies* 29: 4 (2006), pp. 629–655.

Peplow, Simon, *Race and Riots in Thatcher's Britain*. Manchester: Manchester University Press, 2019.

Peretz, Henri, 'The Making of *Black Metropolis*', *The Annals of the American Academy of Political and Social Science* 595 (2004), pp. 168–175.

Perry, Kennetta Hammond, '"Little Rock" in Britain: Jim Crow's transatlantic topographies', *Journal of British Studies* 51: 1 (2012), pp. 155–177.

———, *London Is the Place for Me: Black Britons, citizenship and the politics of race*. Oxford: Oxford University Press, 2015.

———, 'The Sights and Sounds of State Violence: encounters with the archive of David Oluwale', *Twentieth Century British History* 34: 3 (2023), pp. 467–490.

Phillips, Trevor & Mike Phillips, *Windrush: the irresistible rise of multiracial Britain*. London: HarperCollins, 1998.

Pilkington, Edward, *Beyond the Mother Country: West Indians and the Notting Hill white riots*. London: IB Tauris, 1988.

Pitts, Johny, *Afropean: notes from Black Europe*. London: Penguin, 2020.

Pitts, Johny & Roger Robinson, *Home is Not a Place*. London: William Collins, 2022.

Powe, George, *Don't Blame the Blacks*. Nottingham: Five Leaves, 2022 [1956].

Prince, Simon & Geoffrey Warner, *Belfast and Derry in Revolt: a new history of the start of the troubles*. Newbridge: Irish Academic Press, 2012.

Prins, Baukje & Sawitri Saharso, 'From Toleration to Repression: the Dutch backlash against multiculturalism', in Steven Vertovec & Susanne Wessendorf (eds.), *The Multiculturalism Backlash: European discourses, policies and practices*. Abingdon; New York: Routledge, 2010, pp. 72–91.

Ramamurthy, Anandi, *Black Star Britain's Asian Youth Movements*. London: Pluto Press, 2013.

Ramdin, Ron, *The Making of the Black Working Class in Britain*. London; New York: Verso, 2017 [1987].

Rampton, Ben, 'Interracial Panjabi in a British Adolescent Peer Group', *Language in Society* 20 (1991), pp. 391–422.

SELECT BIBLIOGRAPHY

——, *Crossing: language and ethnicity among adolescents*. Manchester: St Jerome Publishing, 2005.

Ranasinha, Ruvani (ed.), *South Asians and the Shaping of Britain, 1870–1950*. Manchester; New York: Manchester University Press, 2012.

Renshaw, Daniel, *The Discourse of Repatriation in Britain, 1845–2016: a political and social history*. London; New York: Routledge, 2021.

Rex, John & Robert Moore, *Race, Community and Conflict: a study of Sparkbrook*. London: Oxford University Press, 1967.

Rhodes, James & Lawrence Brown, 'The Rise and Fall of the "Inner City": race, space and urban policy in postwar England', *Journal of Ethnic and Migration Studies* 45: 17 (2018), pp. 3243–3259.

Rhodes, Martha Robinson, 'Bisexuality, Multiple-Gender-Attraction, and Gay Liberation Politics in the 1970s', *Twentieth Century British History* 32: 1 (2021), pp. 119–142.

Rich, Paul B., *Race and Empire in British Politics*. Cambridge: Cambridge University Press, 1990.

Richardson, Peter, *St Ann's, the End of an Era*. Nottingham: Five Leaves, 2020.

Robinson, Lucy, 'Smiley Culture: a hybrid voice for the Commonwealth', in William 'Lez' Henry & Matthew Worley (eds.), *Narratives from Beyond the UK Reggae Bassline*. Cham: Palgrave, 2021, pp. 101–123.

Rock, Paul & Stanley Cohen, 'The Teddy Boy', in Verdon Bogdanor & Robert Skidelsky (eds.), *The Age of Affluence 1951–1964*. London & Basingstoke: Macmillan, 1970, pp. 288–320.

Rogers, Asha, *State Sponsored Literature: Britain and cultural diversity after 1945*. Oxford: Oxford University Press, 2020.

Romyn, Michael, *London's Aylesbury Estate: an oral history of the 'concrete jungle'*. Cham: Palgrave Macmillan, 2020.

Rose, E.J.B., *Colour and Citizenship: a report on British race relations*. London; New York: Oxford University Press, 1969.

Rose, Sonya O., 'Girls and GIs: race, sex, and diplomacy in Second World War Britain', *The International History Review* 19: 1 (1997), pp. 146–160.

——, 'Sex, Citizenship, and the Nation in World War II Britain', *The American Historical Review* 103: 4 (1998), pp. 1147–1176.

SELECT BIBLIOGRAPHY

Roseneil, Sasha & Julie Seymour (eds.), *Practicing Identities: power and resistance*. Basingstoke: Palgrave Macmillan, 1999.

Ryan, Louise, 'Family Matters: (e)migration, familial networks and Irish women in Britain', *Sociological Review* 52: 3 (2004), pp. 351–370.

Sandhu, Sukhdev, *London Calling: how black and Asian writers imagined a city*. London; HarperPerennial, 2004.

———, *Night Haunts*. London; New York, 2006.

Sanghera, Sathnam, *Empireland: how Imperialism has shaped modern Britain*. London: Penguin Random House, 2021.

Sardar, Ziauddin *Balti Britain: a provocative journey through Asian Britain*. London: Granta, 2008.

———, *A Person of Pakistani Origins*. London: C. Hurst & Co, 2018.

Schaffer, Gavin & Saima Nasar, 'The White Essential Subject: race, ethnicity, and the Irish in post-war Britain', *Contemporary British History* 32: 2 (2018), pp. 209–230.

Schaffer, Gavin, 'Legislating against Hatred: meaning and motive in Section Six of the Race Relations Act of 1965', *Twentieth Century British History* 25: 2 (2014), pp. 251–275.

Schofield, Camilla & Ben Jones, '"Whatever Community Is, This Is Not It": Notting Hill and the reconstruction of "race" in Britain after 1958', *Journal of British Studies* 58: 1 (2019), pp. 142–173.

Schofield, Camilla, *Enoch Powell and the Making of Post-Colonial Britain*. Cambridge: Cambridge University Press, 2013.

———, 'In Defence of White Freedom: working men's clubs and the politics of sociability in late industrial England', *Twentieth Century British History* 34: 3 (2023), pp. 515–551.

Schwarz, Bill, '"The Only White Man in There': the re-racialization of England, 1956–1968", *Race & Class* 38: 1 (1996), pp. 65–78.

———(ed.), *West Indian Intellectuals in Britain*. Manchester: Manchester University Press, 2003, pp. 31–50.

Selbourne, David, *Left Behind: journeys into British politics*. London: Jonathan Cape, 1987.

Sengupta, Saswati, Shampa Roy & Sharmila Purkayastha, *'Bad' Women of Bombay Films: studies in desire and anxiety*. Basingstoke: Palgrave Macmillan, 2019.

SELECT BIBLIOGRAPHY

Sharma, Sanjay, John Hutnyk & Ashwani Sharma (eds.), *Dis-Orientating Rhythms: the politics of the new Asian dance music*. London: Zed Books, 1996.

Shenker, Jack, *Now We Have Your Attention: the new politics of the people*. London: Bodley Head, 2019.

Sherwood, Marika, 'Racism and Resistance: Cardiff in the 1930s and 40s', *Llafur: the journal of the Society of Welsh Labour History* 5: 4 (1991), pp. 51–70.

Shukla, Nikesh (ed.), *The Good Immigrant*. London: Unbound, 2017.

Sinclair, Neil M.C., *The Tiger Bay Story*. Cardiff: Dragon & Tiger Enterprises, 2003.

Singh, Ramindar, *Indians in Bradford: the development of a community*. Bradford: Bradford and Ilkley Community College, 1986.

Sivanandan, Ambalavaner, *A Different Hunger: writings on black resistance*. London: Pluto Press, 1982.

———, 'All That Melts into Air is Solid: the hokum of New Times', *Race & Class* 31: 3 (1990), pp. 1–30.

Slater, T.R., 'Birmingham's Black and South Asian Population', in J. Gerrard and T.R. Slater (eds.), *Managing a Conurbation: Birmingham and its Region* (Studley: Brewin Books, 1996), pp. 140–155.

Smith, Otto Saumarez, 'Action for Cities: the Thatcher government and inner-city policy,' *Urban History*, vol. 47, no. 2 (May 2020), pp. 274–291.

Sobande, Francesca & layla-roxanne hill, *Black Oot Here: Black lives in Scotland*. London: Bloomsbury, 2022.

Sobolewska, Maria & Robert Ford, *Brexitland: identity, diversity and the reshaping of British politics*. Cambridge: Cambridge University Press, 2020.

Solomos, John, *Race and Racism in Contemporary Britain*. Basingstoke: Macmillan, 1989.

Spencer, Sarah, 'Immigration', in Anthony Seldon (ed.), *Blair's Britain: 1997–2007*. Cambridge: Cambridge University Press, 2007, pp. 341–360.

Square, Vicki, '"Integration with diversity in modern Britain": New Labour on nationality, immigration and asylum', *Journal of Political Ideologies* 10: 1 (2005), pp. 51–74.

SELECT BIBLIOGRAPHY

Steedman, Carolyn, *Landscape for a Good Woman*. London: Virago, 1986.

Stevens, Dallal, 'The Nationality, Immigration and Asylum Act 2002: secure borders, safe haven?', *The Modern Law Review* 67: 4 (2004), pp. 616–631.

Stocker, Paul, *English Uprising: Brexit and the mainstreaming of the far right*. London: Melville House UK, 2017.

Studlar, Donley T., 'Policy Voting in Britain: the colored immigration issue in the 1964, 1966, and 1970 General Elections', *The American Political Science Review* 72: 1 (1978), pp. 46–64.

Suleyman, Chimenem 'My Name is My Name', in Nikesh Shukla (ed.), *The Good Immigrant*. London: Unbound, 2017, pp. 22–32

Sutcliffe, Anthony & Roger Smith, *History of Birmingham Volume III: Birmingham 1939–1970*. Oxford: Oxford University Press, 1974.

Swann, Lord Michael, *Education for All: report of the committee of enquiry into the education of children from ethnic minority groups*. London: HMSO, 1985.

Swift, David, 'Competition or Culture? Anti-migrant hostility and industrial decline: the case of West Yorkshire, 1962–81', *Journal of Ethnic & Migration Studies* 47:11 (2019), pp. 1–17.

Tabili, Laura, 'The Construction of Racial Difference in Twentieth Century Britain: The Special Restriction (Coloured Seamen) Order, 1925', *Journal of British Studies* 33: 1 (1994), pp. 54–94.

Taylor, Becky, *A Minority and the State: travellers in Britain in the twentieth century*. Manchester: Manchester University Press, 2008.

Thane, Pat, 'Population and the Family', in Paul Addison & Harriet Jones (eds.), *A Companion to Contemporary Britain 1939–2000*. Oxford: Blackwell, 2005, pp. 42–58.

Thorpe, Charles, 'Participation as Post-Fordist Politics: Demos, New Labour, and science policy', *Minerva* 48 (2010), pp. 389–411.

Thurlow, Richard, *Fascism in Britain: from Oswald Mosley's Blackshirts to the National Front*. London: I.B. Tauris, 1998.

Trilling, Daniel, *Bloody Nasty People: the rise of Britain's far right*. London: Verso, 2012.

Troyna, Barry & Jenny Williams, *Racism, Education and the State*. Beckenham: Croom Helm, 1986.

SELECT BIBLIOGRAPHY

Troyna, Barry (ed.), *Racial Inequality in Education*. London: Routledge, 1989.

Tuan, Yi-Fu, *Space and Place: the perspective of experience*. Minneapolis: University of Minnesota Press, 1977.

Tuck, Stephen, 'Malcolm X's Visit to Oxford University: US civil rights, Black Britain and the special relationship on race', *The American Historical Review* 118: 1 (2013), pp. 76–103.

Tyler, Katherine, 'The Suburban Paradox of Conviviality and Racism in Postcolonial Britain', *Journal of Ethnic and Migration Studies* 43: 11 (2017), pp. 1890–1906.

Vernon, James, *Modern Britain: 1750 to the Present*. Cambridge: Cambridge University Press, 2017.

Vertovec, Steven, & Susanne Wessendorf (eds.), *The Multiculturalism Backlash: European discourses, policies and practices*. Abingdon; New York: Routledge, 2010, pp. 72–91.

Vertovec, Steven (ed.), *Anthropology of Migration and Multiculturalism*. London: Routledge, 2010.

Vinen, Richard, *Second City: Birmingham and the forging of Modern Britain*. London: Allen Lane, 2022.

Visram, Rozina, *Asians in Britain: 400 years of history*. London: Pluto Press, 2002.

Walford, Geoffrey, *Markets and Equity in Education*. London; New York: Continuum, 2006.

Ward, Stuart & Astrid Rasch, *Embers of Empire in Brexit Britain*. London: Bloomsbury, 2019.

Warren, Saskia & Phil Jones, 'Local governance, Disadvantaged Communities and Cultural Intermediation in the Creative Urban Economy', *Environment and Planning C: Government & Policy* 33 (2015), pp. 1738–1752.

Waters, Chris, '"Dark Strangers" in our Midst: discourses of race and nation in Britain, 1947–1963', *Journal of British Studies* 36: 2 (1997), pp. 224–225.

Waters, Rob, *Thinking Black: Britain, 1964–1985*. Oakland: University of California Press, 2019.

———, *Colonized by Humanity: Caribbean London and the Politics of Integration at the End of Empire*. Oxford: Oxford University Press, 2023.

SELECT BIBLIOGRAPHY

Webster, Wendy, *Mixing It: diversity in World War Two Britain*. Oxford: Oxford University Press, 2018.

Wessendorf, Susanne, 'Commonplace Diversity and the "Ethos of Mixing": perceptions of difference in a London neighbourhood', *Identities: global studies in power & culture* 20: 4 (2013), pp. 407–422.

White, Jerry, *London in the Nineteenth Century: a human awful wonder of God*. London: Vintage, 2007.

Whittle, Matthew, 'Hosts and Hostages: mass immigration and the power of hospitality in post-war British and Caribbean literature', *Comparative Critical Studies* 11 (2014), pp. 77–92.

Williams, Raymond, *Marxism and Literature*. Oxford: Oxford University Press, 1977.

———, *Politics and Letters: interviews with the New Left Review*. London: New Left Books, 1979.

Willis, Paul, *Learning to Labour: how working class kids get working class jobs*. Farnborough: Saxon House, 1977.

———(ed.), *Common Culture: symbolic work at play in the everyday cultures of the young*. Milton Keynes: Open University Press, 1990.

Wills, Clair, *Lovers and Strangers: an immigrant history of post-war Britain*. London: Allen Lane, 2017.

Witmer, Robert, '"Local" and "Foreign": the popular music culture of Kingston, Jamaica, before ska, rock steady, and reggae', *Latin American Music Review* 8: 1 (1987), pp. 1–25.

Wynn, Neil A., '"Race War": Black American GIs and West Indians in Britain during the Second World War', *Immigrants & Minorities* 24: 3 (2006), pp. 324–346.

Yemm, Rachel, 'Immigration, Race and Local Media: Smethwick and the 1964 general election', *Contemporary British History* 33: 1 (2019), pp. 98–122.

Young, Robert J. C., *Colonial Desire: hybridity in theory, culture and race*. London; New York: 1995.

Younge, Gary, foreword to Peter Fryer, *Staying Power: the history of black people in Britain*. London: Pluto, 2018 [1984], pp. xi-xii.

———, *Dispatches from the Diaspora: From Nelson Mandela to Black Lives Matter*. London: Faber, 2023.

ACKNOWLEDGEMENTS

The seeds for what has become this book were sewn with the arrival on my desk of Janet Mendelsohn's remarkable archive from her time in late-1960s Balsall Heath. This material allowed me to begin to seriously engage with the nature of my childhood in the same area some twenty-five years later. My experiences in inner-city Birmingham have always informed my work, but until I saw Janet's photography I struggled to work out how I would tackle the subject explicitly. For their initial generosity and enduring friendship, therefore, I am incredibly grateful to both Janet and her husband Marc Levitt. In 2020 I was privileged to be awarded a Fulbright Fellowship at New York University. This turned out to be a terrible time for something of this nature. Within a couple of months of my arrival in New York, the Covid-19 pandemic arrived and I was forced to head home early and into lockdown. But my time in New York bought me invaluable thinking space. It also brought me into contact with St. Clair Drake's archives in Harlem, and his wonderfully evocative record of post-war Cardiff. It was this that allowed me to conceive of this book geographically, as a journey through different cities. I therefore owe a big debt of gratitude to the Fulbright Commission and my host at NYU, Guy Ortolano, for their generosity here.

ACKNOWLEDGEMENTS

My agent, Suresh Ariaratnam, has been a patient, kind and wise source of guidance from the gestation of this book all the way through to its publication. He took a chance on me, for which I am extremely grateful. The many conversations we have shared over the years has shaped this book in indispensable ways. I have also been lucky to have received critical input from friends and colleagues on various parts of the book. Thanks to Mitchell Albert for his help in crafting the sample chapters, to Claire Chambers, who was the first person to read the entire thing on a train journey from hell, and to James Bagan, Peter Cameron, James Cantres, Myra Connell, Monica Connell, Matthew Hilton, Tom Hulme, Josie Kelly (to whom I will one day return her voice recorder), Judith Walkowitz and Keira Williams, all of whom read and provided thought-provoking feedback on various parts. Thanks, too, to the members of the Columbia University British History reading group for their feedback on the Cardiff chapter, to the Europe Center at Stanford, where I brought the manuscript to fruition, and to the people who have engaged with elements of the book at online events and at conferences and workshops around the world.

A large number of people have gone out of their way to help me with my research. In particular, I owe a big thank you to Jayne Aitchison, Simon Baker, Rajinder Dudrah, Ian Francis, Val Hart, the Irons family, Simon Jones, Pat Murphy and Marika Sherwood, as well as each of my interviewees, who generously gave up their time to talk to me. Michael Dwyer and the team at Hurst have been enthusiastic champions of this book, and a pleasure to work with from start to finish. The School of History, Anthropology, Philosophy and Politics at Queen's University Belfast has provided the kind collegial environment that is becoming increasingly unusual in UK higher education. I have received generous departmental funding to be able to make numerous research trips to Cardiff, Nottingham, Birmingham

ACKNOWLEDGEMENTS

and Bradford. But even more important has been the support, friendship and excellent pub camaraderie of many people, especially Maurice Casey, Paul Corthorn, Elaine Farrell, Colm Heatley, Tom Hulme, Ashok Malhotra, Fearghal McGarry, Sean O'Connell, Alex Titov and Keira Williams.

Alicia Field has lived with this book from start to finish. It is impossible to put into words how much her support, generosity, advice, companionship and love means to me. Our children, Connell and Frida Field, have also been with this book from the beginning. Often, when I was trying to reconstruct parts of my own childhood in Birmingham, I had them in mind as future readers. I can't wait to see in what ways their own childhood experiences and hybridised identities will shape them. Connell and Frida, with all my love, this book is for you.

INDEX

Abbott, Diane, 274
Abdullah's, Balsall Heath, 247
Absolute Beginners (MacInnes), 164
Achanak, 245
active citizenship, 252
Aden, colonial (1839–1963), 52, 70
African Americans, 18, 24, 27–41, 43, 69, 85, 91, 192
African Churches Mission, 46
Agard, John, 216
Ajao, Steve, 263
Alamgir, 184
Alfred Street, Nottingham, 75, 88, 105, 106
Ali, Moeen, 282
Ali, Zulfiqar, 229, 234
Aliens Orders (1920; 1925), 42–3, 49, 58, 79
Alsopp, Fred, 95
Alum Rock, Birmingham, 261
Ambala, Haryana, 184
Amin, Idi, 277

Amin, Raja, 227, 228, 229, 230, 232, 235, 253
Andrews, Kehinde, 197
anti-racist activism, 173, 202–14
Apache Indian, 248, 250
Apna Ghar, Balsall Heath, 124, 141, 284
Arab–Israeli War (1947–9), 55
Arabic, 35, 52, 54, 61
Arabs, 7, 16, 115
  1:in Cardiff, 30, 34, 35, 44–57, 60–61, 66, 187
Armaan (1966 film), 184
Ashdown, Jeremy 'Paddy', 225
Asian Weekly, The, 246
Asian Youth Movement, 181, 204, 206
asylum seekers, 254–6, 259–61, 267, 276
Atkinson, Dick, 227, 230, 251–3, 265, 266
Attlee, Clement, 53
Attock, Punjab, 178
austerity (2010–19), 28

INDEX

Australia, 109
Ayub, Muhammad, 244
Aziz supermarket, Balsall Heath, 124, 141, 168

Baker, Shirley, 146
Balsall Heath, Birmingham, 1–2, 5, 8, 12, 13–14, 18, 21–2, 121–74, 221–68, 283–5
   leisure and retail in, 146–52
   Mendelsohn in, 122–8, 137, 139–71, 233, 264
   music scene, 224–5, 238–50
   politicians and, 12, 122, 225–6, 250–61, 264–7
   prostitution in, *see* Balsall Heath red light district
   St Paul's Community Group, 227–8, 230, 251–2, 265, 266
   Travellers in, 135–7, 172
   urban renewal in, 144–6, 152, 283
Balsall Heath red light district, 20, 24, 126–7, 129, 130–31, 145, 148, 152–71, 284
   campaign against (1994), 223–4, 225, 227–37, 252–3, 264, 266
Balsall Heathen, The, 228, 251
balti, 121, 221, 243, 263, 284
Bangladesh, 178
Bangladeshi People's Association, 206
Barbados, 77, 84, 87, 89, 90
Barelwi sect, 178

Bartley Green, Birmingham, 248
Bashir, Mohammed, 183
Bass Culture (Johnson), 216
Bassey, Shirley, 68
Beat, The, 269
Belfast, Northern Ireland, 281
Belgrave Road, Balsall Heath, 228
Bengal region, 161
Bentley, Tom, 252
Bermuda, 81
bhangra, 224–5, 244–50, 264
Bhutt's, Balsall Heath, 243
Bin Laden, Osama, 258
biradari, 177
Birmingham, West Midlands, 1–2, 5, 7, 8, 12–16, 18, 21–2, 121–74, 221–68, 280, 283–5
   Brummie accent, 132, 240
   deindustrialisation, 222, 223
   education in, 188, 222–3, 238
   Handsworth riots (1985), 176, 235
   IRA bombings (1974), 134
   Irish population, 19, 127, 132–7, 155–6
   Mendelsohn in, 122–8, 137, 139–71, 233, 264
   music scene, 224–5, 238–50
   politicians and, 12, 122, 225–6, 250–61, 264–7
   prostitution in, *see* Balsall Heath red light district
   'Rivers of Blood' speech (Powell, 1968), 3, 110, 128, 131, 144, 162, 277

374

INDEX

Travellers in, 135–7, 172
urban renewal in, 144–6, 152
Birmingham Central Mosque, 124, 284
Birmingham University, 122, 227
black Britons, 3, 6, 7, 8–9, 10, 11
Afro-Caribbean, *see* British Afro-Caribbeans
East Africans, *see* British East Africans
West Africans, *see* British West Africans
'black burying', 93, 99
Black Lives Matter, 29, 273
Black Metropolis (Drake and Cayton), 27, 29, 31, 33, 42
Black Power movement, 105–6, 203
Blackwell, Chris, 242, 243
Blair, Anthony 'Tony', 4
Blitz (1940–41), 52
Blunkett, David, 4, 225, 252–61, 264, 266
boarding houses, 34, 47–9, 86–7
Boatang, Ozwald, 282
bodhrán, 243
Bollywood Flashback (Sagoo), 224–5, 249
Bollywood, *see* South Asian cinema
Bradford, West Yorkshire, 7, 14, 160–61, 175–220
bhangra in, 245, 246
education in, 177–82, 192–3, 195, 196–202, 205–20, 264

National Front violence (1976), 202–5
riots (2001), 220, 256–7
self-defence activism in, 202–14
Turning Point (1981 report), 193–5, 200, 206, 208
Bradford Apartheid Group, 179
Bradford City FC, 183
Bradford Council for Mosques, 194, 202, 211–12, 213, 217, 246
Bradford University, 177, 206
Brexit, 4, 14, 110, 218, 274, 275
Brick Lane, London, 249
Bristol, England, 38, 176, 187, 193
British Afro-Caribbeans, 125, 179–80, 210–11, 275
Birmingham, 20, 163, 238–43
Cardiff, 30, 34, 42, 46, 48, 49, 59, 61, 63, 64
education system and, 179–80, 210–11
Empire Windrush, 8–9, 20, 81, 220
London, 18, 79, 100–103, 104, 105, 115
music scene and, 238–43
Nottingham, 15, 18–19, 74, 78–119
British East Africans, 6, 19, 125
in Cardiff, 30, 47–8, 49, 54, 55–7, 60, 70
British Empire, 2, 3, 6, 9–10, 11, 25, 30, 32, 42, 47, 69–70, 76, 81, 125, 197
Aden (1839–1963), 52, 70

375

INDEX

Barbados (1625–1966), 77, 84, 87, 89, 90
Cyprus (1878–1960), 77
decolonisation, 3, 10, 13, 32, 69–70, 76, 113, 127, 137, 180
education and, 215, 268
Gambia (1816–1965), 137
Gold Coast (1821–1957), 77, 84
Guiana (1831–1966), 3, 9, 51, 57, 70, 106
Honduras (1783–1964), 83
India (1612–1947), 10, 32, 69–70, 76, 77, 81, 125, 178, 187
Jamaica (1655–1962), *see* Jamaica
Kenya (1888–1963), 9, 123, 137, 172
Malta (1813–1964), 34, 61, 111, 137
Nigerian colonies (1861–1960), 77, 111
Palestine mandate (1918–48), 55–7
racism and, 43–5, 115–16, 137
Somaliland (1884–1960), 42, 55, 70, 77
Trinidad (1802–1962), 8, 9, 15, 79, 81, 86
Uganda (1894–1962), 8, 79
British National Party (BNP), 4, 179, 254, 259, 260, 275
British Nationality Act (1948), 10, 12, 76, 79, 103, 198
British Nationality Act (1981), 182

British Rail, 131, 227
British South Asians, 6, 7, 10, 11, 12, 19, 77, 91, 259
  in Birmingham, 2, 6, 14, 19, 121, 125, 147–71, 221–38, 244–50
  in Bradford, 7, 160–61, 176–220, 245
  cuisine, 121, 147–8, 162, 168, 183, 187, 221, 243, 263, 281
  in Glasgow, 83
  in Leicester, 231, 245
  in London, 101, 245
  in Middlesborough, 115
  in Nottingham, 15, 107, 108
British Transport Commission, 89
British Union of Fascists, 101
British West Africans, 6, 43
  Nigerians, 46, 68, 73, 100
Brixton, London, 15, 16, 88, 176, 235
Brooklyn, New York, 28
Brown, James Gordon 252
Brummie accent, 132, 240
Bull Ring, Birmingham, 124, 181
Bulldog, 275
'Burma Road', Cardiff, 24, 40–41
Burnham, Roger, 46–7, 48
Burnley, Lancashire, 256–7
Bute Street, Tiger Bay, 34, 35, 52, 59, 60, 69
Butler, Richard Austen, 104, 113
Butlin's, 85

Cable Street, London, 34

376

INDEX

Cadbury's, 215
Café Cairo, Tiger Bay, 17, 60
cafés
  Birmingham, 149, 150–52
  Cardiff, 59–62
Cairo, Egypt, 55
Cairo Lodging House, Tiger Bay, 34
Calthorpe Park, Birmingham, 230, 243
Camden, London, 133
Cameron, David, 4, 11–12, 122, 266–7
Campbell, Robin and Ali, 241–3
Canada, 99, 109
Cannon Street, Middlesborough, 115
Cantle Report (2001), 256–7, 260
Captain Verdic, 81
Cardiff, Wales, 7, 9, 13, 15–16, 18–19, 24, 27–71
  American soldiers in, 18–19, 24, 31, 35–41, 43
  café culture, 59–62
  CIAC, 34, 58, 62–7, 70
  mixed-race people in, 31, 32, 34, 36, 43, 46–50, 63–8, 70
  mixed-race relationships in, 18–19, 24, 31, 32, 34, 35–50
  Muslim community, 7, 33–4, 35, 48, 50–57
  riots (1919), 42, 51, 76, 78
  shipping industry, 30, 34, 35, 41–3, 46, 48, 53–4, 57–9, 61, 68

Cardiff Bay Barrage, 68
Cardiff Rugby Club, 65–7
Caribbean, 6, 11, 15, 64–5, 125
  Barbados, 77, 84, 87, 89, 90
  cricket in, 35, 86
  Empire Windrush, 8–9, 20, 81, 220
  Jamaica, *see* Jamaica
  shipping industry, 30, 34, 42, 46, 48
  Trinidad, 9, 15, 79, 81, 86
  World War II, 9, 11, 18
  see also British Afro-Caribbeans; Jamaica
Carmichael, Stokely, 203
Casey, John, 197
Cayton, Horace, 27, 29, 33
Centre for Contemporary Cultural Studies (CCCS), 122, 153, 238
Chaggar, Gurdip Singh, 204
Chambers, Claire, 179
Chapeltown, Leeds, 175–6, 207
Charles III, King, 278
Chawla, Juhi, 184
Cheddar Road, Balsall Heath, 224, 227, 229, 230, 232, 235, 236–7, 243, 284
Cheshire, Stephen, 248
Chhachh, Punjab, 178
Chic, 247
Chicago, Illinois, 29–30, 32, 35, 42, 50, 63, 69
childbirth, 274
Chilwell, Nottingham, 88, 98

377

INDEX

Chin Yee's Travel Service, Kingston, 81
Chinese people, 281, 283
Chop Suey Café, Tiger Bay, 34
Christianity, 83, 281
Chura Liya Hai Tumne (Sagoo), 249
cinemas, 147, 150
Citizenship Oath and Pledge, 260
'clash of civilisations', 4, 44, 49, 68, 258
Clevedon Road, Balsall Heath, 124, 126, 140, 141, 224, 237, 284
Clive, Robert, 81
Clock, Birmingham, 124
coal, 9
Coard, Bernard, 179–80, 211, 214, 215
Coburn, James, 175
Cochrane, Kelso, 115
'Cockney Translation' (Smiley Culture), 238
Colonial and Social Welfare Club, 88, 97, 104–5, 106, 116
Colonial Defence Association, 33, 51
colonialism, *see* British Empire
Colony, The (1964 documentary), 131–2
colour bars, 10, 17, 39, 79, 87–8, 91–2, 99, 109, 115–16
 bars and hotels, 39, 86, 95
 employment, 20, 78, 87–8, 89, 91, 109, 111–13, 172, 267–8
 housing, 16, 47–9, 78, 87–8, 172, 267–8
Coloured International Athletic Club (CIAC), 17, 58, 62–7, 70
Columbia, 248–9
Colville Road, Balsall Heath, 238
Commission for Racial Equality, 193, 199, 256
Commonwealth, 110, 127, 160
Commonwealth Immigrants Act (1962), 79, 113, 125, 172, 177, 267, 276
Commonwealth Immigrants Act (1968), 172, 221, 276
Communist Party, 51, 57, 63, 106, 271
Connell family, 6, 269–71
Conservative Party
 British Nationality Act (1981), 182
 Cameron government (2010–16), 4, 11–12, 122, 260–61, 266–7
 Commonwealth Immigrants Act (1962), 79, 113, 125, 172, 177, 267
 general election (1964), 114
 general election (2001), 255
 Heath government (1970–74), 186
 Honeyford Affair (1984–5), 209, 210, 214
 Hostile Environment policy (2012–present), 11–12, 260–61, 267, 272, 275

INDEX

Illegal Migration Act (2023), 278
Immigration Act (1971), 186
Macmillan government (1957–63), 79, 108, 113, 125, 126, 140, 172, 177
May government (2016–19), 275
miners' strike (1984–5), 181, 207
Profumo Affair (1963), 126
riots, reaction to (1958), 108, 109, 111, 112
Rwanda policy (2022–present), 274–5
Sunak government (2022–present), 275, 278
Thatcher government (1979–90), *see* Thatcher, Margaret
Constantine, Learie, 86
Consultative Committee, 107–8, 112
Cordeaux, J. K., 109
Cosmopolitan Social Club, 88
council housing, 129
Coventry, West Midlands, 241
Covid-19 pandemic (2020–23), 274
cricket, 35, 58, 64, 67, 81, 86, 106, 257–8, 274, 284
Crooke, Stan, 131
Crossways, London, 282
Cuba, 8, 81
Cuba, SS, 80
Cyprus, 77, 92, 111, 281

Daily Express, 225
Daily Mail, 195, 225, 234
Daily Mirror, 109
'darkest Cardiff', 13, 27, 45, 67
Davis, Alex, 277
Davis, Cliff, 66
decolonisation, 3, 10, 13, 32, 69–70, 76, 113, 127, 137, 180
deindustrialisation, 177, 219, 222, 223, 256
Delf Hill Middle School, Bradford, 179
Demos, 251
Deobandi sect, 178
Derbyshire, England, 91, 101
detention centres, 276
DFC Chicken, Balsall Heath, 123, 147, 168, 171
Dheol, Jaz, 282
'Dhol Tax' (Achanak), 245
dialectical process, 25, 34, 170–71, 223, 250–68, 273
diasporaization, 183, 278
Dickens, Charles, 77
'Dil Cheez' (Sagoo), 250
discrimination
education, 178–82, 187–90, 192–3, 196–202, 205–20
employment, 20, 78, 87–8, 89, 91, 109, 111–13, 131, 134, 172, 186–7, 267–8
housing, 16, 47–9, 78, 87–8, 172, 267–8
shipping industry, 42–3, 49, 57
Diwali, 216

INDEX

Dome nightclub, Birmingham, 246
Dominican Republic, 81
dominoes, 106
Don Christie's, Balsall Heath, 243
'Don't Fence Me In' (Porter and Fletcher), 38
Donnellan, Phillip, 131–2
Douglas, Bill, 64–7, 71
Drake, St Clair, 27–35, 42, 45–50, 51–71, 96, 279
Driberg, Thomas, 111
Drummond Middle School, Manningham, 180–82, 192–3, 196–202, 205–19
Drummond Parents' Action Committee, 205–14
Dubliners, The, 90
Dún Laoghaire, Dublin, 132
Dunkin Donuts, 28–9, 32
Dusseldorf, Germany, 271
Dyer, John, 163

Ealing, London, 190
East Africa, 6, 19, 125
   Kenya, 2, 9, 55, 123, 137, 169, 172, 221, 276
   Somaliland, 30, 42, 47–8, 49, 54, 55–7, 60, 70
East Anglia, 280
Ebony Café, Tiger Bay, 34
Eccleshill, Bradford, 188
Eddo-Lodge, Reni, 6
Edgbaston, Birmingham, 163, 230, 239
education, 177–82, 192–3, 195, 196–202, 205–20, 226, 239, 252–3, 264
Edward Road, Balsall Heath, 229
Egypt, 55
Eid, 216, 219, 281
Ekarte, Daniels, 46
elections
   1964 general election, 114
   1992 general election, 250
   2001 general election, 252, 255
Emigrants, The (Lamming), 87
Émigré Journeys (Hussein), 148–50, 161–3, 168, 173
Empire Day, 81
Empire Windrush, 8–9, 20, 81, 220
employment
   discrimination, 20, 78, 87–8, 89, 91, 109, 111–13, 131, 134, 172, 186–7, 267–8
   unemployment, 30, 43, 54, 80, 96, 108–9, 220, 241
English language, 2, 254, 259
English Travellers, 135
Eribon, Didier, 24
Escalla, 81
Essential Ragga, 248
Ethiopia, 55
Ethnic Minority Election Study (2010), 274
European Union, 4, 110, 255, 267, 275, 280
   Brexit, 4, 14, 110, 218, 274, 275
Evaristo, Bernardine, 282

INDEX

Exodus (Marley), 269

'facts of blackness', 32, 33, 34, 45, 83, 189
Fairford, Gloucestershire, 35
al-Falah, 206
'fallen women', 40
Fanon, Frantz, 32, 50, 83, 189
far right, 101–2, 110, 113, 114–15, 185–92, 195, 196, 197, 202–5
   British National Party (BNP), 4, 179, 254, 259, 260, 275
   National Action, 277
   National Front (NF), 11, 115, 144, 184, 190, 202–5, 230, 233, 239, 275
   Union Movement, 101, 110, 113, 114–15, 276
   see also racism; riots
Farage, Nigel, 4, 11, 218, 275
fascism, *see* far right
Faubus, Orval, 102, 104
Federal West Indies (1958–62), 104
Fellowes, Alex, 201
Filey, North Yorkshire, 85
films, 17, 37, 38, 147, 150, 152, 158, 184, 247, 249
Floyd, George, 29
food, 17, 147–8, 162, 168, 187, 243, 281–2
football, 85, 190, 256, 262, 282
Four Oaks, Birmingham, 223
Fox, Marcus, 209–10
France, 3
Free, Norman, 206
Fryer, Peter, 79
funk music, 224, 244

Gabicci, 238
Gaitskell, Hugh, 113
Galway, Ireland, 7
Gambia, 137
gambling, 62
garage music, 262–3
Garnett, Stanley, 179
Garvey, Marcus, 58
Germany, 4, 6, 22, 269–71, 279
   Nazi period (1933–45), 6, 18, 31, 39, 52, 129, 137, 203, 215, 270
Ghana, 77, 84, 263
ghazal, 150, 171, 250
Ghazal and Beat, 246
Ghulam, Mohammed, 91
Gilroy, Paul, 3
Glasgow, Scotland, 80, 81, 83, 146
Godfrey, Arthur, 67
Gohil, Pravin, 266
Gold Coast (1821–1957), 77, 84
Goldsmith Street, Nottingham, 78
Gordon-Walker, Patrick, 114
graffiti, 78, 131, 170, 184
Grant, Ainsley, 87–8
Greater London Council, 5
Greece, 34, 279
Greek Cypriots, 92, 111

INDEX

Greenock, Inverclyde, 80
Griffin, Nicholas, 4, 255
Griffiths, Peter, 114
grime music, 282
Grunwick dispute (1976–8), 187
Gunaratne, Guy, 282
Guyana, 3, 9, 51, 57, 70, 106, 115, 275

Hafizabad, Punjab, 161
Hague, William, 255
Haiti, 30
al-Hakimi, Abdullah Ali, 35, 51–7
halal food, 180, 189, 207, 211, 219, 238
'Half Caste' (Agard), 216
'half-castes', 18, 20, 37, 43, 45, 46, 63, 64, 163
see also mixed-race people
Hall, Stuart, 7, 12, 77, 78, 80, 122, 123, 153, 227, 238, 268, 272
Hall Green, Birmingham, 261–2
Halwell, Glady, 232–3
Hand on the Sun (Mehmood), 178–9, 191, 204
Handsworth, Birmingham, 88, 176, 181, 235, 241, 242, 244, 248
Handsworth Revolution (Steel Pulse), 269
Happiest Days of Your Life, The (Dighton), 106
Hardy, Bert, 47, 48, 60
Harlem, New York, 27, 29, 59, 101
Harrison, James, 109

Hassan, Norman, 241
Havana, Cuba, 8
Hedges, Nick, 146
'Hey! Jamalo' (Sagoo), 249
Highgate Tower, Birmingham, 134
Hill, Kenneth, 137–9
Hilton, Matthew, 167
Hinduism, 178, 216, 244, 246
hip-hop culture, 37, 224, 244, 245
Hirsch, Afua, 272
Hispanic people, 92
history curriculum, 215
Hoggart, Richard, 84, 122
Holiday Inn, Cardiff, 69
Hollywood, 37
Hollywood Canteen (1944 film), 38
Holyhead, Anglesey, 132
Homepride, 282
Honeyford, Ray, 180–82, 192–3, 196–202, 205–20, 258, 264, 284
Hostile Environment policy (2012–present), 11–12, 260–61, 267, 272, 275
housing
  discrimination, 16, 47–9, 78, 82, 87–8, 172, 267–8
  slums, 68, 129, 131, 134, 144–6, 152
  sub-letting, 233
How the West Indian Child... (Coard), 179–80, 211, 214, 215
Howell, Dennis, 135
Hummingbird nightclub, Birmingham, 246

INDEX

Hussain, Saeed, 204
Hussein, Abdullah, 148–50, 161–3, 168, 173
Husseini, Amin, 56
Hyatt Hotel, Birmingham, 222–3, 250
hybridisation, 132, 141, 156, 183

Ikon Gallery, Birmingham, 165–7
Illegal Migration Act (2023), 278
Immigration Act (1971), 186
Imperial Hotel, London, 86
Imran's, Balsall Heath, 243
income support, 259, 260
India, 10, 11, 32, 69–70, 76, 77, 81, 125
  independence (1947), 10, 32, 76, 178, 187
  see also British South Asians
Indian cinema, see South Asian cinema
Indian food, see South Asian cuisine
Industrial Revolution (c. 1760–c. 1840), 215
infant mortality rates, 219
International Convention Centre, Birmingham, 222–3, 250
International Friendship League, 108
Iqra Academy, Manningham, 218
Ireland, 6, 7, 16, 22, 31, 73, 271, 281
  Birmingham, migration to, 19, 127, 132–7, 155–6
  Nottingham, migration to, 74, 90–91, 113
Irish Press, 132
Irish Republican Army (IRA), 134
Irish Travellers, 134–7, 172
Irn-Bru, 124
Irons, Ben, 118, *118*, 119
Irons, Eric, 19, 80–86, 88–9, 93, 96, 97, 104–7, 116–18, *118*
Irons, Nell, 19, 85–6, 88, 117, *118*
Irons, Paul, 118–19, *118*
Islam, 3–5, 11, 14, 17, 24, 216–19, 256
  bhangra and, 246
  in Birmingham, 23, 124, 161, 223–4, 227, 228–37, 238
  in Bradford, 178, 180, 184, 194, 202, 207, 211–12, 217–19, 246, 256
  in Cardiff, 33–4, 35, 49, 50–57
  festivals, 216, 219, 281
  halal food, 180, 189, 207, 211, 219, 238
  in Nottingham, 108
  pork, prohibition of, 108, 190
  Shi'ism, 238
  Sufism, 52, 244, 280–81
  War on Terror (2001–present), 3–4, 49, 226, 257–61
Islamic Youth Mission, 206
Island Records, 243
Israel, 55–6
Italy, 6, 31, 56, 81

Jackson, Frank, 104

INDEX

Jamaica, 2, 7, 8, 10, 20, 46, 77, 80–82
  Empire Windrush voyage (1948) 8–9, 20, 81, 220
  independence (1962), 79, 113, 137, 171
  music, 11, 80, 106
  patois, 216, 238–41, 242
  riots, reaction to (1958), 104–6, 116
James, Cyril Lionel Robert, 58
jazz music, 37, 106, 244
Jewish people, 101, 102, 176, 184
Jim Crow laws (c. 1870–1964), 29–30, 31, 36, 37, 39, 85, 91, 102–3, 115, 187
jitterbug, 37, 59, 86
Johnson, Linton Kwesi, 216, 269
Jones, Claudia, 106
Jones, Simon, 238–40
Jones, Willie, 66
Joseph, Keith, 210
jungle music, 243–4

Kano, 282
Kapur, Steven, 248, 250
Kashmir, 7, 152
  Mirpur, 125, 161, 178
Kashmir Coffee Bar, Balsall Heath, 17, 126, 147, 150, 152, 171, 237, 284
  Mendelsohn's photographs, *146*, *149*, 152, *154*, 155, *155*
Keeler, Christine, 126
'Keep Britain White', 78, 101, 103, 131

Keighley, Bradford, 196, 200
Kelham, Nell, *see* Irons, Nell
Kenya, 2, 9, 55, 123, 137, 169, 172, 221, 276
Kettering, Northamptonshire, 73
Khan, Nusrat Fateh Ali, 244
Kilburn, London, 133
Kilkerranmore, County Cork, 271
Kilroy-Silk, Robert, 217
King Fuad I University, 55
King's Road, London, 100
Kingston, Jamaica, 7, 80, 81
Kipling, Rudyard, 199
Kumari, Meena, 158, 183
Kureishi, Hanif, 177–8, 183, 199, 218, 219

Labour Party, 4, 5, 251–61, 264, 265, 267–8
  Attlee government (1945–51), 10, 12, 76, 79, 103, 198
  Balsall Heath Travellers eviction (1968), 135
  Blair government (1997–2007), 4, 194, 225, 252–61, 264, 275–6
  British Nationality Act (1948), 10, 12, 76, 79, 103, 198
  Callaghan government (1976–9), 214
  Cantle Report (2001), 256–7, 260
  Commonwealth Immigrants Act (1962), 113, 114, 267
  Commonwealth Immigrants Act (1968), 172, 221

384

INDEX

general election (1964), 114
Greater London Council (1972–7), 5
Honeyford Affair (1984–5), 193, 202, 214
MacPherson Report (1999), 259
Nationality, Immigration and Asylum Act (2002), 259, 276
Race Relations Act (1968), 171–2
Race Relations Act (1976), 193
riots, reaction to (1958), 109, 111
Wilson government I (1964–70), 135, 171–2, 221
Wilson government II (1974–6), 193
LaCorbiniere, Karl, 104
Ladypool Road, Balsall Heath, 238, 243, 247, 285
Lahore, Punjab, 152, 205
Lamming, George, 84, 87
language, 238–41, 242, 282
Lawrence, Stephen, 259
Leadbeater, Charles, 252
League of Coloured Peoples, 51
Leeds, West Yorkshire, 175–6, 207
lehenga, 238
Leicester, Leicestershire, 187, 231, 245, 280
Leigh, Vivien, 86
leprosy, 186
Letts, Donovan, 277
Liberal Democrats, 225, 260
Lindsay, Martin, 112

Lister's Mill, Bradford, 193
Lithuania, 280
Little Rock, Arkansas, 102–3, 104
Little Simz, 282
Little, Kenneth, 45, 53, 59–60
Liverpool, Merseyside, 42, 46, 111, 146, 189
Toxteth riots (1981), 176, 193, 214, 235
London, England, 14–15, 61, 92, 100
bhangra in, 245, 249
Cochrane murder (1959), 115
Grunwick dispute (1976–8), 187
Irish population, 133
Lawrence murder (1993), 259
Notting Hill riots (1958), 18, 79, 100–103, 276
prostitution in, 126
supplementary schools, 180
urban renewal in, 146
Lonely Londoners, The (Selvon), 15
Los Angeles, California, 92
Loudoun Square, Tiger Bay, 35, 36, 56, 61
Louth, Lincolnshire, 103
Lowndes, Mary, 94, 95, 115
Lumb Lane, Bradford, 160–61, 183
Luton, Bedfordshire, 187
Lycamobile, 281
Lyon's Tea Houses, 90

Mabuse, Motsi, 282

INDEX

MacInnes, Colin, 164
Macmillan, Maurice Harold, 79, 108, 140
MacPherson Report (1999), 259
Madden, Maxwell, 202
Maindy Barracks, Cardiff, 31, 35, 39–41, 46, 50
Majid, Shabnam, 250
Majority Rights, 217
Making History (Johnson), 269
Malcolm X, 203
Maloney, Jim, 136
Malta, 34, 61, 111, 137, 279
Manchester Guardian, 100
Manchester, England, 88, 146
Mandela, Nelson, 238
Mangrove restaurant, Notting Hill, 203
Manji, Fatima, 282
Manley, Norman, 104–6, 116
Manningham, Bradford, 14, 177, 180, 182–92, 204
    Drummond Middle School, 180–82, 192–3, 196–202, 205–19
    Manningham Middle School, 202, 204
    self-defence activism in, 202–14
Maple, Sarah, 282
Marley, Robert 'Bob', 241, 242, 247, 254, 269
Marseilles, France, 59, 62
Marxism, 51, 57, 63, 64
Master Sajjad, 184
May Day parades, 56

May, Theresa, 11, 275
Mayfield, Curtis, 284
Mayne, Roger, 146
'McAlpine's Fusiliers', 90
McGynn, David, 243
McKay, Claude, 59, 62, 63
Mehmood, Tariq, 178–9, 191, 204
Mendelsohn, Janet, 122–8, 137, 139–71, 233, 264, 284
Mento music, 80
'Mera Laung Gawacha' (Sagoo), 248
Merchant Navy, *see* shipping industry
Merkel, Angela, 4
Mermaid, Birmingham, 132
Merrick, Jim, 185–6, 196, 208
Mexico, 8, 81, 92
microaggressions, 131
Middle East, 30, 54
Middlesborough, North Yorkshire, 115
Millionairess, The (1960 film), 199
Milton Keynes, Buckinghamshire, 280
miners' strike (1984–5), 181, 207
Mirpur, Kashmir, 125, 161, 178
Miss India, 184
mixed-race people, 18, 20, 36, 46, 279–80
    in Birmingham, 163–4, 169
    in Cardiff, 31, 32, 34, 36, 43, 46–50, 63–8, 70
    in Nottingham 116–19
mixed-race relationships, 1–2, 13, 16, 17–20, 90, 100, 279

INDEX

in Birmingham, 123, 155–71
in Cardiff, 18–19, 24, 31, 32, 34, 35–50, 96
in Nottingham, 19, 85–6, 96, 116–19
Montego Bay, Jamaica, 240
Moody, Harold, 51
Morcambe, Lancashire, 270
Morrison, Majbritt, 100
Moseley, Birmingham, 121, 123, 171, 263, 285
Moseley Road, Balsall Heath, 147, 237–8, 244, 248
Mosley, Oswald, 101–2, 110, 113, 115, 276
mosques, 17
  Birmingham, 23, 124, 228–9, 284
  Bradford, 194, 207, 211–12, 213, 217
  Cardiff, 7, 33–4, 35, 50–57
Moss Side, Manchester, 88, 193
motor industry, 223
Mozambique, 57
Mulgan, Geoff, 252
multicultural slang, 238–41, 242, 282
multiculturalism, 3–8, 181
  dialectical process, 25, 34, 170–71, 223, 250–68, 273
  'street-level multiculturalism', 124, 127, 173, 194, 219, 265, 280
Murphy, Dervla, 184–5, 195, 200, 201, 219

music, 11, 80, 106, 224–5, 238–50, 262–3, 269, 282

Nachural Records, Smethwick, 244
Nakba (1948), 56
namaz, 161
National Association of Headteachers, 209
National Front (NF), 11, 115, 144, 184, 190, 202–5, 230, 233, 239, 275
National Health Service (NHS), 10, 11, 78, 267, 274
National Union of Manufacturers, 91
National Union of Mineworkers, 181, 207
Nationality, Immigration and Asylum Act (2002), 259, 276
Navy, Army and Air Force Institutes (NAFFI), 85, 86, 117
Nayak, Anoop, 242
Nazi Germany (1933–45), 6, 18, 31, 39, 52, 129, 137, 203, 215
Neighbourhood Watch, 229
Nelson Mandela school, Balsall Heath, 238
Netherlands, 3, 4
'New Commonwealth', 127
New Inns pub, Handsworth, 246
New Labour, 4, 194, 225, 251–61, 264, 265, 275–6
New York, United States, 27–9
New Zealand, 109
Newport, Wales, 37–8

INDEX

Nigeria, 68, 73, 77, 100, 111
'No Irish, no blacks, no dogs' signs, 16
Norfolk, Virginia, 37
Northern Ireland, 134, 182, 281
Notting Hill, London, 15, 92, 105
   carnival, 106, 282
   Mangrove restaurant, 203
   Profumo Affair (1963), 126
   prostitution in, 126
   riots (1958), 18, 79, 100–103, 104, 105, 109, 126
Nottingham, Nottinghamshire, 7, 10, 13, 15, 16, 73–119
   Caribbean population, 74, 78–119
   Consultative Committee, 107–8
   Irish population, 74, 90–91, 113
   St Ann's riots (1958), 13, 18, 20, 76, 78, 93–117, 127, 232, 276
Nuneaton, Warwickshire, 22, 75, 76, 269, 280, 281

O'Connell, Harry, 51–2, 53, 54, 56, 57, 58, 62, 173
O'Leary, Dermot, 282
Oadby, Leicestershire, 280
oil industry, 54
Old Mo, Birmingham, 124
Oldham, Manchester, 256–7
Oluwale, David, 176
Orgreave Coking Plant, South Yorkshire, 207
Oriental Star Records, 244, 248, 249

Osborne, Cyril, 103, 111, 112, 115
Ousley, Herman, 256
'overcrowding' narrative, 109, 110

Pakistan, 2, 6, 7, 10, 19, 77, 160–61, 187, 200, 205
   cuisine, *see* South Asian cuisine
   folk music, 244
   see also British South Asians
Pakistani Community Centre, Bradford, 210
Palestine, 55–7, 281, 284
Pan-Africanism, 58, 63
Pannell, Norman, 111
Party for Freedom, 4
'Pass it On' (Marley), 254
Patel, Dhiren, 221
Patel, Priti, 277
patois, 216, 238–41, 242
Patterson, Sheila, 89
People, The, 109
Phillips, Melanie, 234–5, 251, 258
Phillips, Mike, 8
Phillips, Trevor, 8
Picture Post, 52–3
pirate radio, 243, 282
Pitts, Johny, 124
Poland, 8, 137, 280, 281
'Police Officer' (Smiley Culture), 238
policing, 274
Poll Tax (1989–90), 245
Popkess, Athelstan, 94–5, 98–9, 102
Portillo, Michael, 225

INDEX

Portland, Jamaica, 81
Portugal, 47
Powell, John Enoch, 11, 14, 19, 115, 171, 173, 181–2, 185, 196, 201, 228
  political influence of, 226, 255, 276
  'Rivers of Blood' speech (1968), 3, 110, 128, 131, 144, 162, 277
  victimhood narrative, 19, 110, 115, 182, 185, 196
pregnancy, 274
Premji, Naz, 282
Presley, Elvis, 92
prisoners of war, 31, 271
prisons, 274
Profumo, John, 126
progressive individualism, 252
Promises and Lies (UB40), 241
prostitution, 14, 19–20, 61, 97–8
  Balsall Heath, *see* Balsall Heath red light district
Pukka Pies, 284
Punjab region, 125, 147, 161, 176–7, 224
  music, 244–50, 261
Punjabi language, 240
Pure Garage, 263
Pyar Ka Sagar, Balsall Heath, 126, 147, *148*, 150, 152, 158, 171, 237, 250, 284
Pyar Ka Sagar (1951 film), 152, 158

al-Qaeda, 258

qawwalis, 150, 171
Qayamat Se Qayamat Tak (1988 film), 184
Question, The, 272–3

Race Relations Act (1968), 171–2
Race Relations Act (1976), 193
Race Relations Advisory Council, 194, 195
Race Today, 204, 206
racism, 3, 11, 14, 33, 34, 79, 83–5, 110, 127, 131–2, 220, 273–8
  activism against, 173, 202–14
  attacks, 115, 190–92, 204, 259
  awareness classes, 195
  duplicity of, 85, 87, 131
  education and, 178–82, 187–90, 192–3, 196–202, 205–20
  empire and, 43–5, 115–16, 137
  employment and, 20, 78, 87–8, 89, 91, 109, 111–13, 131, 134, 172, 186–7, 267–8
  housing and, 16, 47–9, 78, 87–8, 172, 267–8
  media and, 94, 97, 98, 99, 100
  mixed-race relationships and, 13, 17–20, 31, 32, 36–50, 96, 100, 126, 163, 279
  riots, *see* riots
  War on Terror and, 49, 226, 257–61
Radio One, 224, 249
Radio XL, 246, 249, 262
Rafiq, Azeem, 274
Raja Brothers Supermarket, Balsall Heath, *265*, 266

INDEX

Raleigh Industries, 74
Ranganathan, Romesh, 282
Rastafarians, 239
Rawalpindi, Punjab, 178
'reception centres', 276
'Red Red Wine' (UB40), 242
red-light districts, *see* prostitution
reggae music, 224, 225, 238, 241–3, 244, 248, 269, 281, 282
Rehman, Abdul, 183
Rehman, Abdullah, 12, 266
Reid, John, 254
Religious Education (RE), 195, 196, 211
Rhodes, Cecil, 81
riots, 176, 193, 198, 214, 235, 276
   Bradford (2001), 220, 256
   Brixton (1981), 176, 235
   Burnley (2001), 256–7
   Handsworth (1985), 176, 235
   Middlesborough (1961), 115
   Notting Hill (1958), 18, 79, 100–103, 104, 108, 109, 126, 127, 276
   Oldham (2001), 256–7
   St Ann's (1958), 13, 18, 20, 76, 78, 93–117, 127, 232, 276
   St Pauls (1980), 176, 193
   Tiger Bay (1919), 42, 51, 76, 78
   Toxteth (1981), 176, 193, 214, 235
'Rivers of Blood' speech (Powell, 1968), 3, 110, 128, 131, 144, 162, 277
Robin Hood Chase, Nottingham, 87

Robin Hood Chase Pub, St Ann's, 93, 95
Roma Music Bank, Handsworth, 244, 246
Romance in Marseilles (McKay), 59
romantic relationships, *see* mixed-race relationships
Royal Air Force (RAF), 80, 81, 107, 117, 118
rude boy culture, 11
'Rule Britannia', 81
Rushdie, Salman, 217, 235
Rwanda, 274–5

Sagoo, Bally, 224–5, 247–50, 257, 262
Sailors Institutes, 59
Salah, Khalid, 56
Salam, 52
Salaman, Ali, 60–61
Salford, Manchester, 146
Salisbury Review, 197, 199, 202, 205, 209, 258
Sande Fjord Café, Tiger Bay, 34
Sargom Cassette Shop, London, 249
Satanic Verses, The (Rushdie), 217, 235
Satar's Arab Lodging House, Tiger Bay, 34
Saturday Night and Sunday Morning (Sillitoe), 75, 84–5
Saudi Arabia, 53
Savannah, Georgia, 36

INDEX

Scandinavia, 47
Schumer, Amalia and Wilhelm, 270
Scobie, Edward, 92–3
Scotland, 80–81, 83
Scott, Alex, 282
Scruton, Roger, 209, 217
segregation, 24, 47, 70, 91, 179, 187, 190, 256–7
 Apartheid South Africa (1948–94), 43, 91, 102–3, 115, 210
 Jim Crow America (c. 1870–1964), 29–30, 31, 36, 37, 39, 85, 91, 102–3, 115, 187
Selecter, The, 241, 269
self-defence activism, 173, 202–14
'self-policing society', 252
Selfridge's, 124, 281
Sellers, Peter, 199
Selvon, Samuel, 15
September 11 attacks (2001), 3, 5, 257
sex; sexuality, 17–20
 mixed-race relationships, *see* mixed-race relationships
 prostitution, *see* prostition
Shah, Kafait, 152, 182–3
Shakespeare Street, Nottingham, 78, 86
Shaw, Albert, 136
shelta, 136
Shelter, 146
Sheppard, Alan, 57–8, 62, 63–4, 66, 70, 71
Sherborne Road, Birmingham, 134

Shereen Kadah, Balsall Heath, 147, 171, 237
Shia Islam, 238
Shipley, Bradford, 209
shipping industry, 30, 34, 35, 41–3, 46, 48, 53–4, 57–9, 61, 124
Siddiqi, Abdul Wahhab, 280–81
Signing Off (UB40), 241
Sikhism, 178, 180, 185, 186, 216, 244, 246
Sillitoe, Alan, 75, 84–5
Singapore Café, Tiger Bay, 34
Singh, Santokh, 147
Sivanandan, Ambalavaner, 113, 276
ska music, 11
skanking, 239
skinhead culture, 11
slang, 238–41, 242, 282
slavery, 197, 215, 273
Sliver (1993 film), 241
slum housing, 68, 129, 131, 134, 144–6, 152
Small Heath, Birmingham, 23, 135
Smethwick, West Midlands, 114, 244
Smiley Culture, 238, 250, 264
social entrepreneurs, 251, 252
socialism, 194
Sohal, Suky, 245
Soho, London, 126
Solihull, West Midlands, 112, 263
Solingen, Dusseldorf, 271
Somali Youth League, 55

INDEX

Somaliland; Somalis, 30, 42, 47–8, 49, 54, 55–7, 60, 70
soul music, 244
South Africa, 43, 91, 102–3, 115, 210
South Asian cinema, 17, 147, 150, 152, 158, 184, 210, 247, 249
South Asian cuisine, 121, 147–8, 162, 168, 183, 187, 221, 243, 263, 281
South Down, Northern Ireland, 182
South Shields, Tyneside, 42
Southampton, Hampshire, 46, 81, 271
Spain, 47
Spanish Town, Jamaica, 80, 240
Sparkbrook, Birmingham, 133, 261
Sparkhill, Birmingham, 1–2, 8, 21, *21*, 121
Spearhead, 275
Specials, The, 241, 250, 269
Speedwell Road, Balsall Heath, 243
St Ambrose's Church, Edgbaston, 230
St Ann's, Nottingham, 74, 77, 86, 88, 89, 92–100
riots (1958), 13, 18, 20, 76, 78, 93–117, 127, 232, 276
St George's Day, 202
St Kitts, 131
St Lucia, 9
St Patrick's Day parades, 132, 134

St Pauls, Bristol, 176, 193
St Paul's Community Group, 227–8, 230, 251–2, 265, 266
St Vincent, 46
Stalin, Joseph, 57
steel bands, 106
Steel Pulse, 241, 242, 247, 269
stop and search, 274
Stormzy, 282
Stourbridge, West Midlands, 259
Street Watch, 236–7, 253, 266
'street-level multiculturalism', 124, 127, 173, 194, 219, 265, 280
Streets, The, 282
'structures of feeling', 237
Sufism, 52, 244, 280–81
Sujud, 282
sulu yemek, 281
Sun, 255
Sunak, Rishi, 277–8
supplementary schools, 180
Surat, Gujarat, 178
Swann Report (1985), 214, 216
Sweet Centre, Balsall Heath, 221
Sweet Centre, Bradford, 183
Sylhet, Bangladesh, 178
Szotowicz, Terry, 137

Tampico, Mexico, 8
tea, 82
Tebbit, Norman, 257–8
Teddy Boys, 77, 92–4, 96, 98, 104, 232
Telegraph and Argus, 197, 199
television, 147, 249

INDEX

terrorism, 3–5, 11, 24, 49, 226, 257–61
  September 11 attacks (2001), 3, 5, 257
  Westminster Bridge attacks (2017), 4
textiles industry, 176–7, 183, 193
Thatcher, Margaret
  Balsall Heath and, 225, 251, 252
  deindustrialisation and, 177
  Honeyford Affair (1984–5), 209, 210, 214
  immigration, views on, 186, 239
  miners' strike (1984–5), 181, 207
  Poll Tax (1989–90), 245
'There Will Always Be an England', 81
Tiger Bay, Cardiff, 13, 27, 30–71
  café culture, 59–62
  CIAC, 34, 58, 62–7, 70
  mixed-race people in, 31, 32, 34, 36, 43, 46–50, 63–8, 70
  mixed-race relationships in, 18–19, 24, 31, 32, 34, 35–50, 96
  mosques, 7, 33–4, 35, 50–57
  riots (1919), 42, 51, 76, 78
  shipping industry, 30, 34, 35, 41–3, 46, 48, 53–4, 57–9, 61, 68
Tilbury Docks, Essex, 81
Time magazine, 36
Times, The, 112, 172, 209
Times Educational Supplement, 198
Tolkien, John Ronald Reuel, 262

'Too Fat Polka' (Godfrey), 67
Toxteth, Liverpool, 176, 193, 214
trade unions, 89–90, 91, 111–12
Transport and General Workers Union, 90
Travellers, 134–7, 172
Trenchtown, Jamaica, 240
Tribune, 92
Trinidad, 9, 15, 79, 81, 86
Trotsky, Leon, 57, 58
Trump, Donald, 29
Tualla Muhammad, 55, 56
Turning Point (1981 report), 193–5, 200, 206, 208
Tutu, Desmond, 238
Two Tone music, 225, 241, 269
Tyndall, John, 203
Tyneside, England, 242
typhoid, 186

UB40, 225, 241–3, 250, 264
Uganda, 8, 79, 277
UK garage, 262–3
UK Independence Party (UKIP), 4, 11, 267, 275
Uncle's Continental Stores, Balsall Heath, 147
unemployment, 30, 43, 54, 80, 96, 108–9, 220, 241
Union Movement, 101, 110, 113, 114–15, 276
United Black Youth League, 204
United Nations, 278
United States, 27–41, 115, 140, 219

INDEX

African Americans, 18, 24, 27–41, 43, 69, 85, 91, 102
  Floyd murder and protests (2020), 29
  Jim Crow era (1877–1964), 29–30, 31, 36, 37, 39, 85, 91, 102–3, 115, 187
  Little Rock Crisis (1957), 102–3, 104
  Mexican population, 92
  oil industry, 54
  September 11 attacks (2001), 3, 5, 257
  Trump administration (2017–21), 29
  War on Terror (2001–), 3–4, 49, 226, 257–61
  World War II (1939–45), 17–19, 24, 31, 35–41
Upkar (1967 film), 152
urban renewal, 68, 144–6, 152, 283

Vaisakhi, 244
Varna Road, Balsall Heath, 145, 227, 233
VHS tapes, 147, 177, 184
victimhood narrative, 11, 95, 182, 185, 196, 199
Video Palace, Bradford, 184
Vincent, Gene, 92

Wahba, Hafiz, 53
Wallace Inn, Balsall Heath, 141, 171, 284
War on Terror (2001–), 3–4, 49, 226, 257–61

Ward, John, 230
Webb, Osborne, 52
welfare state, 109, 110
West Africa, 6, 43
  Ghana, 77, 84, 263
  Nigeria, 46, 68, 73, 100
West Bromwich, West Midlands, 90
West Indian Parents' Association, 206
West Indies Federation (1958–62), 104
Western Mail and South Wales News, 44
Western Union, 281
Westminster Bridge attacks (2017), 4
white society, 6–7, 16
  privilege, 7
  racism, *see* racism
  victimhood narrative, 11, 95, 182, 185, 196, 199
white flight, 19, 23, 226
working class, 82–4
'Wild Colonial Boy, The', 132
Wilde, Marty, 92
Williams, Raymond, 237
Williamsburg, Brooklyn, 28
Willows Crescent, Balsall Heath, 228–9
Wilson, Harold, 171
Wilson, James, 41, 43, 50, 61
Wilson, Terance, 241
Windrush scandal (2018), 11–12, 272

INDEX

Wing Yip supermarket, Birmingham, 283
Wolverhampton, West Midlands, 115, 181
Woodborough Road, Nottingham, 117
Woodbridge Road, Balsall Heath, 228
Woodward, Jenny, 205–6, 212
World of Fabric, Balsall Heath, 238
World War I (1914–18), 41–2, 270, 272
World War II (1939–45), 3, 6, 8, 9, 11, 17–18, 24, 30–31, 80–87, 129–30
  Blitz (1940–42), 52, 55, 61, 85, 129, 140
  Germanophobia and, 270, 271, 272
  mixed-race relationships, 17–19, 24, 31, 35–41, 44, 85–6
Wray, John, 99
wudu, 281

Yaadon Ki Baraat (1973 film), 249
Yamacraw, Savannah, 36
Yemen, 1, 2, 6, 7, 35, 51–7, 60–61, 70, 284
Yorkshire Campaign to Stop Immigration (YCSI), 185–6
Yorkshire Post, The, 212
Young, Wilbur, 37–8
Younge, Gary, 278
Yousefzada, Osman, 229
Yugoslav Wars (1991–2001), 234

Zaff's, Balsall Heath, 238
Zee TV, 249
Zephaniah, Benjamin, 242
zoot suits, 92